I0822994

POLAR EXPLORATIONS

TO THE ENDS OF THE EARTH

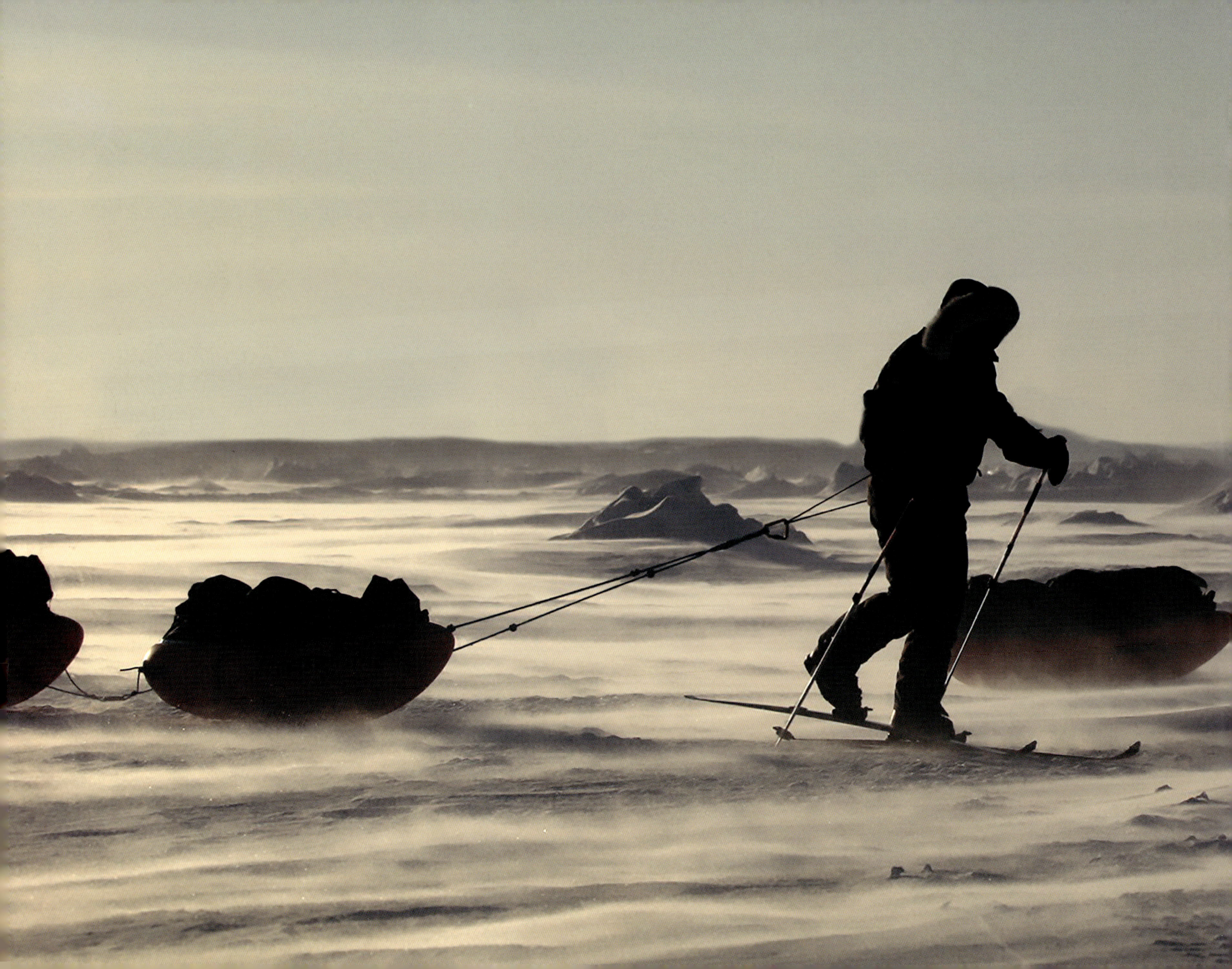

POLAR EXPLORATIONS

TO THE ENDS OF THE EARTH

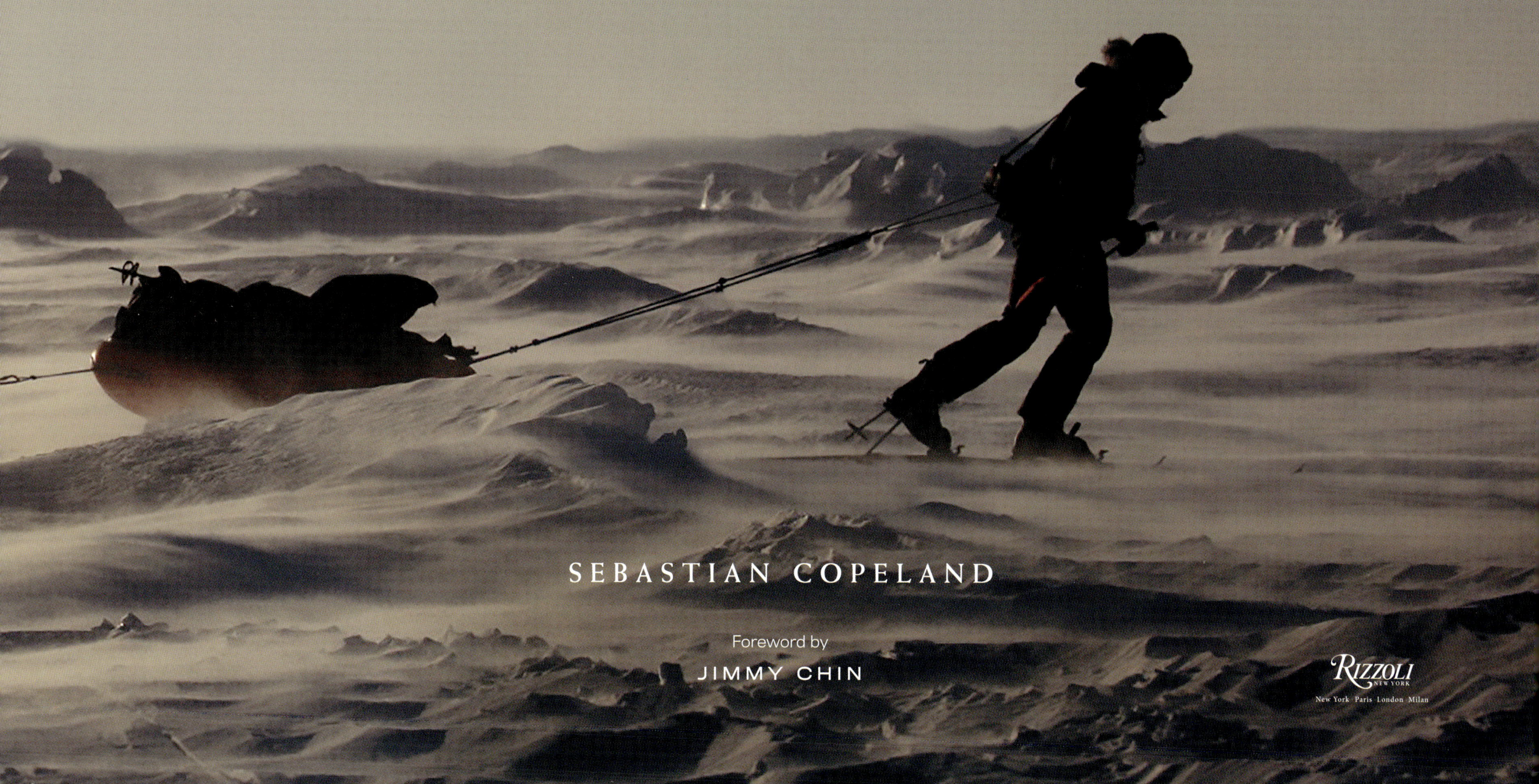

SEBASTIAN COPELAND

Foreword by

JIMMY CHIN

RIZZOLI
NEW YORK
New York · Paris · London · Milan

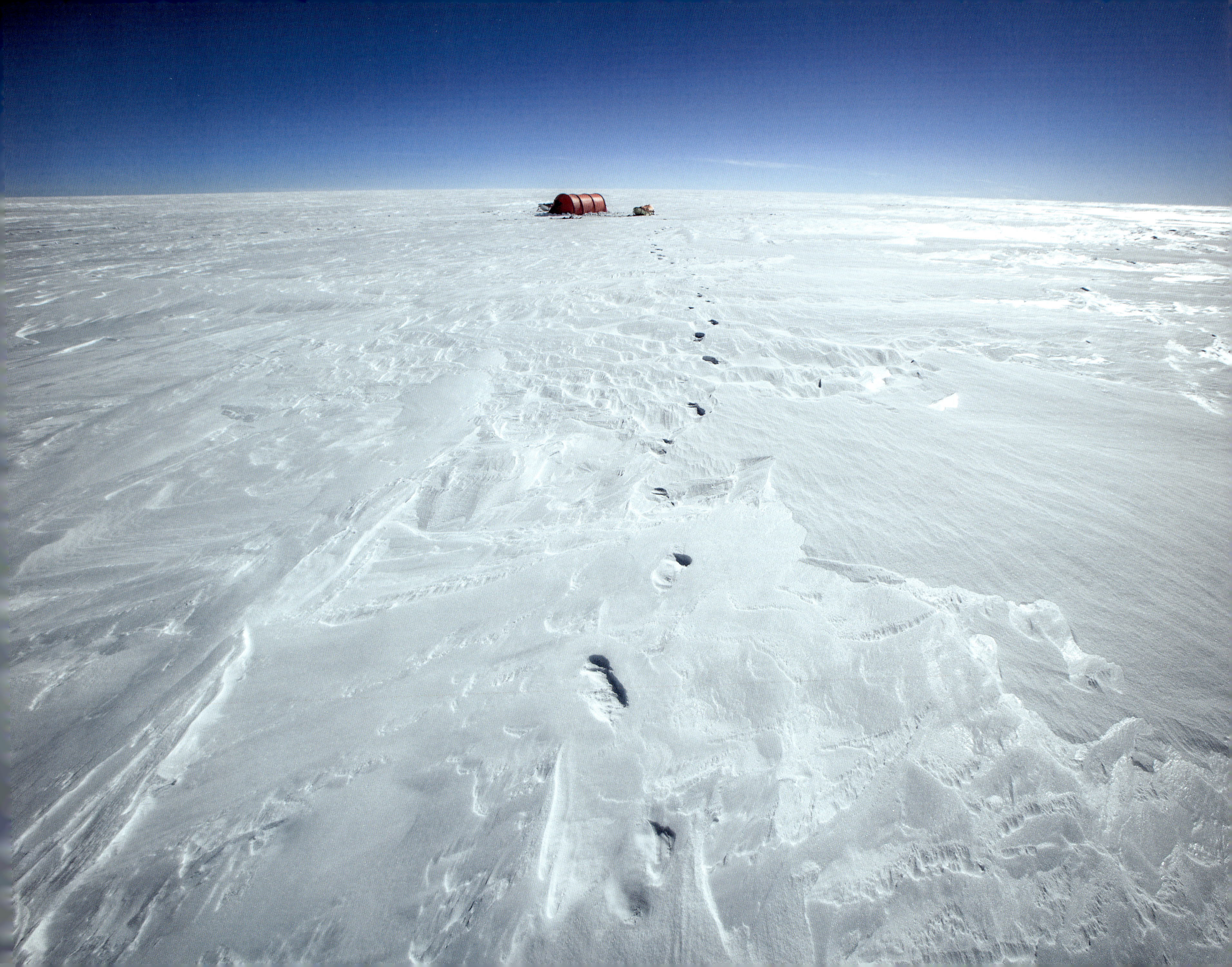

"Only those who risk going too far can possibly find out how far one can go."

T. S. ELIOT

"Men wanted for hazardous journey, small wages, bitter cold,
long months of complete darkness, constant danger,
safe return doubtful, honor and recognition in case of success."

ERNEST SHACKLETON

CONTENTS

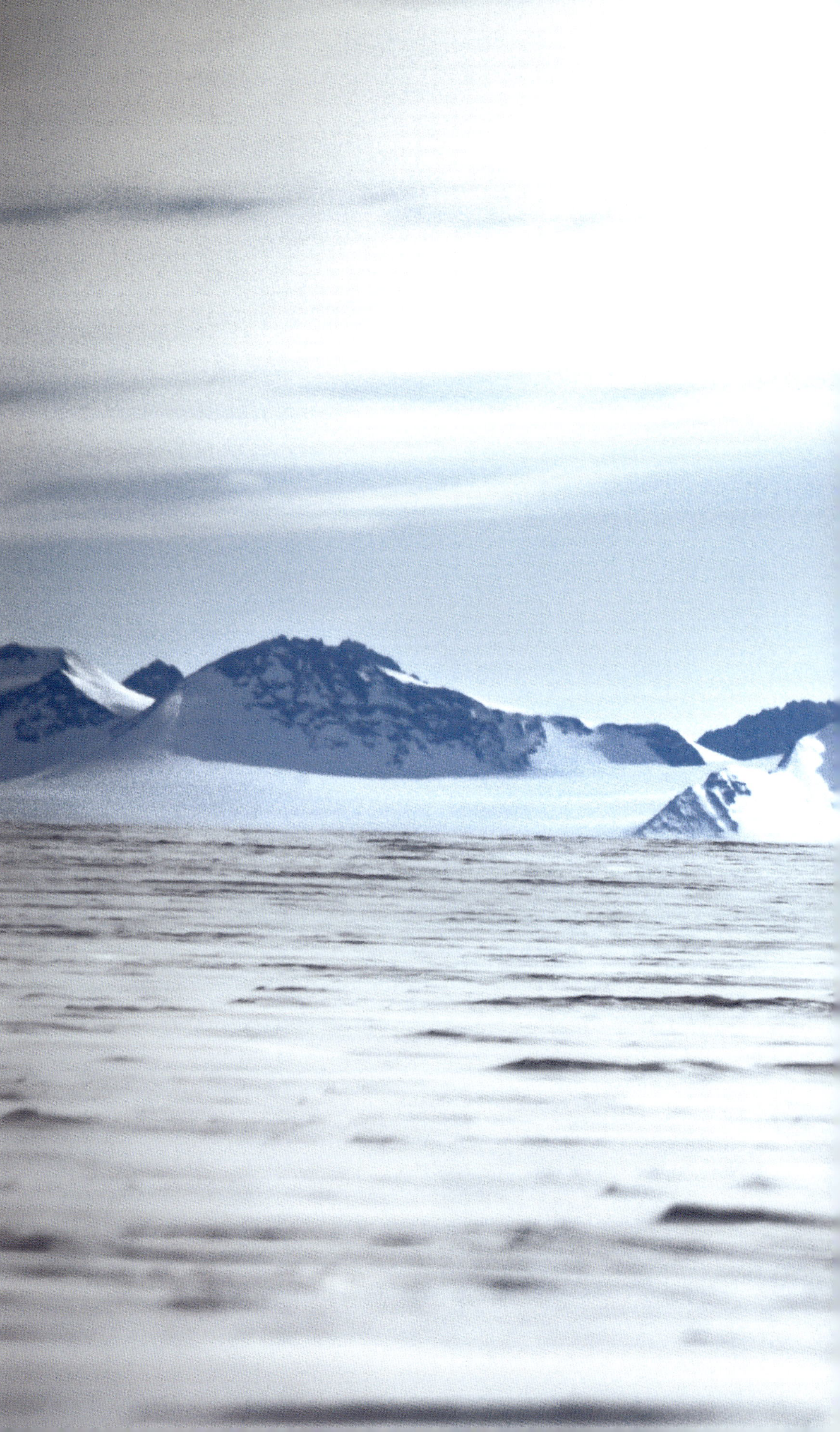

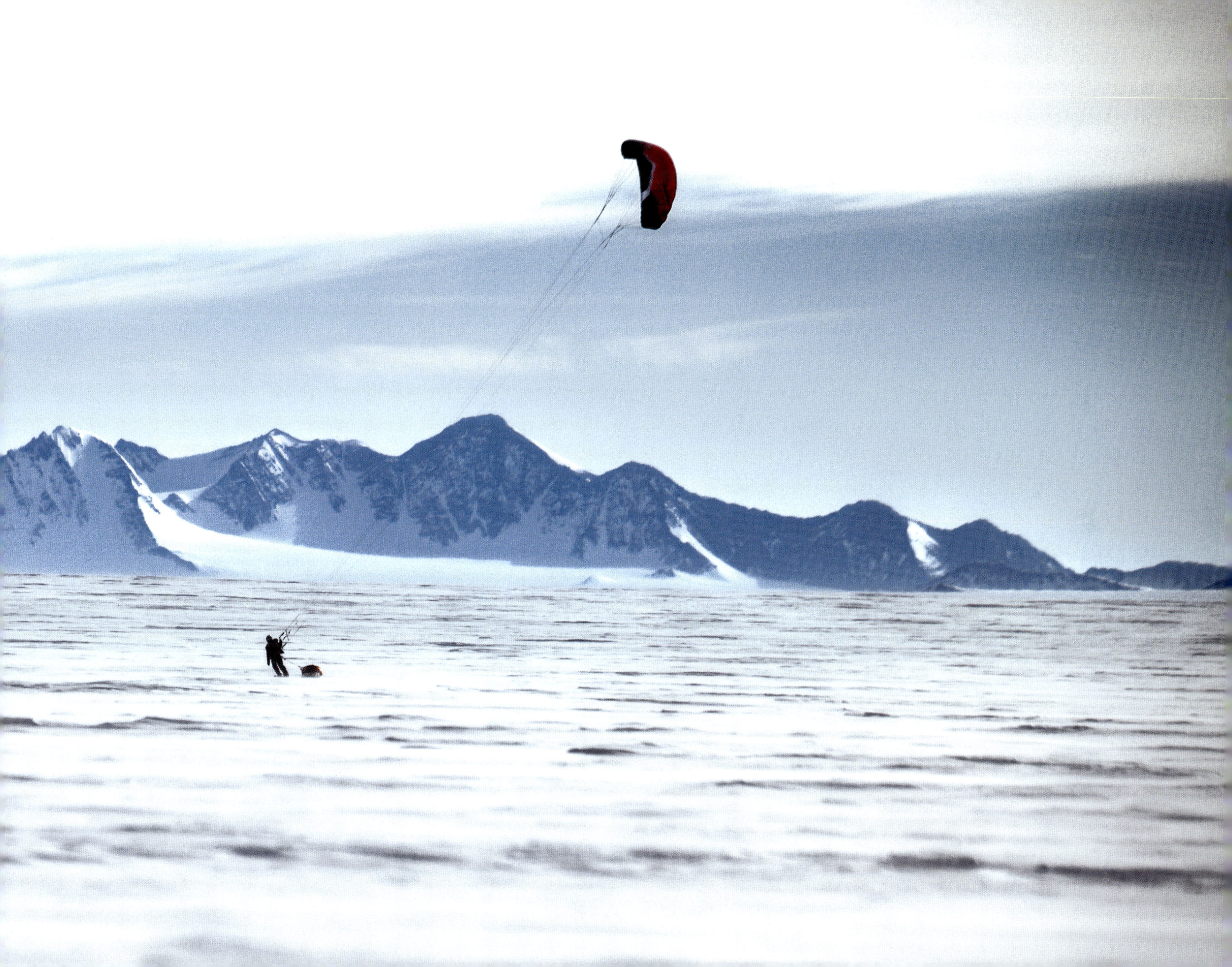

FOREWORD

JIMMY CHIN

Why do people willfully choose pain as a recreational pursuit? It is a good question, which I have spent much of my life pondering, often in the vertical space, when my own life hung by mere metal filaments precariously placed on a rock. After all, to intentionally put yourself in harm's way flies in the face of all evolutionary instincts. Avoiding risk whenever possible has been foundational to the survival of the species. But for some humans, flirting with danger is the badge of a life fully lived. And collectively, at least, whether or not we choose to partake in balancing life and death, we cannot help but cultivate a fascination for that space in between, the place we call extreme.

The great Polish mountaineer Wojciech Kurtyka once said, "Alpinism is the art of suffering." As you'll see while turning the pages of this book, that idea certainly applies to polar journeys too. So much goes into an expedition that is unseen: the preparation, fundraising, training, and, most importantly, the dance with the unpredictable. Expeditions are nothing if not a test of nerves in the face of the unexpected.

And then comes the mission. All the preparation is but a prelude for the quest to have an apex exchange with nature. Nature, at its fiercest, can be a siren call. Its song is both alluring and mischievous. But unlike Odysseus, who asked to be tied to the mast of his ship to ward off the song, expeditioners revel in pursuing the call. Is it selfish? Perhaps. People often refer to adventure as a mistress, but I think that description oversimplifies what is more profound and more innocent. Sure, there are the friendships and loyalties; sharing experiences facing the unknown creates bonds that are unique to that space and cannot be duplicated outside of it.

But it is not just about the sport and fellowships. There is the craft. Climbing helps me understand why musicians make music, why artists make art. The craft formalizes the search for a higher purpose at the edge of ourselves. Inherent to that are the mechanics of pain. Pain is an internal contradiction of these experiences. We manufacture a world of pain and fear, and then go to great lengths to research equipment, techniques, terrain, and weather predictions to incrementally mitigate that fear. A reasonable person doing cost-benefit analysis might simply say, "Cut the pain and enjoy life." If I had a penny for each time someone said to me that I am glutton for punishment, I could probably buy myself a new pair of climbing shoes. But the craft is a doorway to experience the sublime again and again, and that transcends any sport. It is what creates balance in a space that is fundamentally lacking it. It reconciles doubt with personal growth and embracing the process. In the end, we go to these places to find the best versions of ourselves. And that spiritual dimension, I like to think, benefits not only me, but also everyone around me.

Beyond athleticism and personal milestones, there is an inherent connection with nature. Words cannot do justice to the treat of feasting your eyes on your surroundings while cold air cuts your face like razor blades and frozen fingers barely hang on to life. There is simply nothing like the pinnacle of achievement in those conditions; it is bigger than any award. To be fully present and find your center in the midst of this chaos is the quest, and it is a privilege that I have never taken for granted.

Nature is bigger than us, and extreme conditions are quick to settle that score. To pull out a camera in that context and compose a shot is a challenge that few will understand. Arguably, it is less choice than instinct. It is a calling. I have always believed that you become the shooter you were destined to be. And when I experience a feeling about something that I understand in a setting that is uniquely confronting, I feel compelled to share it.

Extreme shooters feel duty bound to share. The best immersive adventure photography aims to do two things: capture the essence of a scene, and lend a feeling of participatory engagement right from your armchair. Sebastian's photography transports me to life on the edge. Through his lens, I get to revisit Queen Maud Land in Antarctica, a place that I climbed in 2017, but from a different perspective. Whether near the North Pole, in Greenland, or in Antarctica, months of trudging are distilled down to the ethos of adventure in his visual diaries. On each page of this epic book, I am reminded that it is often when the soul is threatened that the very best in us shows up. Enjoy the ride!

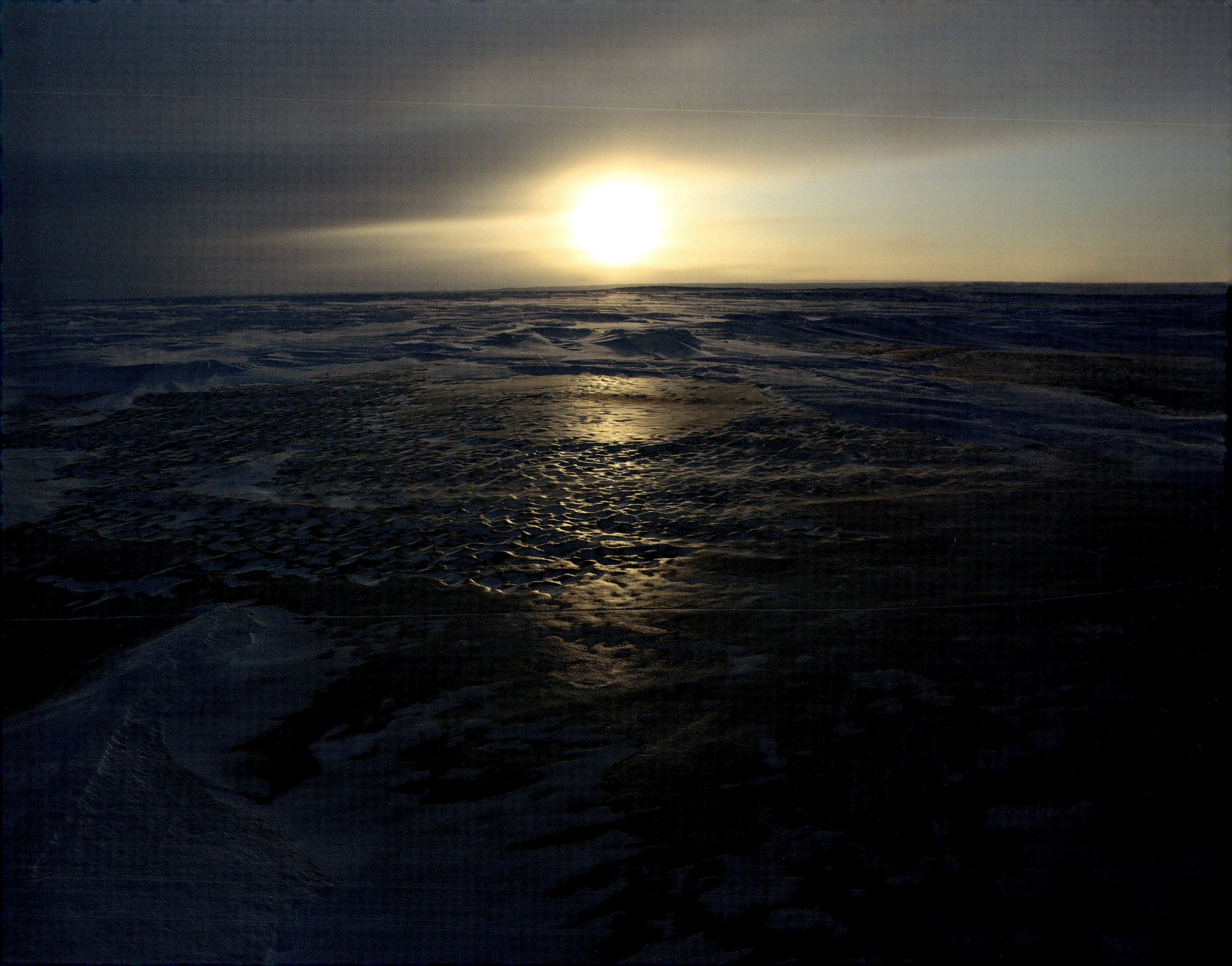

INTRODUCTION

SEBASTIAN COPELAND

"Great God! This is an awful place." Scribbled in Captain Robert Falcon Scott's tragic diary on his return trip from the South Pole in 1912, these words have lived in various iterations in the hearts of every explorer attempting to leave a mark on polar history. Scott and his men would perish on the Antarctic ice from cold and starvation, sealing their place in exploration folklore. But this thinly veiled plea, tormented as it was, has all but roused a very singular human appetite for self-inflicted misery. Technology may have eased critical aspects of modern exploration, namely comfort and safety, but the toil remains, as do many dangers. And polar mystique endures to this day, teasing adventure seekers with myriad possibilities to challenge human grit.

Upon returning from the moon, the Apollo 11 astronauts famously said that they had learned more about themselves on that mission than they had about the moon. With its barren plains, mountains, and valleys, the moon's features display characteristics that echo some of its earthly counterpart. In fact, the moon and our polar caps have a lot in common. To call them welcoming would be a stretch of reason. Both are cold, generally void of life, and entirely antagonistic to human life. They are both deserts; if water is present, it exists mostly in frozen form. And survival in both realms is strictly defined by finite resources that are brought along, putting a de facto limit on our capacity to maintain life. In other words, overextending a visit is not prescribed for good health.

So, what could be more fun than to venture there?

The impulse to discover has been entrenched in human DNA since we began migrating out of Africa two million years ago. Fueled by our most basic instinct—the curiosity to move—exploration is what we do when we are born. It is society that dulls that spirit. The appeal of open spaces harks back to our central mechanical achievement: our ability to walk. And isn't walking the first miracle of life after birth? We commemorate our children's maiden steps on film and in photographs. For most of us who enjoy the privilege, walking is the building block of our independence, freedom, and expression. Despite becoming more sedentary, we continue to cultivate a fascination for nature's untouched spaces, culminating with the ones we understand least, perhaps fundamentally because we find in them a canvas to paint ourselves anew.

In the modern age of remote mapping, exploration of our planet's ice surfaces has turned decidedly personal. The pinpoint accuracy of satellite observation makes obsolete the toil of early pioneers and cartographers and narrows the need for ground-level surveys. Consequently, crossing a frozen landscape on foot today can seem mostly aspirational, and a fool's errand. But the poet W. H. Auden must have had the ice deserts in mind when he coined the phrase "altogether elsewhere." Because the exotic appeal is not just external. A desert is the landscape of the imaginary and the sacred. It is where we go to have conversations with God. And there is something inherently human about introspection in the void of these giant spaces. The isolation can confront us with questions about ourselves that we had not sought to ask: Who am I, and why am I here? In the stark vastness of the great white, answers come easier because there aren't many places to hide.

I have never faced an enemy combatant. The army turned me down, which is just as well since I'm averse to killing anything. But there was something about combat that I felt naturally drawn to. Whatever it was that lived inside of me, which I struggled to understand, I figured I could channel and put to good use in nature. I didn't romanticize heroism or whatever notion adrenaline is inextricably associated with. The best I could come up with was polar exploration.

This has meant spending months at a time immersed in grueling circumstances in the horizontal space, conquering nothing especially important other than cold distance. "Conquerors of the useless," as Yvon Chouinard would say. Polar exploration is at once the most overstated skill and misunderstood misery. A journey to the heart of the ice will mix bliss and despair in equal parts. It is foundational and a wrecking ball at the same time, arbitrarily shuffling tedium with fury. But coming out of it will lead, always, to one formidable place: transformation. I was lucky to cross thousands of miles on skis in some of the most remote locations on

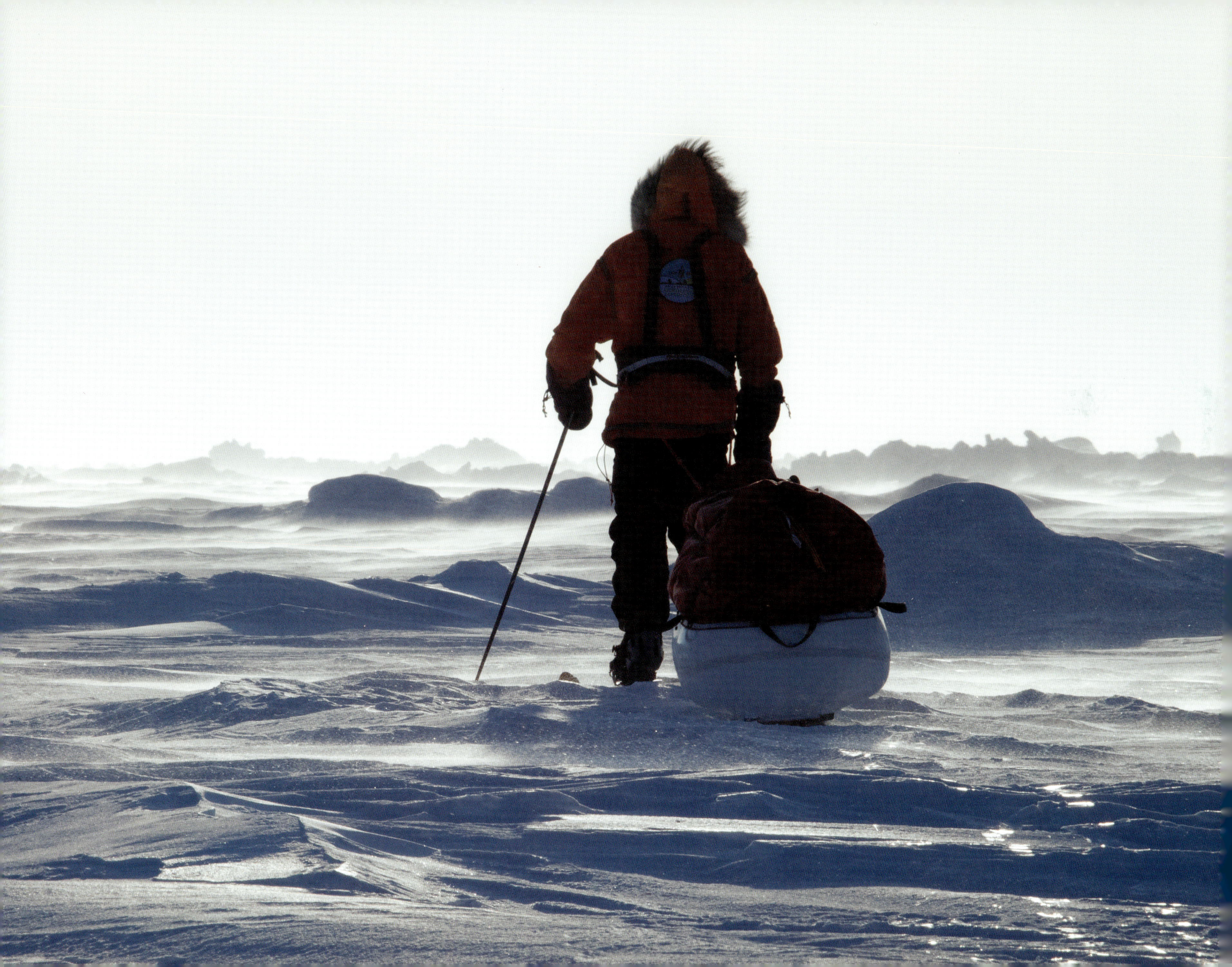

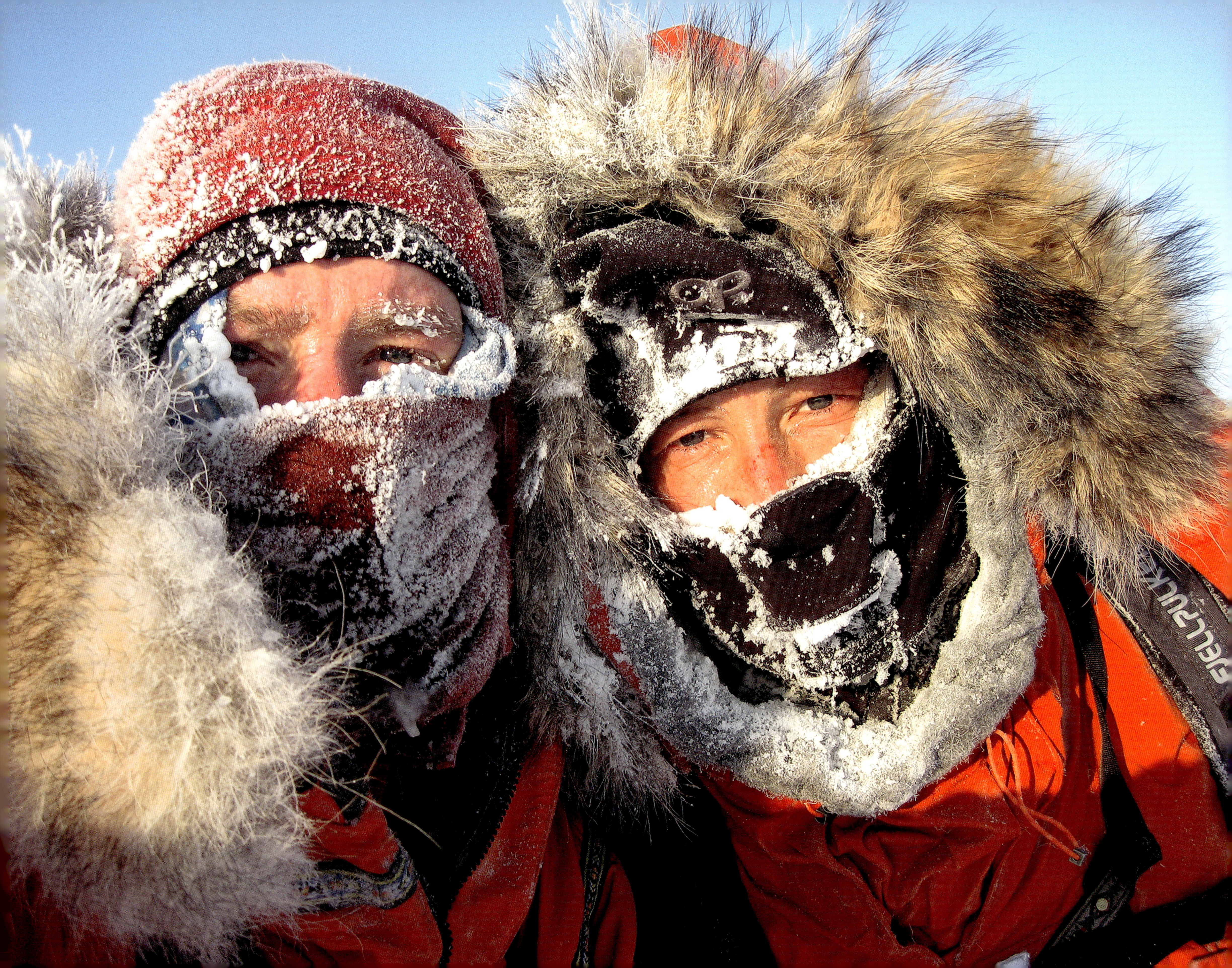

Earth. In Antarctica alone, this meant 2,500 miles over 84 days, on skis and kites, with temperatures hardly warming beyond -22°F.

I am sometimes asked about the residual effect of those expeditions. Long, unsupported ice missions typically imply isolation, most notably from external interactions and people. Whether traveling alone or with a partner, the weeks and months of limited sensorial exposure, the simplicity of purpose, and the monastic, virtually meditative existence in a brutally antagonistic environment that commands prolonged hyperfocus can make for a rough reentry. Sights, smells, sounds, communications, technology: all are sudden assaults that require adaptation. The behavioral adjustment and flashbacks can trigger a lingering condition that resembles post-traumatic stress disorder (PTSD). Physiologically, the body's breakdown from the sustained effort, diet, and cold is startling. On the ice, it is so gradual as to be imperceptible; besides, there are no mirrors. But before-and-after photos tell a story that words cannot. When the dust settles and bruises heal, what remains from the immersion is empowerment that comes from learning a new language and the intense exchange with nature that transpires. Additionally, the bonds created from blind trust in a partner must resemble those forged on the battlefield. I cannot give enough thanks for the many times my partner has been central to my safety or helped preserve pieces of me—not to speak of their cold stoicism during my shooting sessions. There is closeness that can only derive from the strength of those shared experiences.

With this book, I wanted to give a snapshot of life on the trail in the frozen space. It is more diary than a deliberate attempt at making art, and certainly does not represent an anthology in any sense of the word. I apologize in advance to those who will see in this volume the indulgent mark of a narrow point of view. Undeniably, it is, since it chronicles just my experiences, and a slim slice at that. My intention is simply to send a postcard from the edge, by assembling a visual account of some of my seminal trips. I focused mostly on the ones that include what I loosely refer to as the Polar Grand Slam, covering distances greater than 100 nautical miles on all three of the largest ice concentrations on the planet: the Arctic Ocean, Greenland, and Antarctica. The choice of distance is arbitrary, of course, but defining it that way is a deliberate attempt at showcasing immersive commitments while minimizing adventure milestones. Those hold great value, to be sure, and I have pursued some myself with both successes and failures. But the accounts detailed in this book, visual and otherwise, focus on the experiences themselves: the grind, the sweat, the struggles, the joy. And, most importantly, the deep communion with the elements.

To call this the path less traveled would be an understatement; these paths were seldom and sometimes never traveled at all. And it is the gift of photography to capture glimpses of what are undeniably unique experiments at the edge of ourselves. Sharing them is also a way for me to relive them with you. See you on the trail.

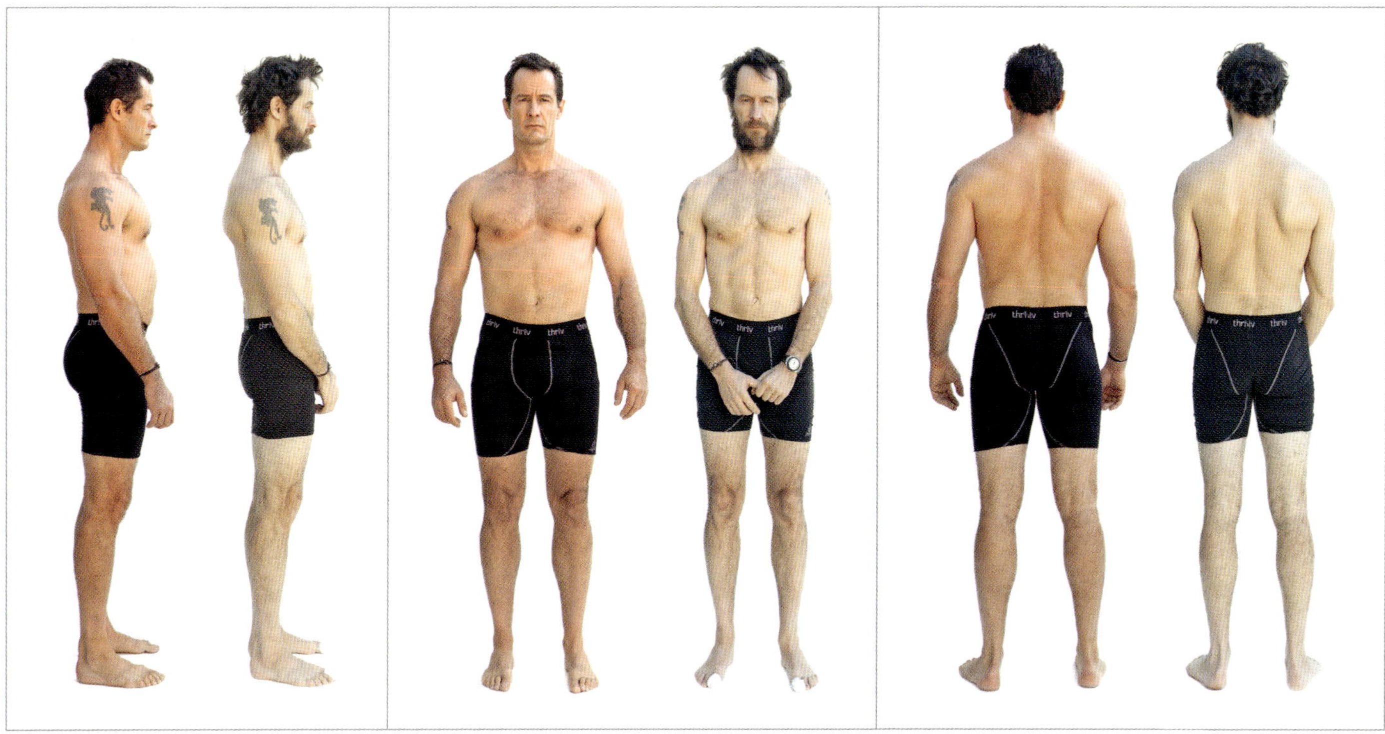

THE COLD ART OF POLAR TRAVEL

SEBASTIAN COPELAND

THE ENDS OF THE EARTH

The Arctic tern may well be the greatest voyager of all time. Long before Aristotle theorized about a *terra australis* at the bottom of the Earth, the tern was already journeying there, migrating from the Arctic to Antarctica and back, as it does annually, covering distances of up to 50,000 miles. The British explorer James Cook would surely have crossed paths with these extraordinary fliers when he first entered the Antarctic waters on January 17, 1773. Even then, Antarctica would not be discovered for another 50 years. The landmass remained theoretical until 1820, when Fabian Gottlieb von Bellingshausen and Mikhail Lazarev first caught sight of a body of ice that turned out to be East Antarctica.

A year later, the sealer John Davis allegedly set foot on land, opening exploration and commercial prospects on what became the Earth's seventh continent. Indeed, the discovery captured the imagination of intrepid travelers keen on the promise of fortune and fame on this *terra incognita*. But for most of them, the journey did not extend far from the coast. Out there, the feeling went, was only death. In fact, it would take another 90 years after Davis for Antarctica's most iconic destination—latitude 90° south—also known as the South Pole, to be reached by humans. When the Norwegian explorer Roald Amundsen crossed this vast expanse of white and planted his flag at the South Pole on December 14, 1911, life had not been present there for at least 34 million years. Venture inland on an ice desert and not even the valiant tern will be found. With no food source anywhere, life simply vanishes. Ice sheets are some of the most barren and inhospitable expanses on Earth.

At the opposite end of the world, the Arctic had long been a place where humans were tested in resolve and grit as they sought opportunity. Unlike Antarctica—a landmass surrounded by oceans—the Arctic is primarily an ocean surrounded by coastal lands. Despite easier access in the Northern Hemisphere, the region remained onerous for its harsh climate and desolation. A geological uplift closed the Arctic Ocean gateways, like the Bering, 2.6 million years ago. The Arctic became thermally isolated, and the ice buildup generated a cooling that once extended all the way south to where New York City is now. The Pleistocene or Ice Age lasted until about 11,700 years ago, but given the polar regions' limited exposure to sunlight, it has remained frigid even while the rest of the world has thawed.

That harshness was no barrier for human enterprise. After leaving Africa two million years ago, and on our way to explore Eurasia and then farther east, we eventually crossed into the Americas 25,000 years ago, on foot, in pursuit of mammoths. Indeed, the Last Glacial Maximum exposed the Bering Land Bridge between Asia and North America when sea levels would have been 400 feet lower. The Beringian ice corridor enabled hunting populations to push into the North American Arctic, and then into Greenland from Siberia, around 3,000 BC. Hunting and gathering these unfamiliar lands would have been full of tragic uncertainty, but undoubtedly, our ancestors experienced the timeless wonder of discovery when crossing a bridge that revealed some of the more spectacular vistas filling our polar world. Through the millennia, the visual impact hasn't relented.

With more sophisticated farming and engineering practices and their impact on economies, we became more sedentary. Our ancestral urge to explore was diminished by external forces and building walls. Civilization eventually brought claims of territorial ownership, hindering our freedom to get on the move. But the siren call of wild places remains deeply anchored in human DNA. Each expansion of geographic statehood and colonization bears the signature of human temerity, and with it comes a push to explore further. At scale, the most recent illustration is the North American experiment. Notwithstanding the abject treatment of Indigenous populations, as happened prior in South America, India, and Africa, the movement of early settlers is a testament to human's brazen curiosity. Ever expansive, the edge of our exploration can now be found in the depths of the oceans and the outer reaches of the solar system. Not much of the Earth's skin has been unseen, except in large deserts. And that predominantly means the ice.

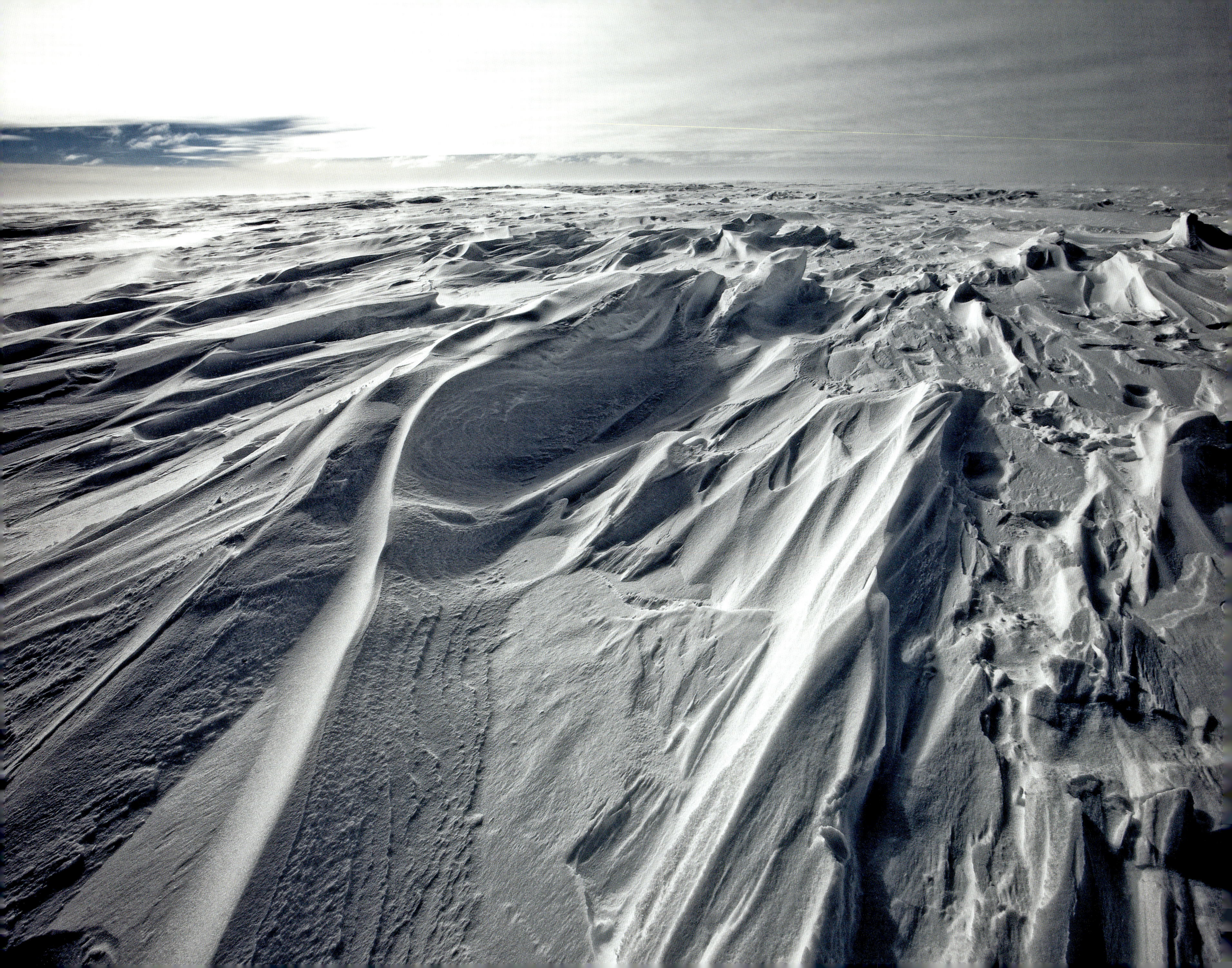

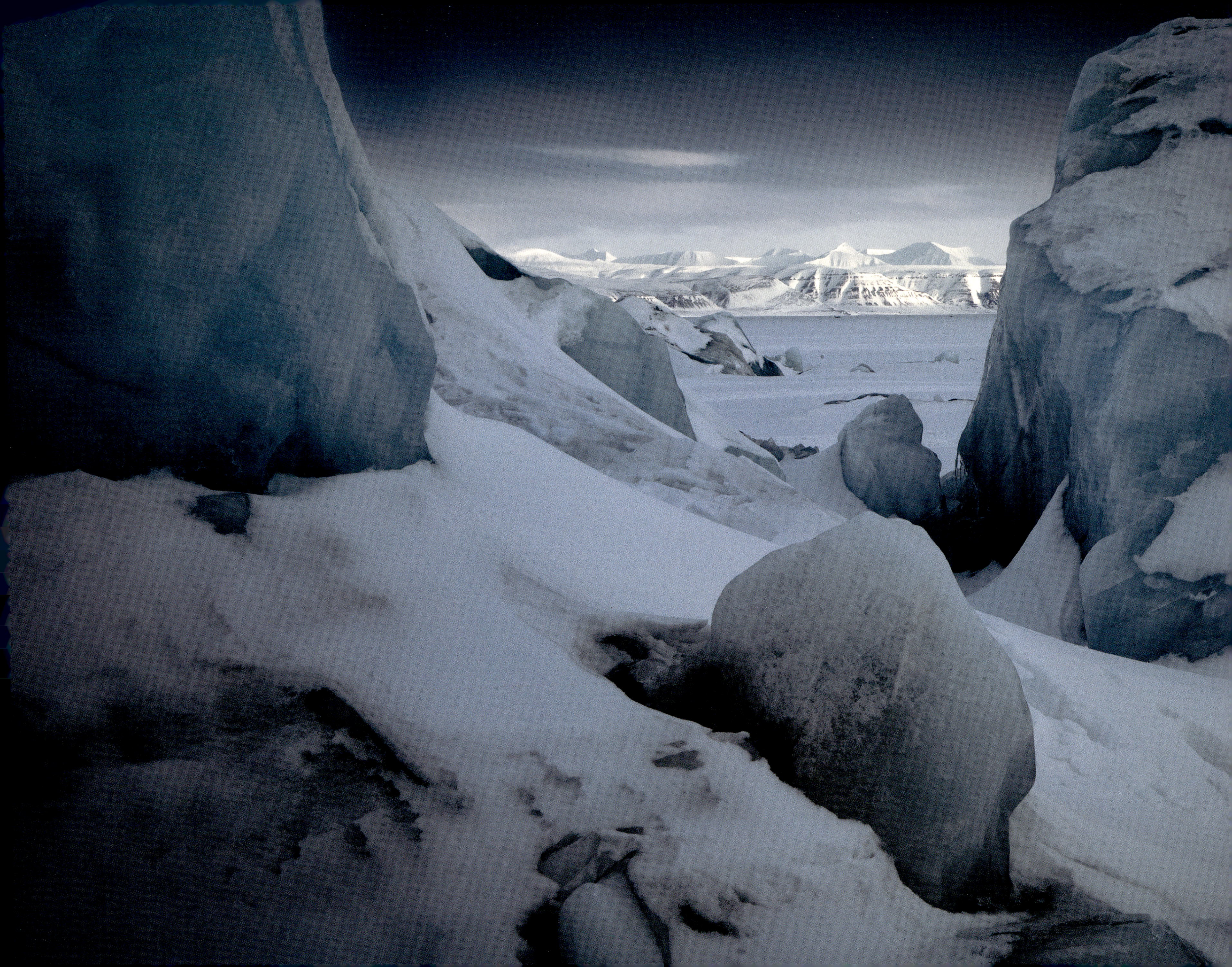

THE WEIGHT OF HISTORY

Polar exploration historically served national economic or scientific interests. Throughout the 18th and 19th centuries, cartographers set off in earnest to define the Earth's landmasses. That also meant the northernmost regions. The Norse settlers arrived in Greenland in 985, led by the Viking adventurer Erik the Red, and populated the edge of the world until they disappeared 400 years later. But the earliest record of a European-funded discovery mission to southeastern Greenland is the Pining-Pothorst Expedition of 1472, solicited by King Christian I of Denmark. With the discovery of the New World two decades later came the search for the holy grail of maritime missions, one that held the lucrative promise of cutting shipping routes for the Northern Hemisphere between Asia and Europe: the fabled Northwest Passage. In 1497, England's King Henry VII commissioned John Cabot to explore the route. On the way to Alaska and the Bering Strait, icebergs blocking multitudes of channels between small islands in the northern territories of Canada made this a treacherous undertaking. Cabot failed.

For the next 450 years, some of history's best navigators tried their luck to find a passage. Names like Jacques Cartier, William Baffin, Jens Munk, Vitus Bering, Martin Frobisher, Henry Hudson, John Davis, Captain James Cook, and John Franklin valiantly represented the crowns of England, Russia, France, and Norway. All failed, many meeting their fate in the process. Of those explorers, none is more famous than the British Royal Navy officer Sir John Franklin. His two vessels, the HMS *Erebus* and HMS *Terror*, and 128 men vanished in 1845 in search of the passage. They would never be found (although the wrecks of *Erebus* and *Terror* were finally located on the seabed in 2014 and 2016, respectively). Ships were notoriously forced into the brutal and often fatal vise of the Arctic winters, trapped, and then crushed by the ice. Crews had to overwinter, sometimes multiple seasons, before being slowly killed by scurvy, hunger, and cold, or drowned in storms. Some were lost after setting off on foot in desperate attempts to reach southerly colonies. Some simply went mad.

But in 1906, over the course of three years, the Northwest Passage was finally navigated from one end to the other by none other than Roald Amundsen, five years ahead of his South Pole discovery. (It would take until 1944 for a Royal Canadian Mounted Police sergeant, Henry Larsen, to successfully make the 900-mile Northwest Passage journey in one season.) With much of the open-water coastlines surveyed, maritime exploration in the Arctic faded. The British proclaimed the Dominion of Canada in 1867; Greenland went to Denmark after the Napoleonic Wars in 1814; and the United States purchased Alaska from Russia in 1867. The other two Arctic nations, Norway and Russia, were sovereign states; therefore, territorial designs from Europe came to an end. Settlers went to work prospecting for resources, to the detriment of Indigenous people. And Arctic exploration turned from sea to ice; from ships to human- or dog-powered enterprises.

At the other end of the world, James Cook was the first to circumnavigate Antarctica, between 1772 and 1775, although he did so unknowingly. The mapping that he undertook of nearby islands, notably of South Georgia and the South Sandwich Islands (which he claimed for Britain's Overseas Territories), opened the way for a spate of important maritime discoveries. James Weddell, Charles Wilkes, and Jules Dumont d'Urville all contributed invaluable charting of the region's geography. Sealers and whalers had long since navigated the sub-Antarctic Southern Ocean, but were reluctant to cross into the Antarctic Circle. An old mariner's idiom warns that below latitude 40° south, there is no law; below 50° south, there is no God. Antarctica begins at 66.5° south. Facing vicious storms in iceberg-laden seas, and the unpredictable onset of the sea ice, made pushing south into the Antarctic Circle a roll

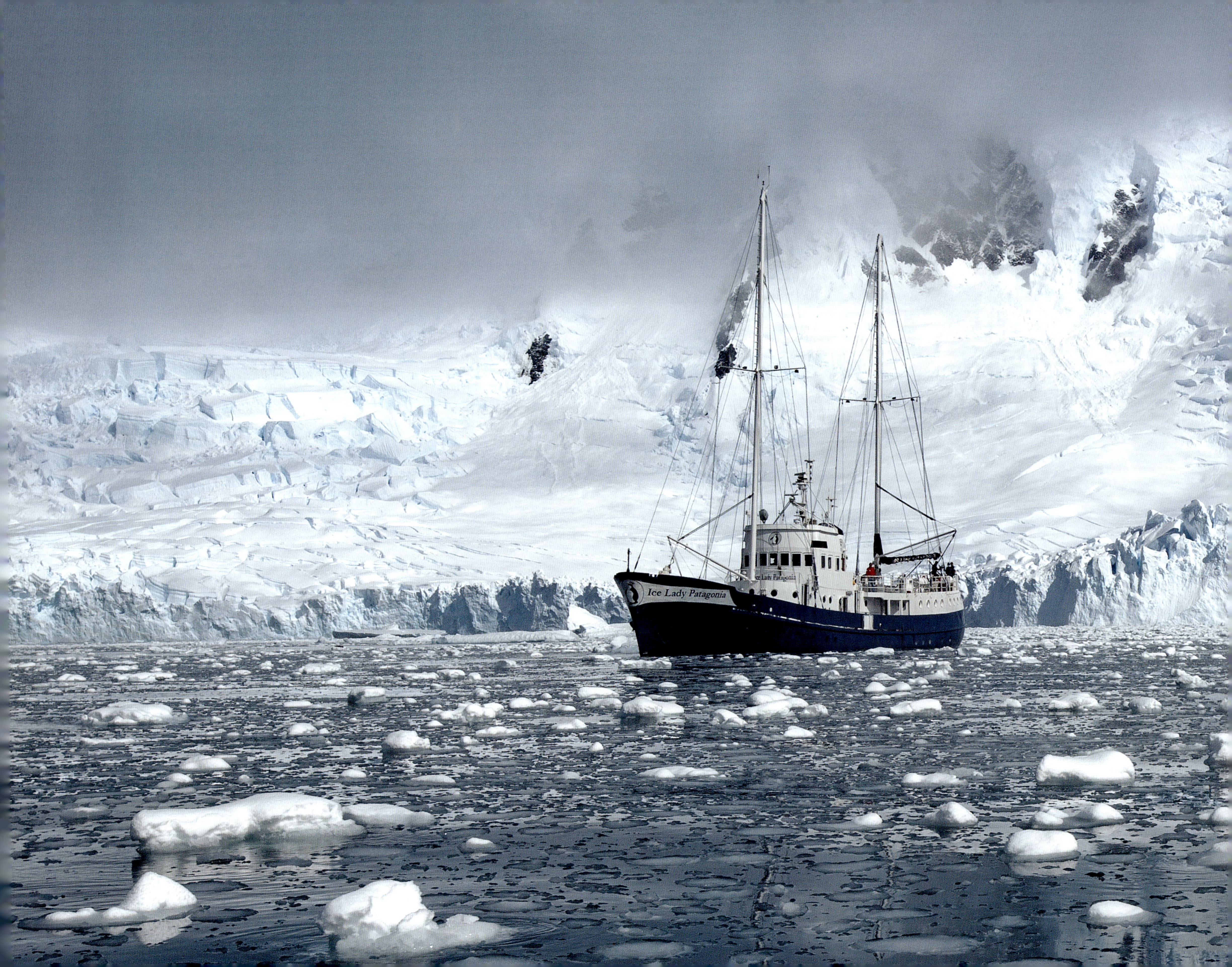
Ice Lady Patagonia

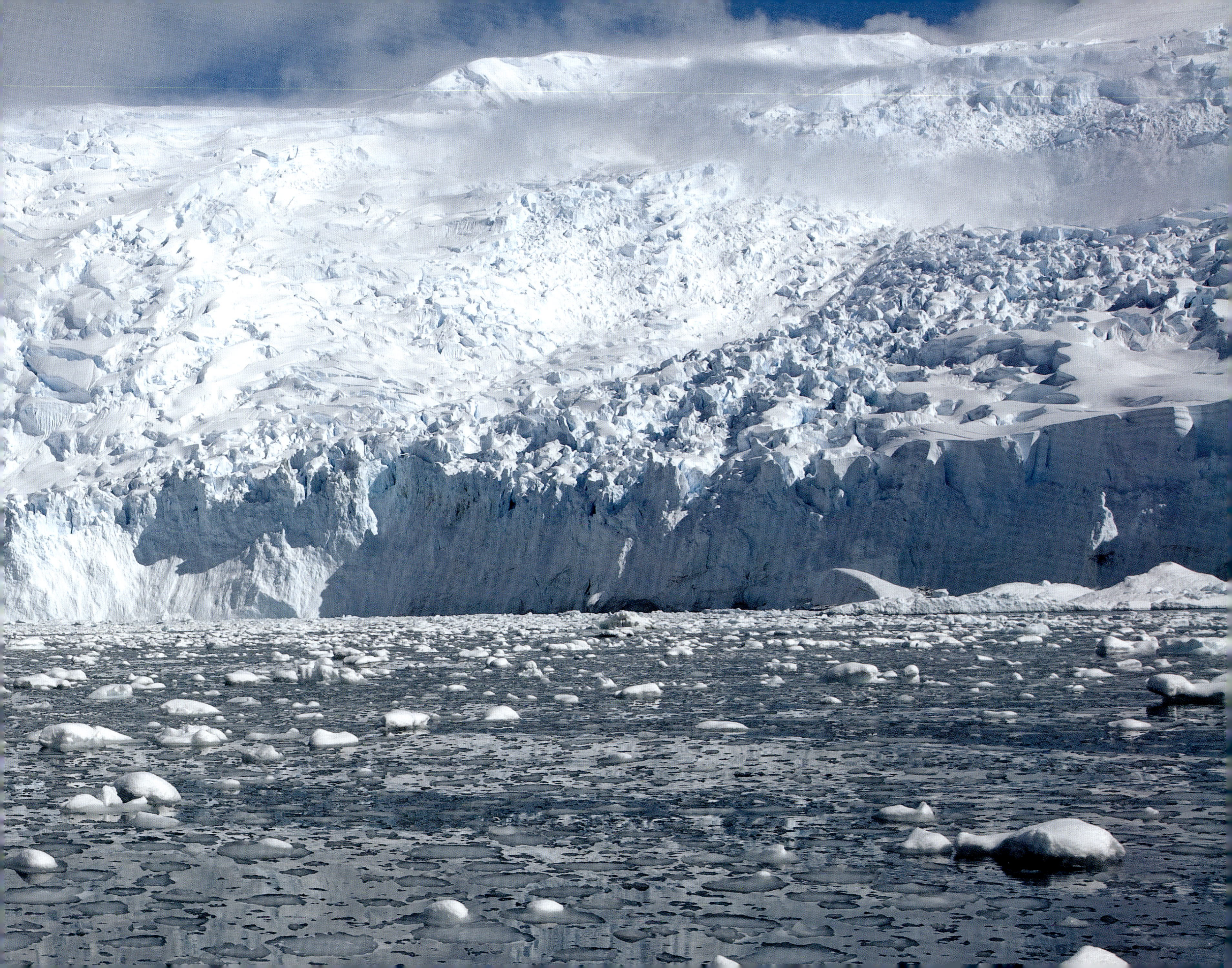

of the dice at best. Those perils explain why Antarctica's massive landmass was not discovered sooner.

As with the High North, missions to Antarctica were often financed and sometimes sanctioned by the crown or governments hoping to secure economic or geostrategic benefits. The Falkland Islands had been claimed by the British in 1765, and by 1819 they added the South Shetlands archipelago to their growing portfolio. For France, after Louis XV had laid claim to the Kerguelen Islands in 1772, Dumont d'Urville asserted sovereignty for the French over Adélie Land, which he had discovered during his 1837–1840 mission. But the middle of the century brought a lull to Antarctic exploration. After discovering the Ross Sea and the Victoria Land coast during his epic four-year expedition starting in 1839, the British Royal Navy officer James Clark Ross would then declare that there were no discoveries left of interest in Antarctica. The continent's lifeless interior was, by all accounts, daunting—though tantalizing. But it did not suggest economic rewards. And while all matters of plundering levied onto the Antarctic marine ecosystem were ongoing, by the end of the 19th century, the general sense was that most of the world had been explored and carved. Much like in the Arctic, it left an empty white space at the bottom of the world's maps: the ice.

ON THE SHOULDERS OF GIANTS

The history of polar exploration abounds with epic tales of human survival. But one stands out for its sheer scope of ambition and ultimate accomplishment. With much of the polar coasts mapped out, all eyes turned to the poles. In 1888, Fridtjof Nansen, a young Norwegian scientist, accomplished the first successful crossing of Greenland on skis, from east to west. Ridiculed at the start for shunning previous strategies, his stripped-down approach, and the audacity of his inexperience, Nansen was welcomed as a national hero upon his return from the daring and successful mission. On the strength of that notoriety, Nansen planned for a much more ambitious expedition, one that garnered the support of his government and galvanized the press: the discovery of the North Pole.

After coming across a new study on ocean currents over the Arctic Ocean, Nansen theorized that if he were to build a ship sturdy enough to sustain being trapped in the ice over many months, the Transpolar Drift Stream—the dominant ocean currents moving from Russia to Greenland—would transport him close to, if not directly over, the North Pole. *Fram* was built with the singular purpose of navigating into the ice. Experienced navigators and polar explorers were dubious and critical of the plan, but on June 24, 1893, *Fram* left Norway, traveling north toward Russia. By September, the pack ice had solidified around the hull, and the ship started drifting. One year later, progress was slow, and the ship's path led Nansen to believe they would never reach the pole that way. On March 14, 1895, he and partner Hjalmar Johansen set off on skis with some dogs and enough food supplies for 50 days to cover the 410-mile distance to the North Pole. *Fram* and its crew would continue drifting, and Nansen estimated that the ship would eventually break away near the Norwegian archipelago of Spitsbergen. He and Johansen would also head for Spitsbergen on foot after reaching 90° north. From there, they would catch a ride home from a local whaler. They would all meet back in Norway.

It did not go as planned.

Travel on the winter sea ice is slow and exceedingly tough. The broken terrain makes hauling heavy loads over fields of ice boulders and open-water cracks (known as leads) challenging. But the men's progress was further hampered by what they understood to be a negative drift: for each mile covered, a portion was lost to the ice crust moving backward due to currents and wind. Like walking on a treadmill. There are no food sources on the winter sea ice, so their survival relied exclusively on the provisions they had brought with them. By April 7, Nansen asserted that even if they reached their objective, they might not make the return trip alive. The decision was made to forgo the pole and head south. But on a fateful day in April, Nansen forgot to wind his watch, thereby losing indispensable information to accurately measure their heading by sextant. From then on, as they searched for the Russian islands of Franz Josef Land, their bearing would merely be approximate.

By the end of May, fox tracks and bird flights overhead intimated that land was nearby. But journeying on increasingly unstable ice from the seasonal melt was painstaking and dangerous, and it was August 6 before the men reached land on the Russian archipelago. By then, they had killed all their dogs, and the land gave them meager opportunities to hunt and scavenge. Traveling from island to island, they continued south. With the approaching cold and darkening of the winter season, they were forced to hunker down in a makeshift shelter and overwinter. The men fed off seal, walrus, and bear meat, narrowly escaping death from their encounters with polar bears. On May 19, 1896, they again began moving south, using the sleds they had turned into kayaks as the sea ice opened. By an astonishing turn of luck, upon resting on shore on June 17, they ran into an exploring party surveying the newly discovered islands. Three years and two months after the start of their mission, on August 13, 1896, long after being thought dead, Nansen and Johansen made landfall in Norway, where they were greeted as heroes.

As an epilogue to the story, the men learned that *Fram* had in fact been released from the ice as predicted and made its way to Spitsbergen. In a Hollywood-style ending, after spending barely five days home, Nansen and Johansen ferried in a hurry to Spitsbergen, where they were reunited with their ship and the original crew. *Fram* entered the harbor of Kristiania (now called

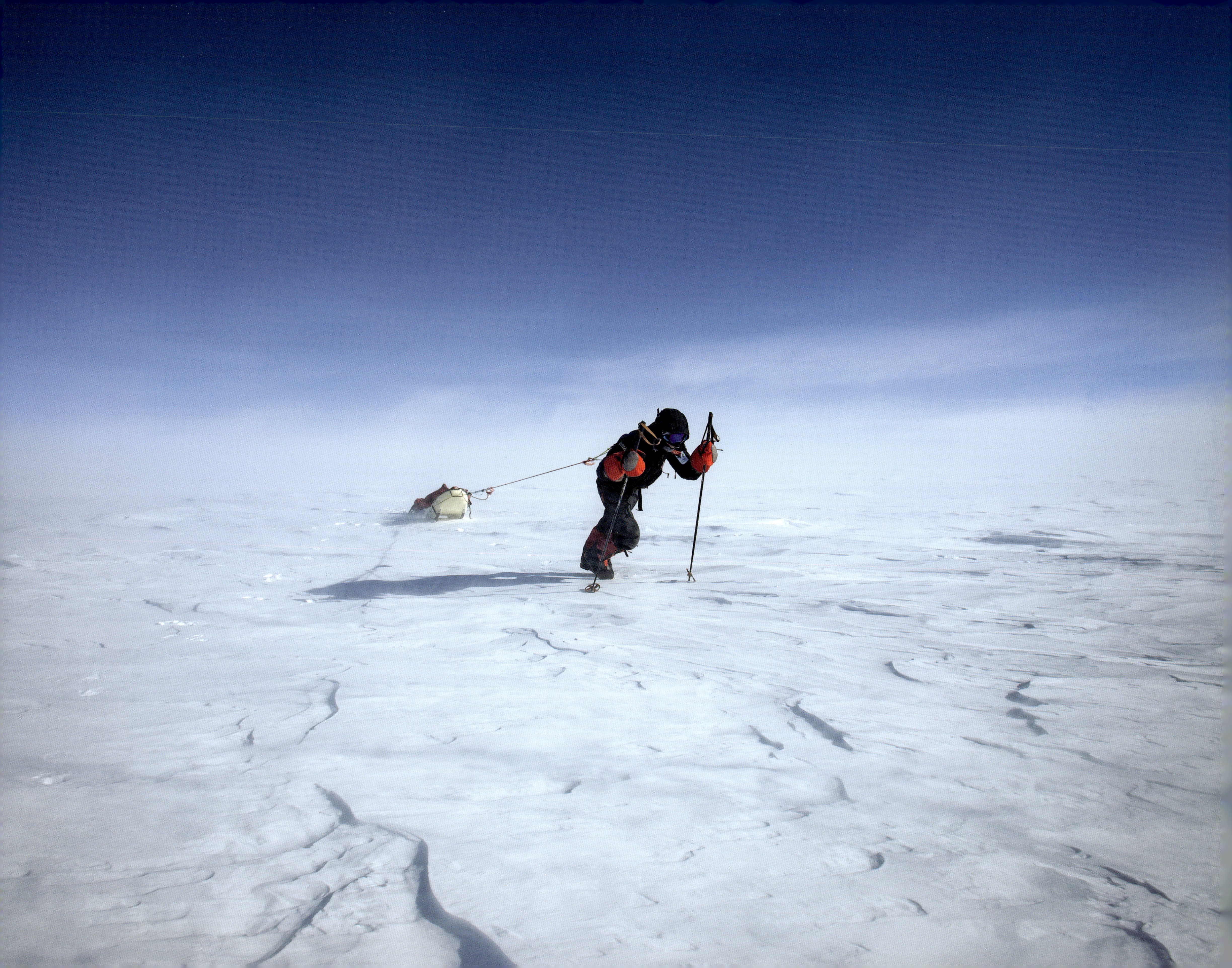

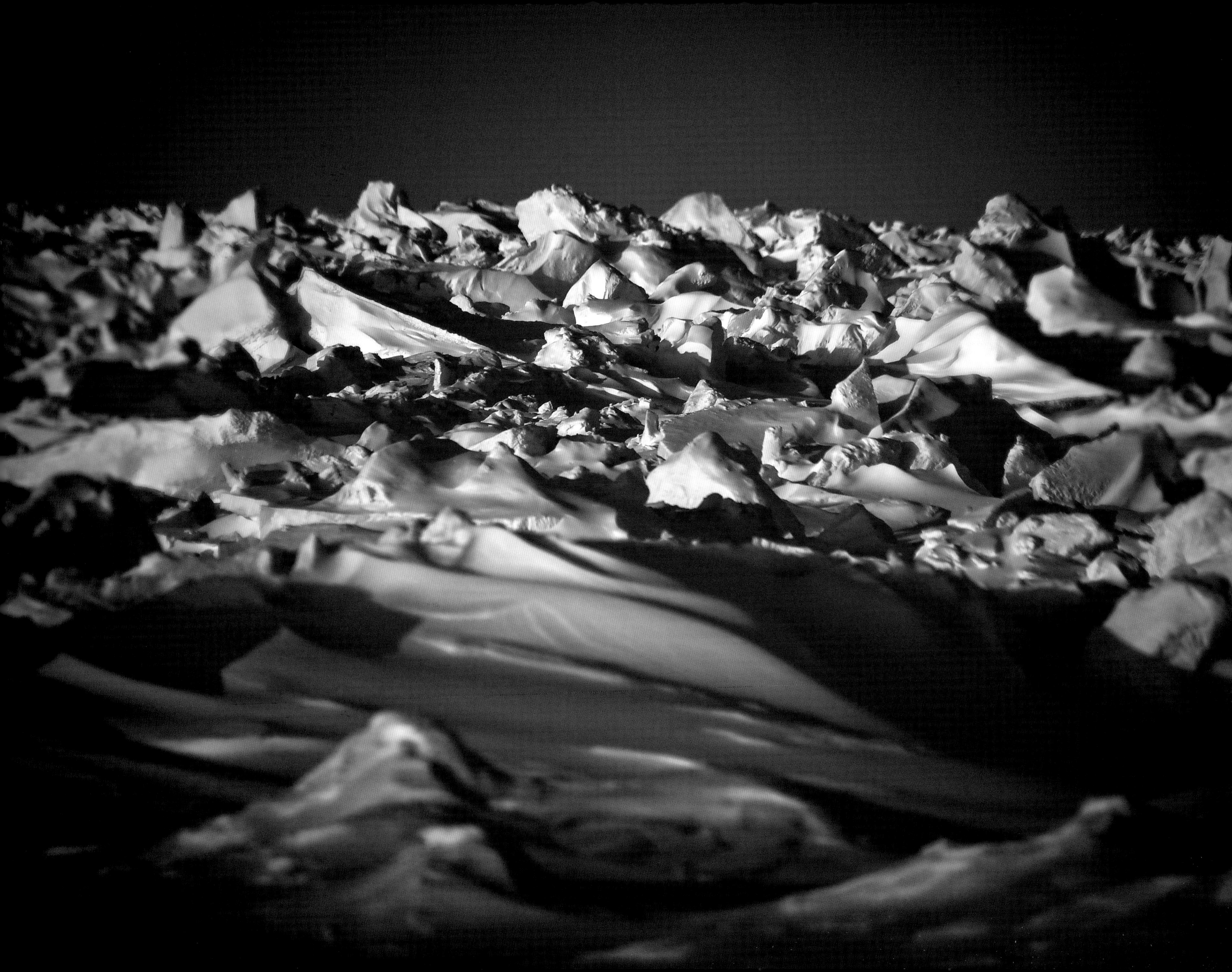

Oslo) a few days later, where the king and packed crowds celebrated their return. The men instantly walked into the pages of history. In so doing, Nansen ushered in a new age of exploration.

THE HEROIC AGE OF EXPLORATION

By pushing the boundaries of human endurance, and acquiring global fame, Nansen and Johansen emboldened scores of adventure seekers to dream bigger in their polar pursuits, all the way to the present day. In 1995, when Richard Weber and Mikhail Malakhov completed the first and only there-and-back trip from Canada to the North Pole without outside assistance—110 days in the harshest environment on Earth—they were channeling history. The Norwegian explorer Børge Ousland completed five superb expeditions on the Arctic Ocean between 1994 and 2020, two of which retraced sections of Nansen and Johansen's steps. Others, such as the Tara Arctic or MOSAiC Expeditions, emulated *Fram* when they deliberately trapped their ships in the Arctic pack ice to conduct scientific surveys lasting more than a year (they returned in 2006 and 2020, respectively). In fact, *Tara*—a 130-foot schooner—followed the path that *Fram* had taken almost exactly a hundred years prior, with one notable difference: at 507 days, it took the modern ship about half the time that *Fram* had taken to drift over the same distance, a conclusive indication of the sea ice volume's retreat due to climate change.

But to compare any of these missions to the early pioneers' journeys would be misguided. Modern explorers are tethered to outside communication, benefiting from modern fabrics, engineering, and navigation technology. And the region is simply more accessible. Today, we are typically dropped off and picked up by planes, avoiding the imperative of overwintering before setting off and the drawn-out and grinding return that was customary a century ago. Modern explorers have it unquestionably easier, even if the dangers remain, particularly as conditions on the sea ice, in the north at least, are increasingly complicating Arctic missions on foot due to climate change. But the glory belongs to the past. It isn't that the human spirit has dimmed since; it's just a case of being born in the wrong era.

Nansen, in the end, did not capture the North Pole. He did, however, accomplish reaching a "farthest north," at latitude 86°13'6" north—200 miles beyond the previous record. His mission also contributed to a better understanding of the Arctic Ocean's currents. *Fram*'s drift on the Arctic pack ice provided proof of concept to the Belgian Adrien de Gerlache. In 1898, he duplicated *Fram*'s experiment, in Antarctica this time, overwintering his ship, *Belgica*, for one year in the Bellingshausen Sea. But the North Pole was still up for grabs, and one who took notice was Robert Peary.

Peary had been on Nansen's radar since 1886 following the American explorer's unsuccessful Greenland crossing (where he nevertheless posted a second-farthest distance into the interior), a performance that informed Nansen's own crossing two years later. This time, it was the Norwegian who inspired Peary to go for the North Pole. On the heels of his failed mission, Peary had organized further travel into northern Greenland and then to the Canadian Arctic. The skills he acquired over that time gave him the confidence to go for 90° north. And he did, twice: first in 1906, without success, and more conclusively in 1909. After overwintering with his team at the edge of Canada's northernmost island, Ellesmere, Peary used multiple teams, including many Inuit, to open sections of the route and lay depots along the way. With the best dogs and five team members, he made the final dash, allegedly reaching the place where "the north wind becomes a south one," as he would later say.

While controversy later developed surrounding the veracity of his claim, Peary was said to have reached the North Pole on April 6, 1909. It then took him five months to reach Indian Harbour in Newfoundland, where he was able to send a wire to alert the world: "I have the Pole, April Sixth." Whether he did or not will never be settled, but Peary undoubtedly traveled closest to the North Pole by applying sound strategy and execution developed from his time spent with Inuit observing their way of life. Using dogs, wearing animal skin for clothing, and building igloos were some of the skills that Amundsen would also use during his successful mission to the South Pole two years later. That knowledge was eschewed by Captain Robert Falcon Scott and arguably accounts for his and his party's tragic deaths in Antarctica in 1912 on their way back from the South Pole.

THE POLES, AT LAST

With the generally accepted view—initially, at least—that Peary had reached the North Pole in 1909, there were no further known surface attempts there for another 58 years. When a determined crew of four men led by Ralph Plaisted left on snowmobiles from Minnesota—on a dare—to reach the North Pole in 1967, no one took them seriously. But they did reach into the Arctic pack ice at latitude 83°20' north before aborting their first attempt. They returned the following year and set off from Ward Hunt Island, near Ellesmere, and succeeded in being the first humans to verifiably stand on the North Pole on April 20, 1968. History was made.

Undoubtedly, this was a Herculean task. But the use of mechanical transportation, the necessary resupplies of fuel, and the fact that they were picked up by plane at the North Pole brings this accomplishment outside the scope of nonmechanized missions, and certainly away from tradition. In fact, Amundsen—again—is credited for the first verified flight over the North Pole, a claim that had been disputed by Richard E. Byrd, who—questionably—professed to having been there first, if only by a few days, in 1926.

But Wally Herbert's 1968–1969 British Trans-Arctic Expedition, spanning 3,720 miles, is officially credited as the first nonmotorized reach of the North Pole. After years of training and preparation, on February 21, 1968, Herbert and three expedition partners crossed onto the sea ice from Point Barrow, Alaska, with four dog teams. Their heading? The Norwegian archipelago of Svalbard in a straight line over the north polar cap. The team first traveled 1,200 miles on the pack ice before setting a winter camp to wait out the seasonal darkness. They drifted at the mercy of currents, facing a midwinter scare in February when their ice floe shattered, splitting their camp in the pitch darkness. Rescue is sketchy on the best of days on the northern sea ice, but it is nonexistent in the polar darkness. Connected to the world only by a radio, the team drifted around the pole without directly reaching it.

With the approaching spring equinox and the seasonal return of daylight, they broke camp and set off again in March. Their mission was facilitated with plane resupplies, an imperative for this length of travel, especially with a team of 40 dogs. On a frigid and windy day, 60 years after Peary, the men planted the Union Jack at the Geographic North Pole on April 16, 1969, the first verified expedition to reach 90° north without mechanized transportation. On May 29, 1969, they would set foot on the northernmost island of Svalbard, effectively completing the first and only surface crossing of the Arctic Ocean. The journey of 464 days spent on the pack ice—facing attacks by polar bears, vicious winter storms, open water, and temperatures reaching -76°F—is one of the more epic polar missions in modern times. (Three months later, Neil Armstrong and Buzz Aldrin would plant a flag on the moon. They covered that 234,000-mile distance in just three days.)

Peary's perceived North Pole accomplishment in 1909 left the second-most sought-after polar trophy up for grabs, and theoretically within human grasp: the Geographic South Pole. Much speculation swirled about Antarctica's interior. The enormity of the landmass was well documented as the new century turned, but the interior remained a mystery. Could an inland sea shield access to the South Pole by foot? Were dangerous predators something to prepare for? Was Antarctica the only continent on Earth where botany research had no place? The Anglo-Norwegian explorer Carsten Borchgrevink would provide answers that laid the groundwork for the subsequent success of Amundsen's and Scott's South Pole reaches. Borchgrevink's Southern Cross Expedition earned him and his men the distinction of the deepest reach into the interior at the time—at latitude 78°50' south—on February 16, 1900. And his party of 10 men was the first to overwinter on land after their ship departed for New Zealand on March 2, 1899, not to return until January of the following year. Their effort confirmed that no weapons were needed against predators in Antarctica. And their use of the Primus stove, invented in 1892, would prove essential to the missions of Amundsen and Scott, facilitating lighter expedition loads to supply heating for cooking and melting snow (the technology is still widely used today). Amundsen had joined the de Gerlache mission in 1897, gathering valuable polar knowledge that he refined in the Arctic, notably during his Northwest Passage discovery.

But it was a 33-year-old British captain, Robert Falcon Scott, who first mounted a legitimate assault of the South Pole between 1901 and 1904. Along with two men, including a 27-year-old navy officer named Ernest Shackleton, Scott's inland Discovery Expedition passed Borchgrevink's farthest-south record on November 11, 1902, pushing deeper toward the South Pole. On December 30, they reached latitude 82°17' south, approximately 500 miles from the pole, when dwindling supplies forced them to turn back. The men were slowed by bouts of snow blindness and scurvy, a vitamin C deficiency disease that had plagued many polar expeditions and was particularly hard on Shackleton. By the time they reached their ship, they had trekked a total of 960 miles over the 93-day mission. Tension had grown on the return trip, but Shackleton was convinced that better preparation could deliver the pole. To Scott's great displeasure, Shackleton believed he was the one to do it.

Shackleton led the British Antarctic (Nimrod) Expedition as it sailed away from New Zealand aboard *Nimrod* on August 11, 1907. After overwintering on the Ross Ice Shelf, as he had done with Scott six years prior, Shackleton and three men departed for the South Pole on October 29, 1908. The ponies they relied on perished on the way up the glacier, forcing the team to man-haul instead. Food rations were periodically adjusted to factor a longer, more arduous journey. Their initial plan for 91 days would likely stretch to 110 to cover the estimated 1,719-mile journey. On January 9, 1909, it was clear that the party would not survive the return should they continue for the pole. At latitude 88°23' south, with a mere 112.2 miles to go, the decision was made to turn back. "Better a live donkey," Shackleton would later famously tell his wife, "than a dead lion. I chose life over death for myself and my friends . . . I believe it is in our nature to explore, to reach out into the unknown. The only true failure would be not to explore at all."

Even in retreat, however, their survival was hardly assured. This was day 72 of a mission that had been planned and rationed for 91 days, using ponies to boot. Battling frostbites, hunger, and storms, the first of the party reached the coast on February 28, 1909, mere days before *Nimrod* was scheduled to depart due to the oncoming seasonal freeze of McMurdo Sound. It had taken the team 122 days to cover 1,495 miles. Emaciated and on the verge of death from weakness and starvation, Shackleton had, by far, pushed farthest into the heart of Antarctica. The men were also the first to set foot on the Antarctic Plateau beyond the Ross

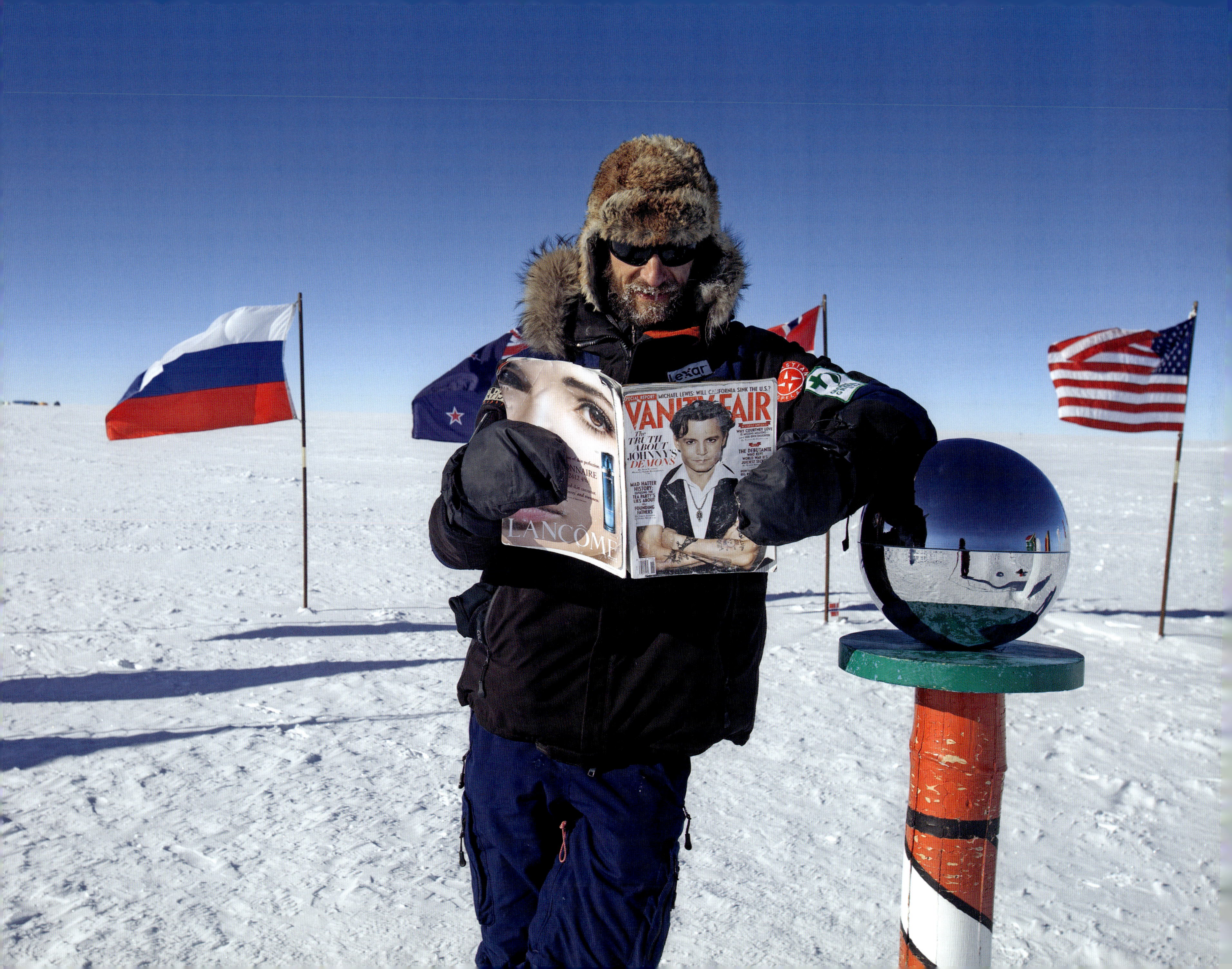
Lexar
SPECIAL REPORT
MICHAEL LEWIS: WILL CALIFORNIA SINK THE U.S.?
VANITY FAIR
The TRUTH ABOUT JOHNNY'S DEMONS
MAD HATTER HISTORY:
FOUNDING FATHERS
WHY COURTNEY LOVE
THE DEBUTANTE
LANCÔME

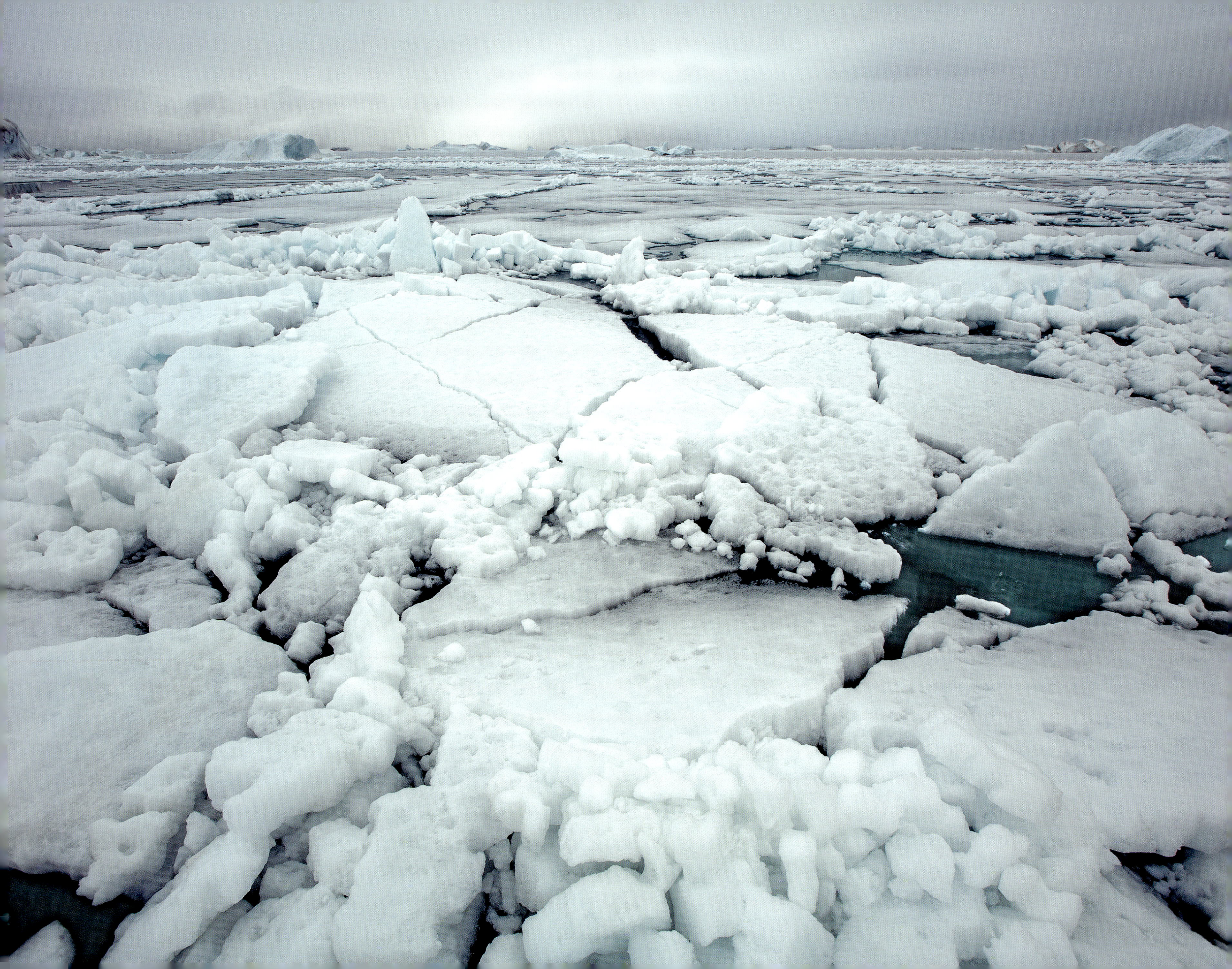

Ice Shelf and the ascending Beardmore Glacier (named after one of Shackleton's patrons). Their daily food rations in the very last stretch were reduced to one single biscuit per man, which Shackleton relinquished one day to boost a weakening partner, a sacrifice that bolstered his reputation as one of the greatest leaders of all time.

WHAT A TERRIBLE PLACE

Shackleton returned a hero, even if deeply in debt. He drew praise from fellow explorers like Nansen and Amundsen. But Scott, his boss on the Discovery Expedition, must have finally exhaled when he learned of the near miss. Scott had enjoyed national fame and success from his exploits in Antarctica and had been plotting a return to conquer the South Pole with the blessing of the navy and the crown. A darling of the British public, and with the alluring polar prize still intact, Scott departed for the Southern Ocean at the helm of the whaler *Terra Nova* on June 15, 1910. On a stopover in New Zealand, however, he received a startling telegram from Amundsen: "Beg leave to inform you *Fram* proceeding Antarctic." On the guise of a scientific mission to the Arctic with the stated intent to drift over the North Pole as Nansen had attempted to, the Norwegian to whom Nansen had given use of his ship unexpectedly changed bearing and headed for the Ross Sea.

A race was on. Unlike Scott, Amundsen had struggled to raise funds and resented what he felt was a lack of attention for his diligent polar work. His dream to be first at the North Pole had suddenly been dashed by Peary's claim. So he secretly reset his aim for the Antarctic Plateau instead, blindsiding Scott, who had anticipated their mutual missions to develop concurrently at opposite ends of the globe. Scott had even gone so far as to lend the Norwegian equipment so they could both conduct similar scientific measurements.

Fram left Oslo on June 3, 1910, and reached the Ross Sea on January 14, 1911. Amundsen set off in earnest, arranging supply depots along his intended route. His impatience led to a false start too early in the season, which practically derailed the mission from the staggering cold. That was the only crack in Amundsen's otherwise poker-faced facade, and it stemmed from his obsession with beating the dashing English captain and his intended use of motorized contraptions. Relying on dogs and animal fur for clothing, techniques that he had acquired from his time spent with Inuit communities in the High North, Amundsen and his five-man team left for the South Pole on October 19 with 52 dogs, intending to feed on the meat they provided as the expedition progressed. The journey south was remarkably smooth. They ascended the Axel Heiberg Glacier and enjoyed relatively stable weather and a flawless execution from the meticulous—if often cruel and aloof—leader.

On December 14, 1911, Amundsen planted the Norwegian flag at 90° south and left a tent and a letter for Scott. The British team would discover it one month later, having shared an altogether different experience on the Antarctic ice. Amundsen returned with 11 dogs and he derided the British for their reluctance to use them in the way the Inuit had taught him. This may have come down to cultural differences as much as anything. In the High North, Inuit have no emotional attachment to canines, whom they consider strictly at the service of their needs. Europeans, on the other hand, have a tradition of domesticity with dogs that famously adorned the royal courts. Either way, Scott had bet on ponies and machines, both of which failed him miserably shortly after setting off for the South Pole. That, regrettably, left man-hauling as the only option.

Suffering weather delays and getting trapped in the sea ice, the Terra Nova Expedition had a late start laying the groundwork for the mission before overwintering. Like Amundsen, the party left depots along the route for the return journey, splitting the work between two seasons. The rush led to a lame decision that would prove fatal to Scott's mission. Fresh off the ship and not acclimated to conditions, the ponies they used to lay depots were dying from exposure during a bout of bad weather. Scott ordered the last load for the return journey to be laid 30 miles short of its intended location. This would mean 30 miles farther for the returning party, when the team would arguably be at its weakest. The ascending party left the coast on November 1, 1911, and began the long haul across the Ross Ice Shelf before ascending the Beardmore Glacier. They did so with three teams of four men. A team of five would ultimately push for the South Pole.

On January 17, 1912, short of breath from the thin air of the high plateau at 9,300 feet, Scott squinted. In the distance, he could barely make out a dark spot sticking up from the ice on the horizon, like a stain on a canvas. And his heart sunk. As the five men approached, their faces hewed from the relentless cold and headwinds that marked their ascent, they found Amundsen's tent and letter, and with it, the bitter confirmation of their defeat. The Norwegian had beat them to the South Pole.

Exhausted and dispirited, they began the long haul back. Shunning dogs had made the journey slow; it took Scott's party 77 days to reach the pole, whereas Amundsen had done it in 56. The season would prove especially cold, and with the onset of fall, temperatures rapidly plummeted. Badly frostbitten and exhausted, the first of the men died on February 17, as they approached the Ross Ice Shelf. Conditions there quickly deteriorated, worsened by tactical and communication errors at the start, which left the men short on fuel and waiting in vain for a dog party that never came. On March 16, the valiant Lawrence Oates stepped out of the tent during a storm and simply said, "I am just going outside and may be some time." With gangrene setting into his feet from cold injuries, Oates was aware of the burden that he placed on his teammates, hindering their chance of survival. He was never seen again.

Tragically, his sacrifice did not help. Pummeled by consecutive storms, the team managed only 20 miles more before getting pinned down by a blizzard. Their meager food and fuel rations running out, the men huddled in their tent, unable to move from their position on the Ross Ice Shelf. They were a mere 11 miles from the next provisions depot, the same depot that had been misplaced four-and-a-half months prior and would have otherwise been reached days earlier. Scott laid next to his men as they slowly faded into hypothermia and starvation-induced comas. He would be the last to perish, shortly after filling his final heartrending journal entry: "The end cannot be far. It seems a pity, but I do not think I can write more. For God's sake, look after our people." This was March 29, 1912, almost five months after setting off.

When Amundsen reached Australia on March 7, 1912, he announced to the world the success of his mission. "Victory awaits him who has everything in order—luck, people call it. Defeat is certain for him who has neglected to take the necessary precautions in time; this is called bad luck." He was unaware of the demise of the Terra Nova Expedition, news that took months to reach the world. In Britain, Scott was swiftly canonized as a tragic hero, and the tale of his loss overshadowed Amundsen's flawless achievement.

BEYOND THE POLES

Polar exploration shifted after the conquest of the North and South Poles. The high cost of outfitting a mission made scientific research and the potential upside from mineral discoveries and unknown resources more enticing to private investors, rather than sheer performance-driven milestones. The Australian geologist Douglas Mawson had accompanied Shackleton on the 1907–1909 Nimrod Expedition, where he notched a first at the magnetic South Pole and the top of Mount Erebus. Scott, unlike Amundsen, saw the merit of scientific studies on his trips and had invited Mawson on the Terra Nova Expedition, but Mawson chose to lead his own mission instead. His Australasian Antarctic Expedition of 1911–1914 featured another harrowing tale of survival.

Mawson and two teammates set off to survey unexplored sections of the continent's coast. When one in his party fell to his death in a crevasse, he took six dogs with him and a sled carrying the bulk of their provisions, including their tent. They were weeks into the trip and 300 miles from the base. The second teammate died of poisoning from feeding on dog liver. Mawson would miraculously crawl back to camp weeks later, the sole survivor of that tragic outing, only to see his ship pull away in the distance, as prescribed to avoid the seasonal freeze. Mawson was rescued the following year. During his time in Antarctica, he and a small party that had stayed for him mapped 2,600 miles of unexplored coastlands. Mawson conducted geological and botanical studies, prospected for minerals, and pushed scientific surveys that paved the way for modern research that is ongoing. Academics today credit the early explorer-scientists for informing our appreciation of Antarctica's unique value in fields as varied as astronomy, biology, geology, glaciology, and more.

Meanwhile, Amundsen's conquest of the South Pole also took the prize away for Shackleton. The polar hero now saw one crown jewel left for Antarctic exploration. When the German Wilhelm Filchner attempted but failed a full crossing from coast to coast via the South Pole in 1912, Shackleton began plotting his own attempt in earnest. The plan involved two ships. *Aurora* departed from Australia with a support party that landed on Ross Island. From there, they would lay depots right up to the Beardmore Glacier to supply the main party. Shackleton approached the continent from the opposite side, leading the main party aboard *Endurance*. The Imperial Trans-Antarctic Expedition left with the world on the brink of war, on August 3, 1914.

The mission was rapidly met with its own disaster. Soon after entering the Weddell Sea, *Endurance* was seized in the hardening sea ice on January 19, 1915. The ship was brand new, but its design specifications did not meet the rigorous stress of the pack ice. After drifting for 10 months, *Endurance* finally sank on November 21. The story of the journey back to safety is the stuff of legends. Defying moving ice and the ferocious onset of the Antarctic winter, the men camped for five months on an ice floe. With diminishing food supplies, they set off on open skiffs to reach the deserted Elephant Island. From there, Shackleton deftly led a team of five men across 800 miles of storm-laden seas to reach a whaling station on South Georgia Island. But rescuing his stranded men was an ordeal that took another three months and as many ships. Multiple attempts to approach the island were foiled by barriers of sea ice. Four-and-a-half months after departing Elephant Island, and 636 days after leaving Britain, all 27 of his men were finally rescued, surviving on little more than blind trust in their leader and the endurance they had cultivated as a result.

But this was far from the mission's only setback. The Ross Ice Shelf's support party had experienced harrowing circumstances of its own. *Aurora*, its ship, had ripped her moorings in a storm and was blown to sea, leaving a party stranded on shore with limited fuel and food. The ship got trapped in the sea ice and drifted 1,600 miles over nine months before being released to the sea and making its way to New Zealand. The stranded men survived with successive missions retracing their steps to the depots that had been laid for the main party. Ironically, it was fortunate that the crossing never happened. Nineteen months, two winters, and three deaths after the calamity, on January 10, 1917, *Aurora*

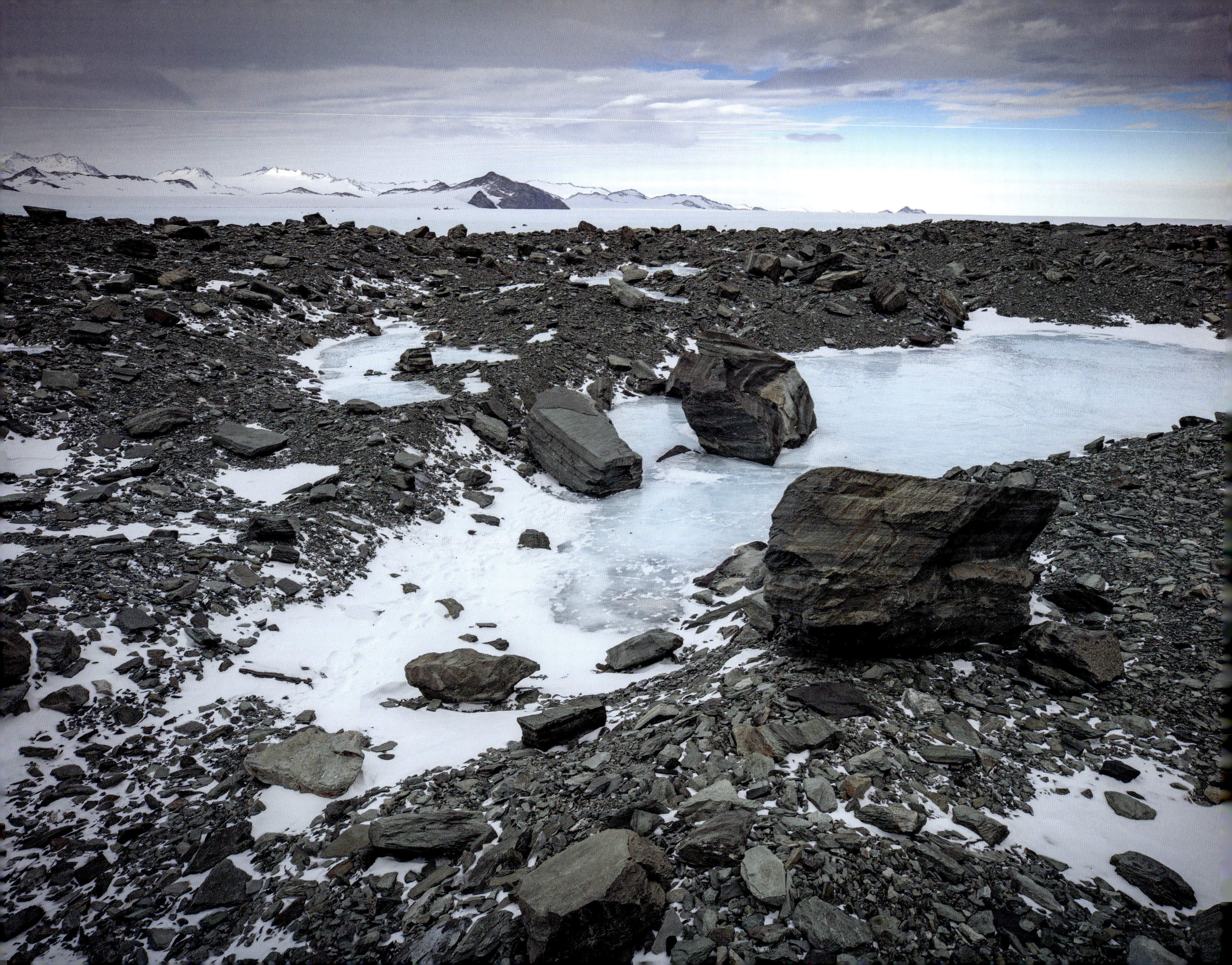

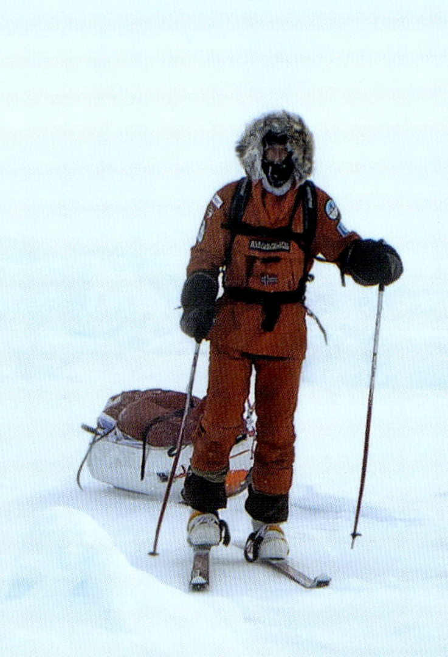

appeared on the horizon. On board was Shackleton, who had scraped together the money to rescue his men. Keeping to his pledge, the Boss left no men behind. (On March 9, 2022, the last member of the expedition—the ship *Endurance*—was located on the seafloor, 106 years after it had disappeared below the ice.)

Despite two failed missions, the name Shackleton will forever be etched in the annals of polar exploration, his reputation best illustrated by fellow explorer Sir Raymond Priestley when he said, "For scientific discovery, give me Scott; for speed and efficiency of travel, give me Amundsen; but when disaster strikes and all hope is gone, get down on your knees and pray for Shackleton."

A POSTCARD FROM THE EDGE

World War I and advances in mechanical engineering put an end to the Heroic Age of Antarctic Exploration. The postwar reconstruction and the Great Depression refocused public interest away from expensive civilian missions on foot to the North and South Poles. But polar history was kept alive by its visual custodians—photographers doubling as expeditioners, or vice versa—men whose extra work and sacrifice had earned their leaders' unconditional trust. When Frank Hurley pleaded, Shackleton gave the order to protect and save 150 heavy, fragile, and cumbersome glass-plate photographs to haul on their open-boat survival journeys. With the Terra Nova Expedition, Herbert Ponting delivered Antarctica's drama into people's homes through the pages of newspapers and magazines, bringing into sharp focus the exotic beauty and the heroes' hardships from the ends of the Earth and immortalizing their bravery. Short on convenience, but long on historical relevance, their large cameras opened doors for future trailblazers and made dreamers out of legions of budding adventurers.

They still do. George Lowe knew them well when he joined the Commonwealth Trans-Antarctic Expedition in 1955, following Vivian Fuchs and Edmund Hillary's vehicle crossing of Antarctica. Lowe was the official photographer on that mission, the first to reach the South Pole from the coast since Scott more than 40 years earlier. Wally Herbert, also in 1955, would surely have pondered over the implication of those early photos when he embarked on his 3,000-mile sled survey of Antarctica. He later insisted that Allan Gill photograph their Arctic crossing over the North Pole. These visual records, as much as the written ones, anchor us in tradition and continue to inspire adventurers to push further. Børge Ousland completed Shackleton's dream of crossing the ice in one shot in 1994, and Rune Gjeldnes went even longer in 2006 when he traveled almost 3,000 miles across the continent. His use of kites helped refine a new mode of transport in Antarctica. If these men benefited from air transportation to reach the ice, they made up for it by traveling alone and without support.

With little left to discover, today's polar exploration has increasingly grown into a privilege, a fancy of athleticism. The high cost of logistics is but a rite of passage into the realm of the past, an era that, by modern standards, seems quaint and romantic in its pursuits. Putting one foot in front of the other is no match for today's rocket ships that carry tourists to the dark side of the moon. And yet it is that notable feeling of being untethered from technology that is the appeal of polar travel and high mountains. Like the Arctic tern, we are connected to our profound nature of independence and our freedom. Today, we are neither hunting nor gathering, but we feel our way across adversity and pain, exploring as we did at birth, for no precise purpose other than, as George Mallory would say of Everest, because it is there. By traveling the pristine and forlorn regions of the frozen space, we are presented with not only the beauty that lives at the edge of our world, but also the one that lives at the edge of ourselves.

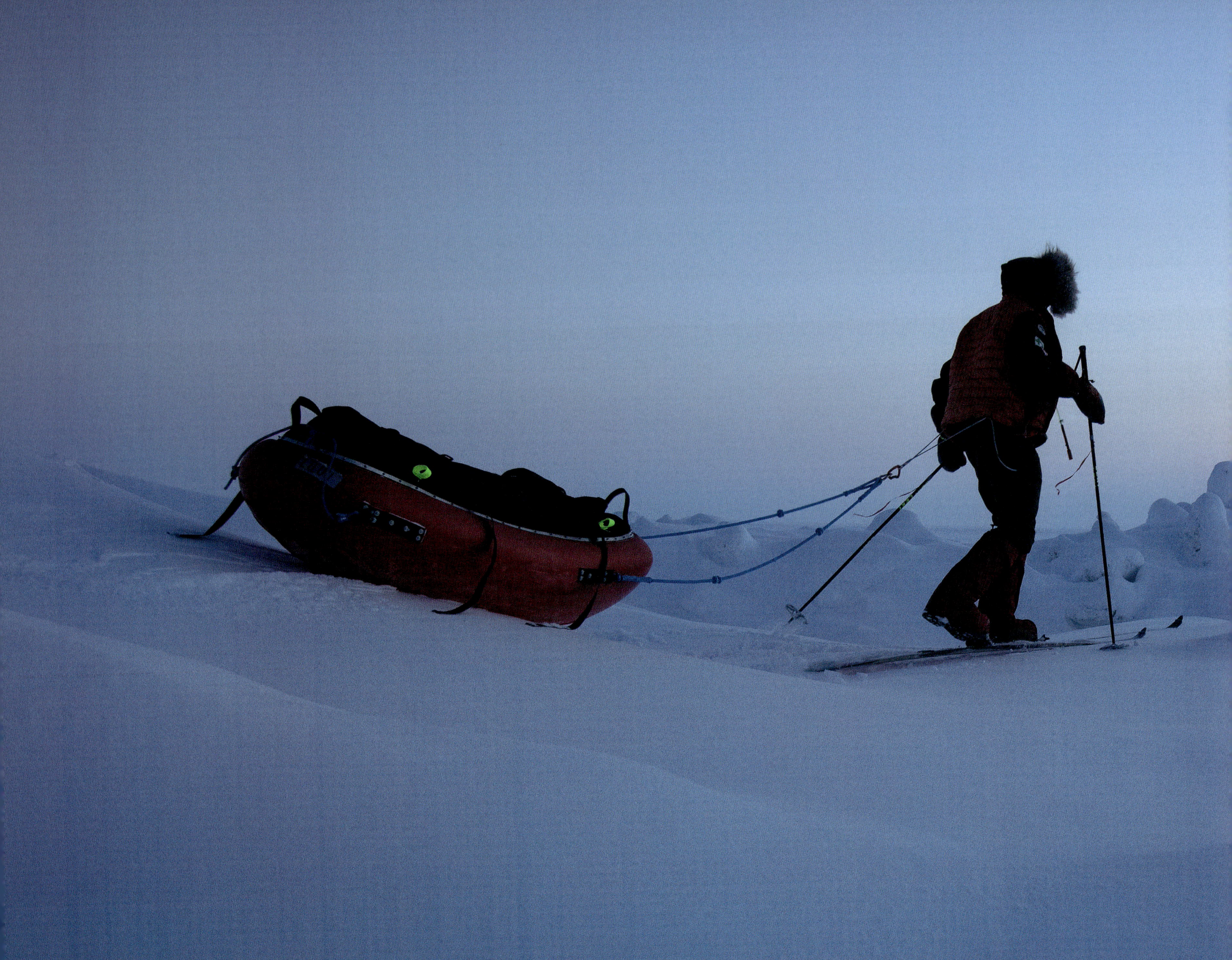

NORTH POLE

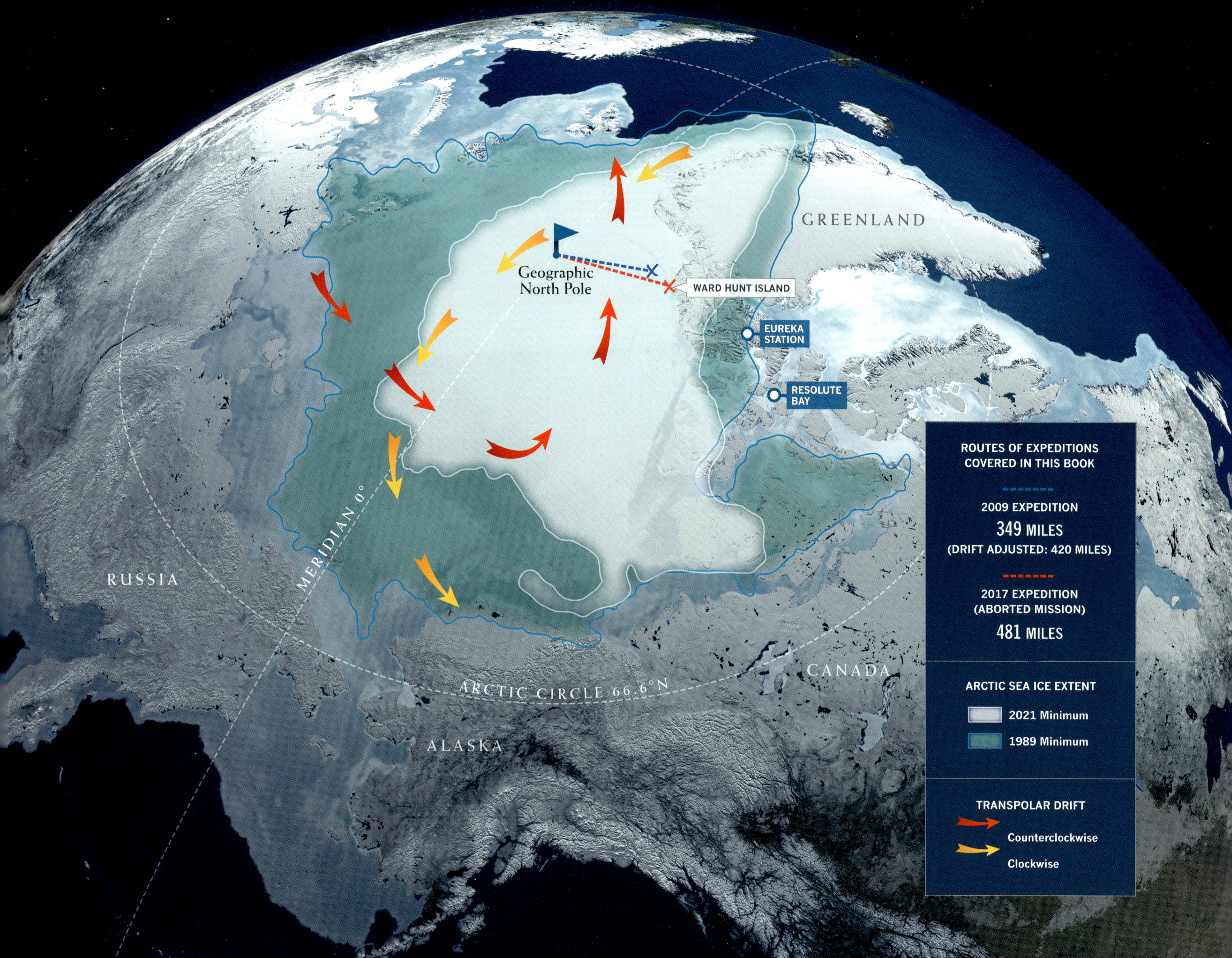
GREENLAND
Geographic North Pole
WARD HUNT ISLAND
EUREKA STATION
RESOLUTE BAY
RUSSIA
MERIDIAN 0°
ARCTIC CIRCLE 66.6°N
CANADA
ALASKA
ROUTES OF EXPEDITIONS COVERED IN THIS BOOK
2009 EXPEDITION
349 MILES
(DRIFT ADJUSTED: 420 MILES)
2017 EXPEDITION
(ABORTED MISSION)
481 MILES
ARCTIC SEA ICE EXTENT
2021 Minimum
1989 Minimum
TRANSPOLAR DRIFT
Counterclockwise
Clockwise

In the winter of 2009, my partner Keith Heger and I set off on foot from latitude 85° north on the Arctic Ocean ice, heading north. After 420 fierce miles over six weeks, losing daily distances to the transpolar drift (the dreaded "Arctic treadmill"), we reached 90° north, the Geographic North Pole, on April 26, 2009. It was not an easy task, as the North Pole sits on floating ice and is in constant nonlinear motion. It is one of two points on which the world rotates. And there is no denying it: it feels good to stand on it! An M16 helicopter ferried us to Barneo, the temporary floating station at 88° north, where an Antonov AN-74 plane flew us to Longyearbyen on Svalbard. Barneo used to service expeditions for six weeks in the early 2000s. It now operates for just three weeks due to the rapid seasonal melt, and its future is uncertain. The North Pole is undeniably on the front line of climate change. As with all my missions, this one was made carbon neutral. The following excerpts are journal entries from my 2009 mission.

Open Leads
Day 7, March 31, 2009
85°38'959" N, 76°52'321" W

Today was tough. If indeed the human body has a hundred million trillion cells in constant communication with one another, mine were all screaming at the same time, "I am cold!" The sound of heavy breathing, the scratching of skis on the ice below, the whistle of the wind on our faces—those were the faithful companions of our solitary journey.

We've now been here for 10 days. From morning to night, hardly a word is exchanged. When I lead, I occasionally check for Keith's shadow near my feet from the low sun behind us. I stop when I hear the words "Fuel!" or "Drink!" shouted from behind me. When Keith leads, my eyes focus on the tracks directly in front of me, and I lose myself in contemplation, occasionally remembering to look up for polar bears. When the time comes, I too shout for a food or drink stop. We hurry through the breaks before the sweat on our skin turns to frost.

As each day rolls into the next, there are no signs of life to break the quiet solitude of our journey. Not a bird, not a bug, no planes high above in the sky. The feeling of loneliness in this white stillness could, for some, scream louder than despair. Temperatures have remained around -40°F or so, dropping somewhat by day's end. The sun does not rise above 15 degrees from the horizon at its apex, but it no longer sets either. We are now in 24-hour daylight.

Today we traveled for eight hours and covered five nautical miles true north, but likely walked eight miles on account of the meandering navigation forced on us by the broken ice and the distance lost to the southerly drift. At the end of the day, we crawled into our tent and pried open our sleeping bags from their frosty grip; we literally cracked the ice from the frozen moisture in the fabric.

Getting in the tent at the end of a day is all we think about now. Keith has developed lesions on his legs, which are worrisome. Is it chilblains? I guess we'll soon find out. But now it's time for hot chocolate and calories. And sleep.

Older and Rubble Free
Day 10, April 3, 2009
86°05'316" N, 76°37'365" W

Frostbite is like a burn. The body secretes a pocket of liquid to protect itself; it is essentially a blister that needs to be carefully protected to prevent the fluid from freezing again and again. But how? Out here, everything wants to hurt you. If the wound goes deeper into the flesh, the risk could be loss. By now, Keith and I have several frostnips—his toes, my fingers. Handling a camera in -40°F temperatures is tough on the hands. I am presently keeping an eye on the middle finger of my right hand. I would hate to lose that digit; it has been of good service to me.

We started late today, as a wind from the north shook the tent all night. We felt no rush and were slow to hit the trail. Most of the day, the wind beat us up, and the mandatory hood and goggles greatly limited our field of vision.

I don't even think of bears anymore. Food stops are cold, and the wind lashes our faces like a fist of needles. "You ok?" "Good." That is about the extent of our dialogue out here, other than the occasional expletive not aimed at anyone, but to reflect how tough this experience really is. Like Sisyphus and his rock, we pull our heavy sleds across this uneven icy landscape, one step after the next. The simplicity of purpose can, at times, create flashes of sheer bliss. But not for long.

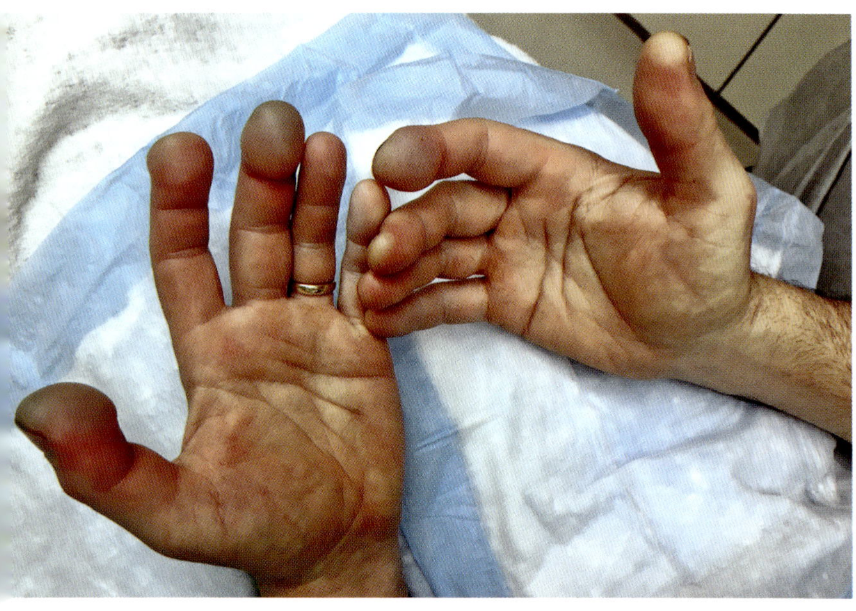

Luckily, today's terrain was mainly open pans of relatively flat ice. Three hours in, however, we came across our first open lead—a crack in the ice, which looks an awful lot like a river and can go on for miles. With it came the black color of the Arctic Ocean, which, of course, is constantly below our feet and the thin crust of ice we walk on. The lead was running east-west, or squarely in our way. It was a complex system of cracks in the ice generated by the awesome power of currents and winds, and after following its banks for a while, we finally found a crossing point. We hurried, as the environment was rapidly changing and the lead widening. A couple of hours later, we came upon another freshly refrozen lead, too wide and too fragile to cross over. We decided to camp near it and let it thicken overnight.

We have some fixing to do in the tent tonight, a buckle and a pole basket, but it must be quick as we have been burning more than our fuel ration for heat, which is easy to do out here. We traveled from 11:30 a.m. until 6:30 p.m. today and covered about five miles. Temperatures were between -32.8°F and -43.6°F. But the wind made it feel more like -76°F. This was another tough day, but we keep heading north. Today was my birthday, but I almost forgot.

A Good Day

Day 12, April 5, 2009
86°16'383" N, 76°35'633" W

Today we saw signs of life! First, a fresh set of fox tracks (what would a fox be doing at this latitude with no food for thousands of square miles—definitely an eccentric), and soon thereafter, a set of bear tracks—a mother and two cubs (also probably confused, unless of course she was looking for us). The tracks were probably days old.

With plenty of thinking time, today I got lost examining the nature of choices. I thought of the men and women who chose to temporarily live in Eureka, Nunavut, Canada, where we overnighted last month waiting for weather. The last bastion of civility before heading for the ice, Eureka is a station battered by the merciless lashings of the Great North. The vehicles that make it there know that they have reached the end of the line and are resolved to finish without ceremony. The men who drive them have stern faces shaped by their pioneering spirit. As with frontier towns of the past, people are lured there by opportunity. But as the lines on their faces deepen, they all seem to soften internally, moved by the power of this harsh desert and surprised by answers that come to them from questions they had not sought to ask. The cold is the great equalizer. But this world of ice is a privilege that must be experienced to be understood.

We traveled 10.3 nautical miles in nine hours today in pretty nice conditions. There were some nice big, open pans, but also some fields of rubble that slowed us down. There were many freshly frozen leads to cross and much warmer temperatures at around -25.6°F. Today, we were warm—no joke!

A Grind

Day 13, April 6, 2009
86°25'530" N, 76°27'047" W

Today was a grind. There were no gimmes. No freebies. No mulligans. No "This one's on the house," or "First ball in!" Nothing but hard-earned, slow miles.

The Arctic terrain can be unrelenting and unflinching. Temperatures today were around -25 to -33°F. Yard by yard, we negotiated the broken ice boulders and pressure ridges the size of two-story houses. The mix of cruddy or powdery snow swallowed up the sleds' rails as if dragging them through syrup. Each section led to another chaotic and random display of nature's forces.

In this grand theater, it is hard not to feel insignificant. And the purpose of our mission, in its simplicity, felt even more absurd. Sometimes the best thing to do is just put one foot in front of the other and move without thinking.

After nine hours and as many nautical miles, we noticed steam rising ahead. A giant melt area perhaps four miles across laid in front of us. A bit of trivia: a way to expect an open lead in winter is to look for the steam that rises from it. Strange though it is to think of freezing water as steaming, the temperature differential with the cold air can exceed 50°F. Occasional slivers of black Arctic water broke the frozen surface. We decided to camp by the "river's" edge, hoping that the slivers would freeze over. Either way, in the morning we will don our emergency swim outfits and dive in. With the coming full moon, neither one of us wants to tempt the monthly powerful tides in this area. Wish us luck.

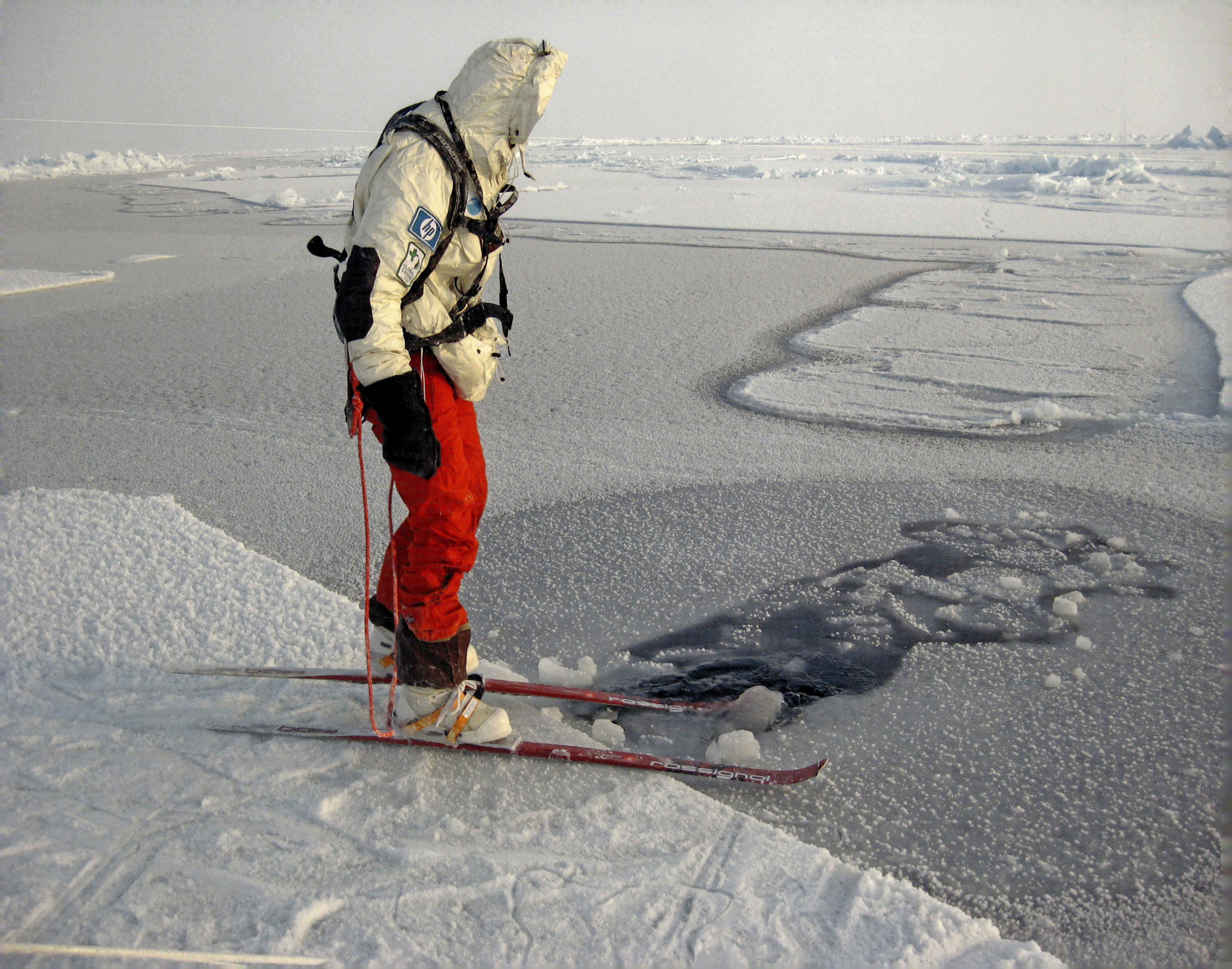
hp
rossignol

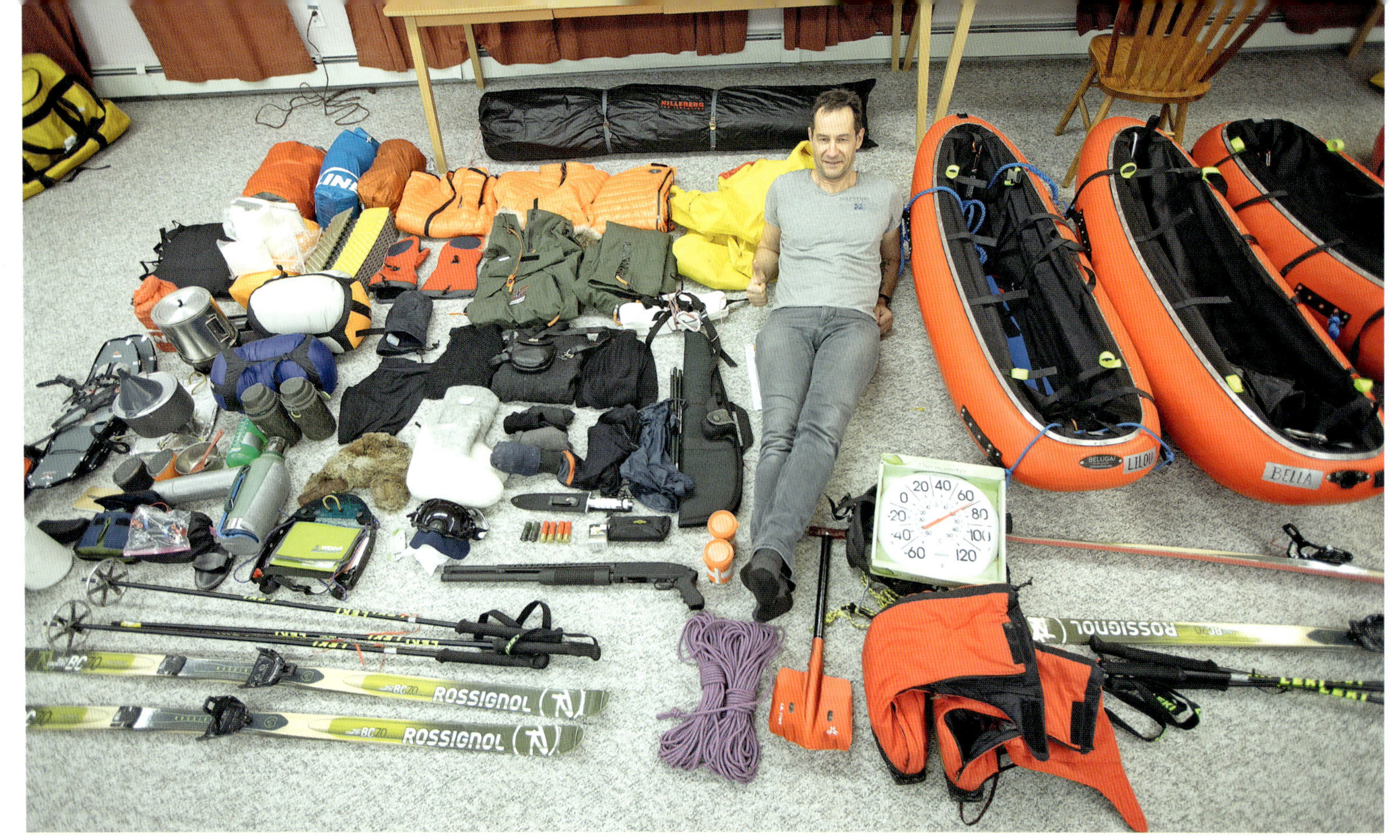
ROSSIGNOL
ROSSIGNOL
ROSSIGNOL
BELLA

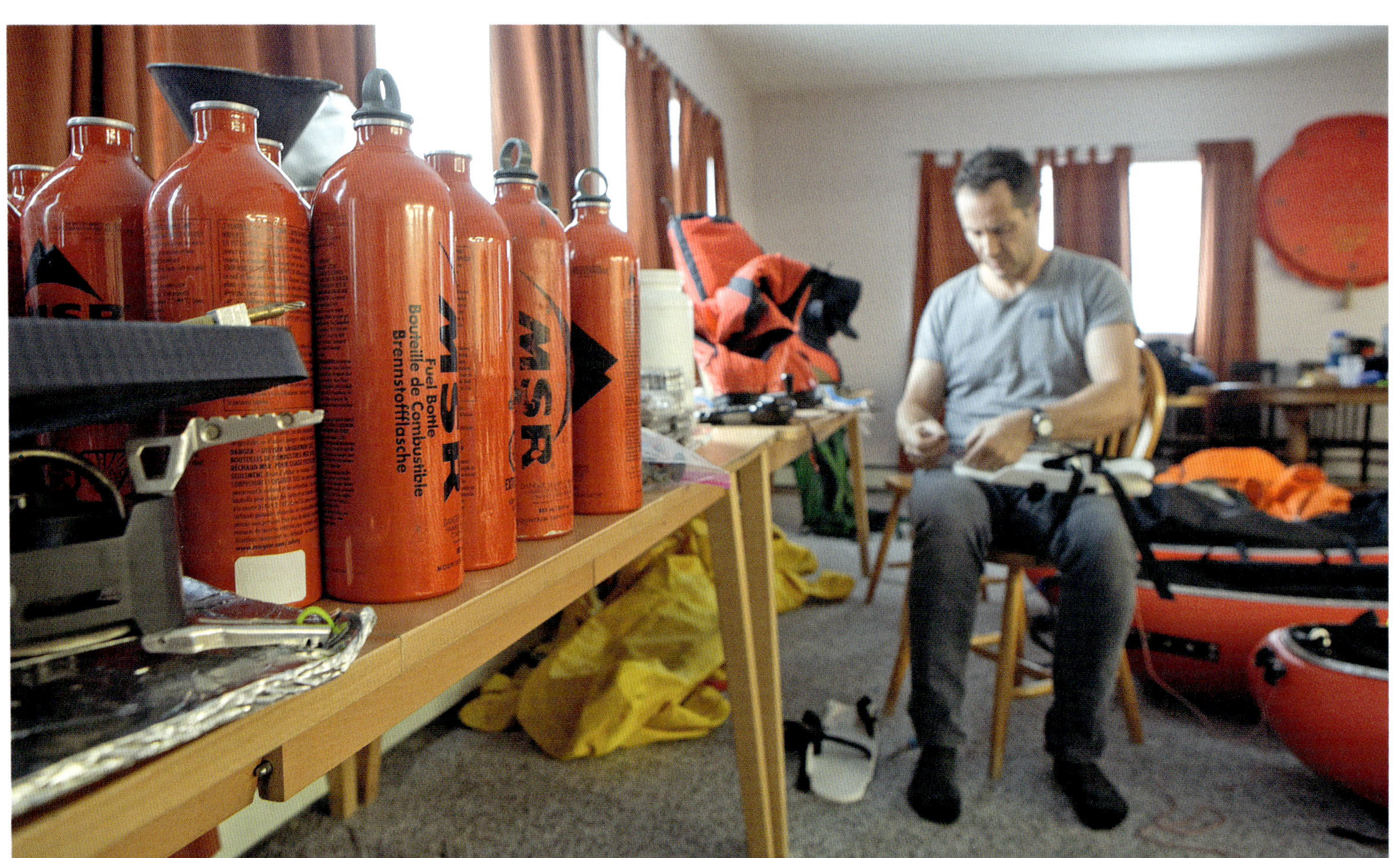
MSR
Fuel Bottle
Bouteille de Combustible
Brennstoffflasche
MSR

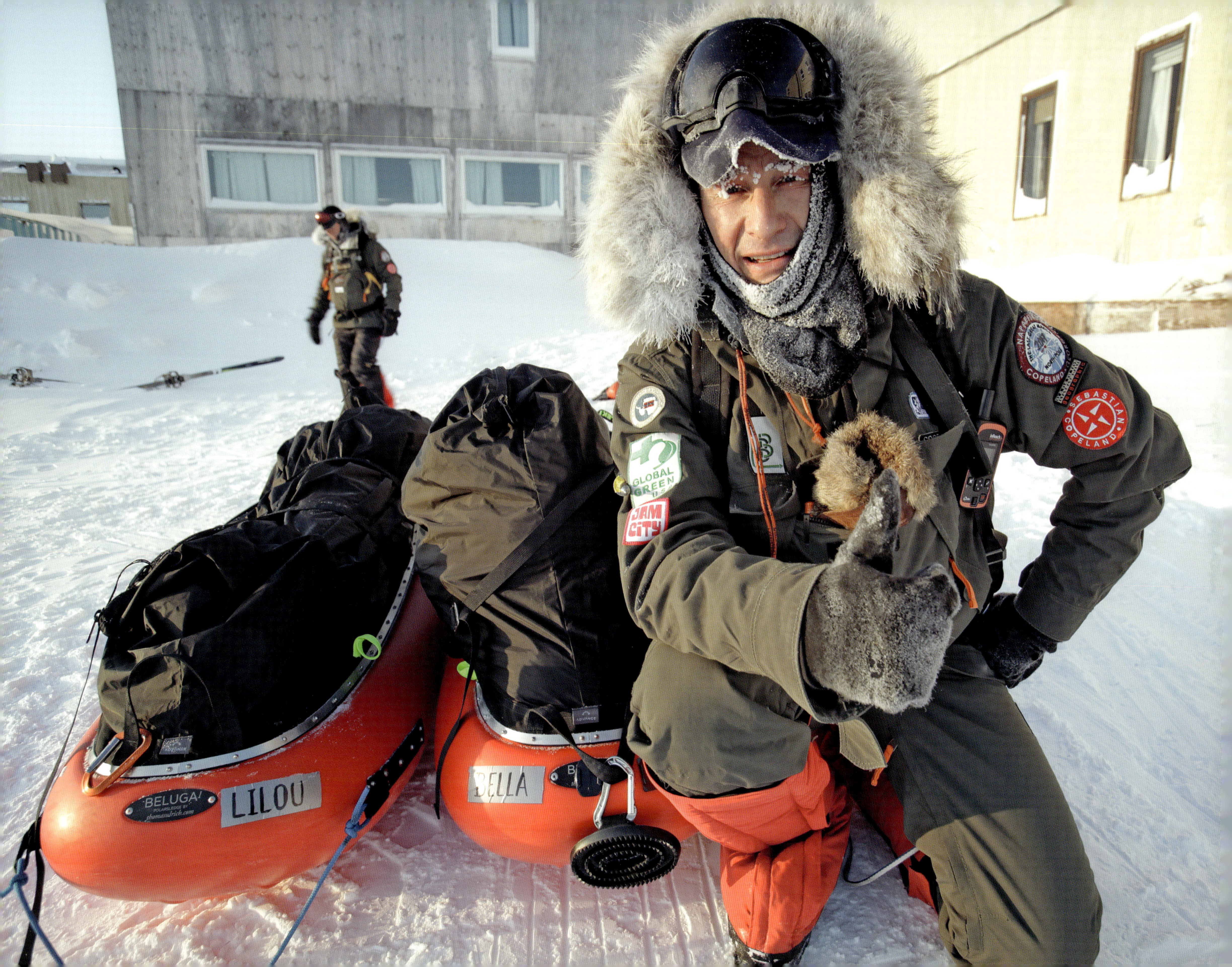
BELUGA
LILOU
BELLA
GLOBAL GREEN
JAM CITY
SEBASTIAN COPELAND

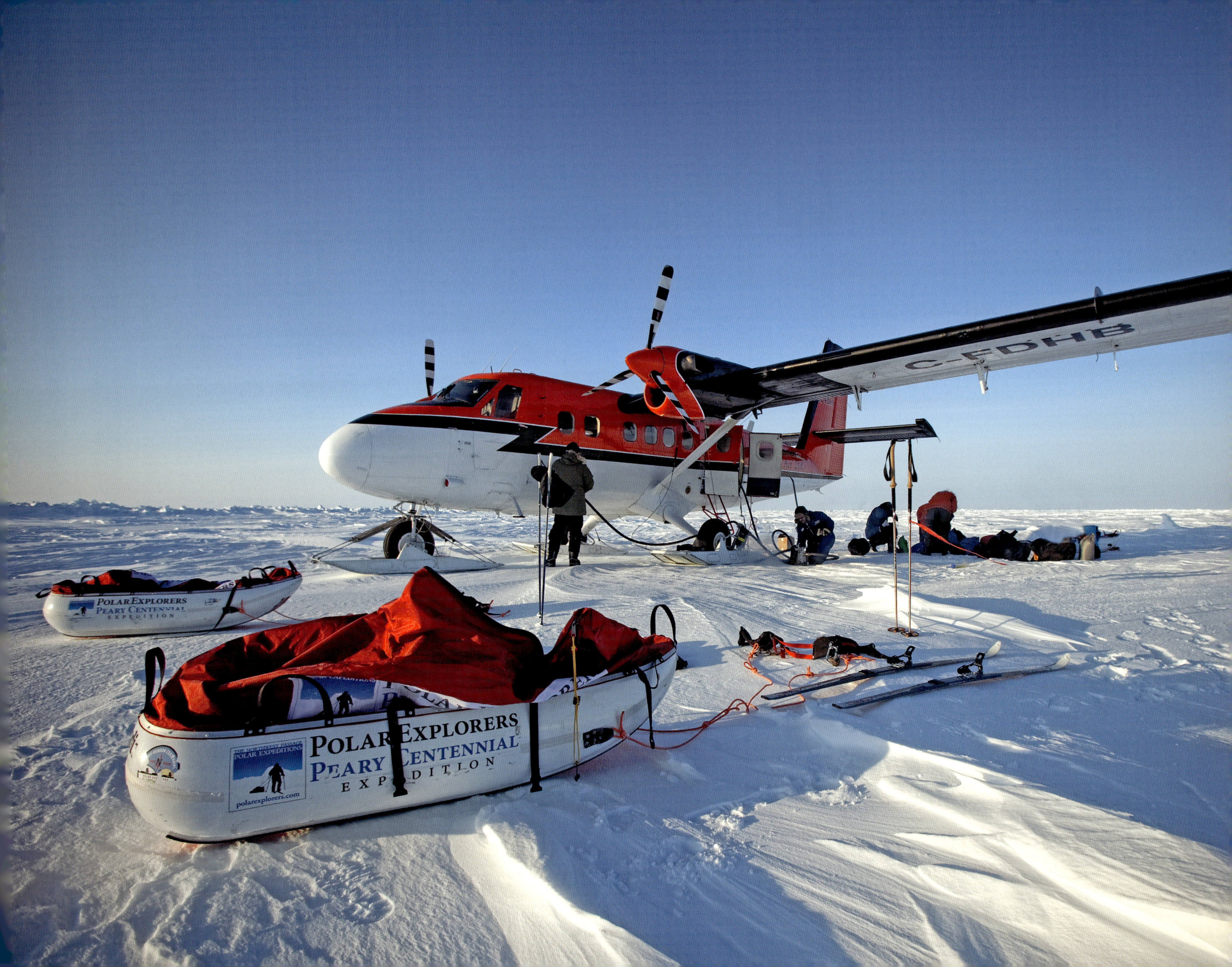
C-FDHB
POLAR EXPLORERS
PEARY CENTENNIAL
EXPEDITION
polarexplorers.com

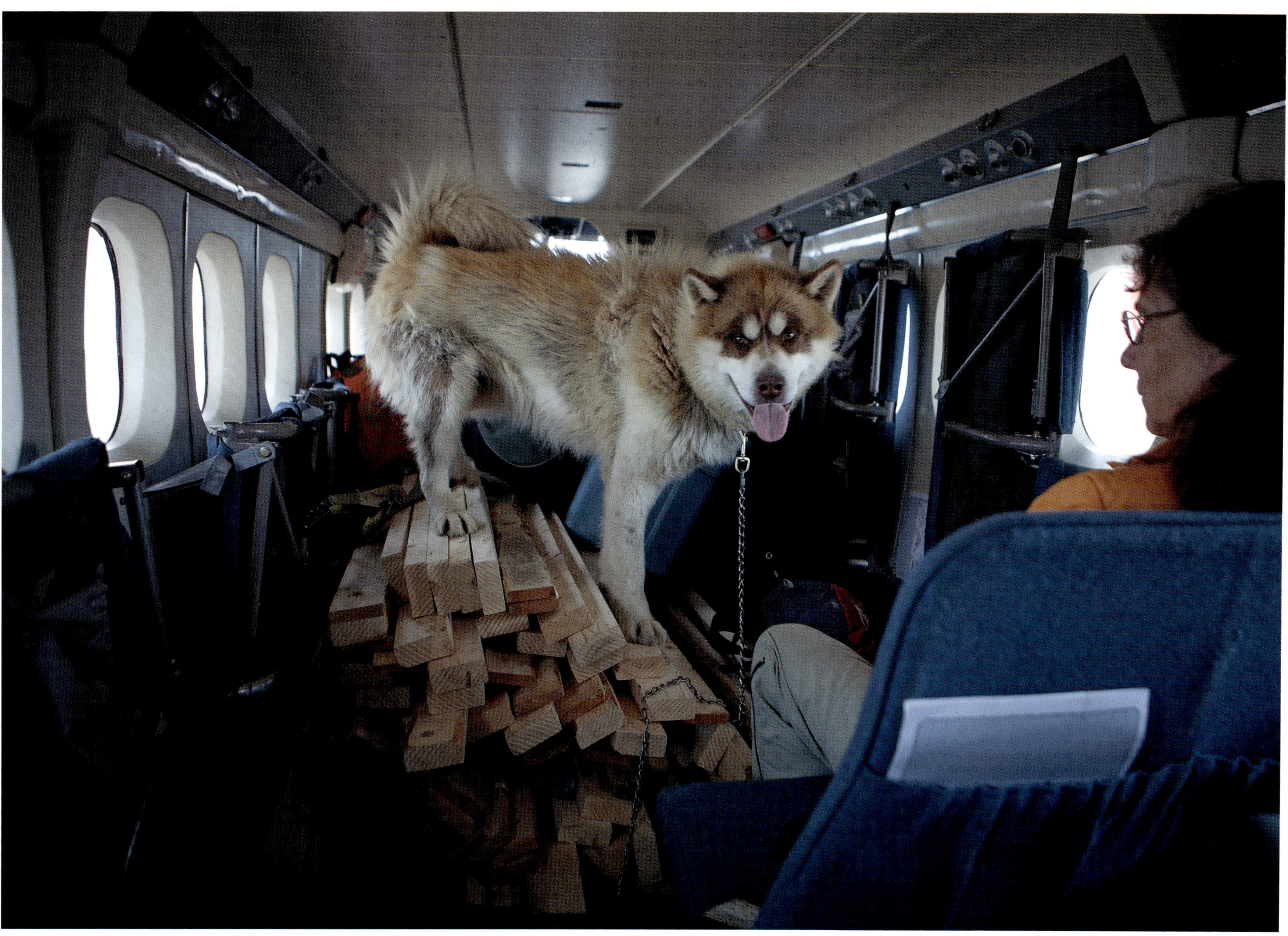

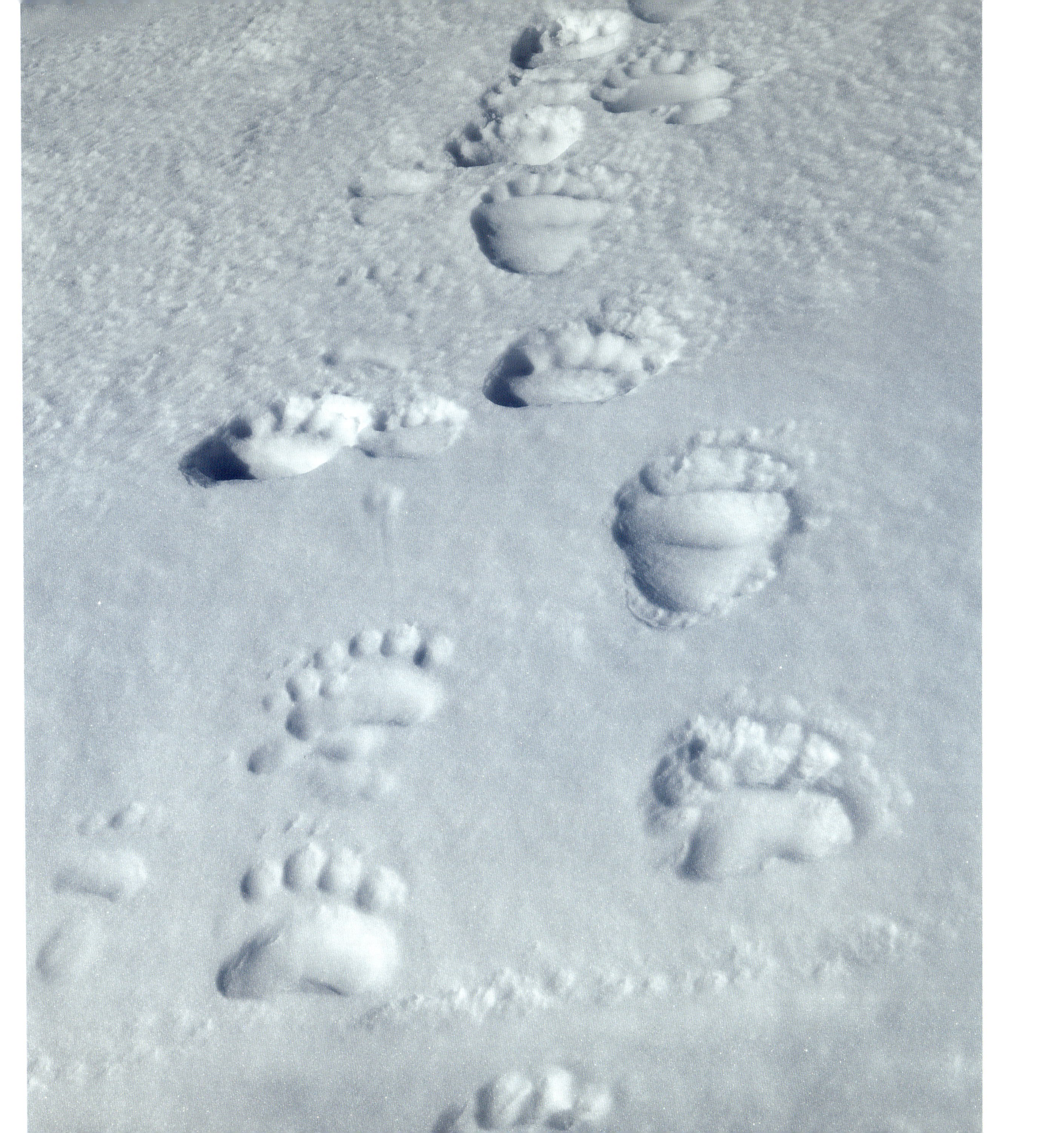

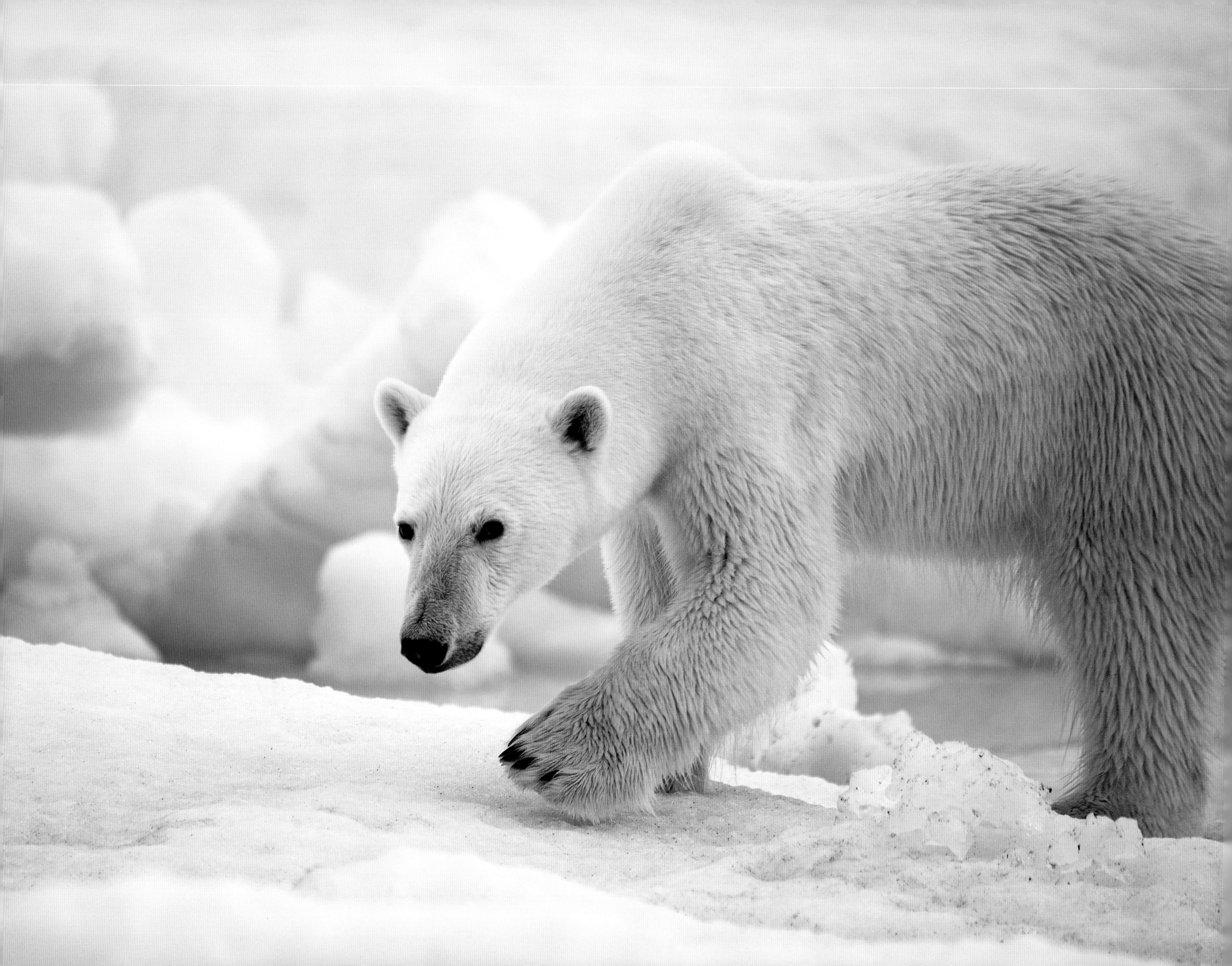

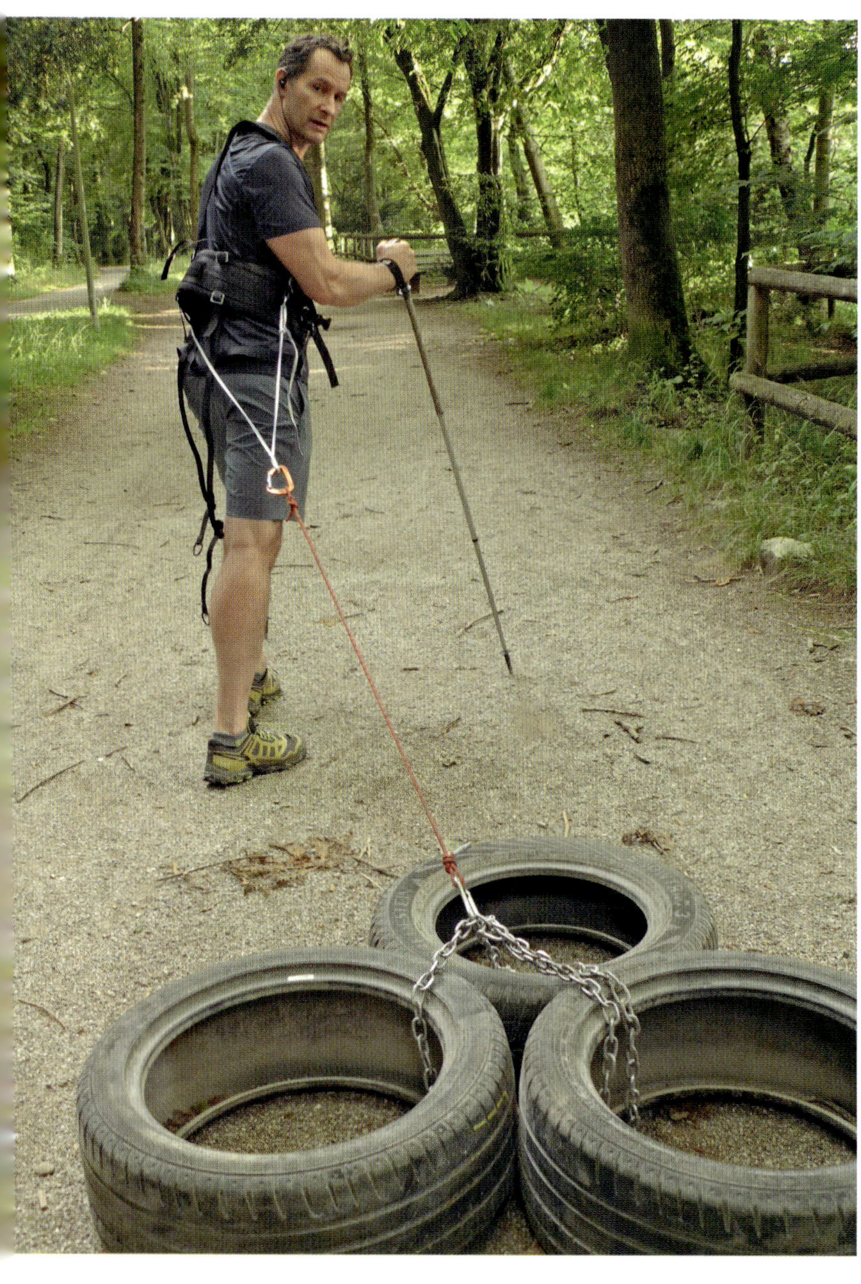

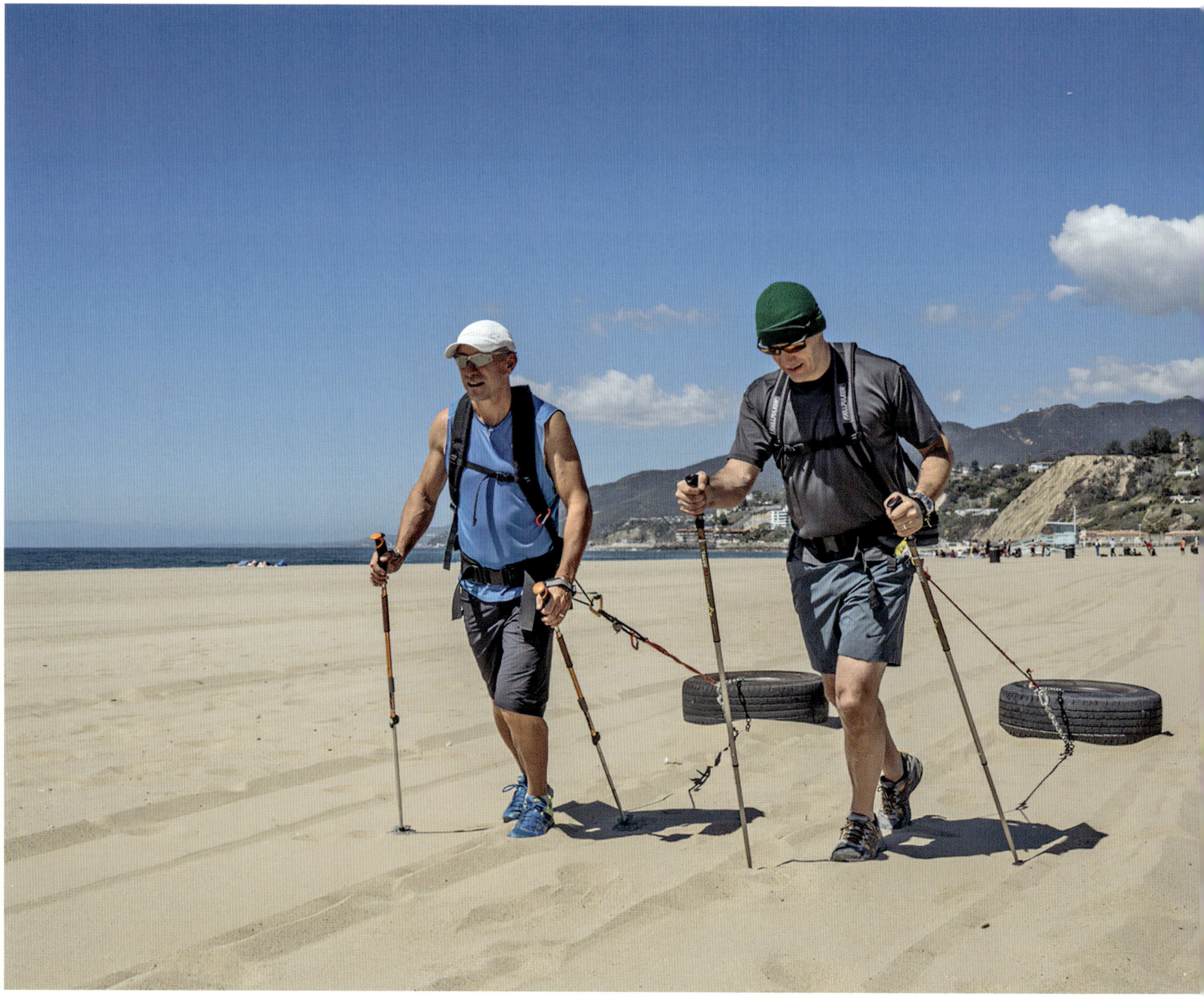

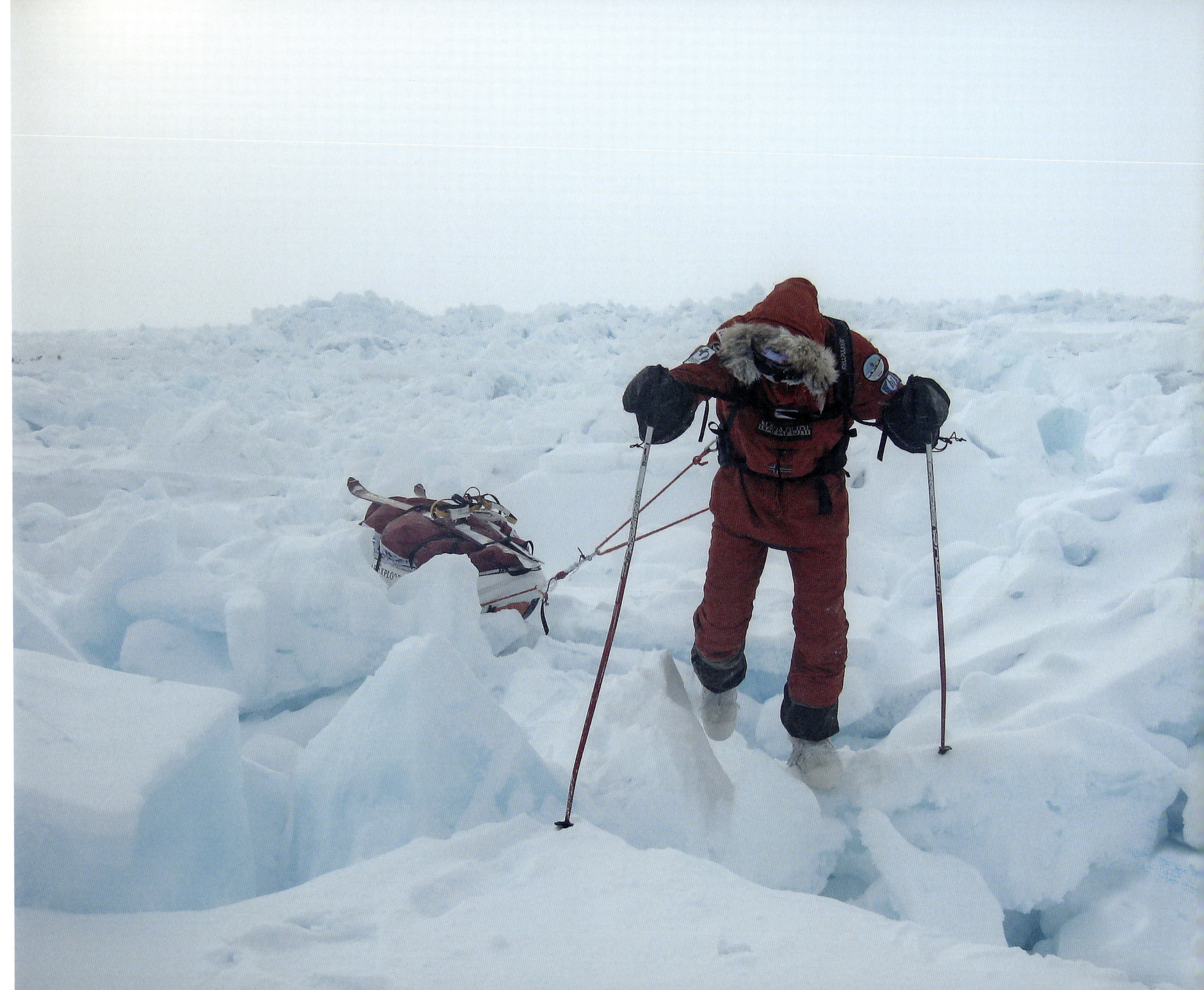

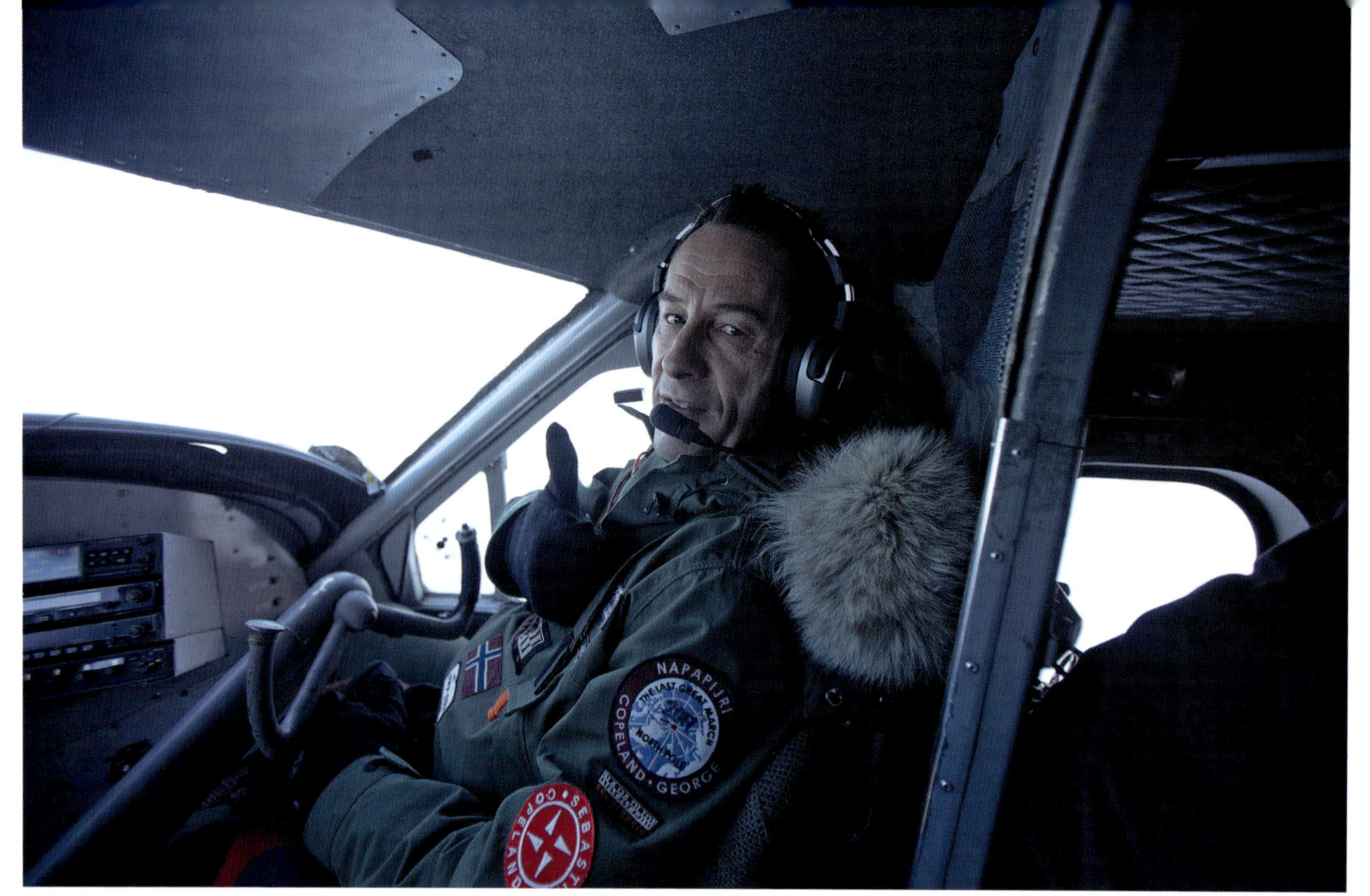
NAPAPIJRI
COPELAND • GEORGE

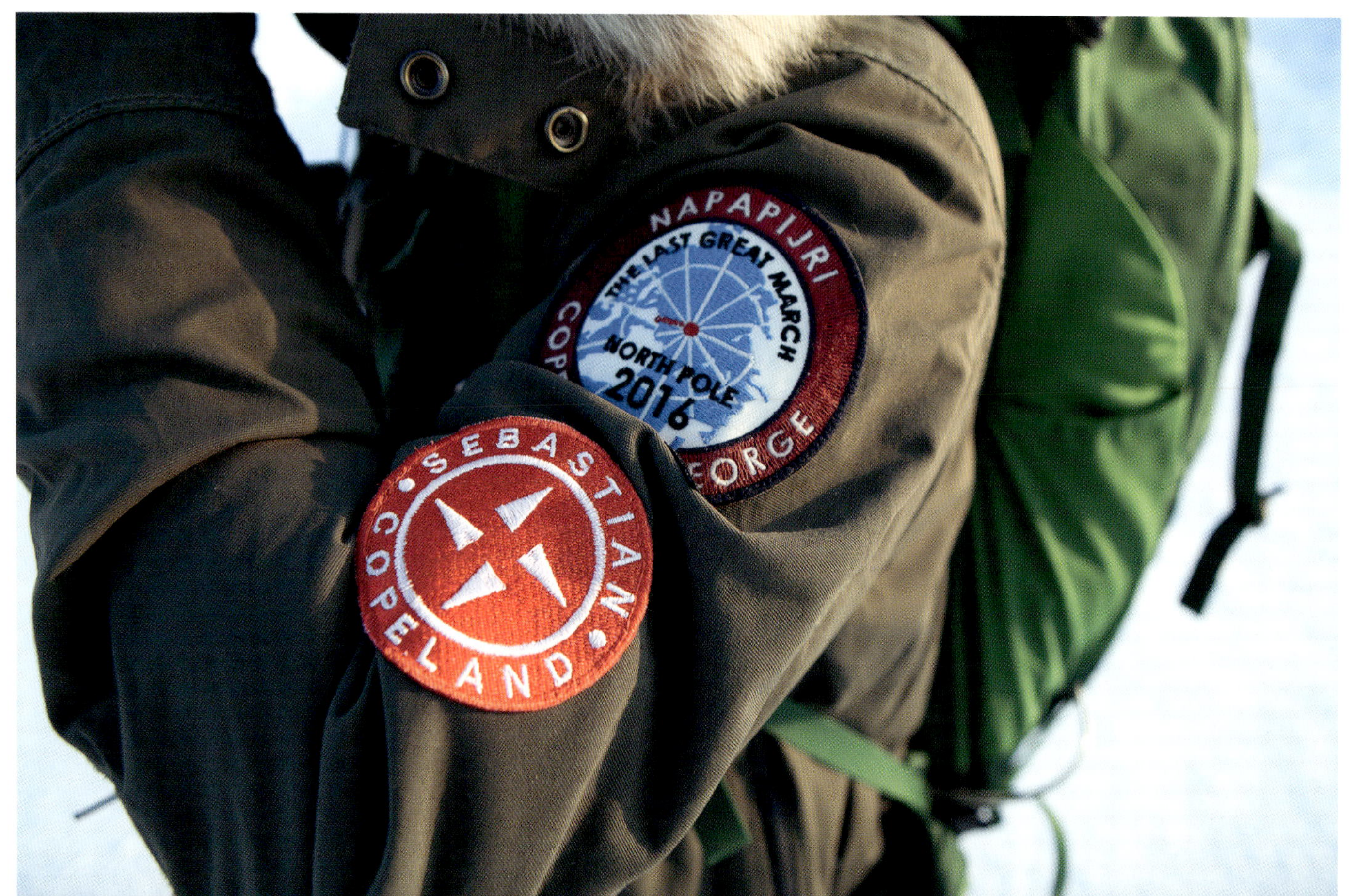
NAPAPIJRI
THE LAST GREAT MARCH
NORTH POLE
2016
SEBASTIAN
COPELAND

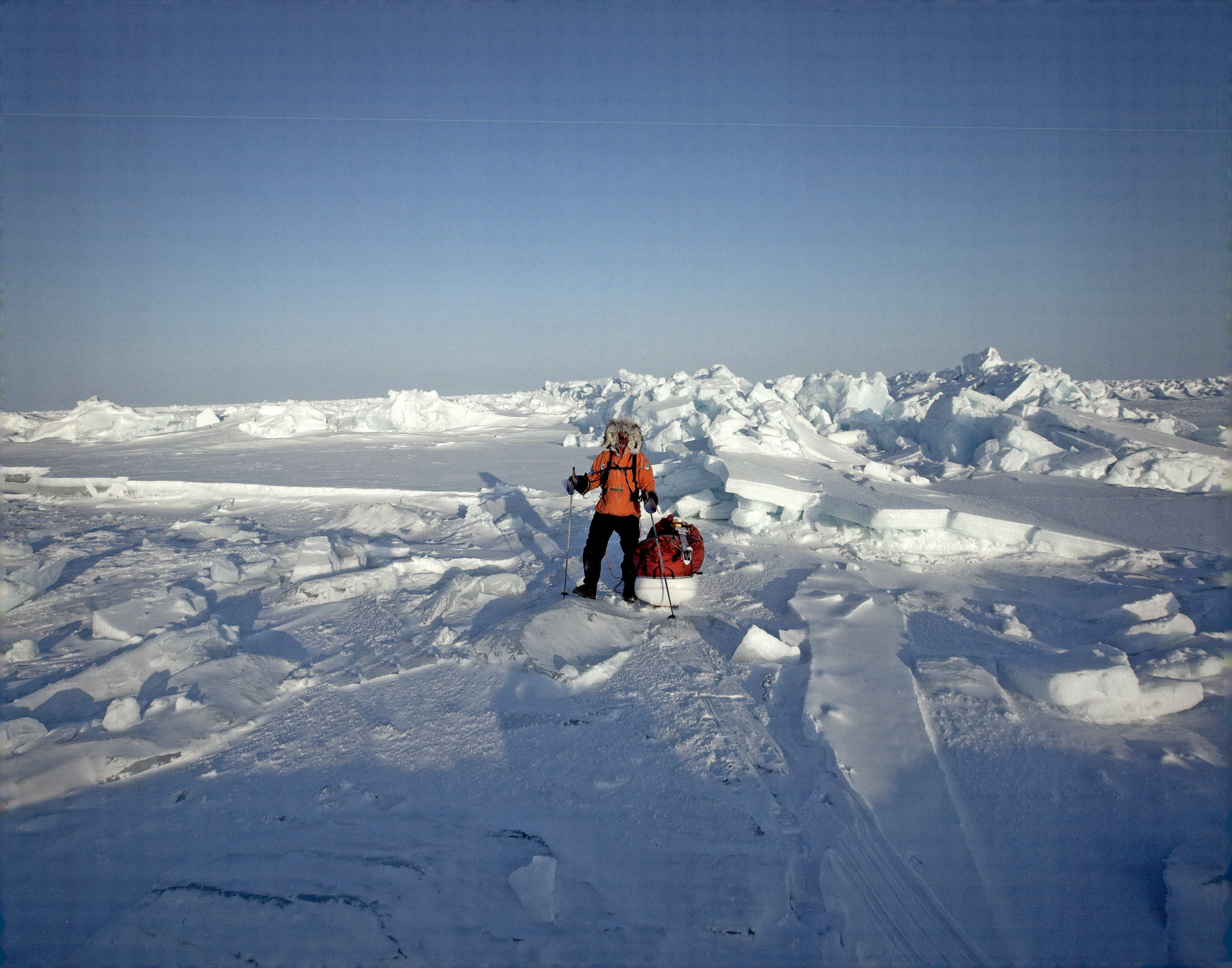

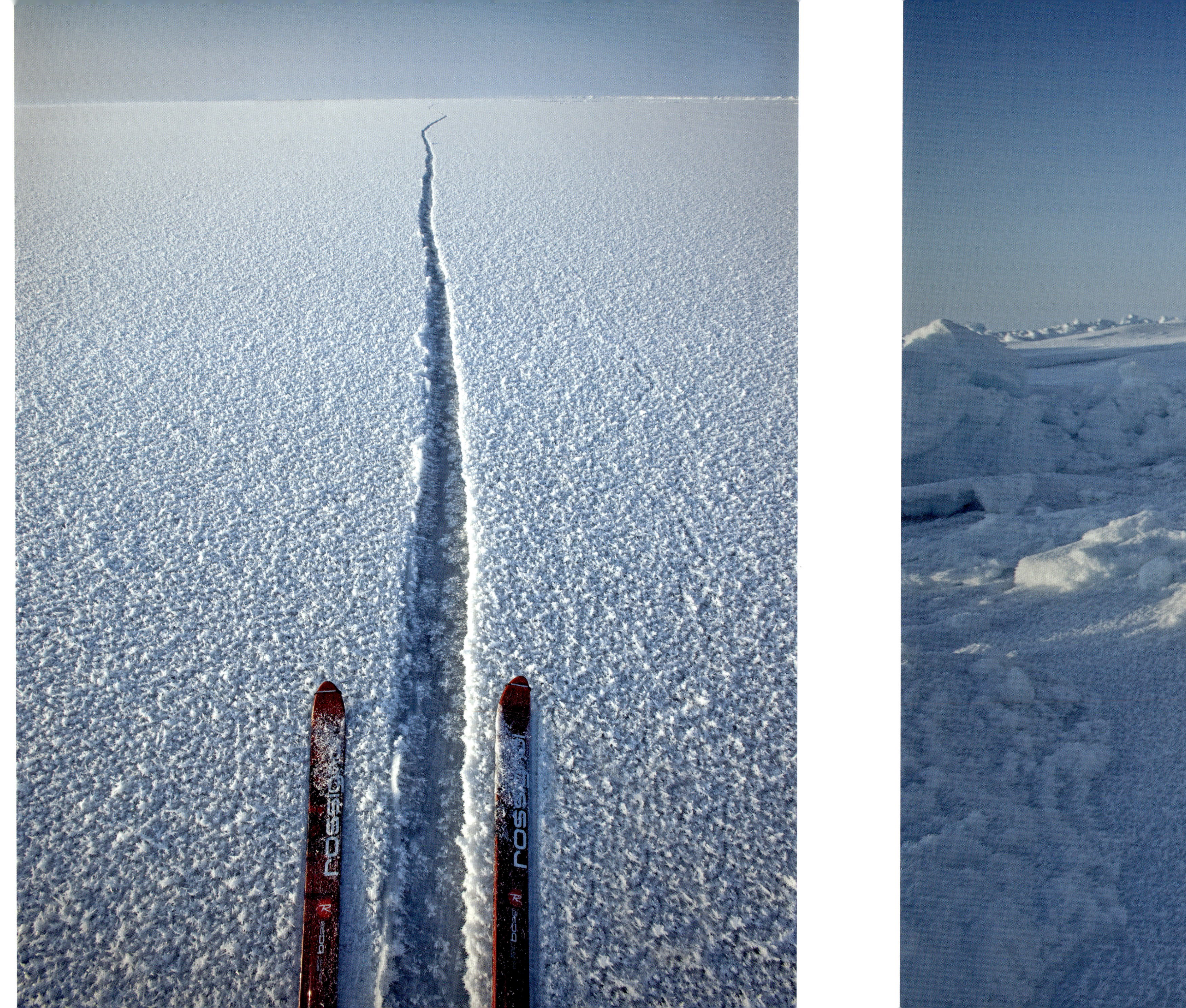

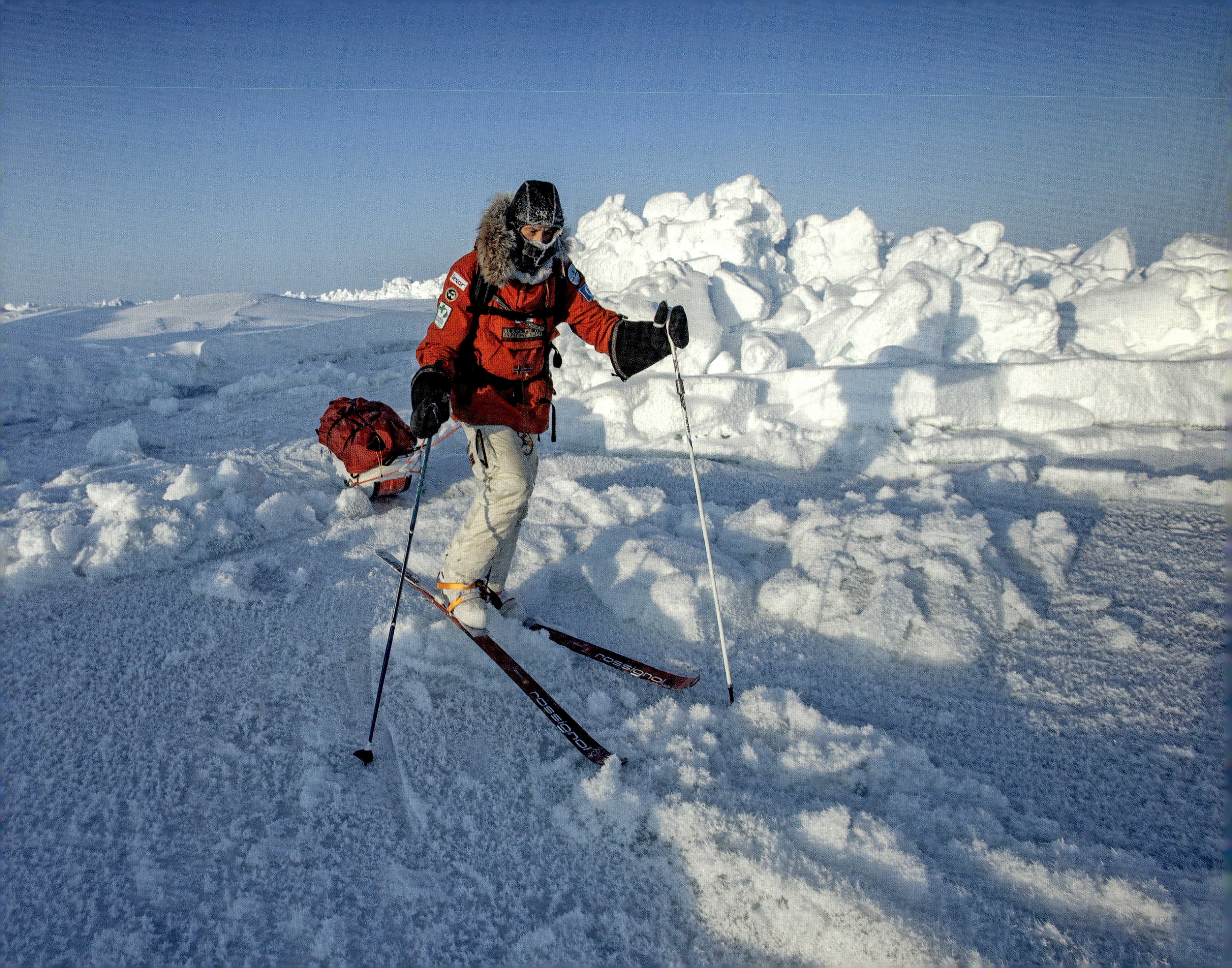
rossignol
rossignol

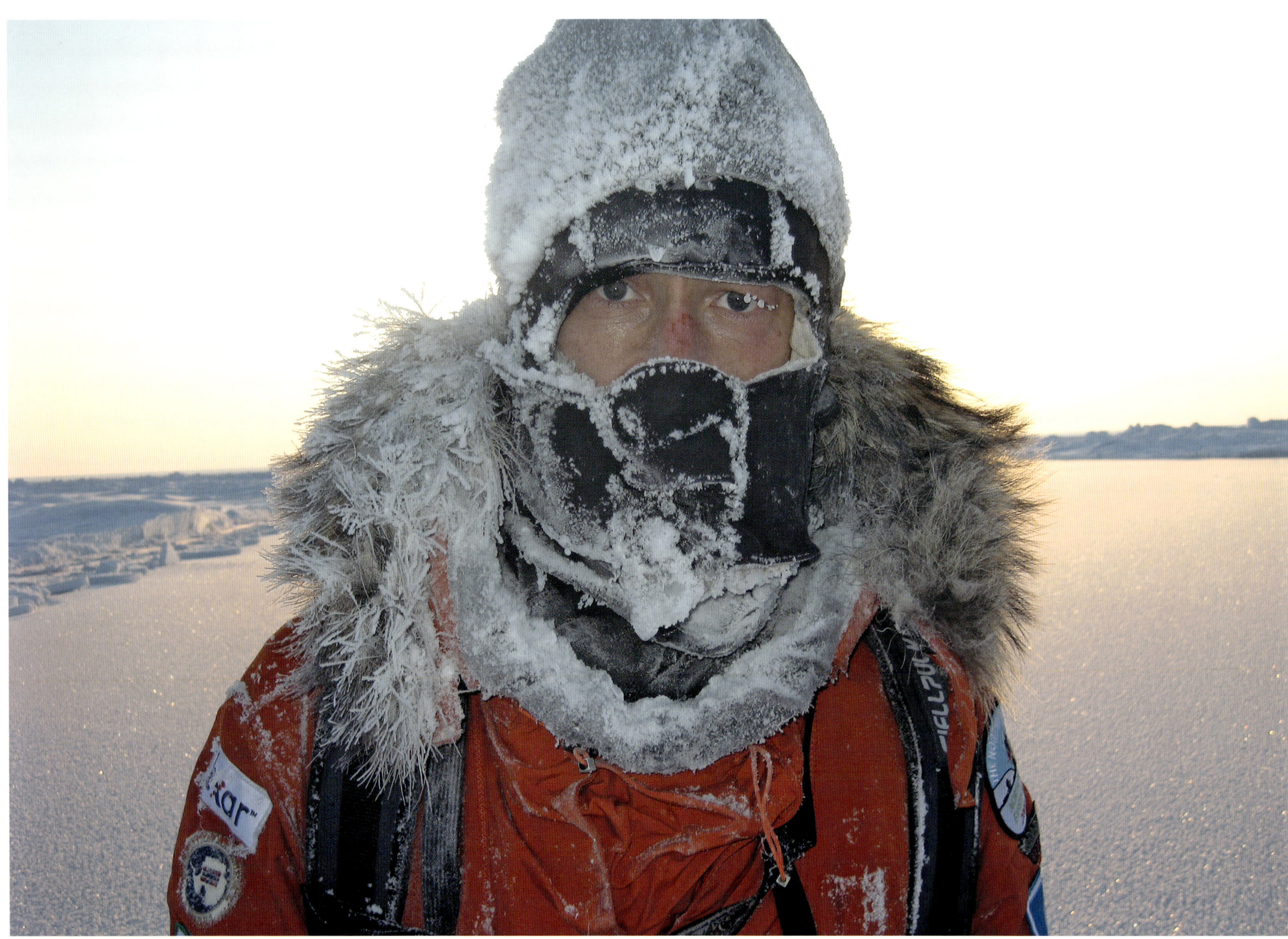

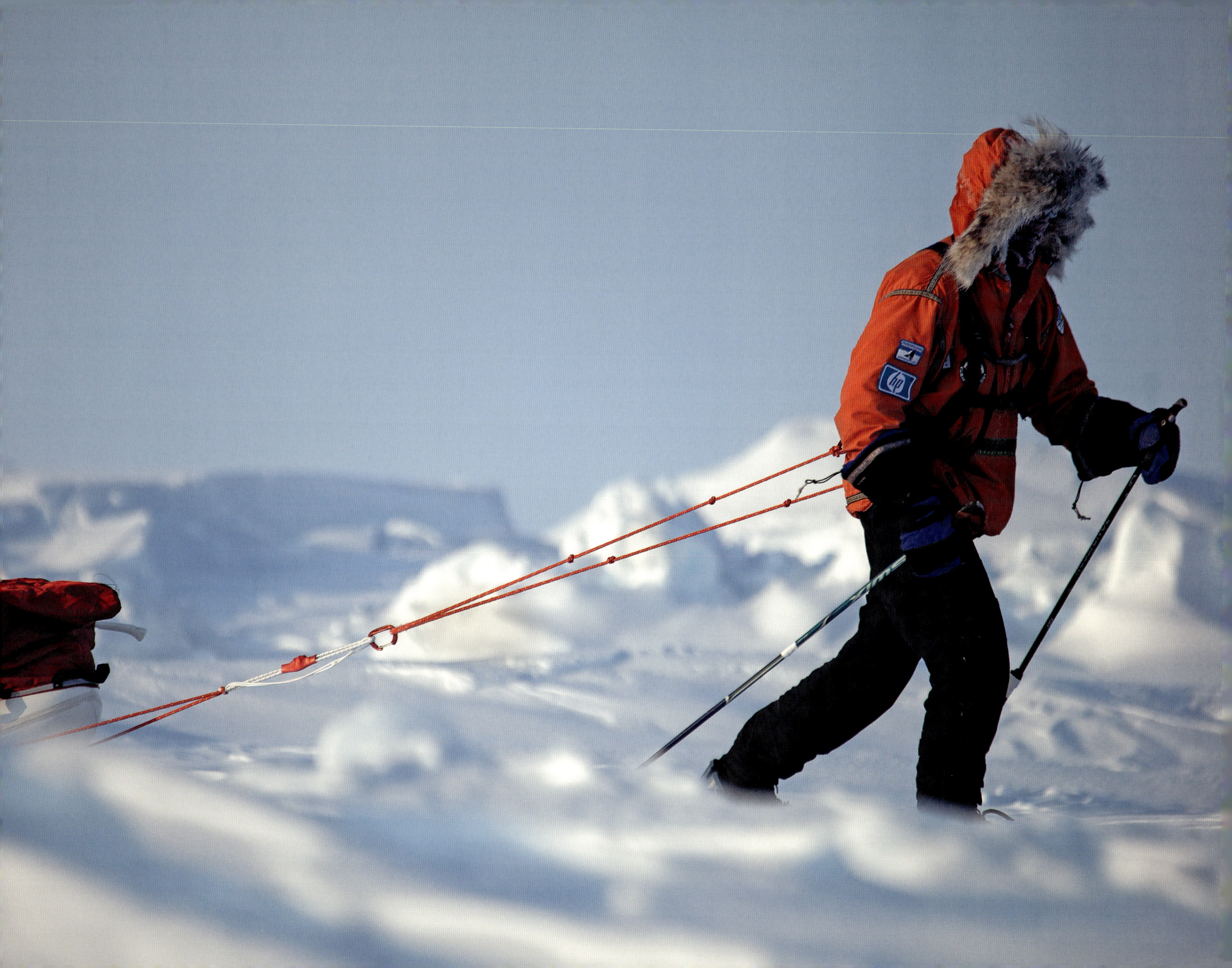

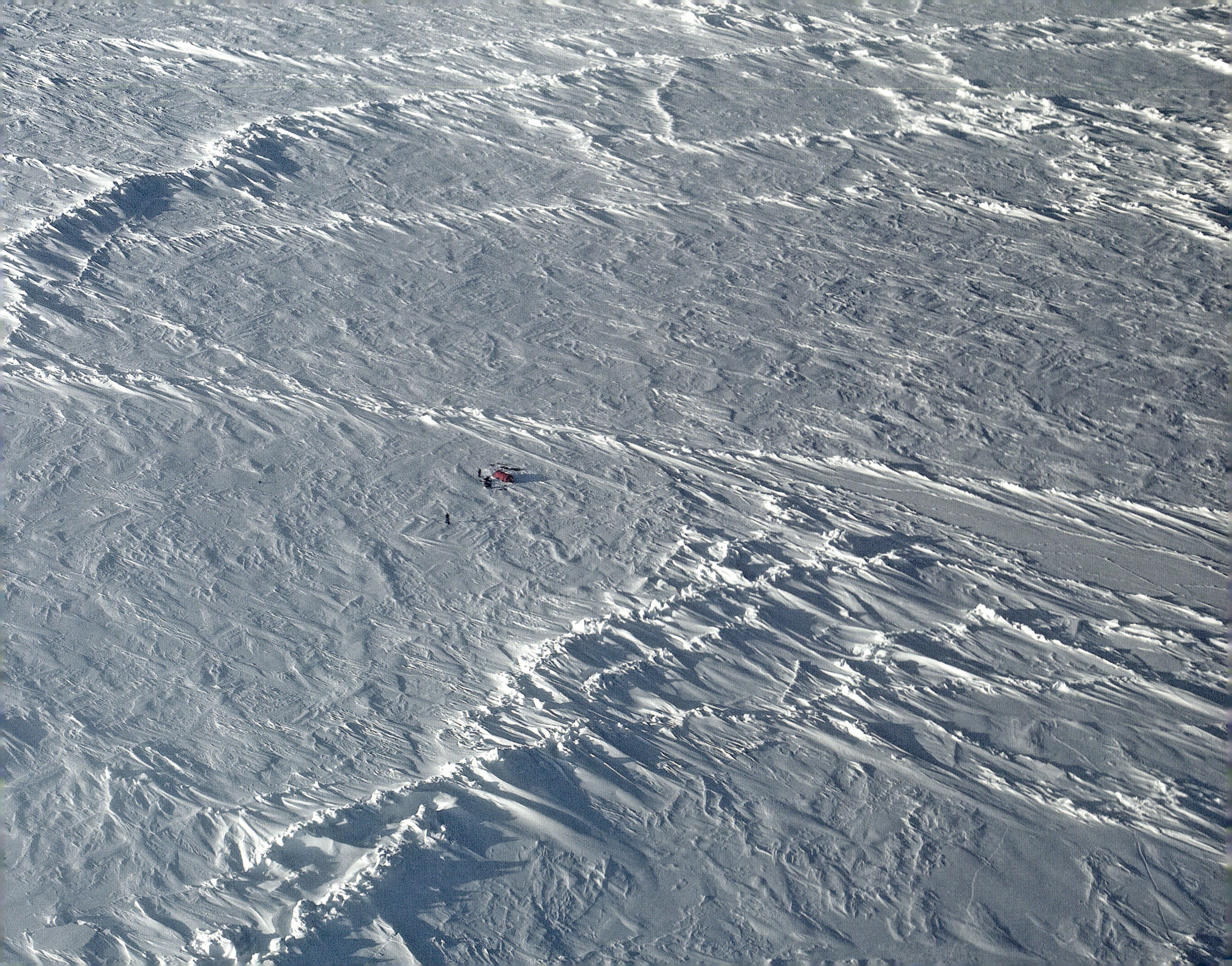

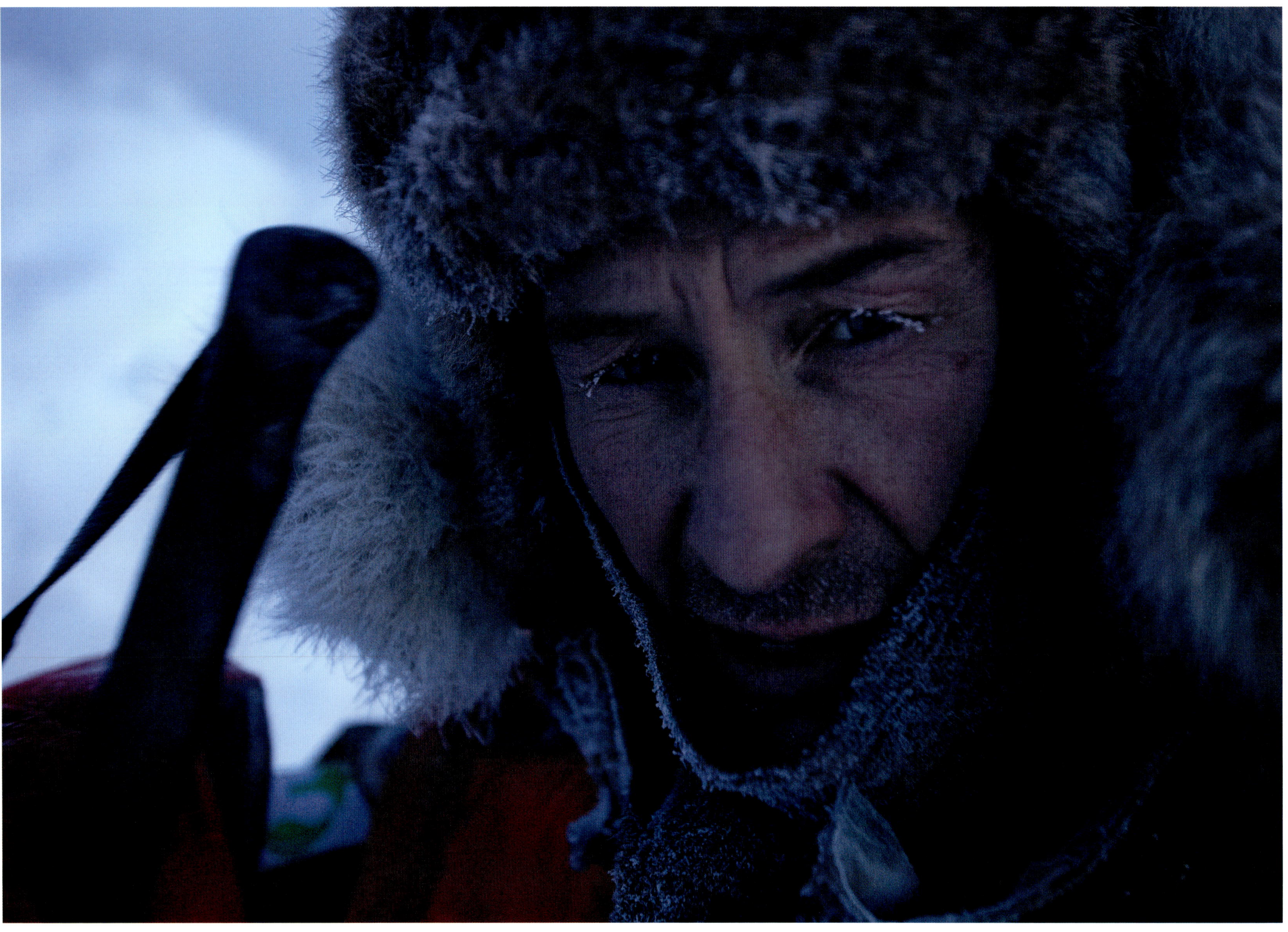

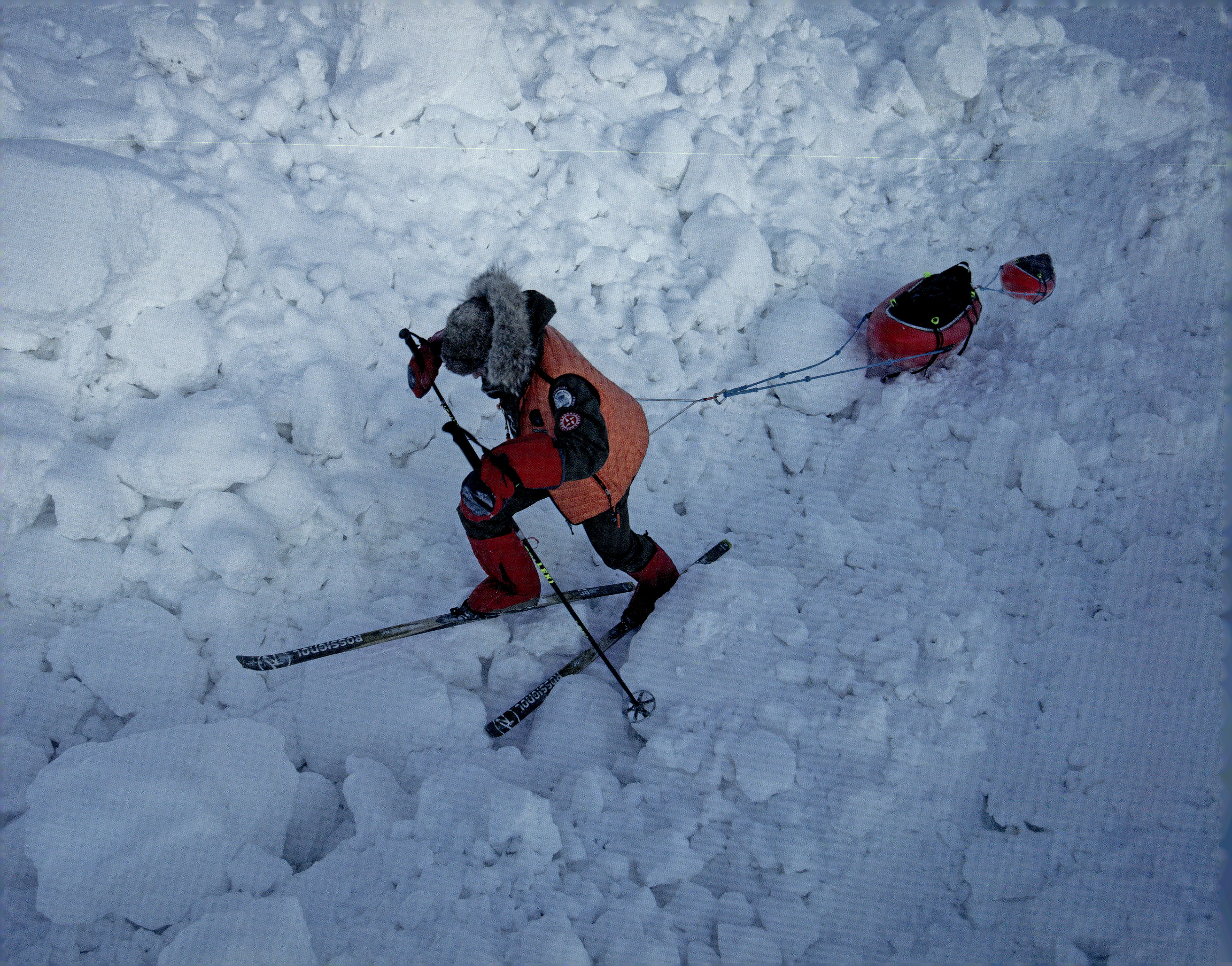
ROSSIGNOL
ROSSIGNOL

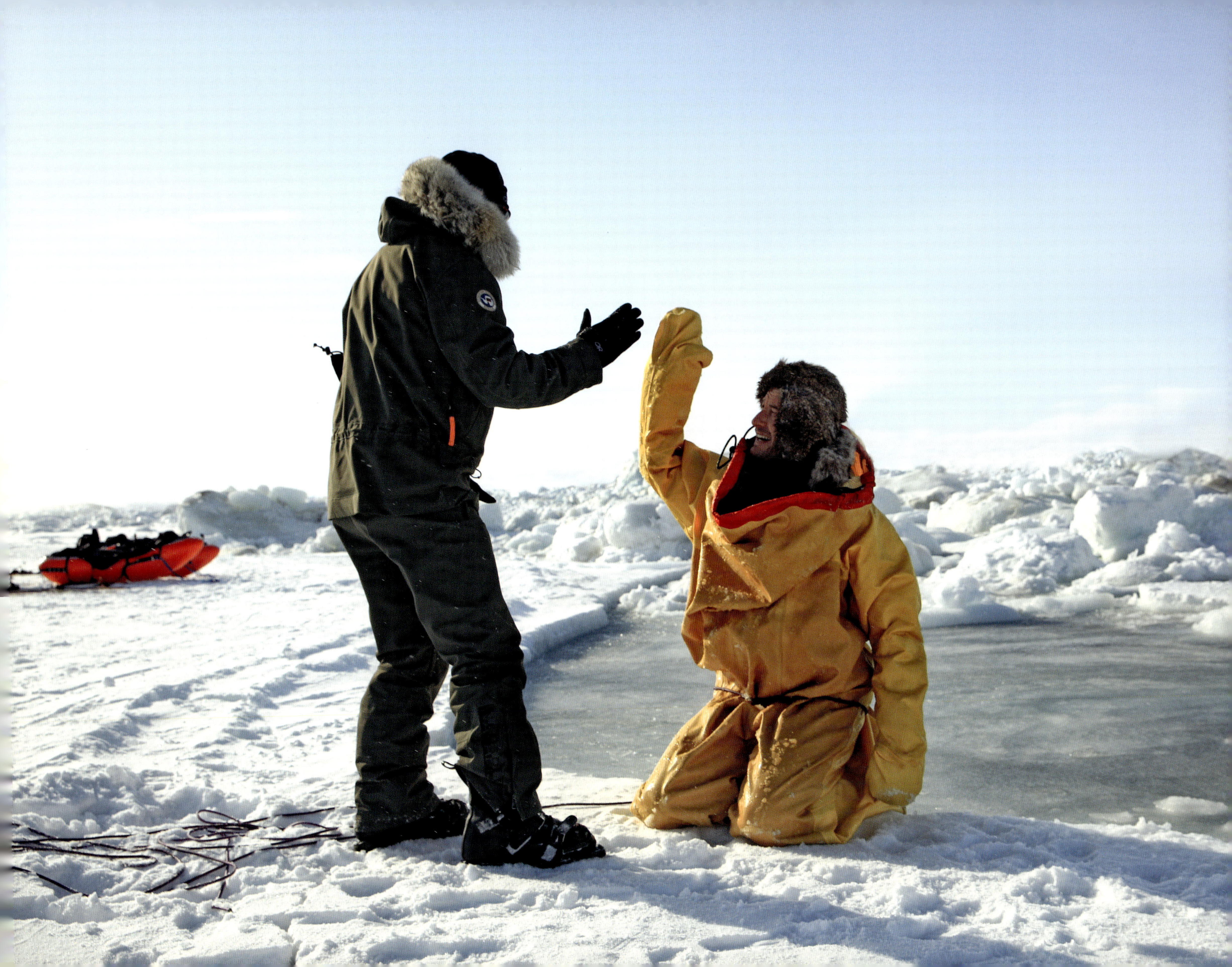

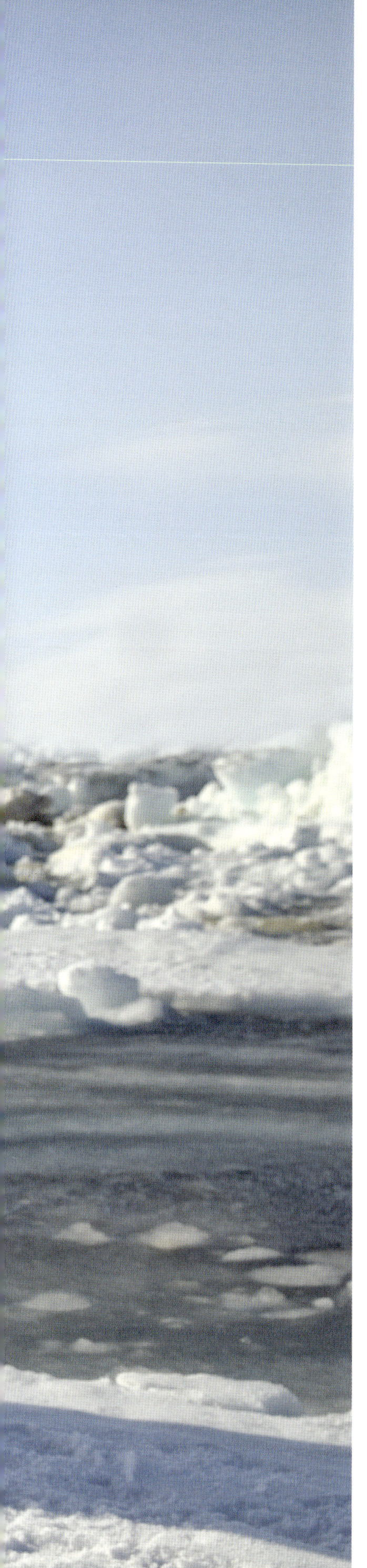

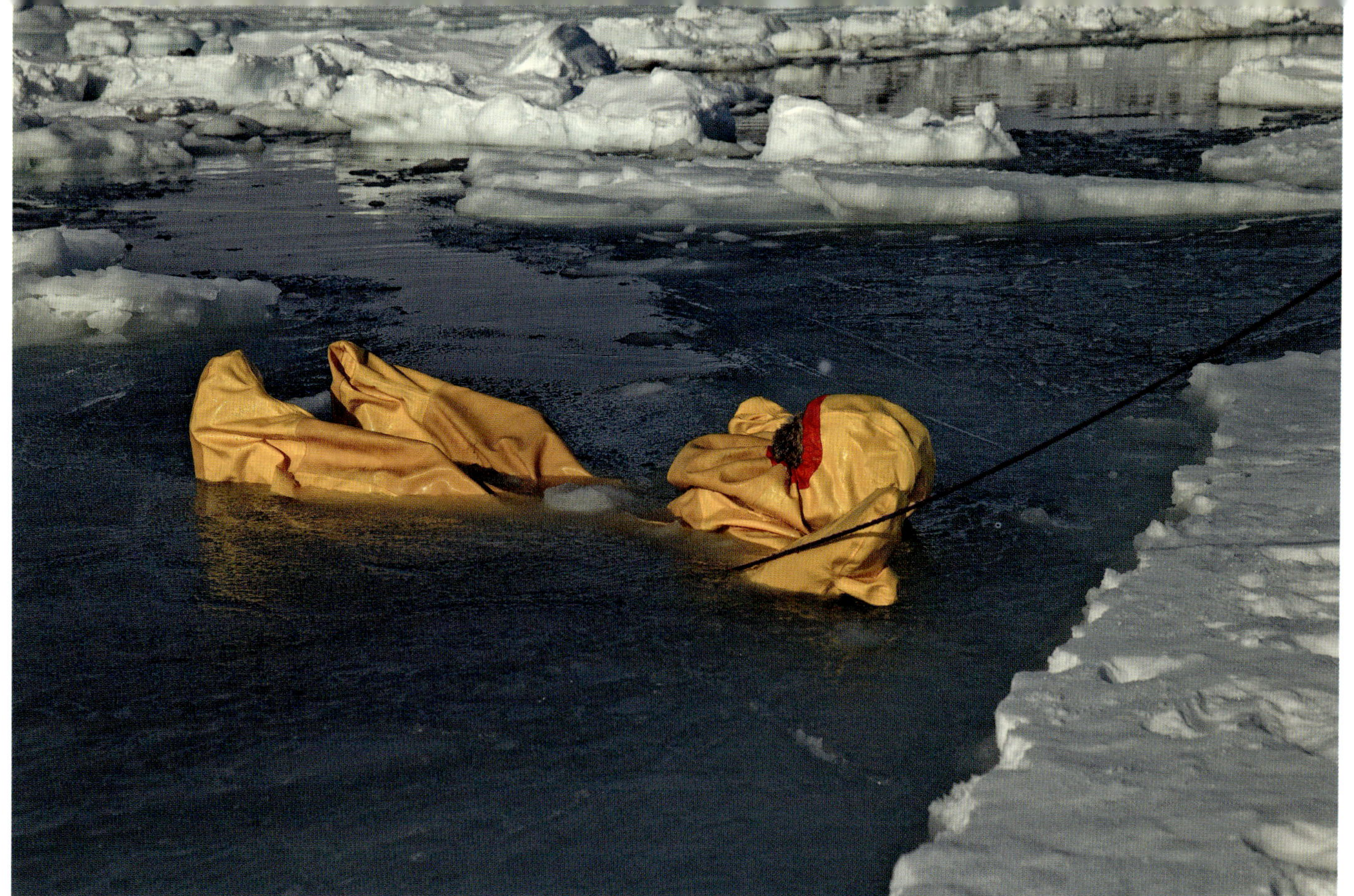

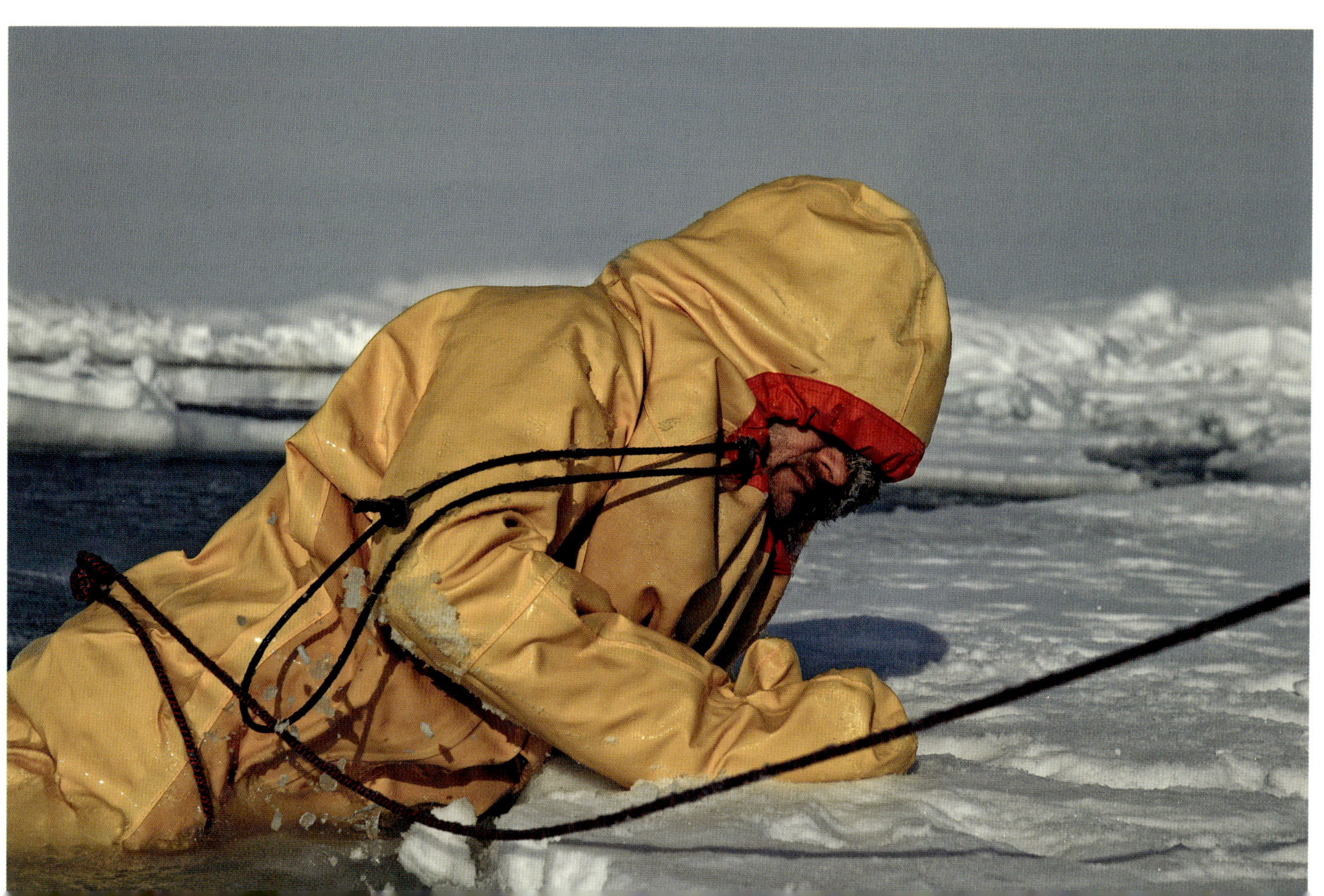

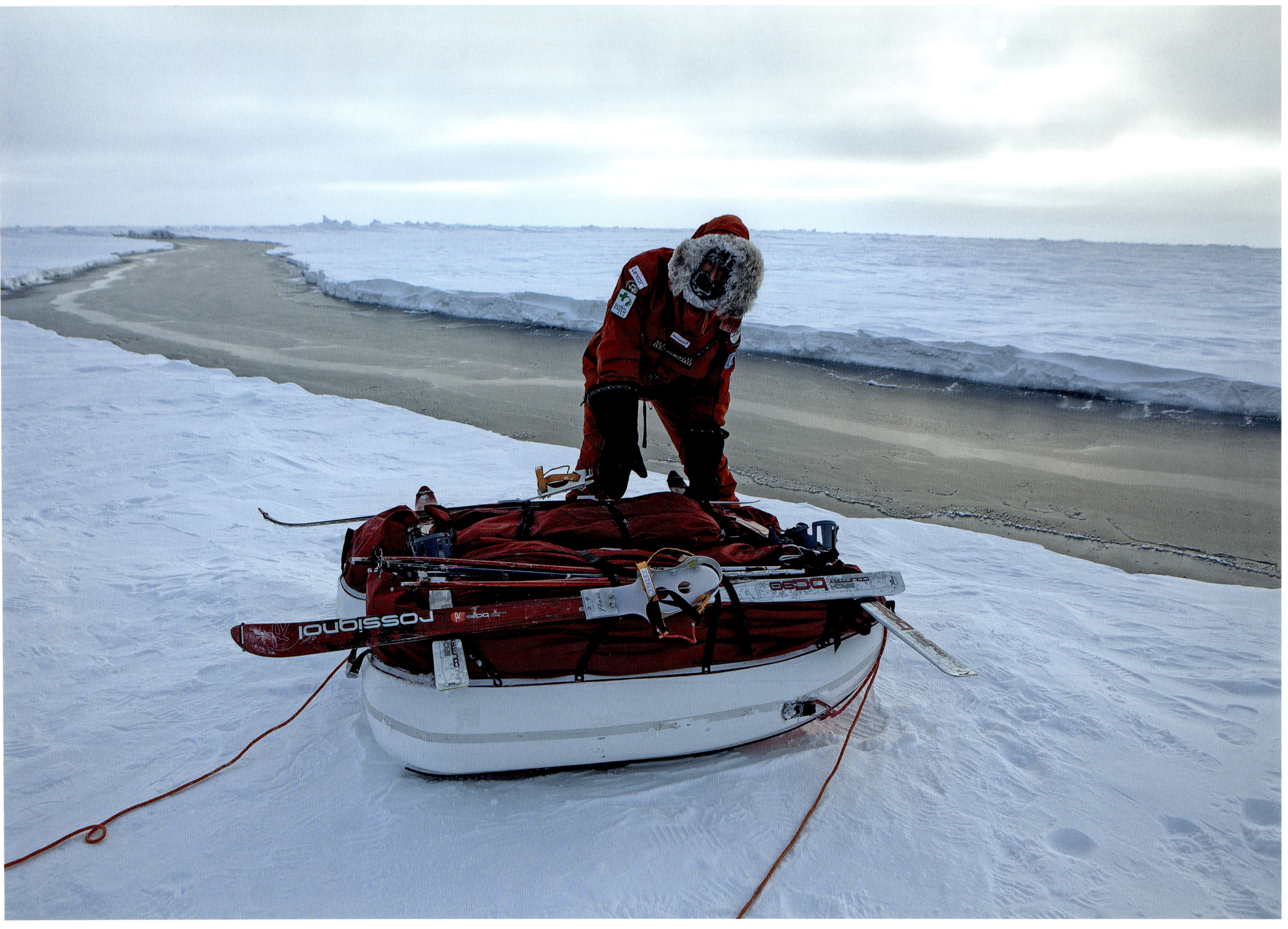

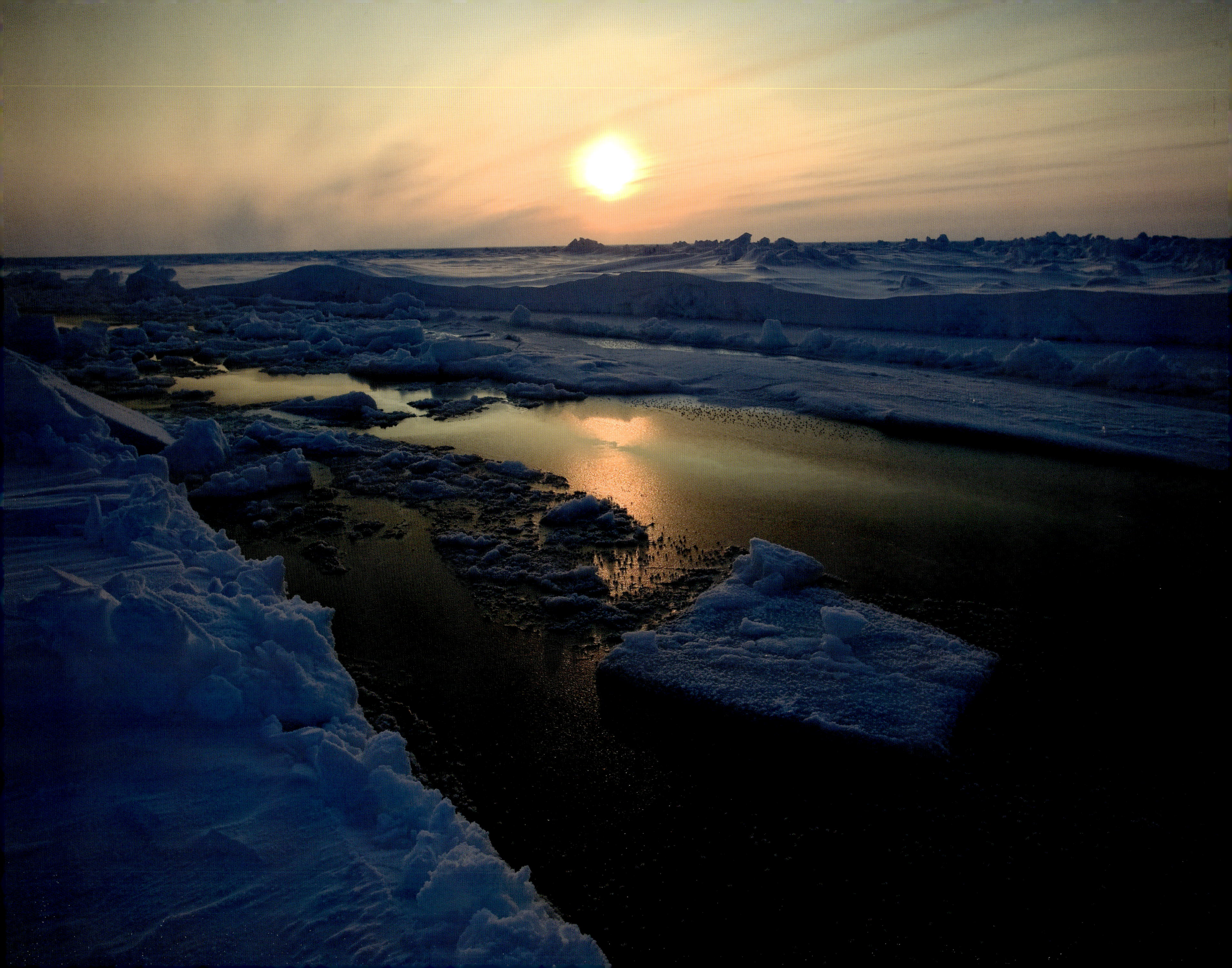

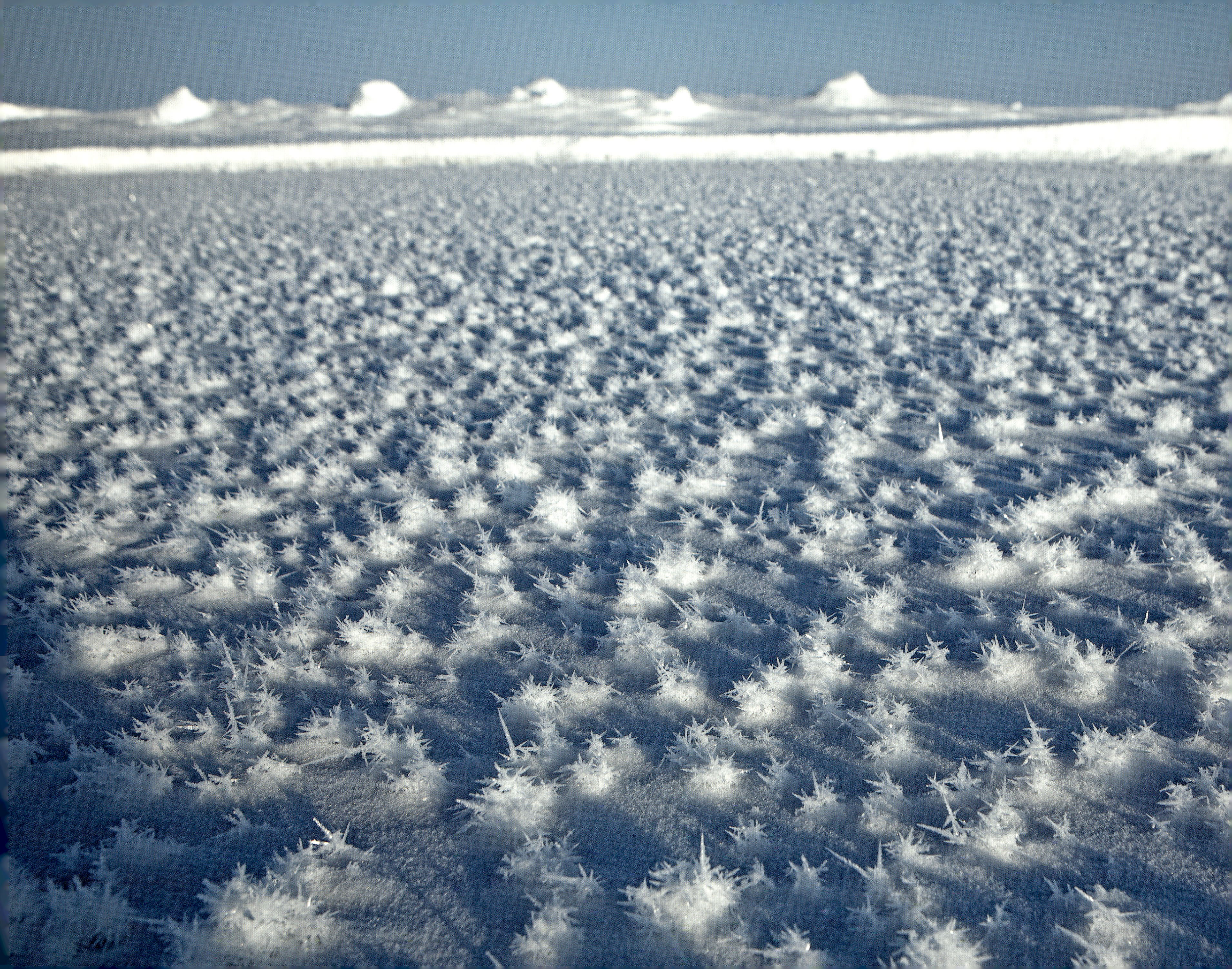

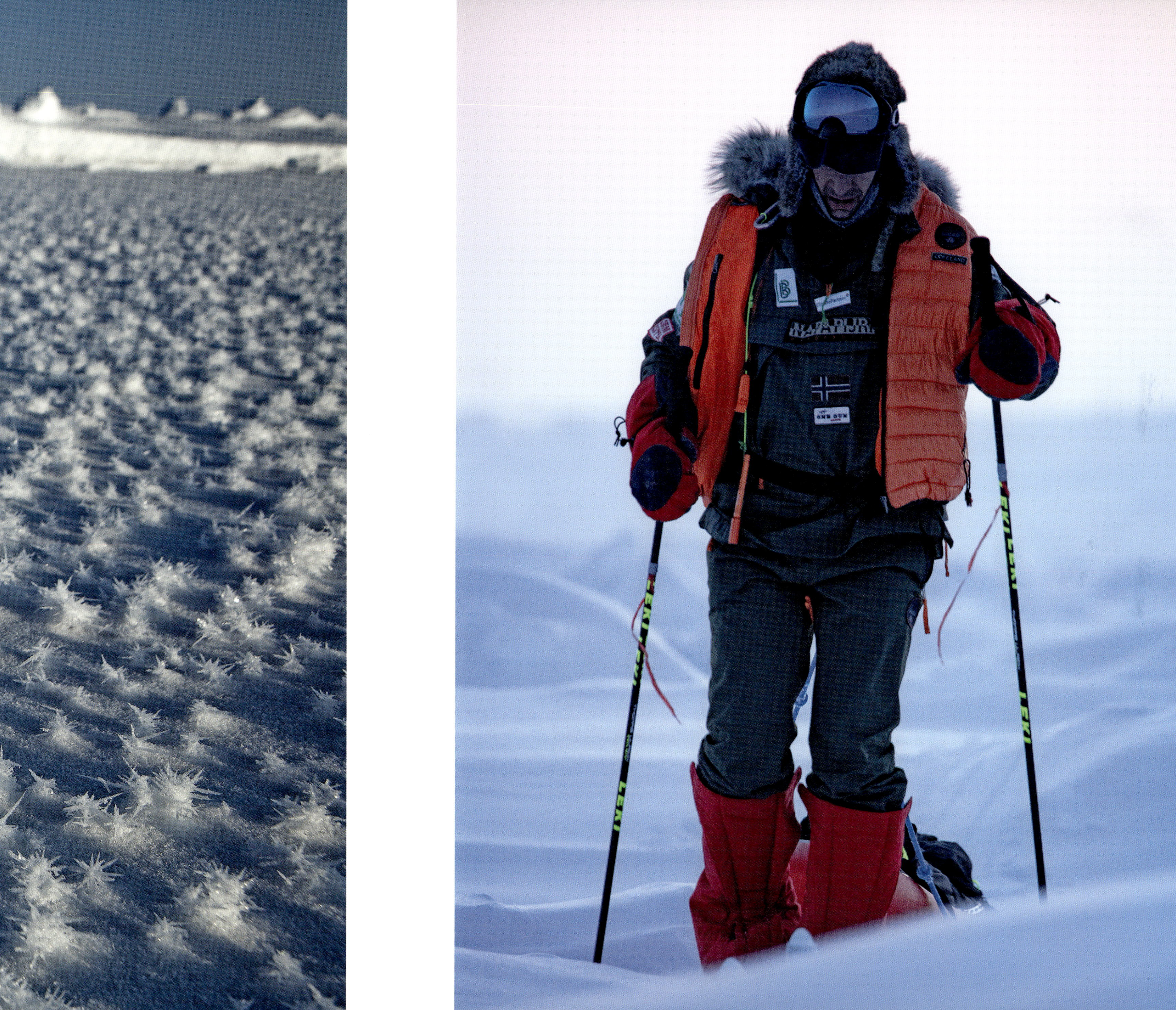
LEKI

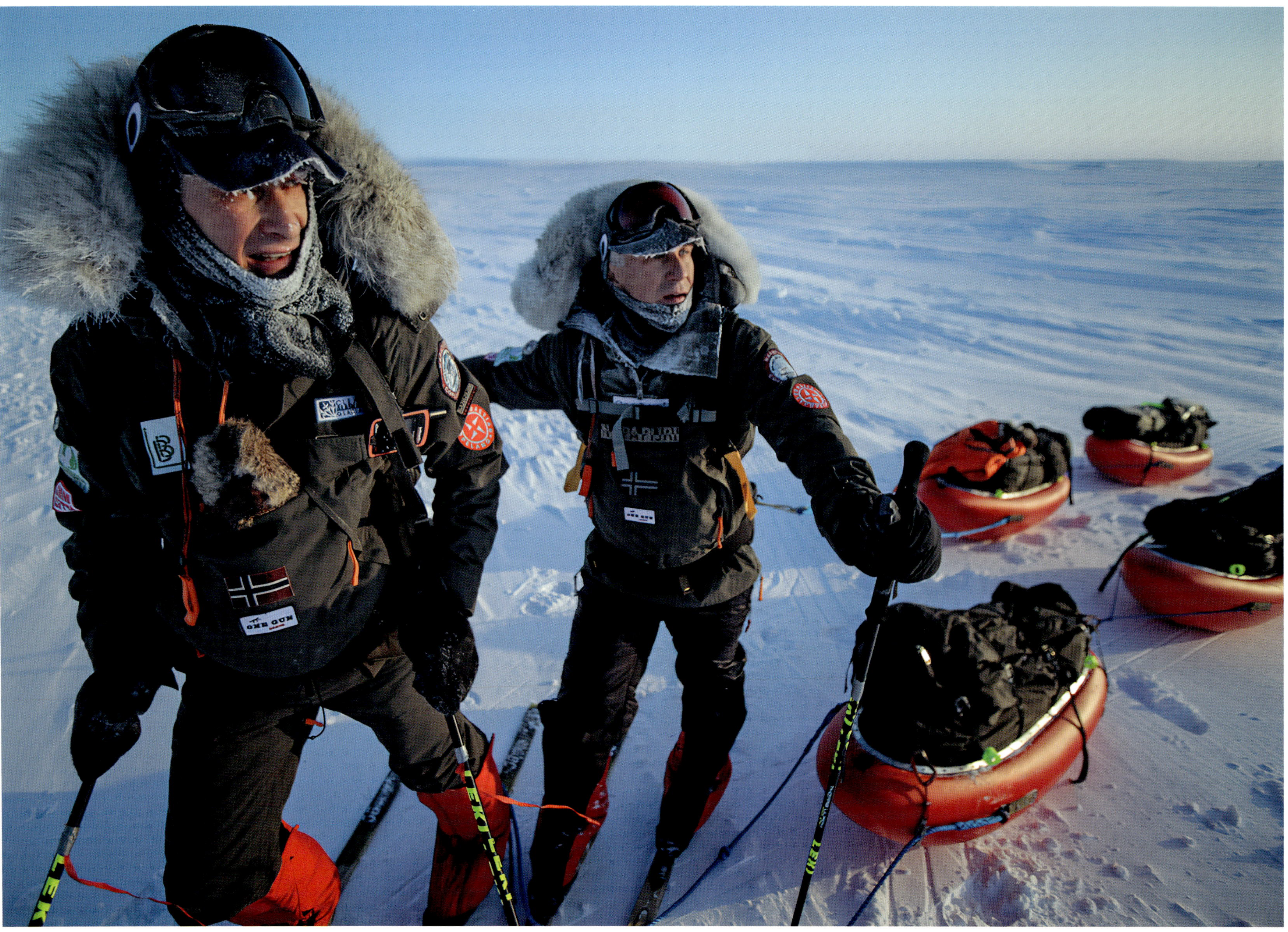

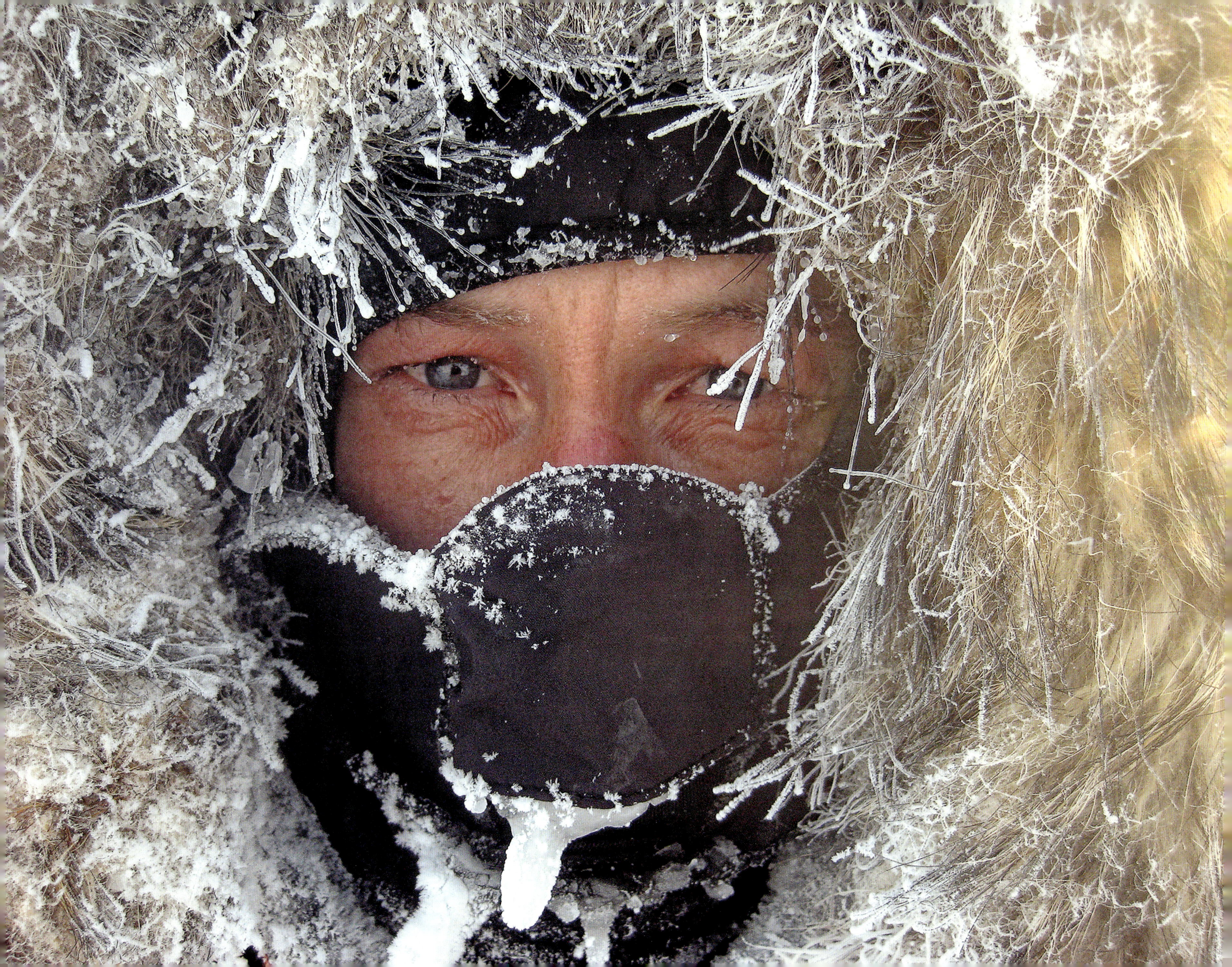

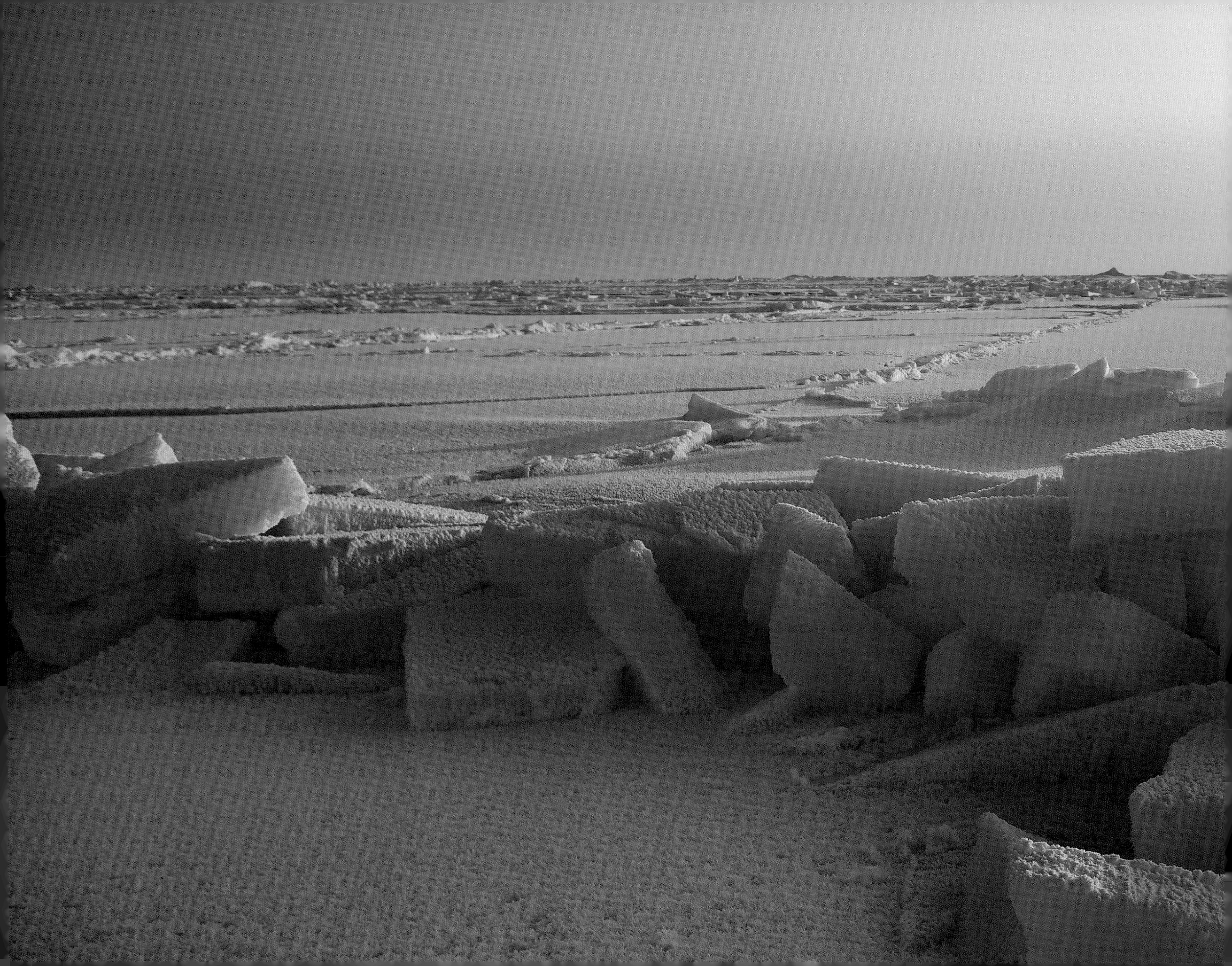

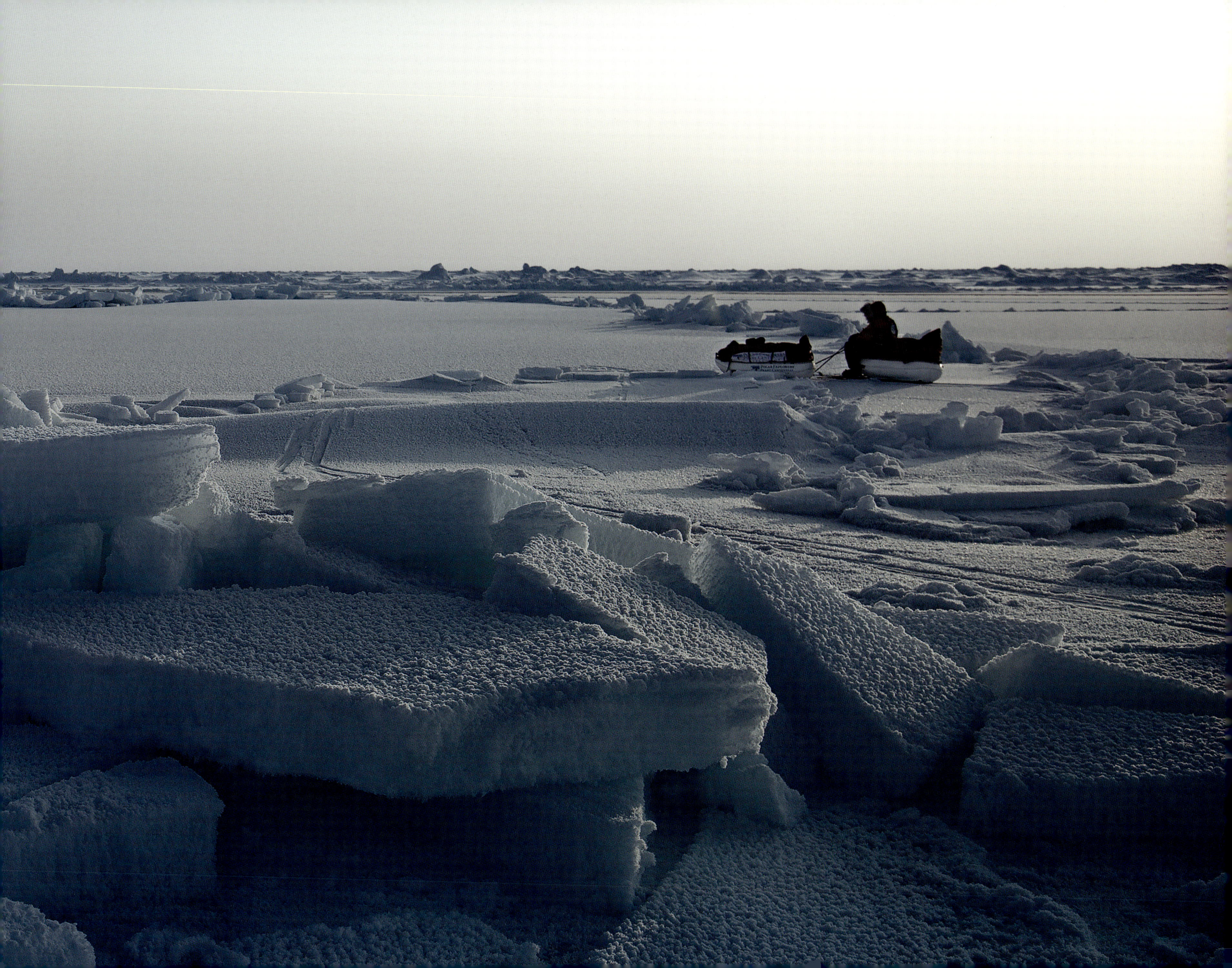

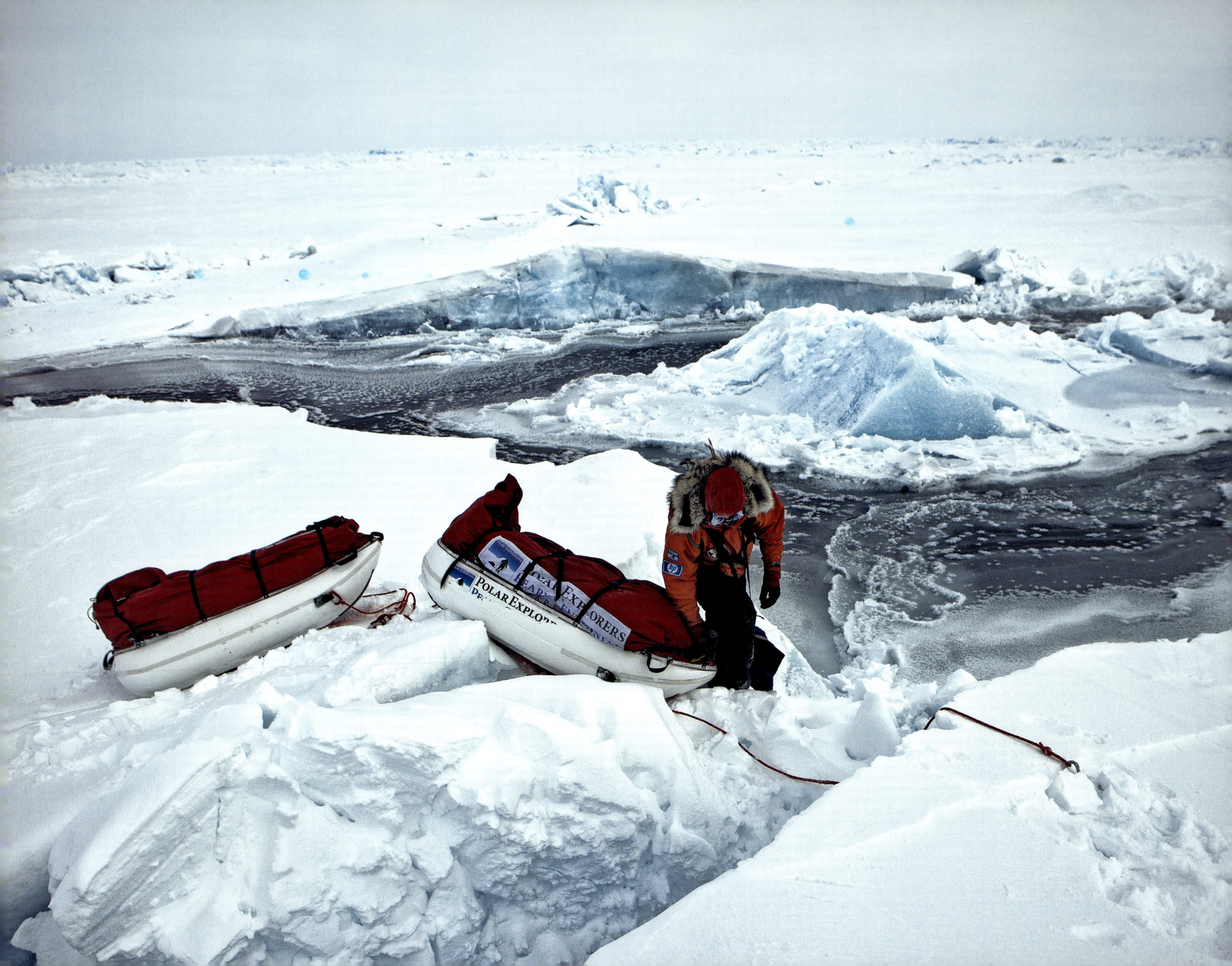
POLAR EXPLORERS

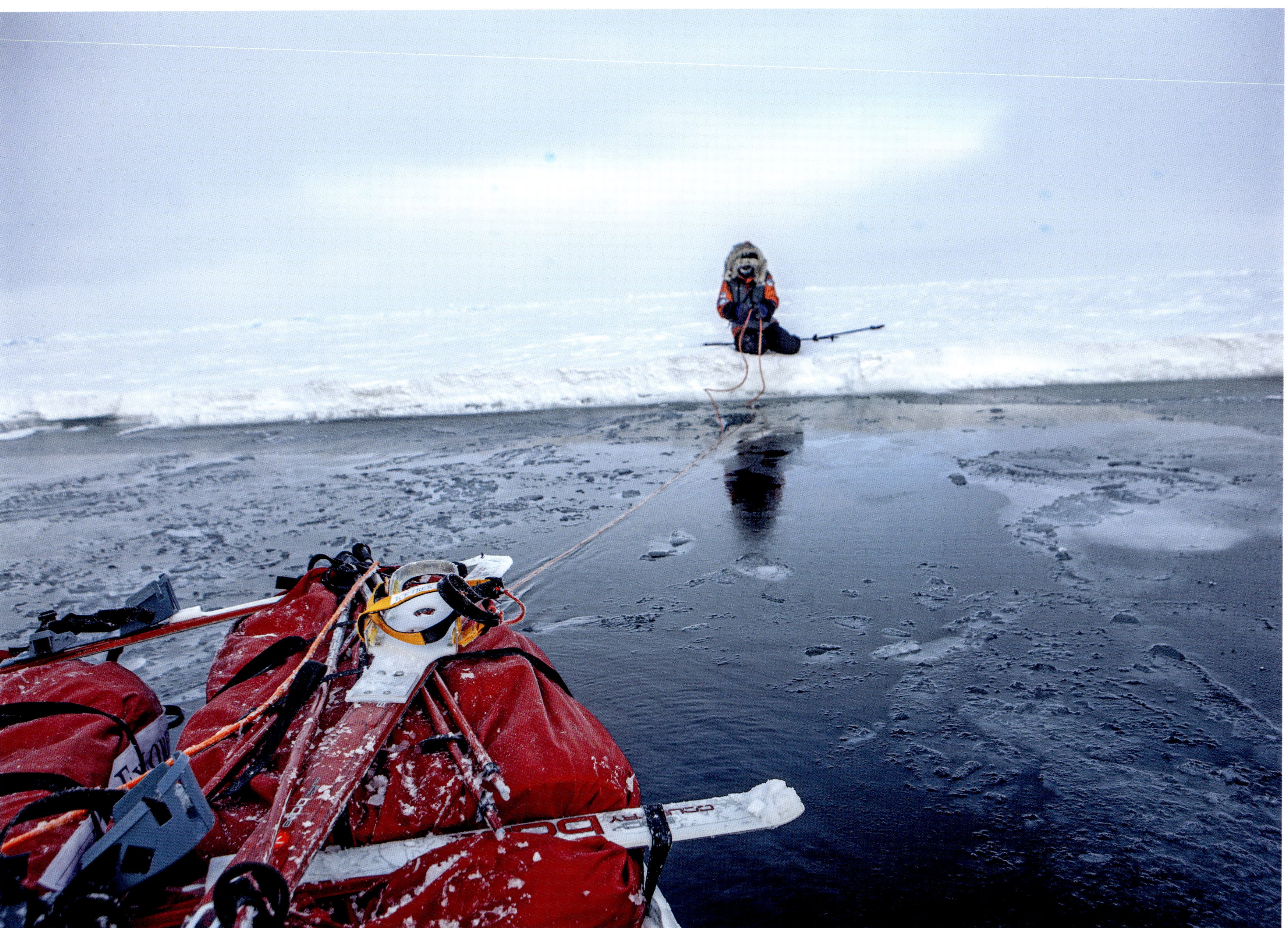

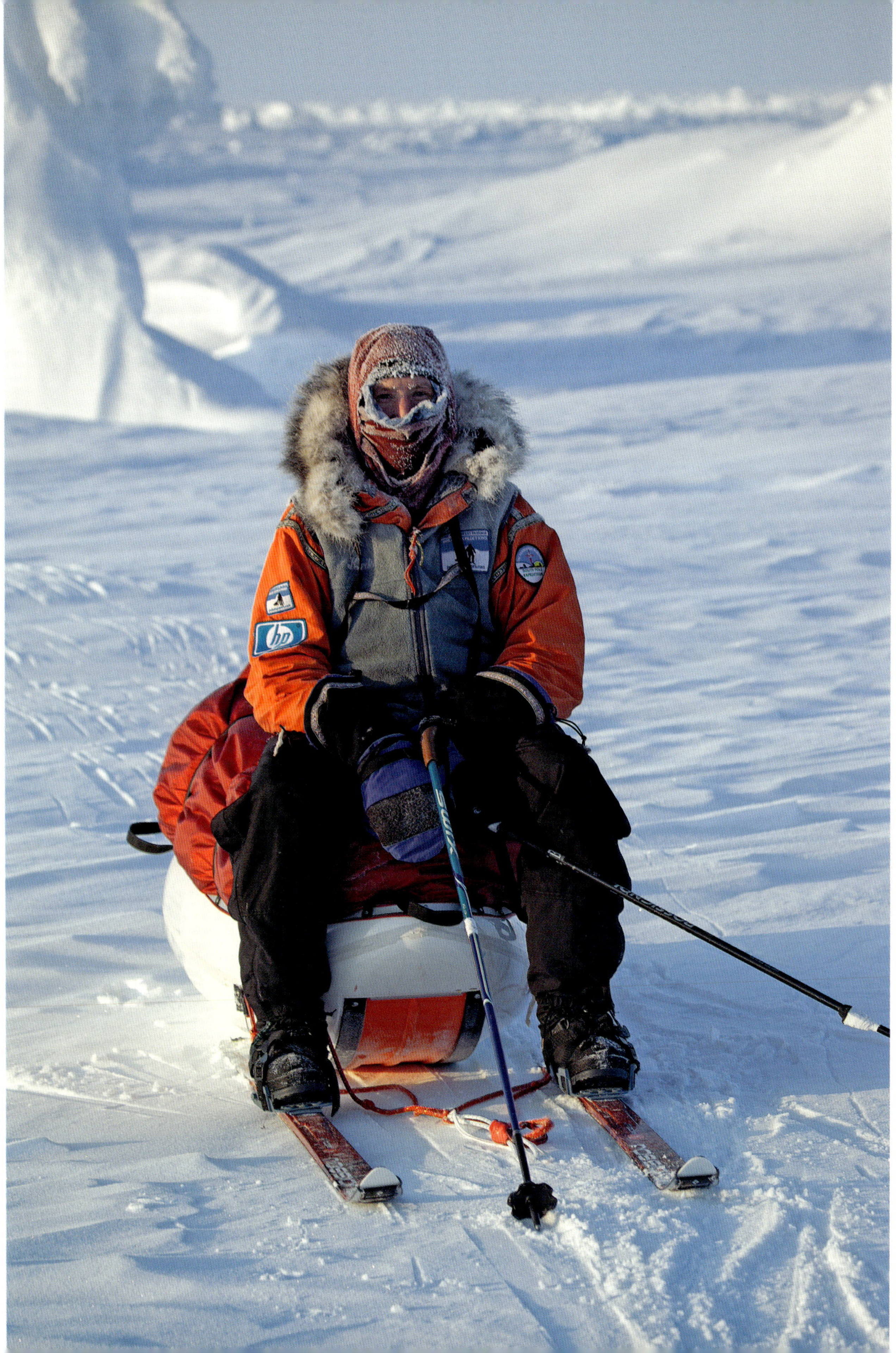

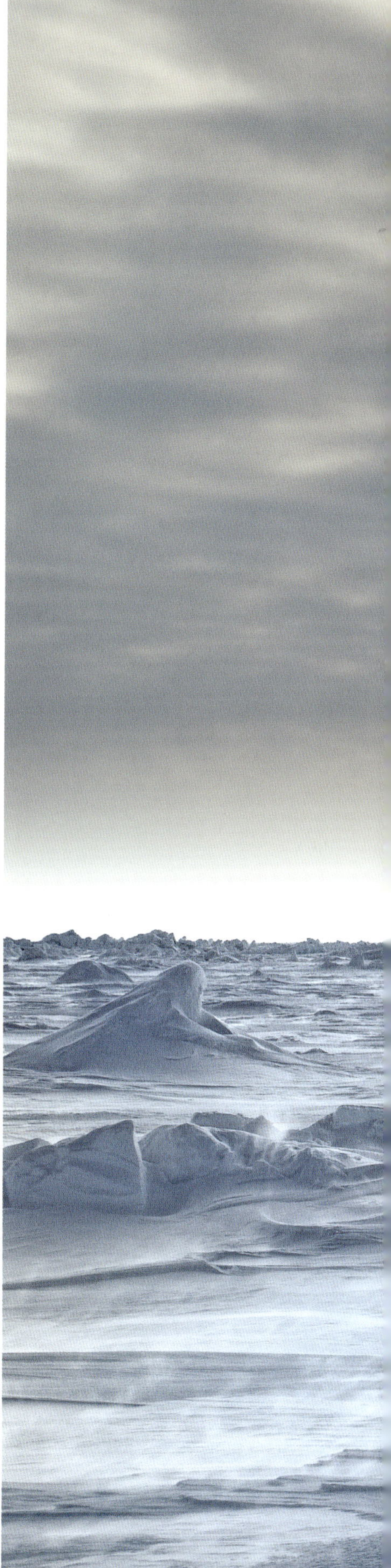

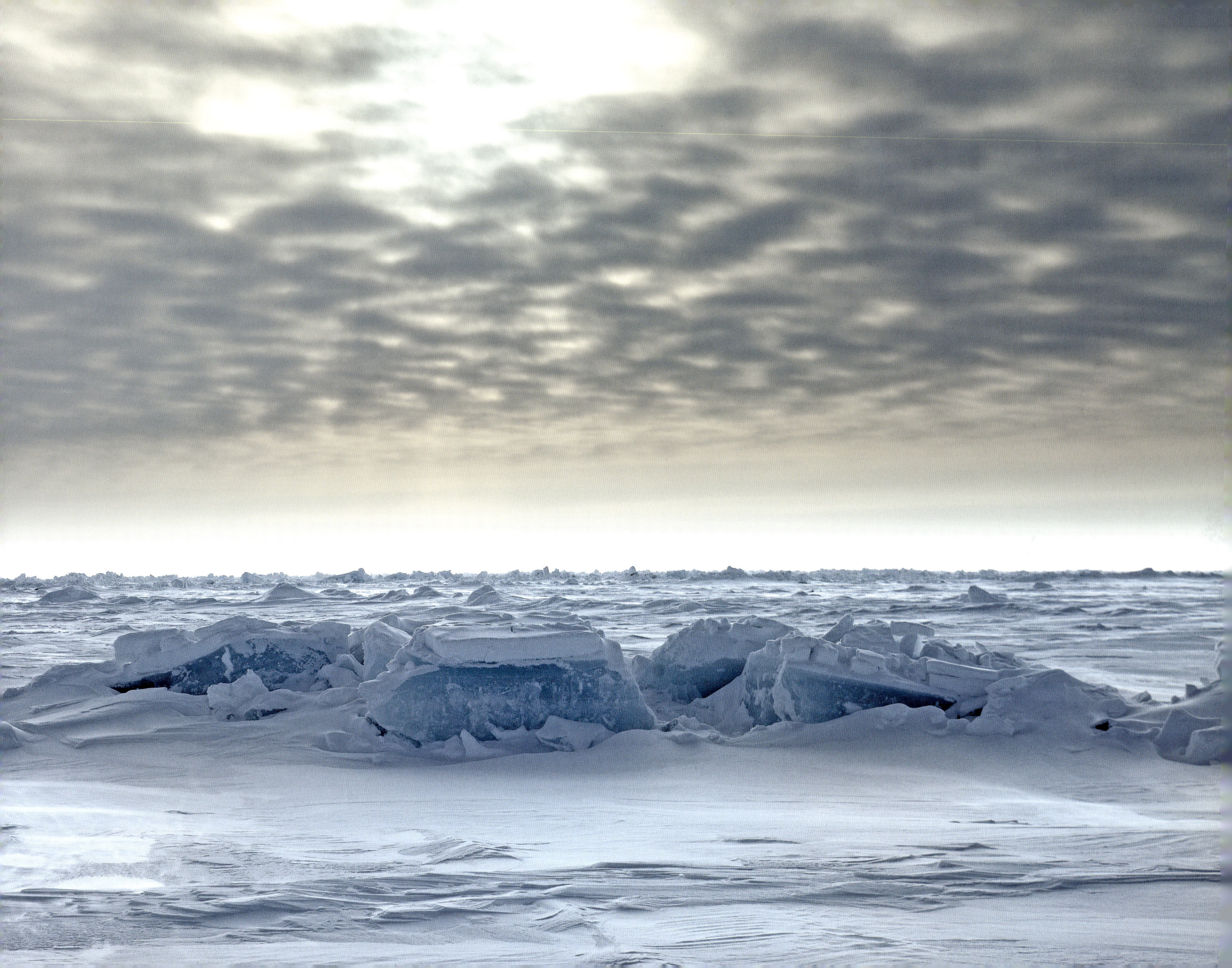

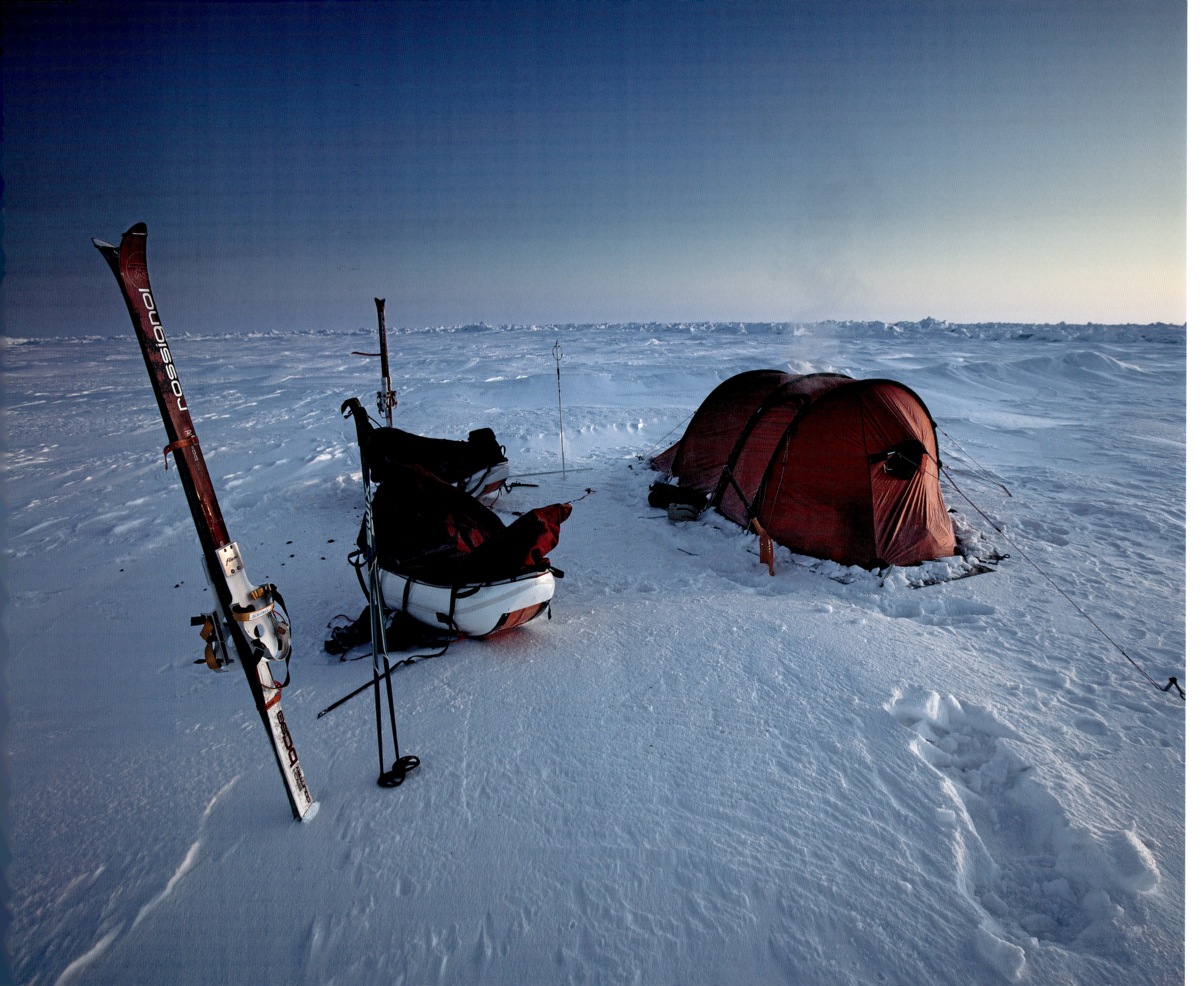
rossignol

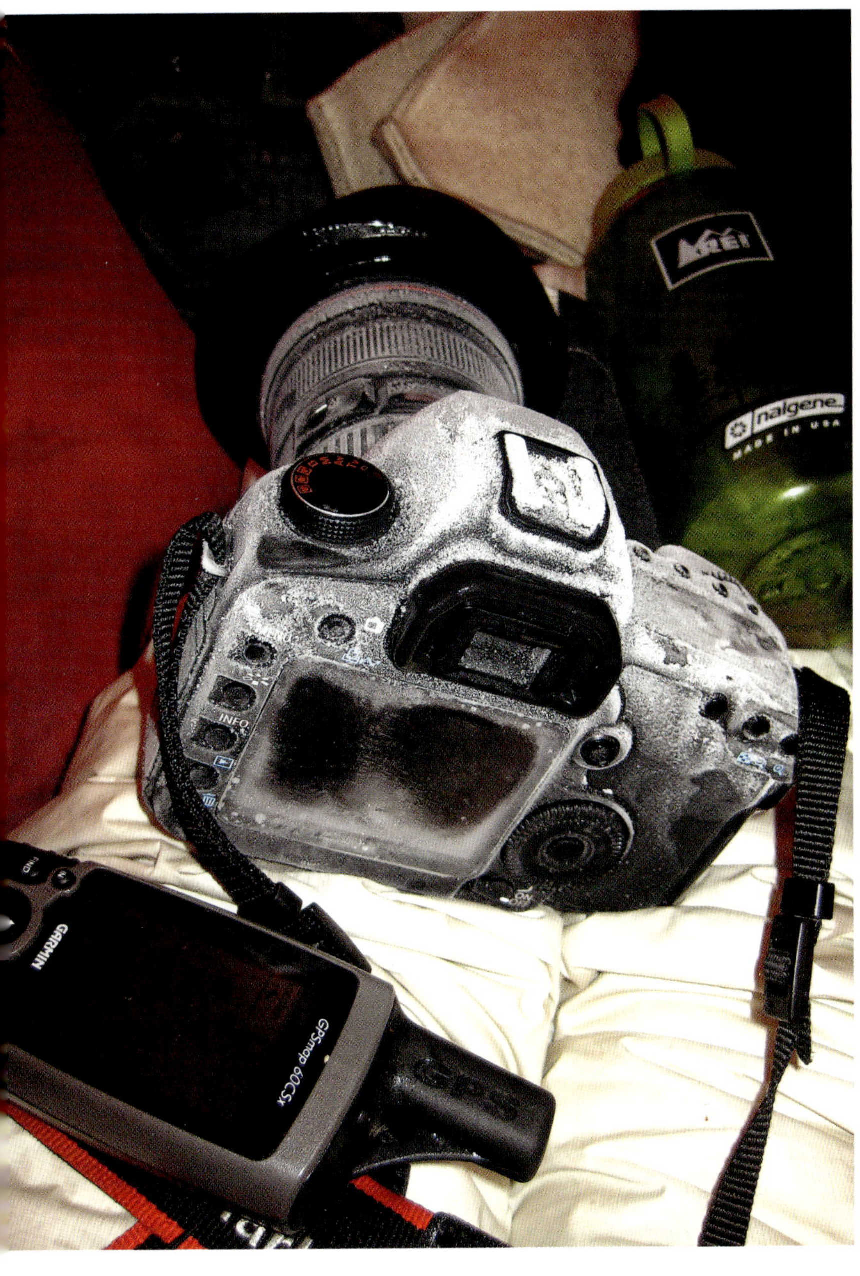
nalgene
MADE IN USA
GARMIN
GPSmap 60CSx

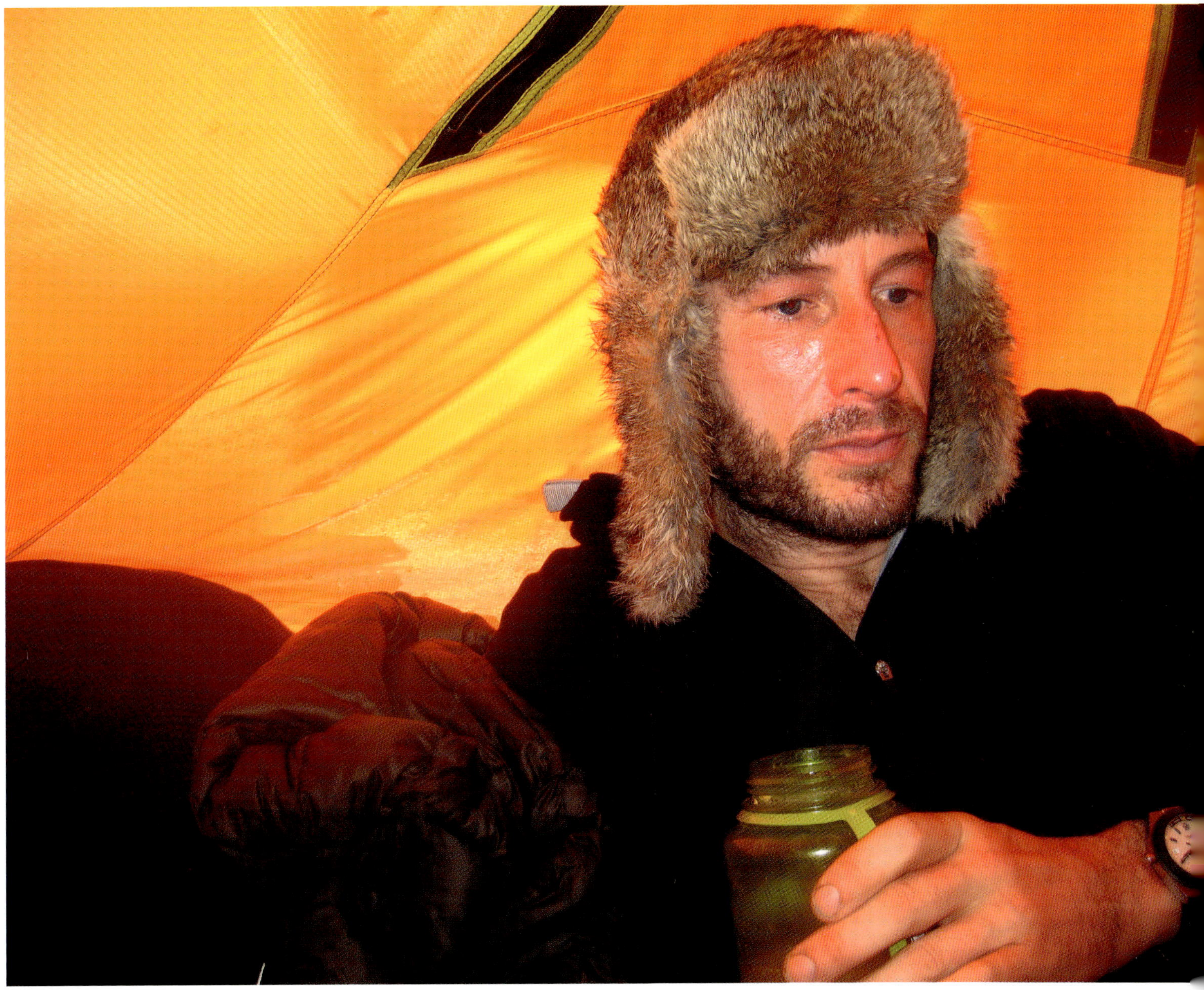

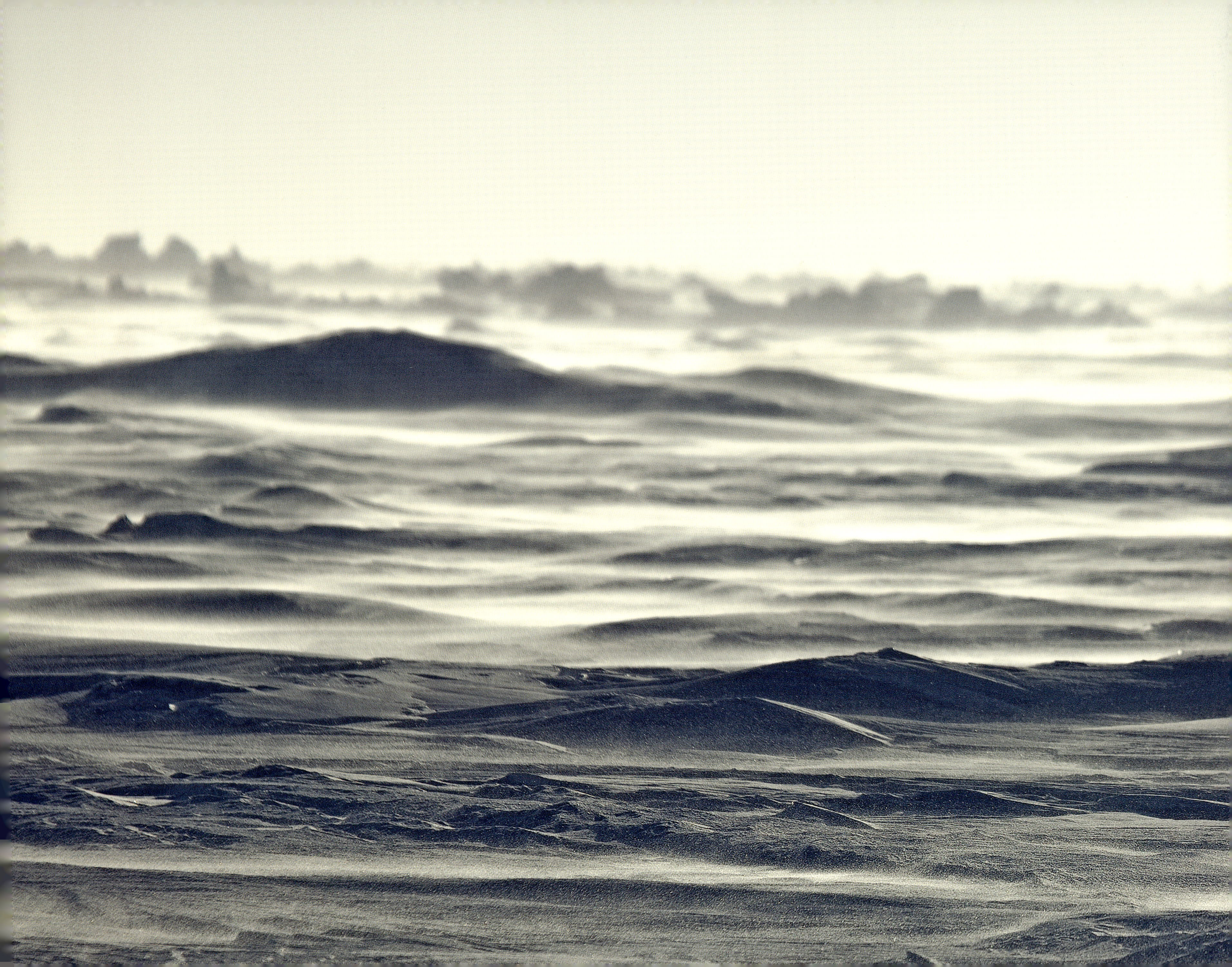

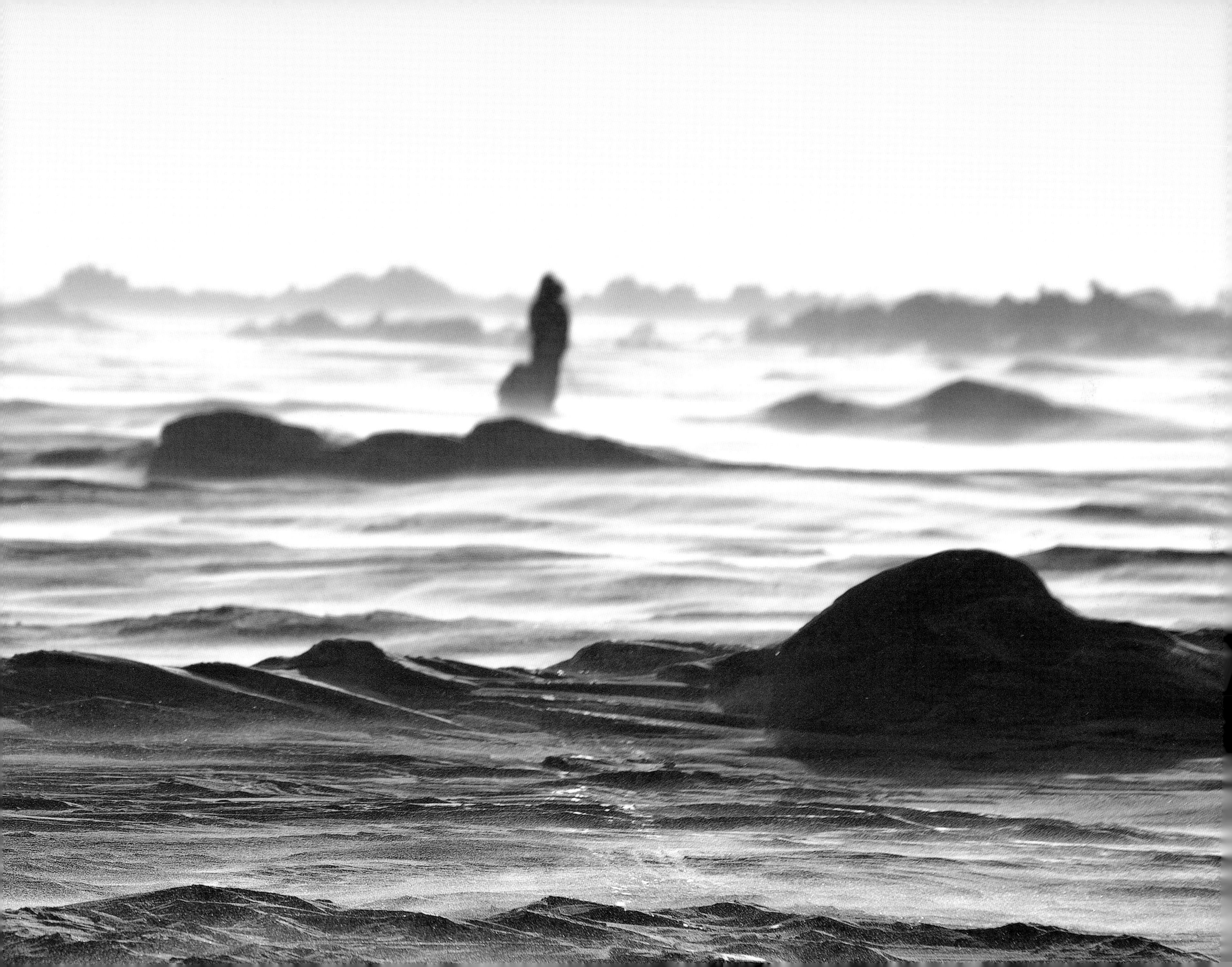

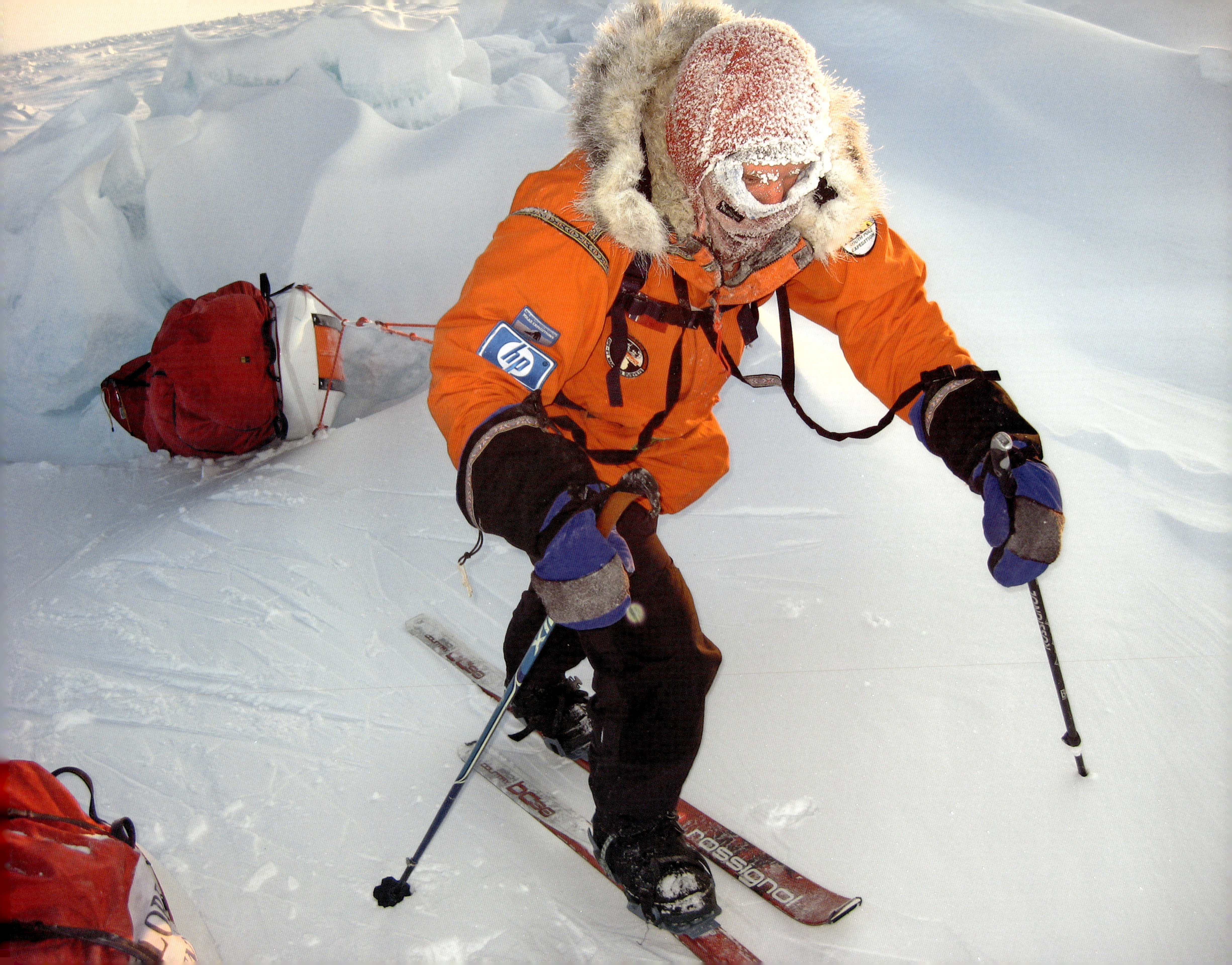

hp
rossignol

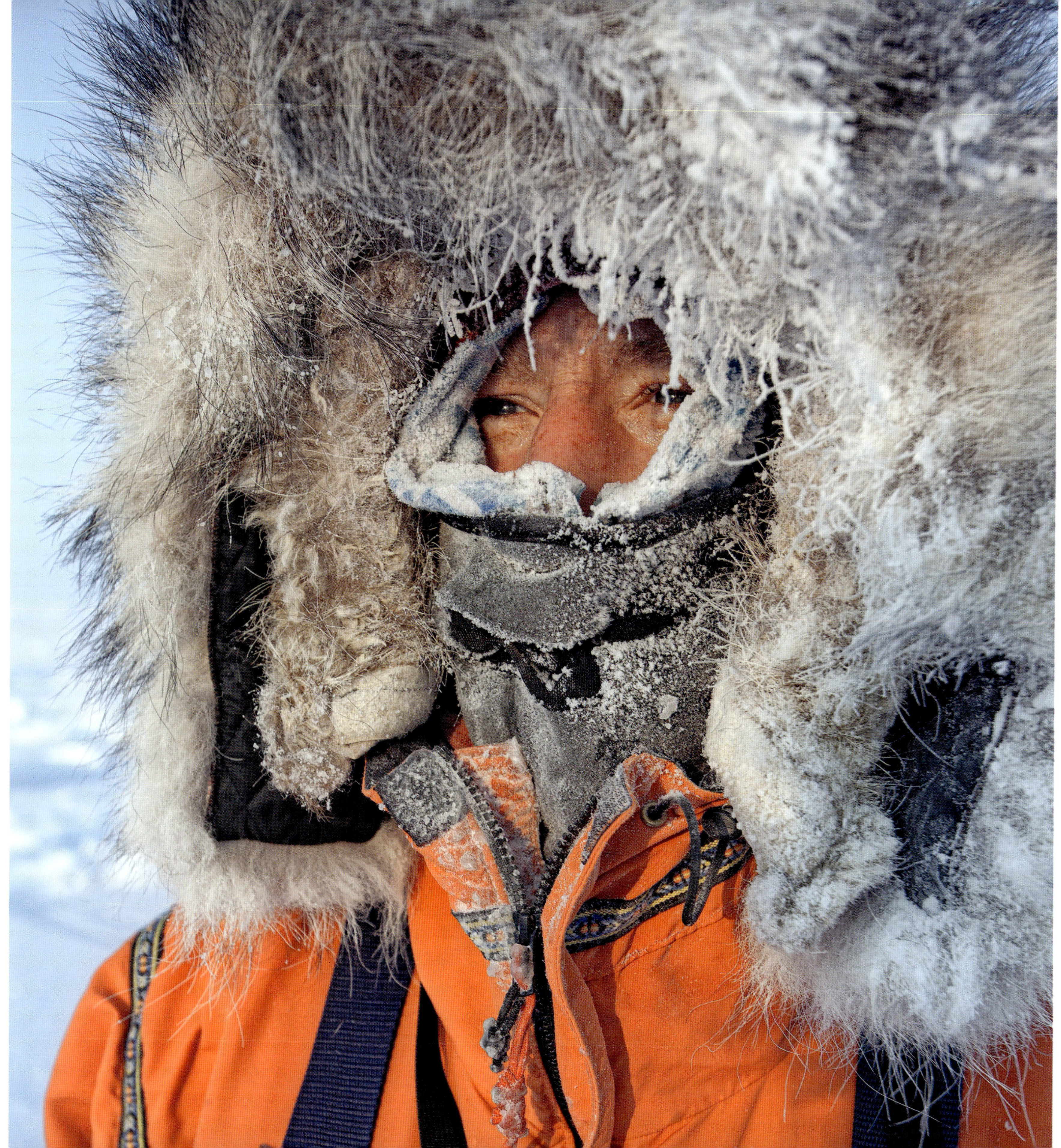

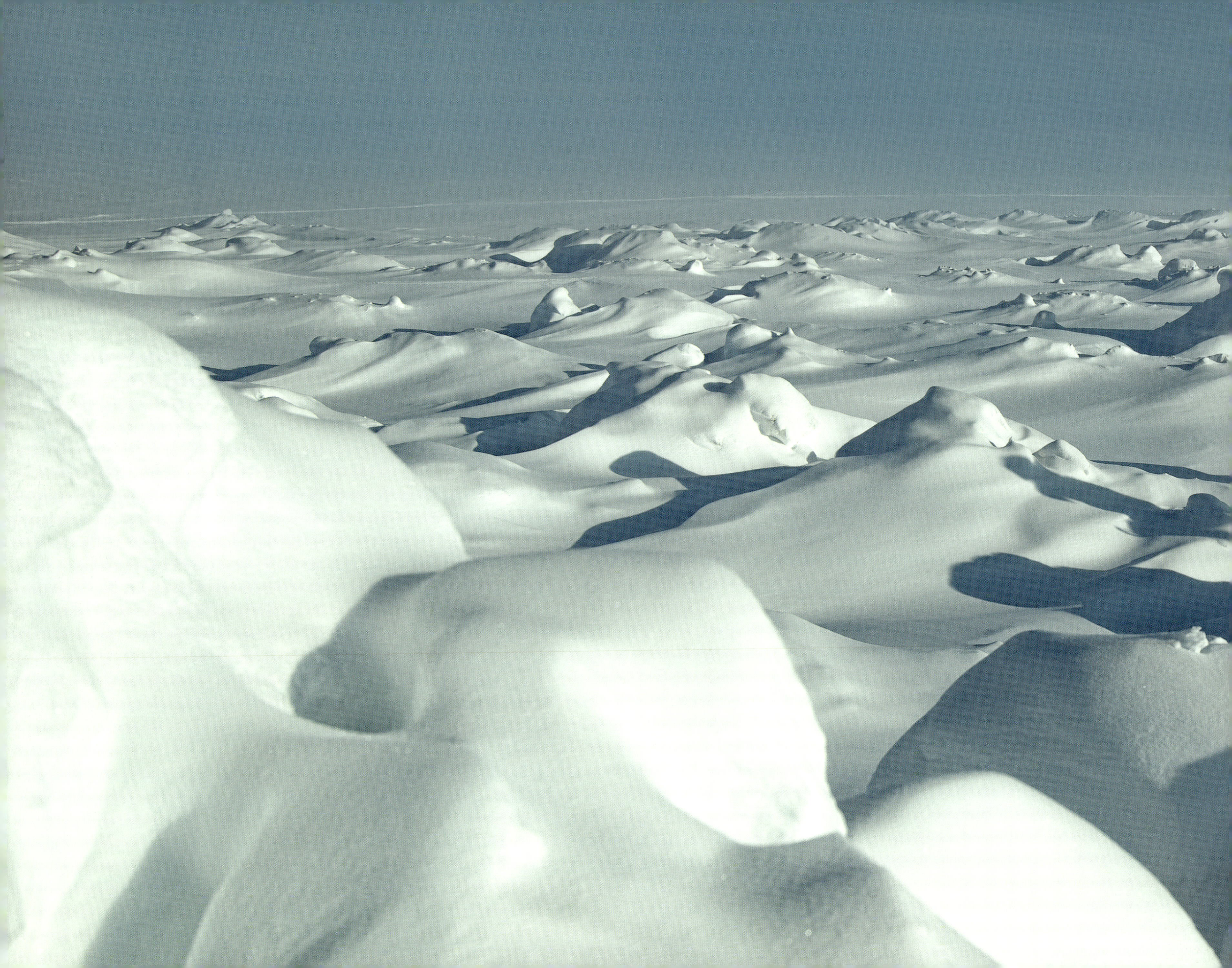

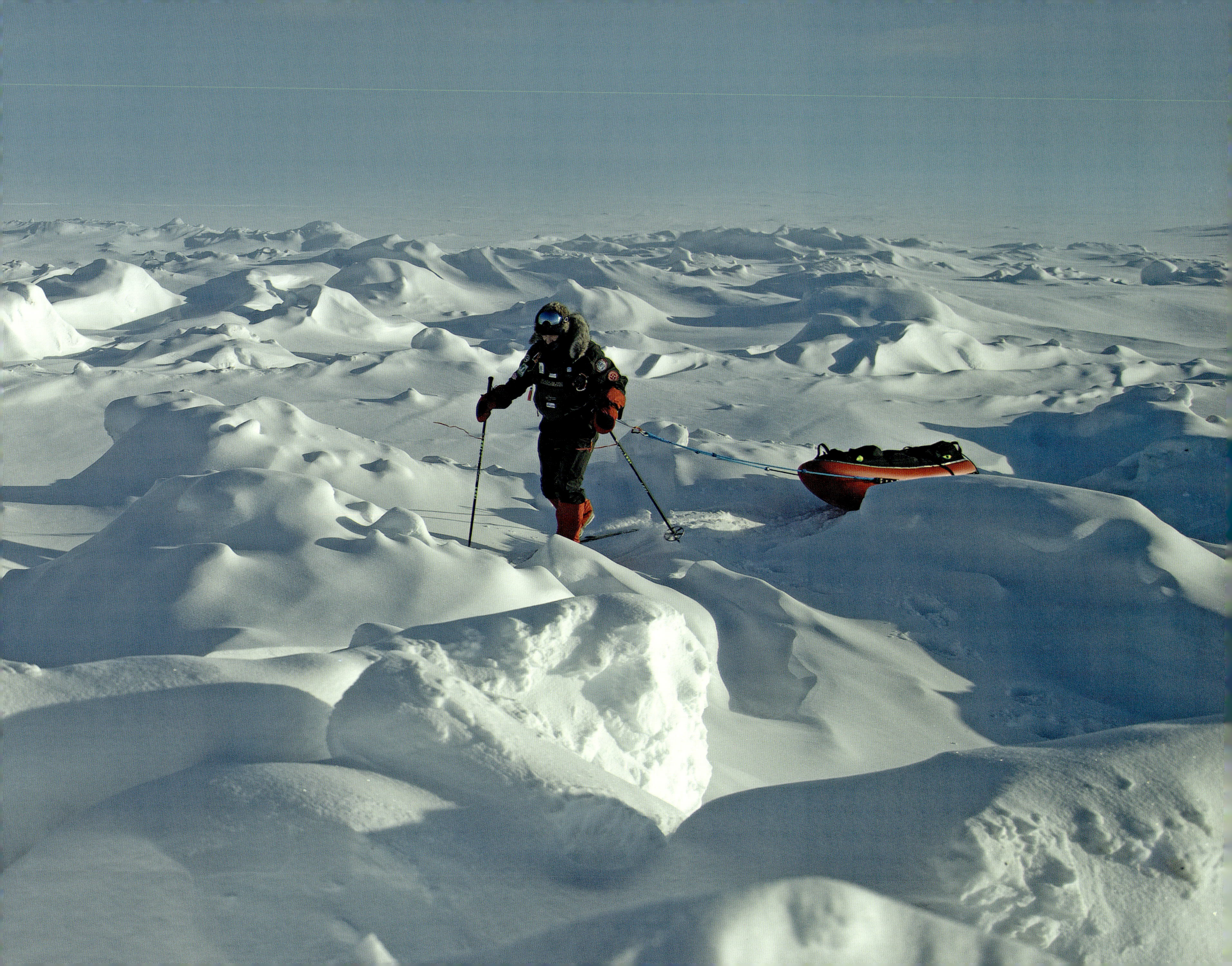

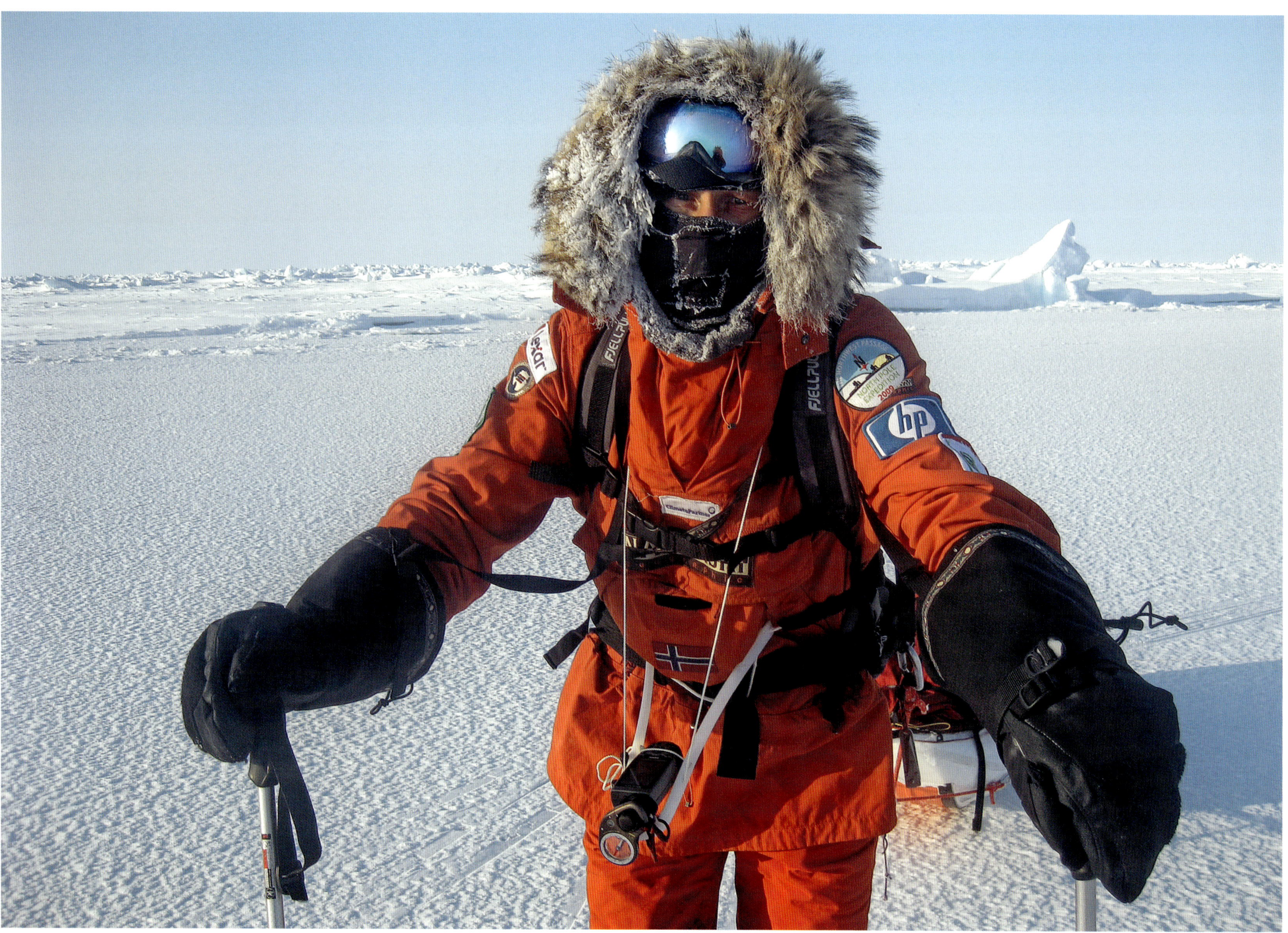
lexar
hp

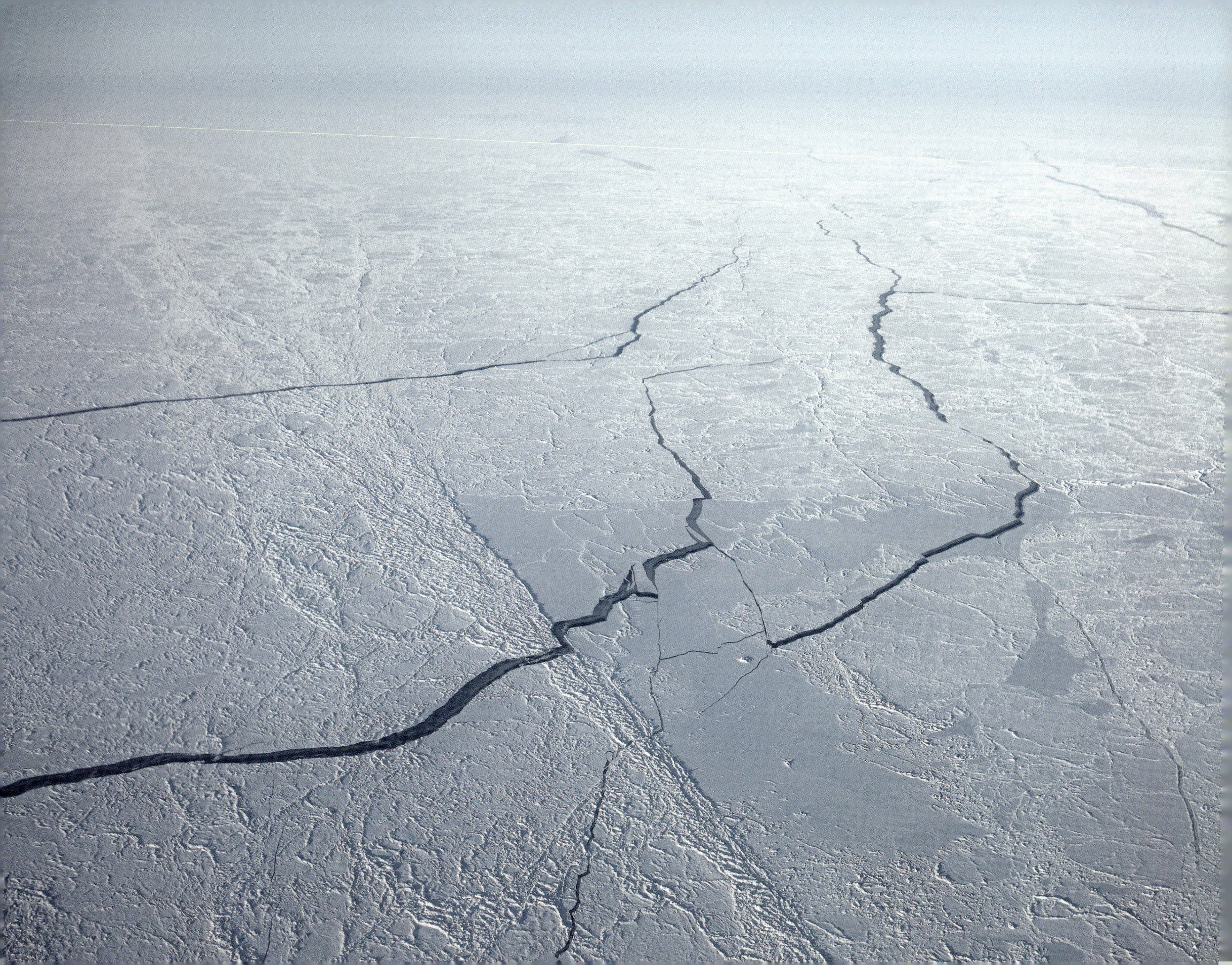

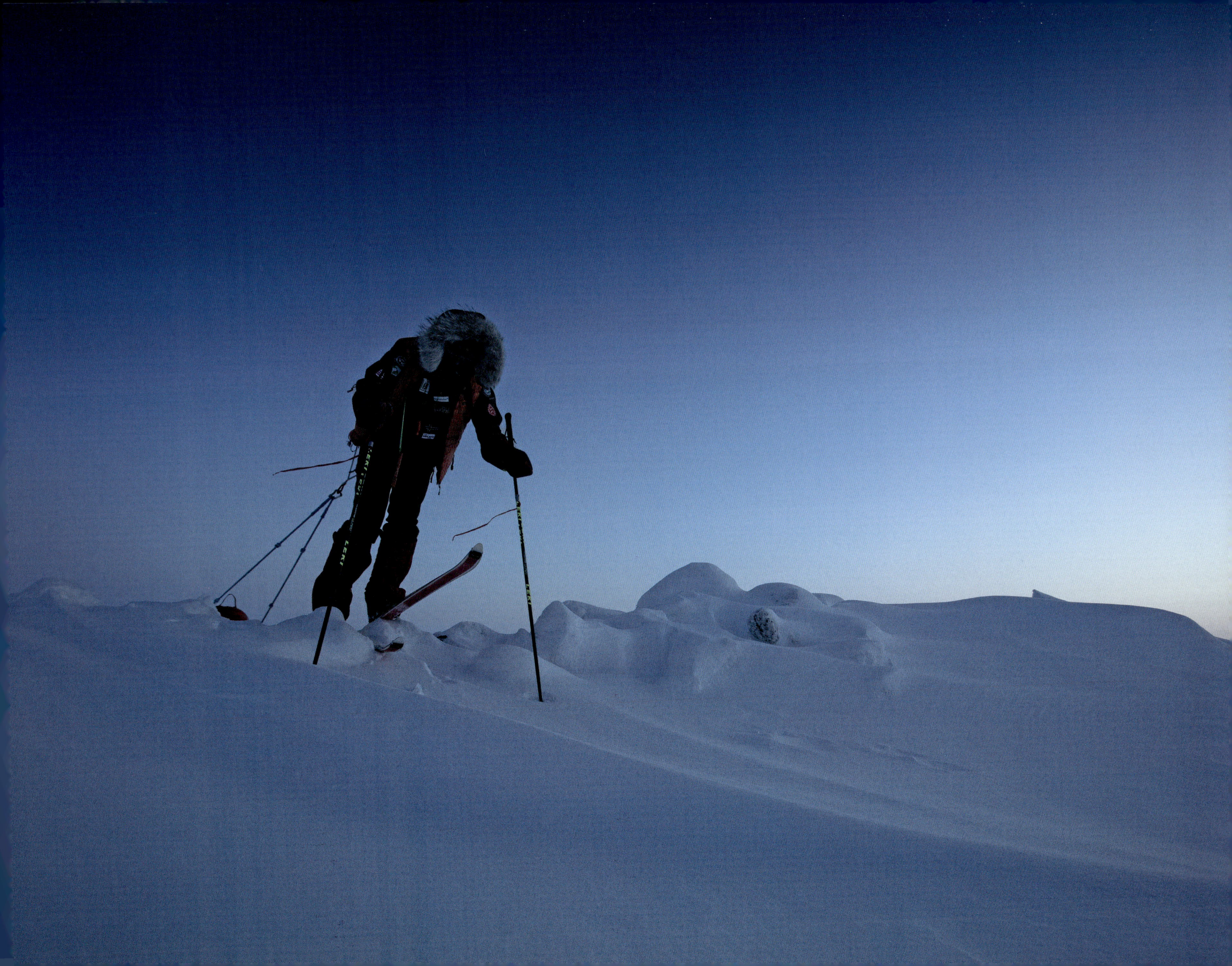

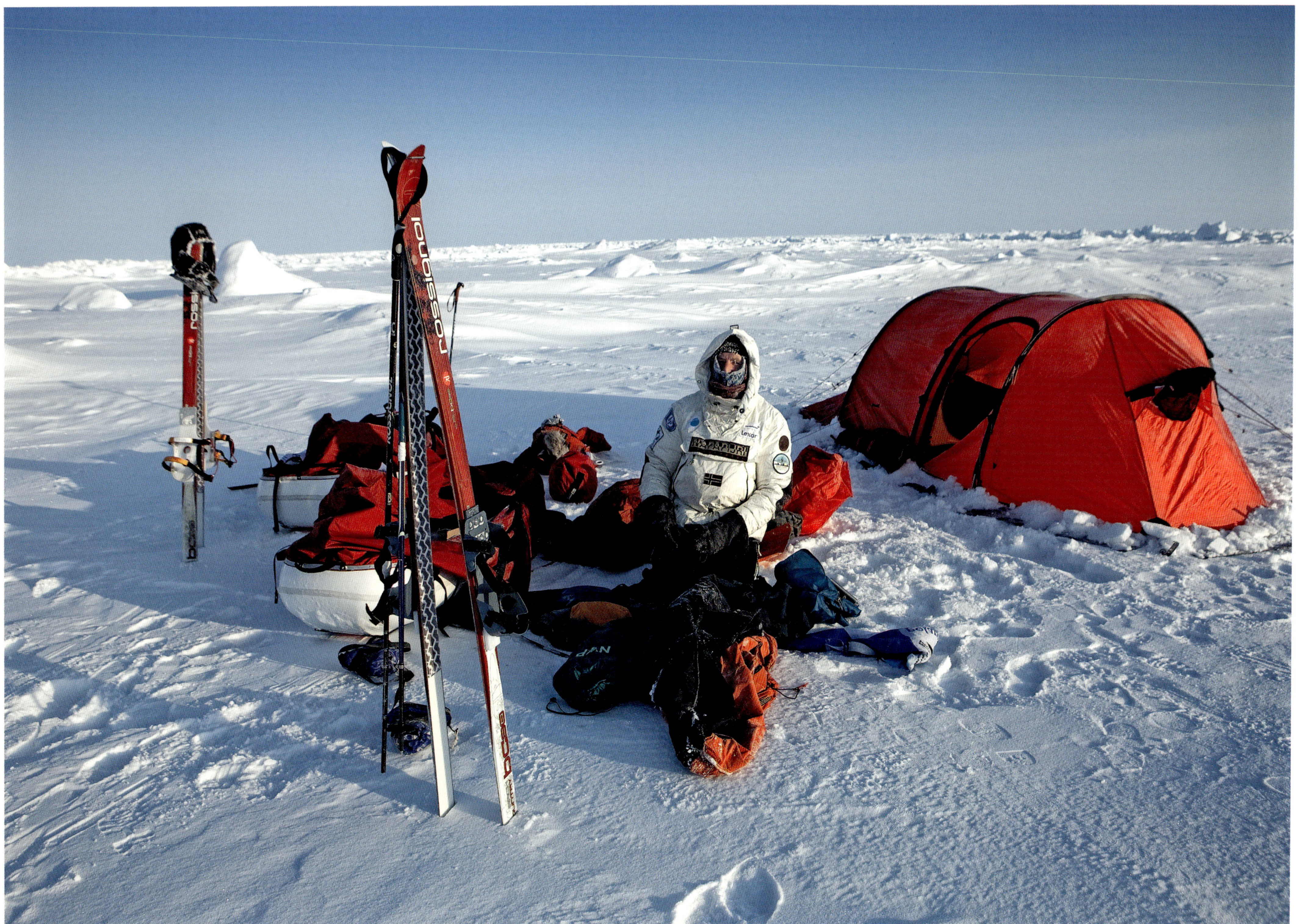
rossignol

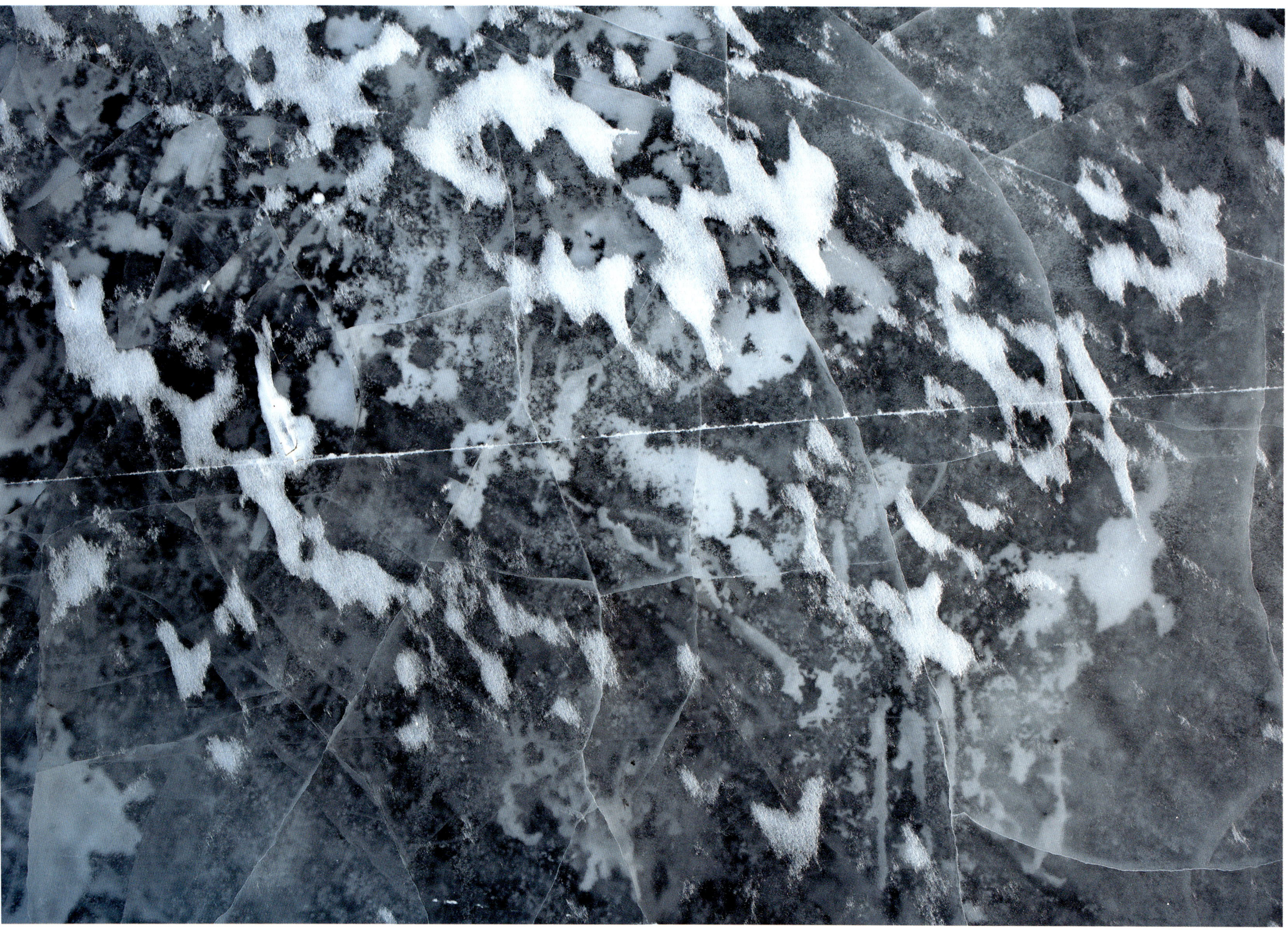

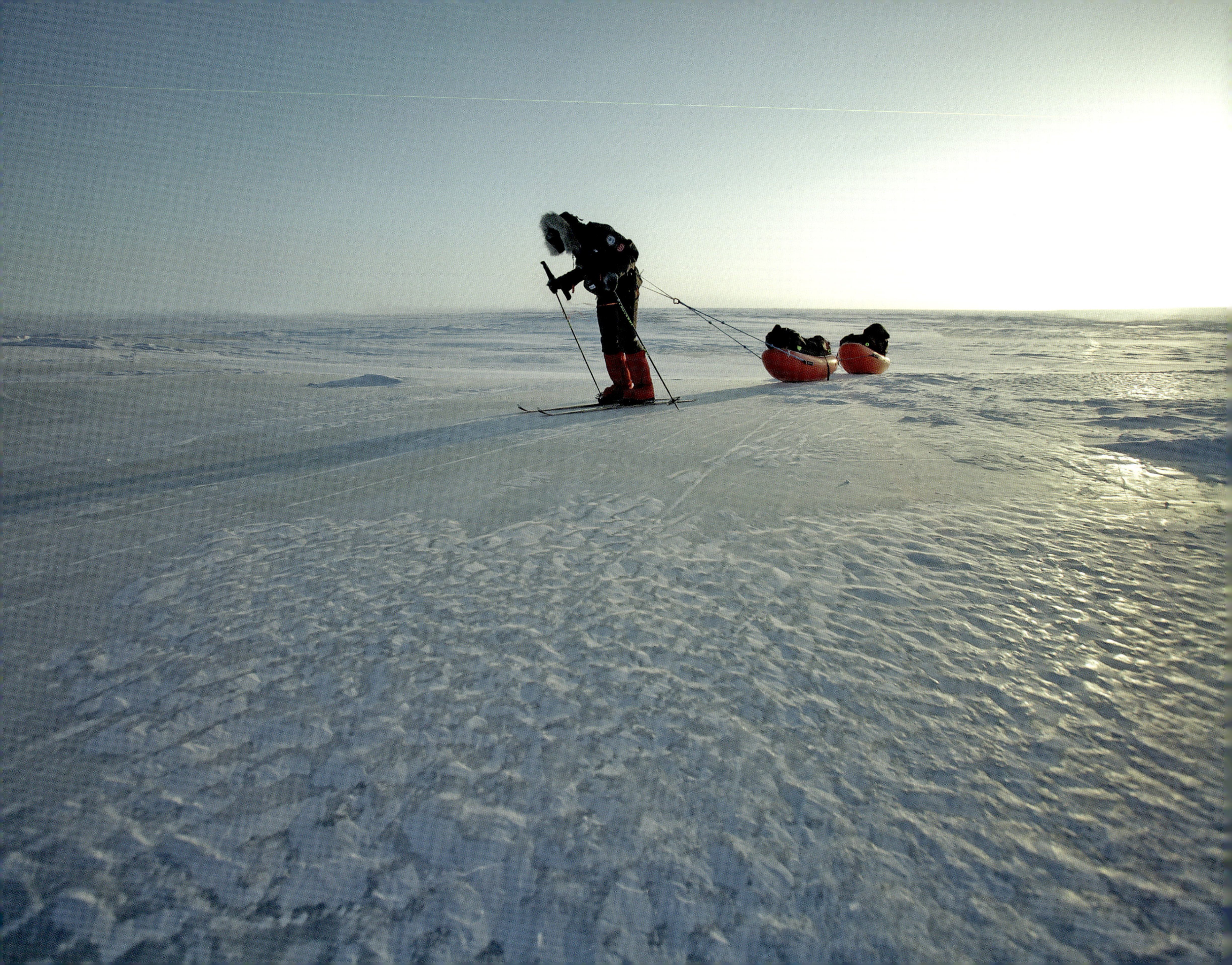

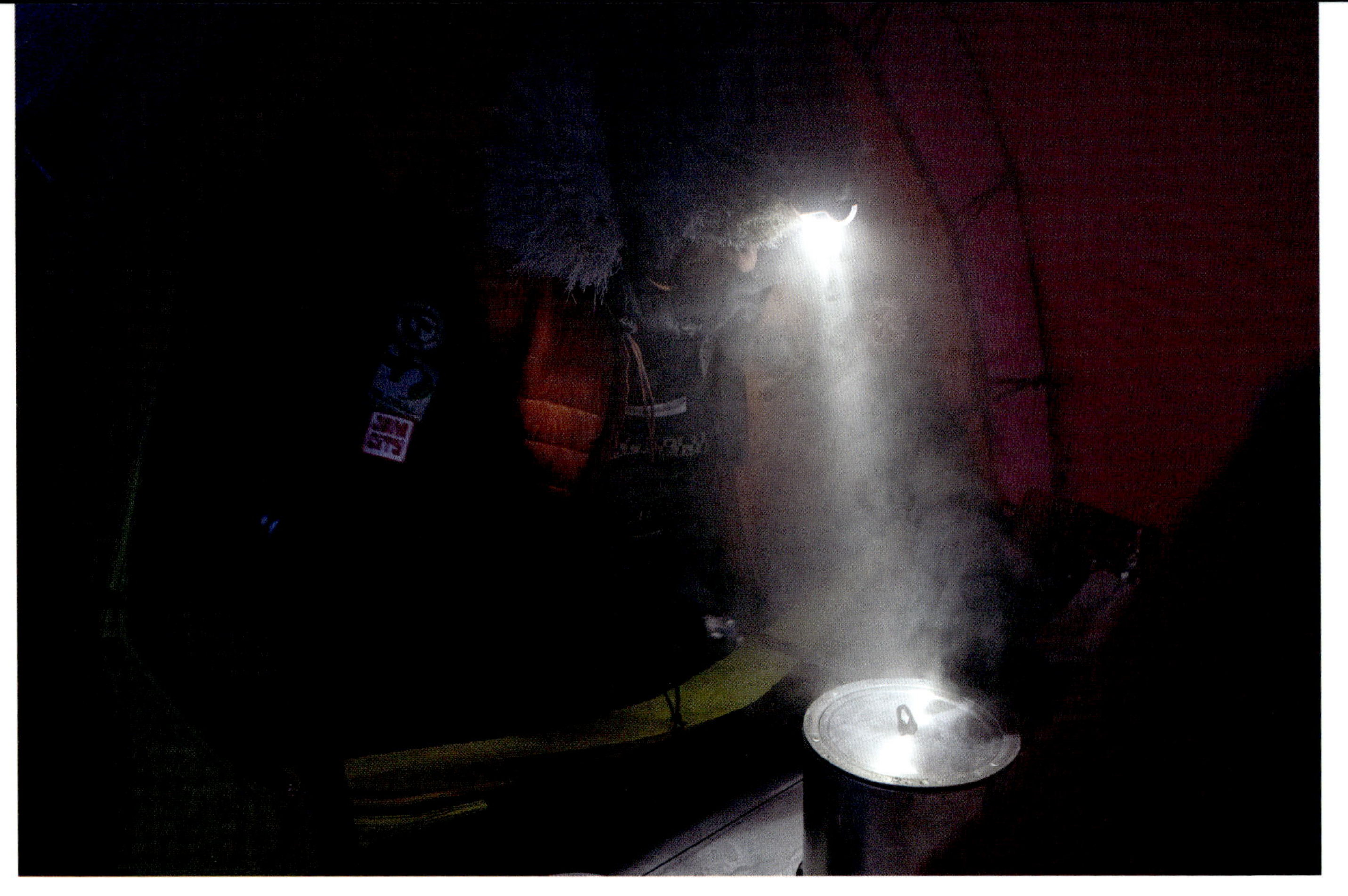

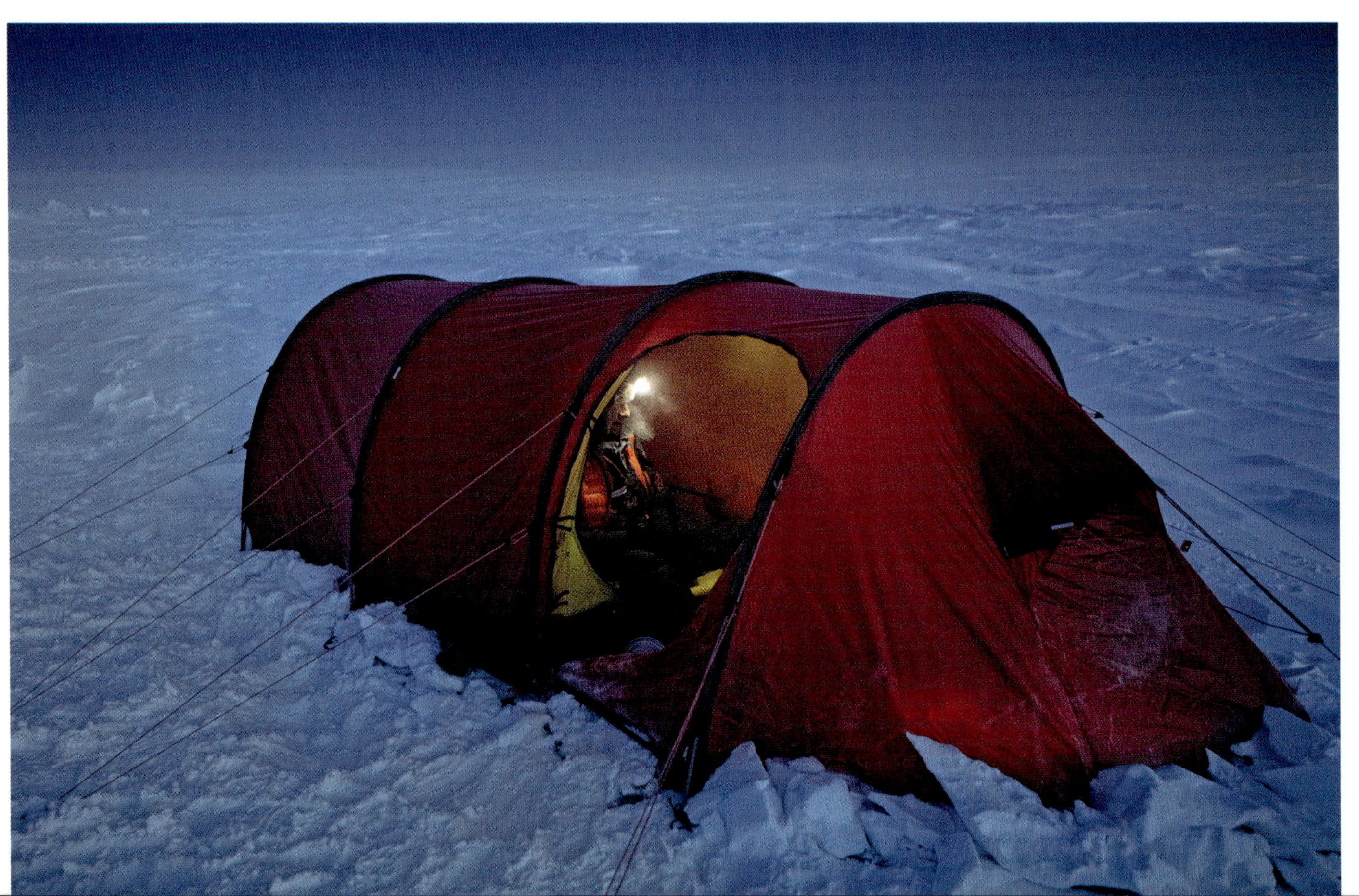

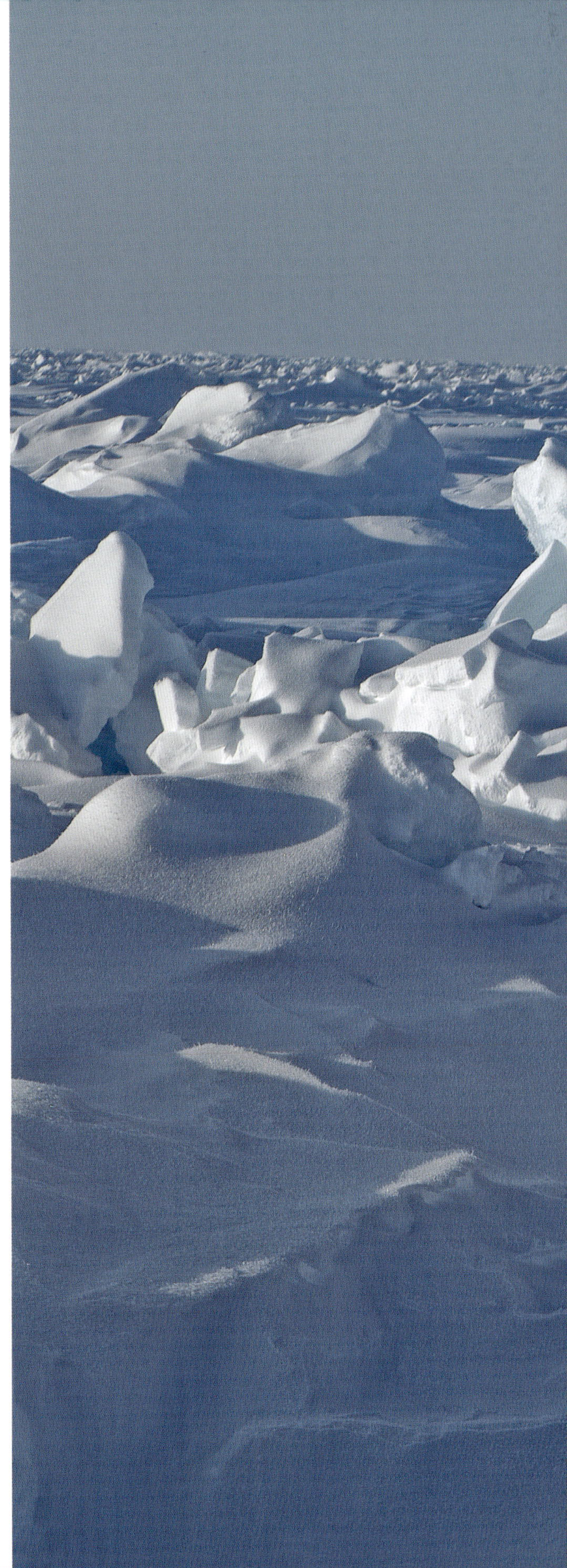

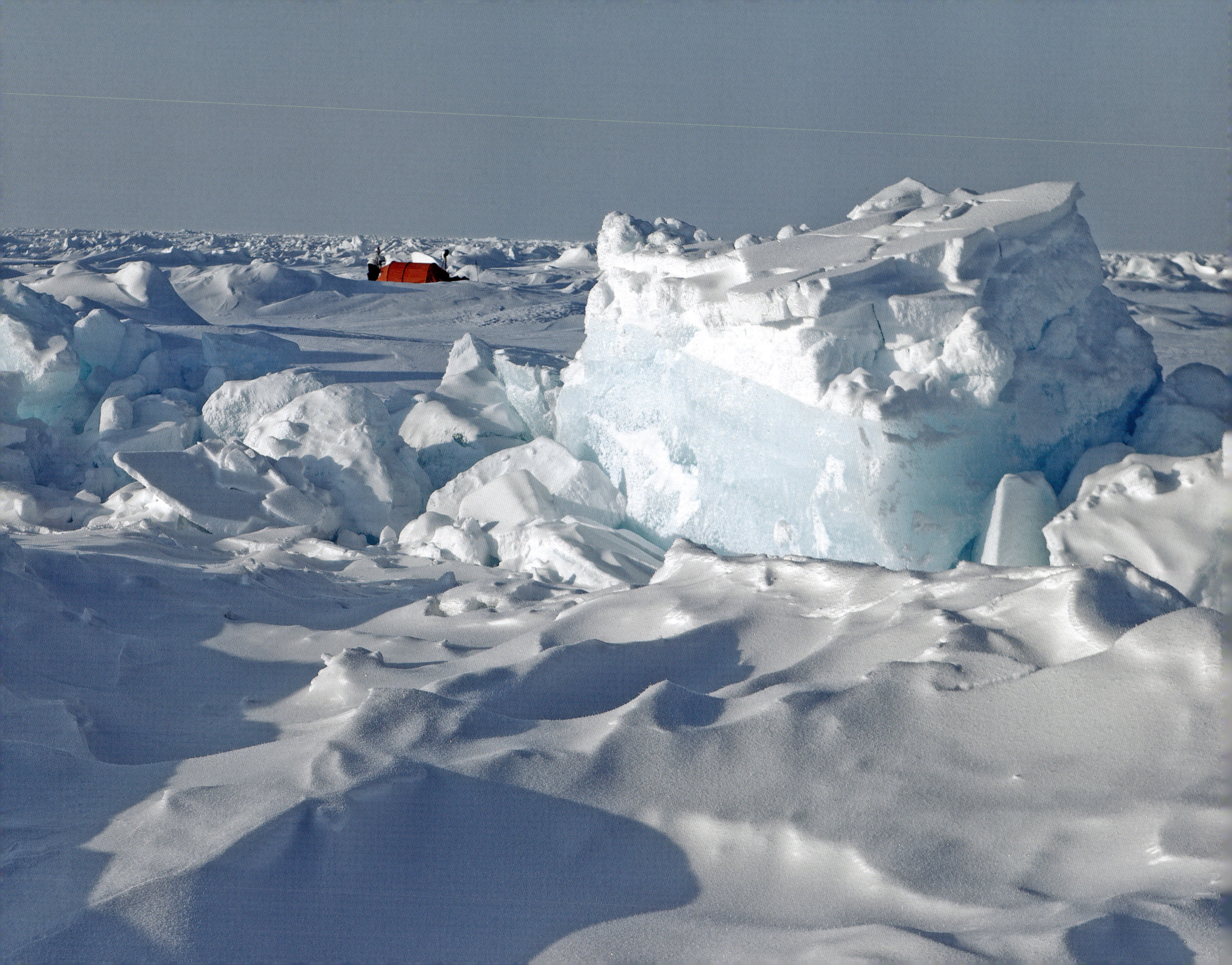

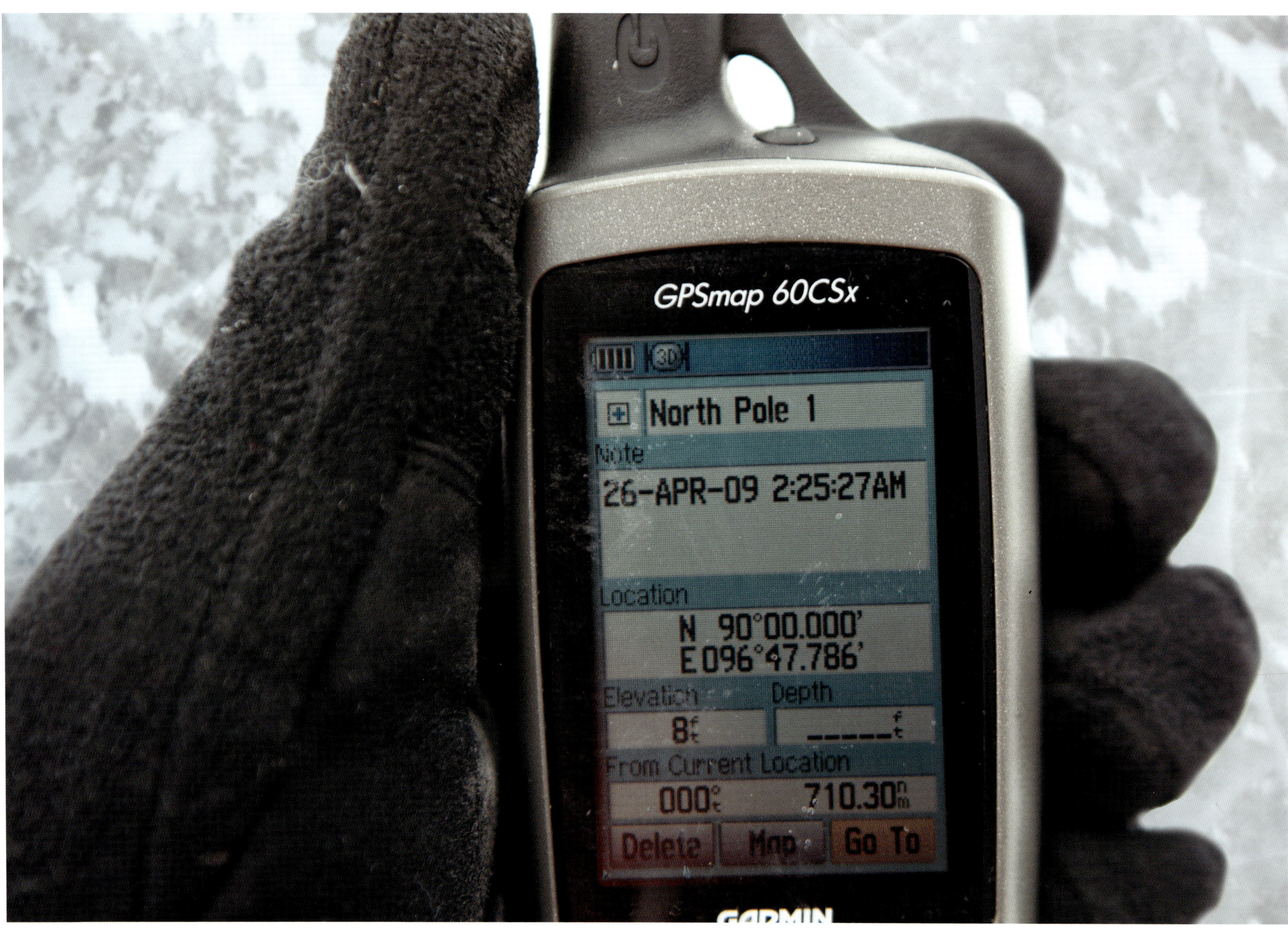
GPSmap 60CSx
North Pole 1
Note
26-APR-09 2:25:27AM
Location
N 90°00.000'
E096°47.786'
Elevation
Depth
8ft
From Current Location
000°t
710.30m
Delete
Map
Go To

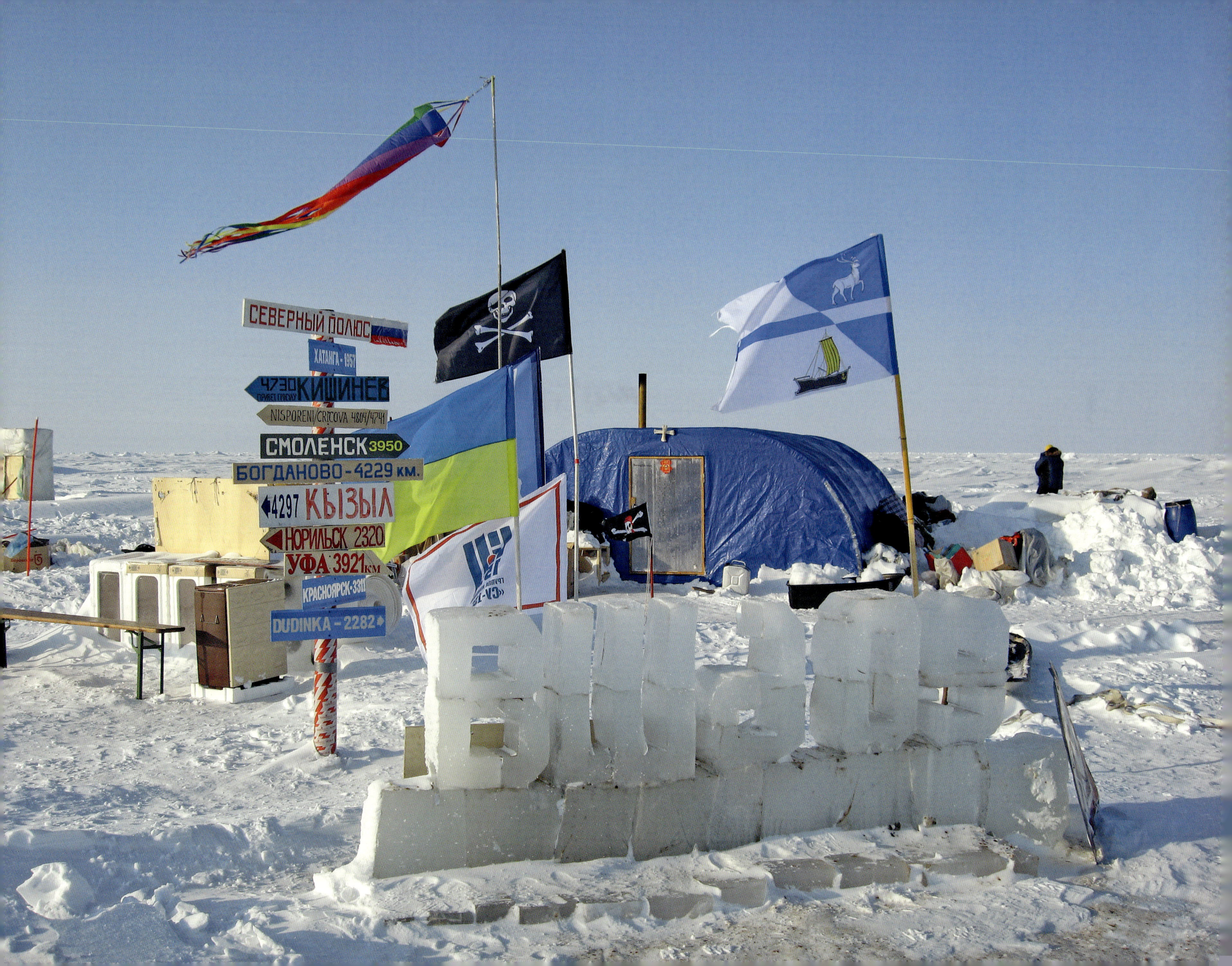
СЕВЕРНЫЙ ПОЛЮС
ХАТАНГА - 1957
4730 КИШИНЁВ
NISPORENI/CRICOVA 4804/4741
СМОЛЕНСК 3950
БОГДАНОВО - 4229 км.
4297 КЫЗЫЛ
НОРИЛЬСК 2320
УФА 3921 км
КРАСНОЯРСК
DUDINKA - 2282

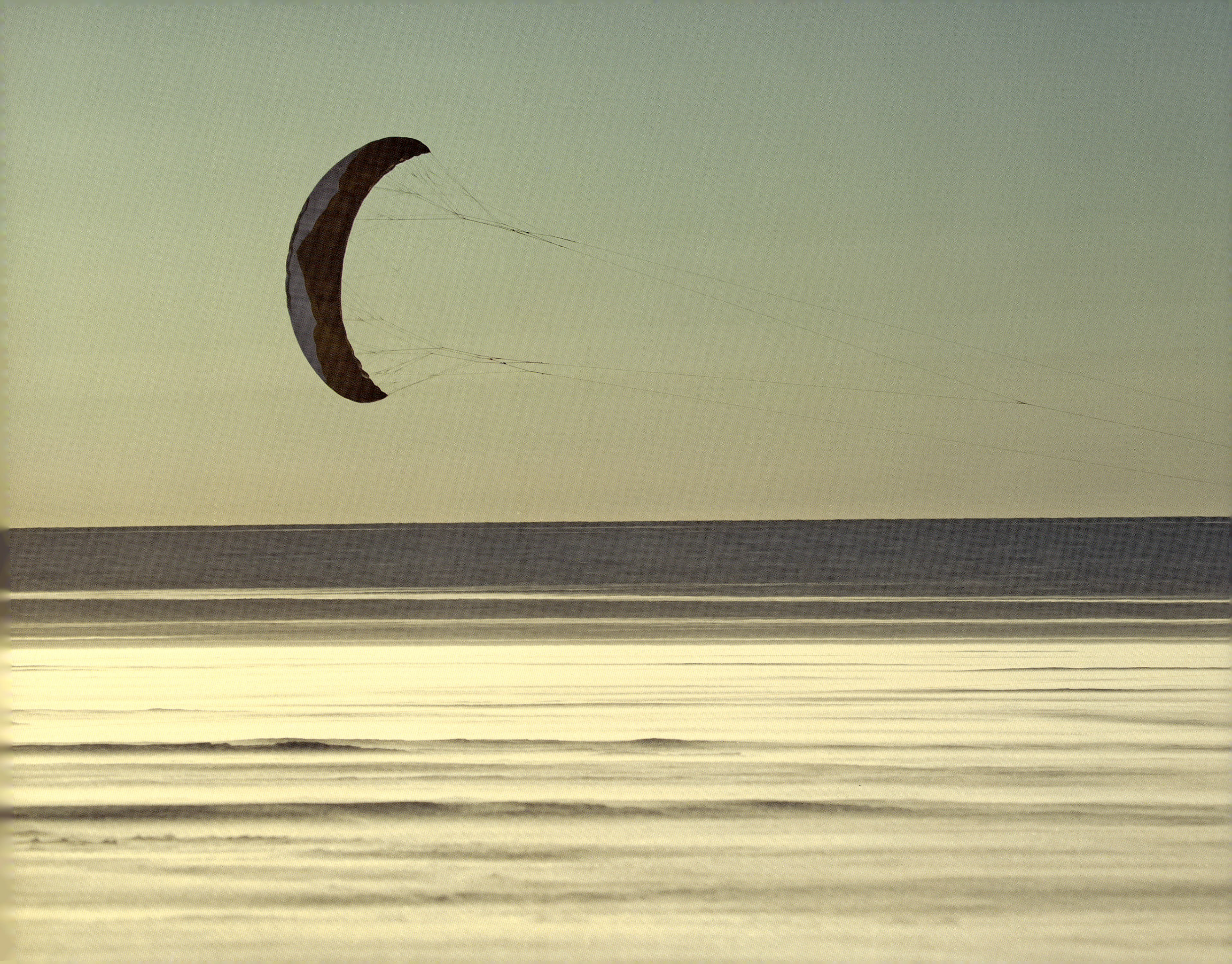

GREENLAND

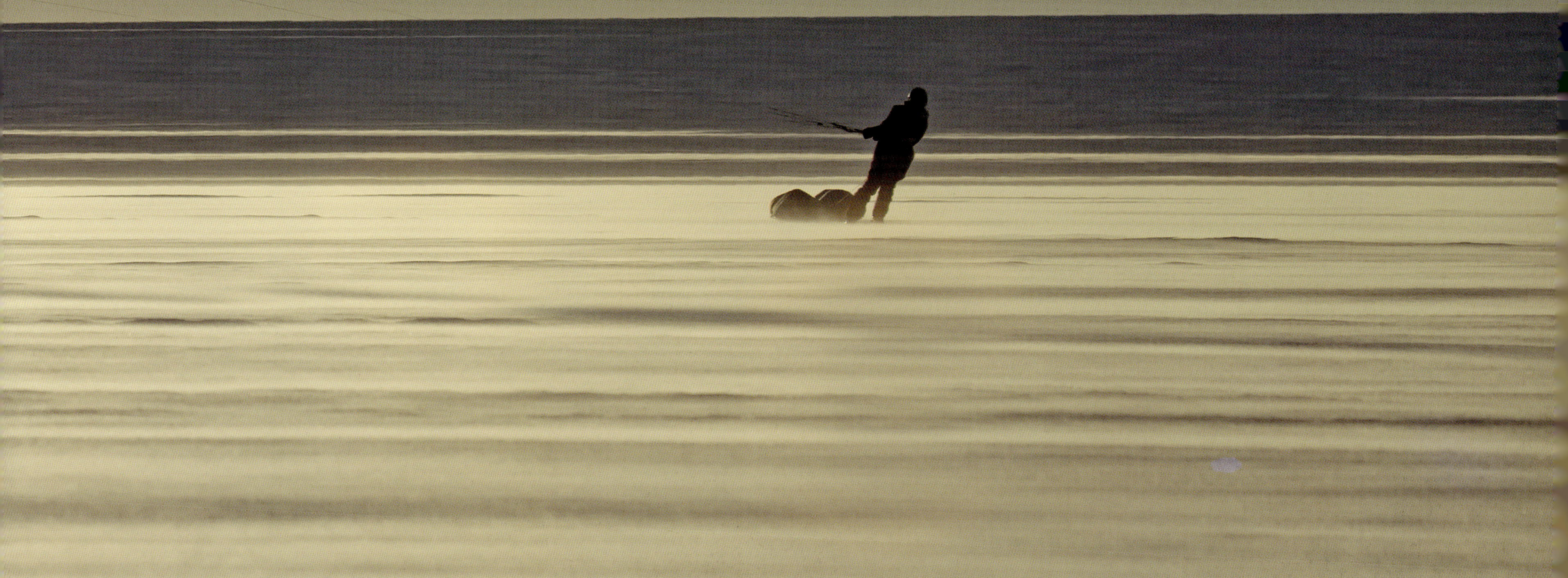

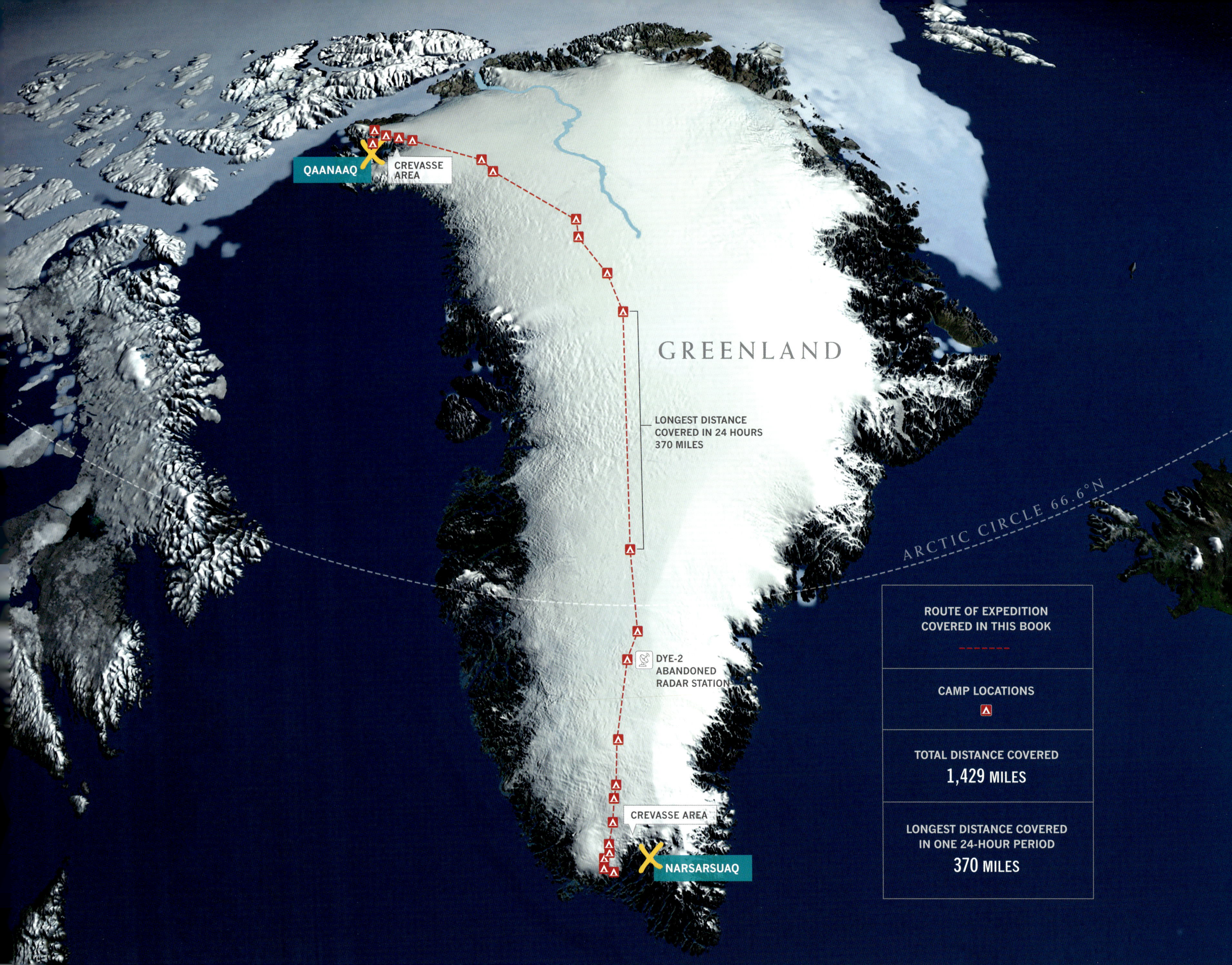
QAANAAQ
CREVASSE AREA
GREENLAND
LONGEST DISTANCE COVERED IN 24 HOURS 370 MILES
ARCTIC CIRCLE 66.6°N
DYE-2 ABANDONED RADAR STATION
CREVASSE AREA
NARSARSUAQ
ROUTE OF EXPEDITION COVERED IN THIS BOOK
CAMP LOCATIONS
TOTAL DISTANCE COVERED
1,429 MILES
LONGEST DISTANCE COVERED IN ONE 24-HOUR PERIOD
370 MILES

After visiting the North Pole, and in preparation for my Antarctica crossing, I wanted an interim trip over what many consider the "third pole." Greenland, in terms of climate change, holds as much drama as the other two—if not more. Its melting ice cap sits on solid ground, above sea level, and releases fresh water into the ocean. This presents a triple threat to life as we know it on the planet. My partner Eric McNair-Landry and I set off to cross its ice sheet on skis and kites, from south to north: 1,429 miles over 42 days. On June 6, 2010, we attempted to beat the record for the longest distance traveled on skis and kites. The following excerpts are from my journal during that trip.

Crevasses
Day 3, May 16, 2010
61°38' N, 46°13' W
Elevation 5,638 feet

When the ice suddenly gives out from under you, and your legs dangle above a void the depth of which is unclear, you get about the same jolt as when a car screeches to a halt inches from running you over.

We camped midafternoon yesterday, hoping that by evening the surface of the ice would harden some. Pulling the sleds uphill is all the more tedious when your foot sinks to the knee into soft snow with every other step from the warmer-than-usual day temperatures. By 7:00 p.m., we broke camp and set off. The sun was hanging low, casting a golden glow on the ice ridge ahead of us. The ice sheet was within sight, though distances in this environment can be deceiving. But the warm colors of the sky belied the biting grip of the wind that picked up. And the placid setting hid the drama that was unfolding below us. We were now square in the middle of the crevasse field! Each variation in color had to be carefully considered, for what might pass for hard ice could in fact be a flimsy bridge.

There is a point of diminishing returns when the dropping light makes challenging the deciphering of color or textural changes. Often, we might make out the curving droop of gravity doing its work on a weak bridge. But for the most part, we probe each step ahead of us with a ski pole, extracting information that can mean the difference between going through or not. On occasion, however, adrenaline shoots up when a leg goes clean through the ice.

To worsen matters, the ice's surface in the end had not hardened enough to support our weight, and we sunk to our ankles with each step. In all, we mostly labored through making a little more than a mile. Temperatures had dropped to 14°F.

On the morning of our third day, we stretched our time in the tent as we began to roll the clock. The winds died down to a deadly stillness, and the sun beat down on the tent. With the vents closed, it was like an oven in there. What a contrast to the previous night, when I went to sleep with a mask over my face.

Flying
Day 6, May 19, 2010
62°20'236" N, 46°48'358" W
Elevation 7,050 feet

Kite skiing is the surest and cleanest way to improve polar journeys from the drudgery of walking with a heavy load in tow. The appeal is in the simplicity: a kite, long lines, skis, and wind. And there is a feeling you get when the lines tighten and the nylon sail fills with air and lifts off. The tug on the harness propels you forward and you're off using nothing but the power of the wind. It's the same feeling that has captured the imagination through the ages since Icarus. It is called flying! And flying, unfortunately, has always had a close relationship with crashing.

We had spent the day resting, and we were reluctantly preparing for another cold night of headwinds and uphill pulling, when the winds timidly shifted more to the east. It didn't take much discussion to agree that a better plan would be to sit, let them build, and then take off in the night. In the end, we dozed in and out of sleep until morning. Nothing. But by midmorning, the tent began to flutter enough to get us motivated, and soon we were packing camp.

With the tent packed, the sled bags zipped up, the kite lines laid out, and the click of boots in the binding, we hooked the sled's line into the harness's carabineer, picked up the kite's handles, gave it a tug, and—nothing! Another gentle tug, followed by a few less diplomatic tugs. Nothing doing. I could not lift off. Eric had more luck—and skill—with his Ozone 12-meter Yakuza handle kite with extended lines than I did with my 14-meter. The kite would fly, but the sled's load would stall it.

After a few frustrated attempts, we switched kites and I managed to get moving. The extra line length, especially in light winds, makes for a very slow response time, but the feeling of gliding over the ice even at slow speeds is exhilarating compared to walking. Every foot of ground covered feels like a victory, and as the uphill miles glide under our skis, the last of the mountains behind us slowly disappear behind the curve of the ice sheet. In one hour, we covered more ground than we did during an entire night on foot!

Soon, the wind strengthened, and our speed picked up. The ice was like a frozen ocean and we were gliding over it at speeds reaching nearly 20 miles per hour. The ice was racing below us, and the sun was out. We took off around 1:00 p.m., and while a system of clouds was forming to the south, the weather was remarkably pleasant—just below freezing to keep the ice nice and hard, and very little sastrugi, which makes it easier on the knees. The open space stretched unlimited in all directions, just like in the open sea.

The wind turned more to the southeast as the sun began to drop. I was obsessed with capturing as much on film as I could, capitalizing on the slightest change in the monotony. With our increasing speed, and Eric slightly downwind from me, I decided to turn on my helmet cam and commit more to film. I removed my mitten and felt my way on top of the helmet, looking for the "on" switch. Distracted, I inadvertently dived the kite just as my skis hit sastrugi and—WHACK! I face-planted into the ice at nearly 25 miles per hour.

Now, the thing about most crashes is that they generally stop at impact. Not with kites! It took another 200 feet, and a couple of lofts bouncing me around the hard ice, before I could grab hold of the brake line, as the kite was still gingerly powering downwind and dragging me like a rag doll along with it. Luckily, the helmet took the impact, and aside from slight bruising—mainly of the ego variety—I dusted off and regained composure.

At 1:00 a.m., we decided to pack it in for the night, especially as the winds had pulled back slightly. In all, we traveled nearly 68 miles over 11 hours excluding stops, and we are now at an elevation of 7,050 feet. All in a good day's work. My legs are slightly wobbly and my body is sore. Time for a hearty, warm meal to counter the cold of the tent, and then lights out.

Not a Teacup Storm

Day 9, May 22, 2010
62°20'236" N, 46°48'358" W
Elevation 7,122 feet

The storm has not relented, increasing in strength and intensity for the third consecutive day. The tent shook all night long, and the wind pounding at the flimsy nylon walls is so loud that trying to catch sleep inside can only be described as resting inside a roaring jet engine. Eric and I scream to each other in order to communicate, up until the point when we decide that such effort is not worth the price of admission, and fall back to our respective activities. The violence displayed here is some of the fiercest I have experienced. We estimate the gusts to be reaching more than 80 miles per hour—and we hope the tent will hold up!

The spindrift is intense, finding its way through the slightest opening. Outside, drift banks are constantly building on the side walls and have to be monitored so as not to collapse the tent. When we step out, the drifting snow immediately freezes on our outerwear and lashes our faces as it races across the frozen ground. Reaching about six-and-a-half feet in height, this liquid smoke reduces visibility down to 70 feet or so, but above, the sky is generally visible. Occasionally, the clouds part, allowing the sun's rays to shine through, which makes for an odd, apocalyptic juxtaposition. It is hard to imagine that three days ago we were in shorts and T-shirts, in melting snow, with no wind and clear blue skies!

A Twenty-Four-Hour Run

Day 24, June 6, 2010
74°45'233" N, 46°39'134" W
Elevation 8,820 feet

Before leaving on this expedition, I had privately mentioned that if the conditions were right, I wanted a shot at the kite-skiing world record for greatest distance covered in a 24-hour period. While I stayed coy about it, I was determined to give it a go. But I could now see what a daunting prospect it would be. The record was 322 miles and our personal best of 162 miles in 16 hours from the previous day was roughly half that.

After that big day ended at 5:00 a.m., we spent the following day resting. I struggled with staying in my sleeping bag, as I could hear the wind outside; it did not let up all day. But our sore bodies needed recovery. By 9:30 p.m., the last items were packed in the sleds, our kites were laid out on the ice, and we were clipped in the harnesses. The winds were moderate but consistent. After the previous day's adrenaline rush, I was hungry for more.

I tugged at the bar. The lines tightened. The open cells filled with air and the familiar crescent bounced off the ground, its shape defined against the white landscape. Another tug and the

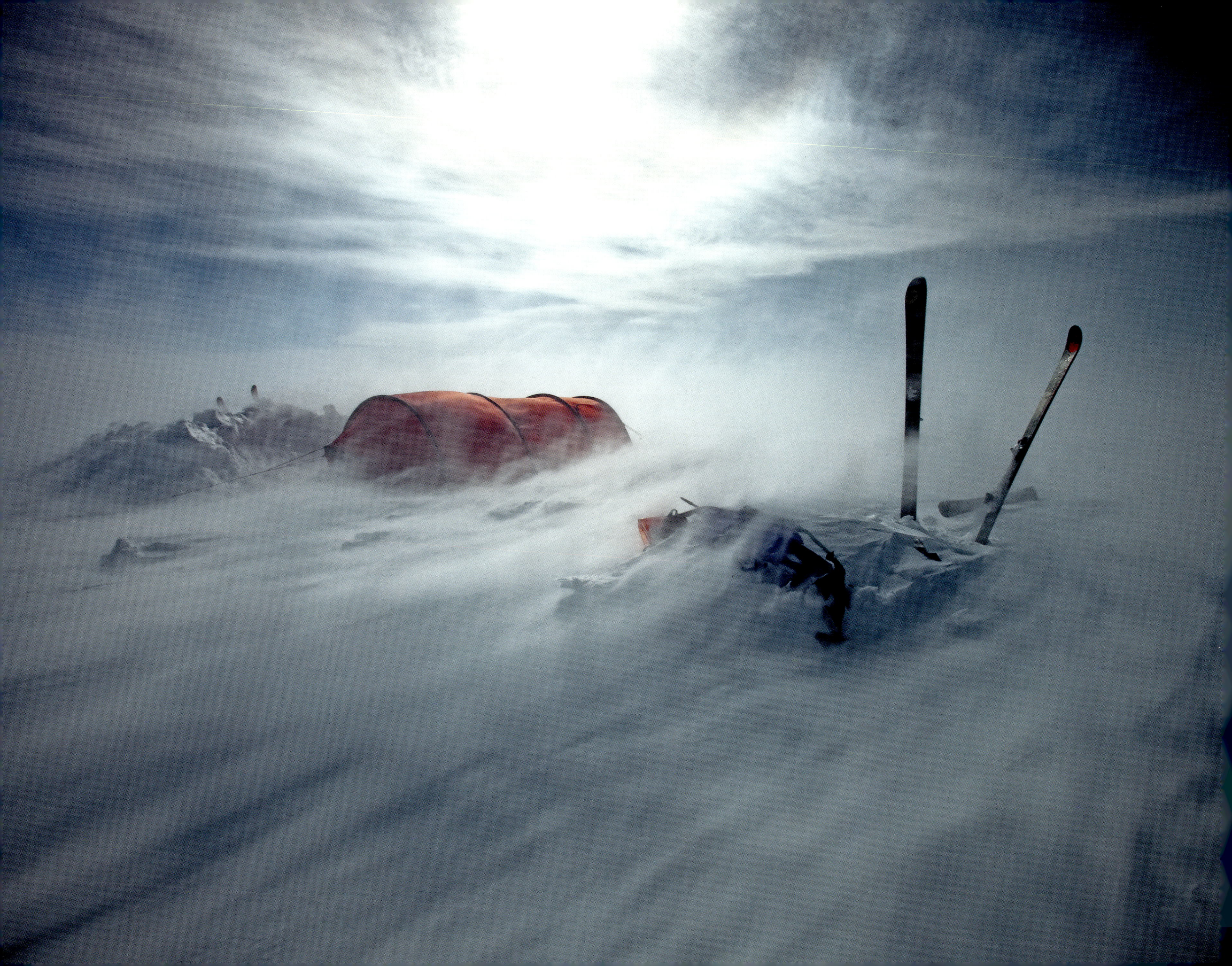

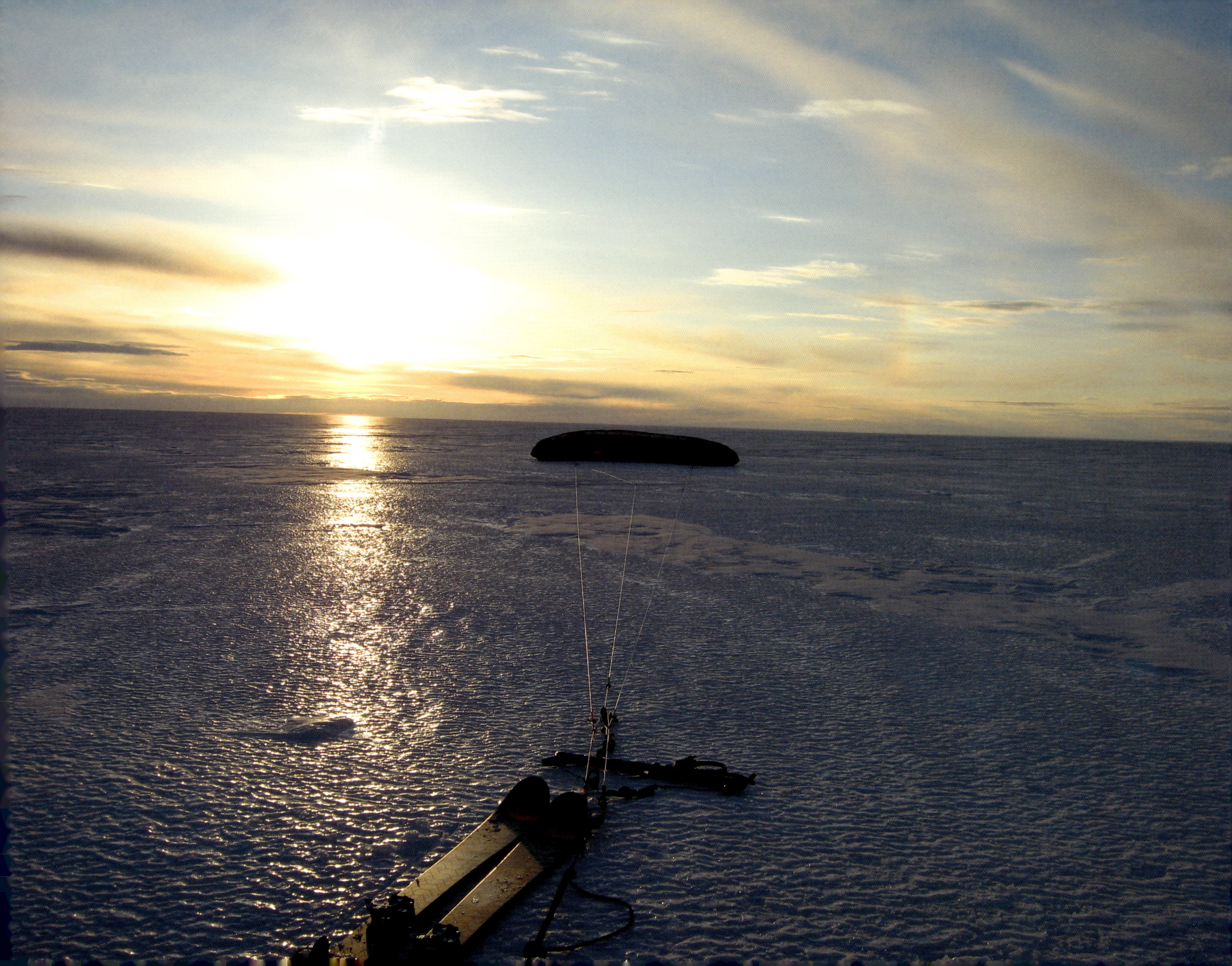

kite lifted in the air. Within the first hour and a half, we had covered almost 62 miles.

"Let's go for it," I told Eric. We had talked a bit about the record, and he had been hesitant. "Silly and dangerous mistakes happen when you subject your body and mind to this type of duress in a highly dynamic environment," he said. But he had had a go at it a couple of years back and posted a not-shabby 256-mile day. I had come to find him quite competitive, and tonight the conditions were there. "OK," he said, "we can give it a try."

The wind grew through the first part of the night. By 4:00 a.m., snowdrift covered the ice in all directions as we chased the midnight sun, sometimes reaching speeds of 37 miles per hour. It was intense. The terrain was shredded enough that riding over it rattled your fillings and gave the right and left hemispheres of your brain a chance to meet. And the temperatures were clearly dropping. We had now passed the 621-mile mark on our trip, crossed into the Arctic Circle, and were headed into the cold. Frost built over our face masks, and, given the windchill, no skin can be exposed in these conditions. In five hours, we had traveled more than 155 miles.

But as the day rose, the winds were faltering. For 48 hours, they had held strong, but as they pulled back, we were now struggling. Fatigue set in. By our next break, it was clear that the rising day would not work in our favor. "If this keeps up, we won't make it. Are we subjecting ourselves to a 24-hour day if we're not going to break the record?" I said. "If we do it, we push the edge of our own limits, record or not. But if we agree to do it, there is no turning back," Eric replied. "That's the spirit," I said. "Let's go!"

The wind kept dropping, and it became debatable whether the kites could even stay up in the air. The monotony of the slow speed was wreaking havoc on our minds and bodies. Skiing on the same tack for endless days places stress on certain areas of the body, and this long day was definitely adding to it. Our left calf muscles were especially sore, as were the flats of our feet. Because holding the kite's handles puts our hands above our hearts, they go cold a lot from lack of circulation, and after hours of gripping, our fingers get stiff and numb. As for our thighs and knees, the first few hours of our rocket-fueled travel had put serious strain on the muscles. Imagine skiing downhill around a mountain without changing direction—for 12 hours!

We kept chipping away at it, and by hour 14, we had covered 280 miles, with nine hours still to go. Light though they were, if the winds kept up, we still had a real shot at it. By now, the snow cover on the ground had deepened and the strange granular consistency added considerable drag to both the skis and the sleds—even though the softness was a godsend on my sore knees.

The winds teased us up and down, but we surprisingly managed to increase our pace. We had traveled 311 miles, with eight hours to go. At this stage, it would have been devastating if the wind died, as the record was within reach. I gripped the handles and felt each foot of distance glide below my skis, getting us closer to that record.

The final three hours were agony. After unclipping the bindings during a short break, I could barely walk. My calf had seized up, both my feet were numb, my knees were sore, and I was so exhausted that I could barely eat the fuel I so needed at this stage. I had finished the tea in my thermos, and my last half-empty Nalgene bottle had frozen. There would be no more liquid until the finish. During the last hour, I listened to the same song on my iPod. Somehow, I must have pressed the repeat option, and it tediously played the same tracks over and over. But I was too tired to mind. In fact, with each minute painfully dragging on, I used the track as a rough estimate of time. We knew we had beat the record, but we'd stopped checking and so did not know by how much.

The last stretch was pure mind over matter, and the final 15 minutes dragged on forever. There was no finish line, and no cheering crowd. We would arrive at a point determined by the clock, and when that 24th hour closed, our position would be our place of rest for the night. We had been up for 31 hours and exerting for 24.

The kites finally dropped from the sky for the last time that day, and I crawled over to fold mine. We wobbled into the tent, made some food, and agreed it was time to check our distance. We had beat the record by a whopping 48 miles! At 370 miles, we were now, until proven differently, the world-record holders for the longest distance traveled on skis and kites over one 24-hour period. I passed out once during dinner and then fell into a deep slumber that lasted 13 hours.

We are 466 miles from our objective and have now covered 963 miles. Outside, there is not a sound; it's a complete whiteout, with light snowfall. But we will reap the reward of our labor with a day off, a glass of electrolytes, and a bowl of granola and water. Don't be jealous now!

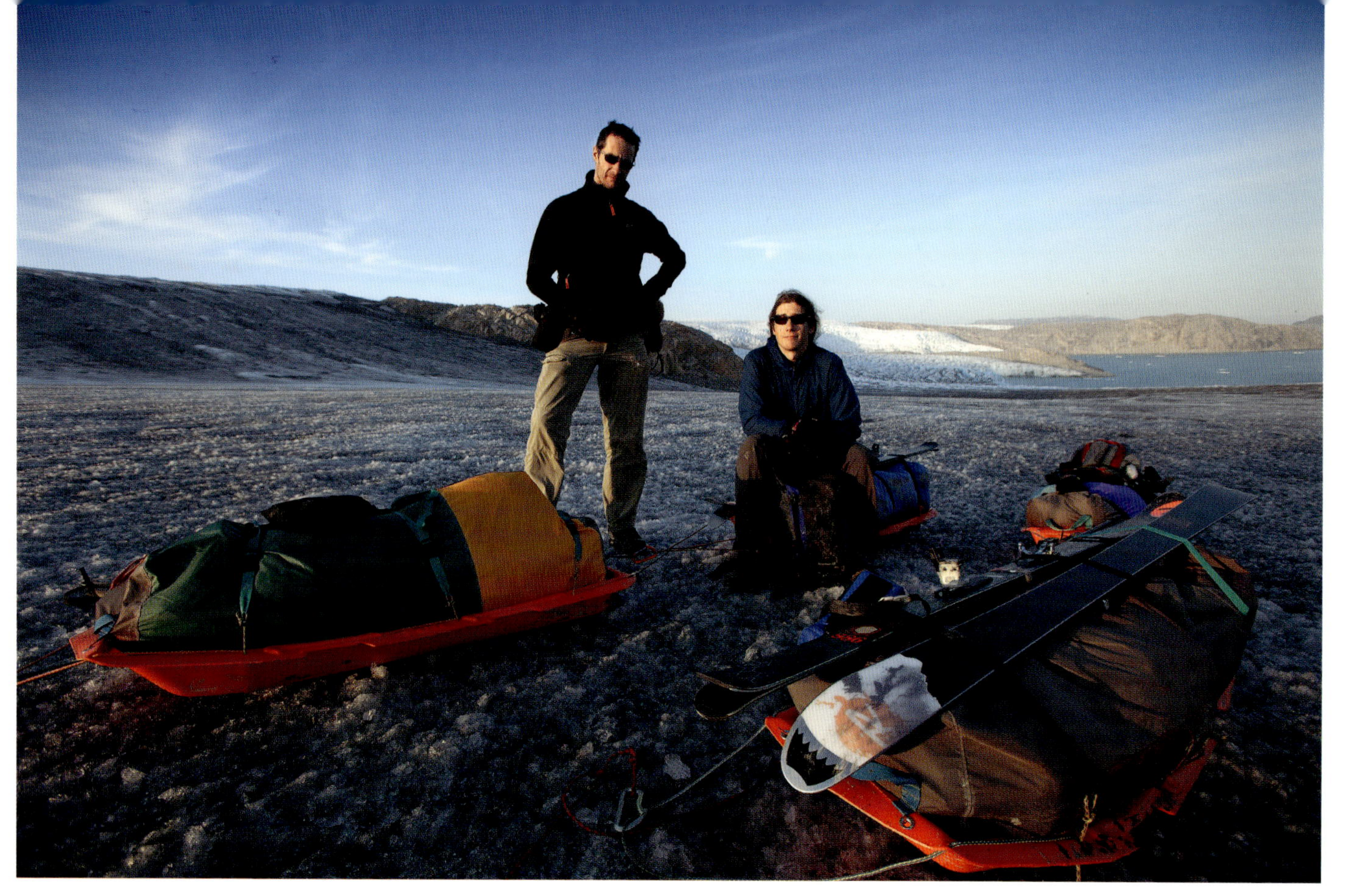

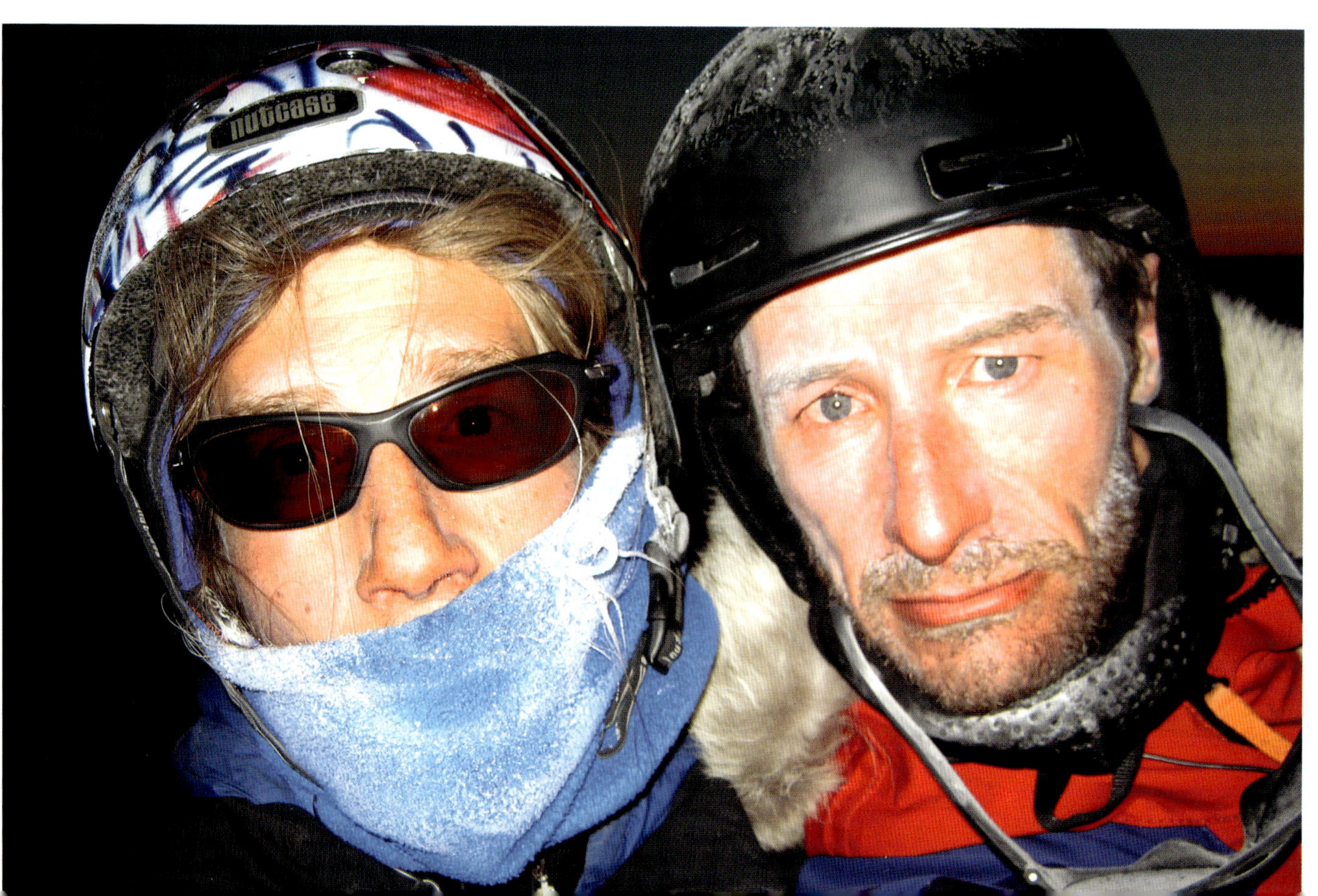
nutcase

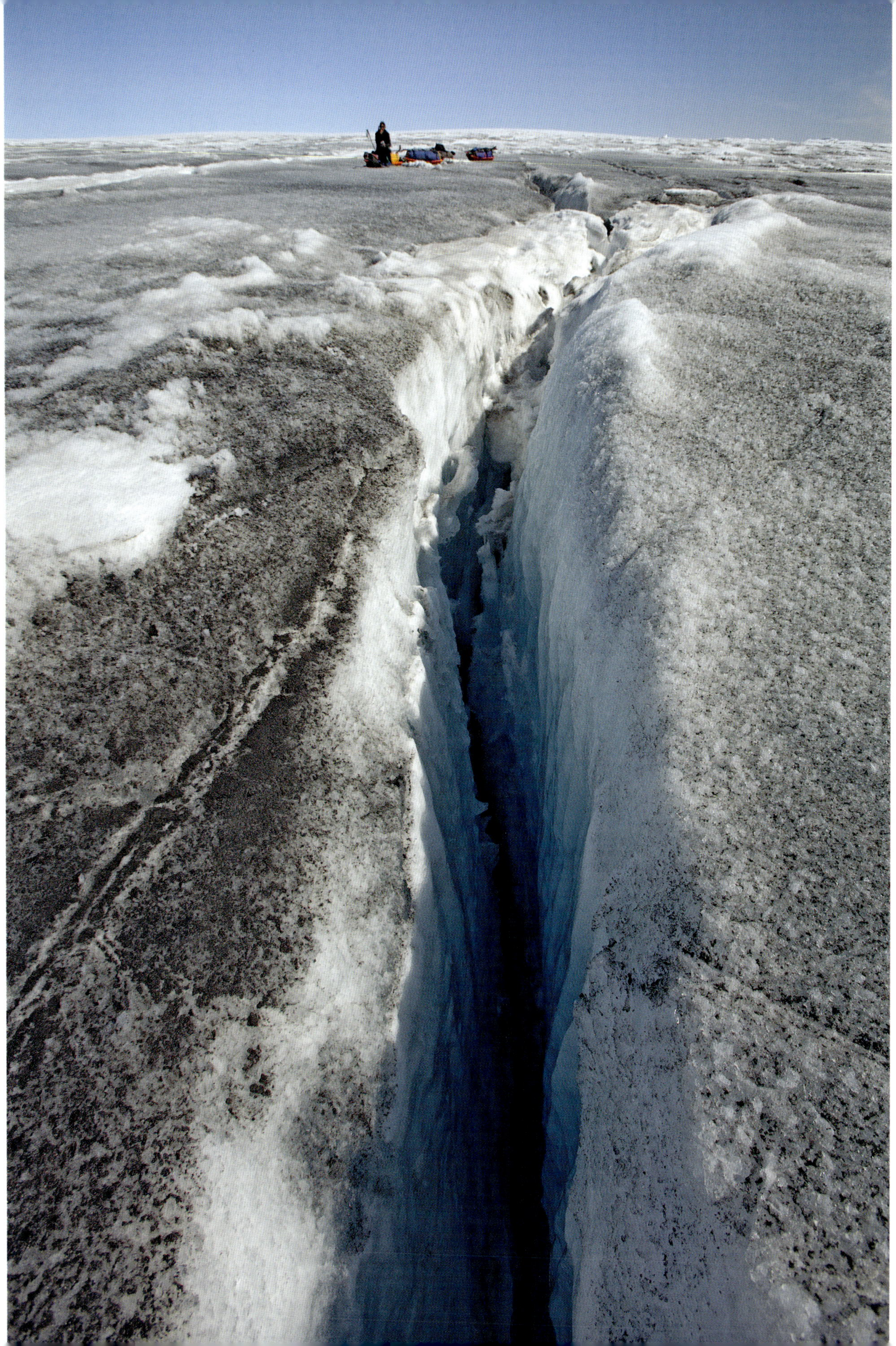

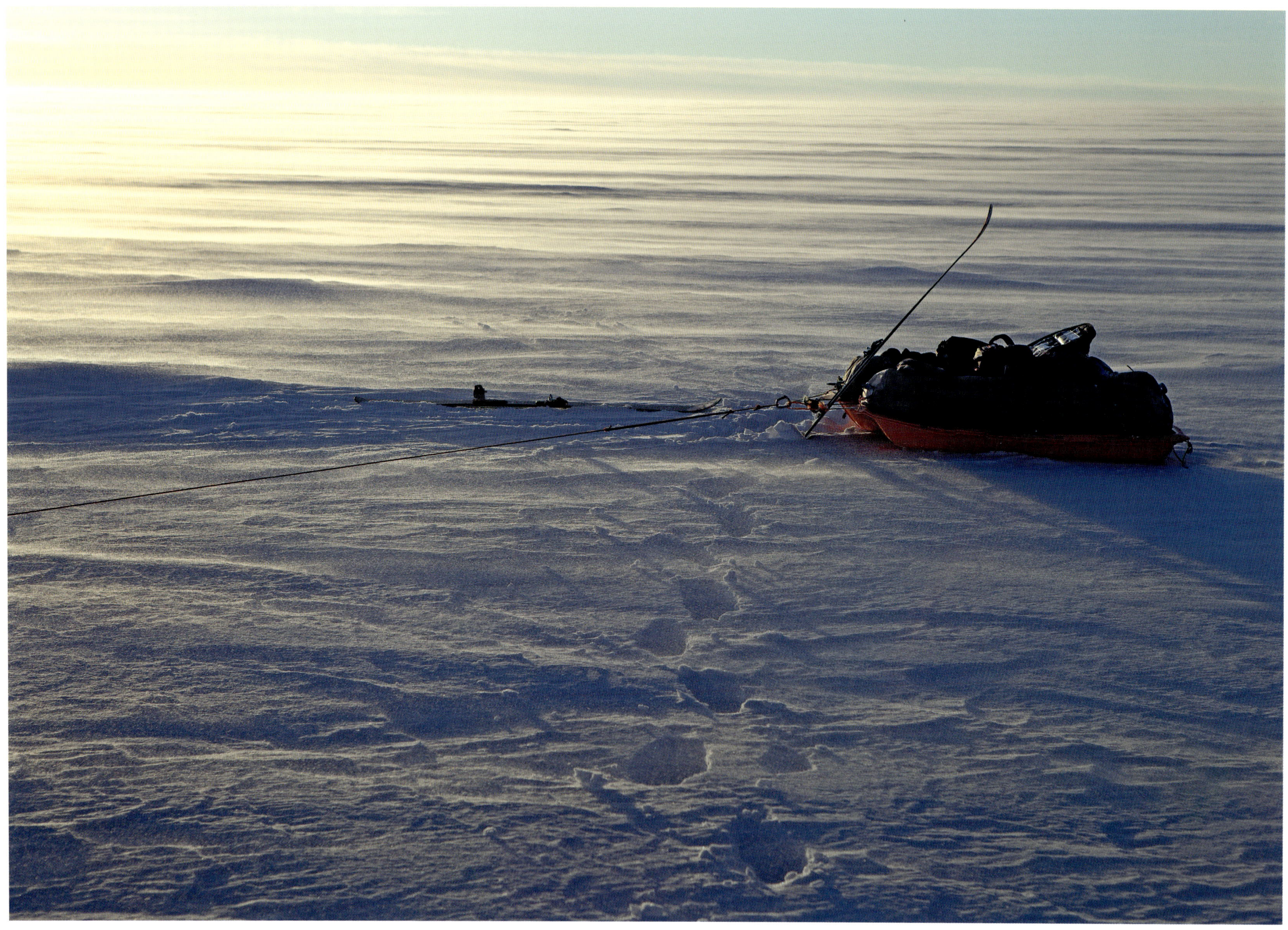

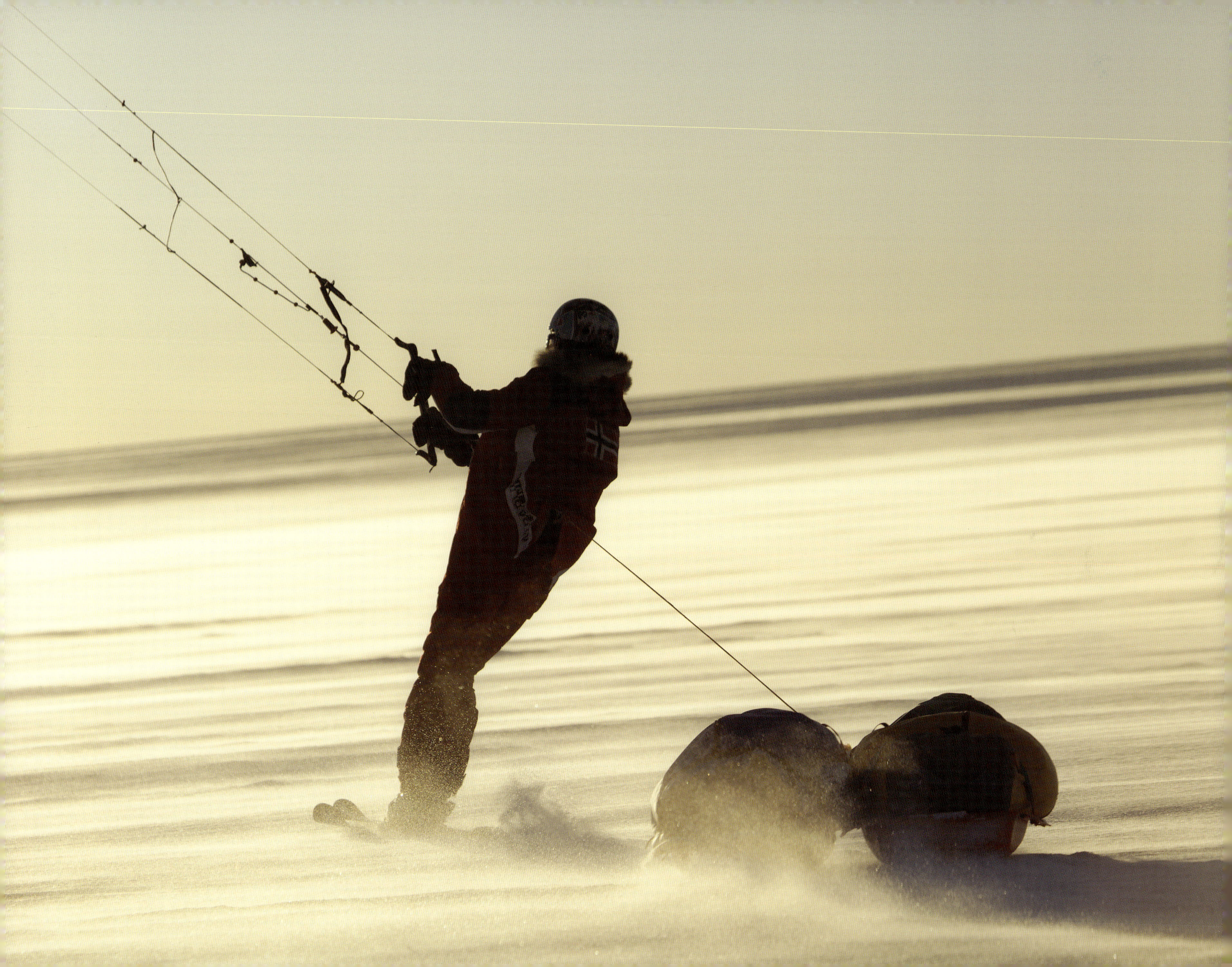

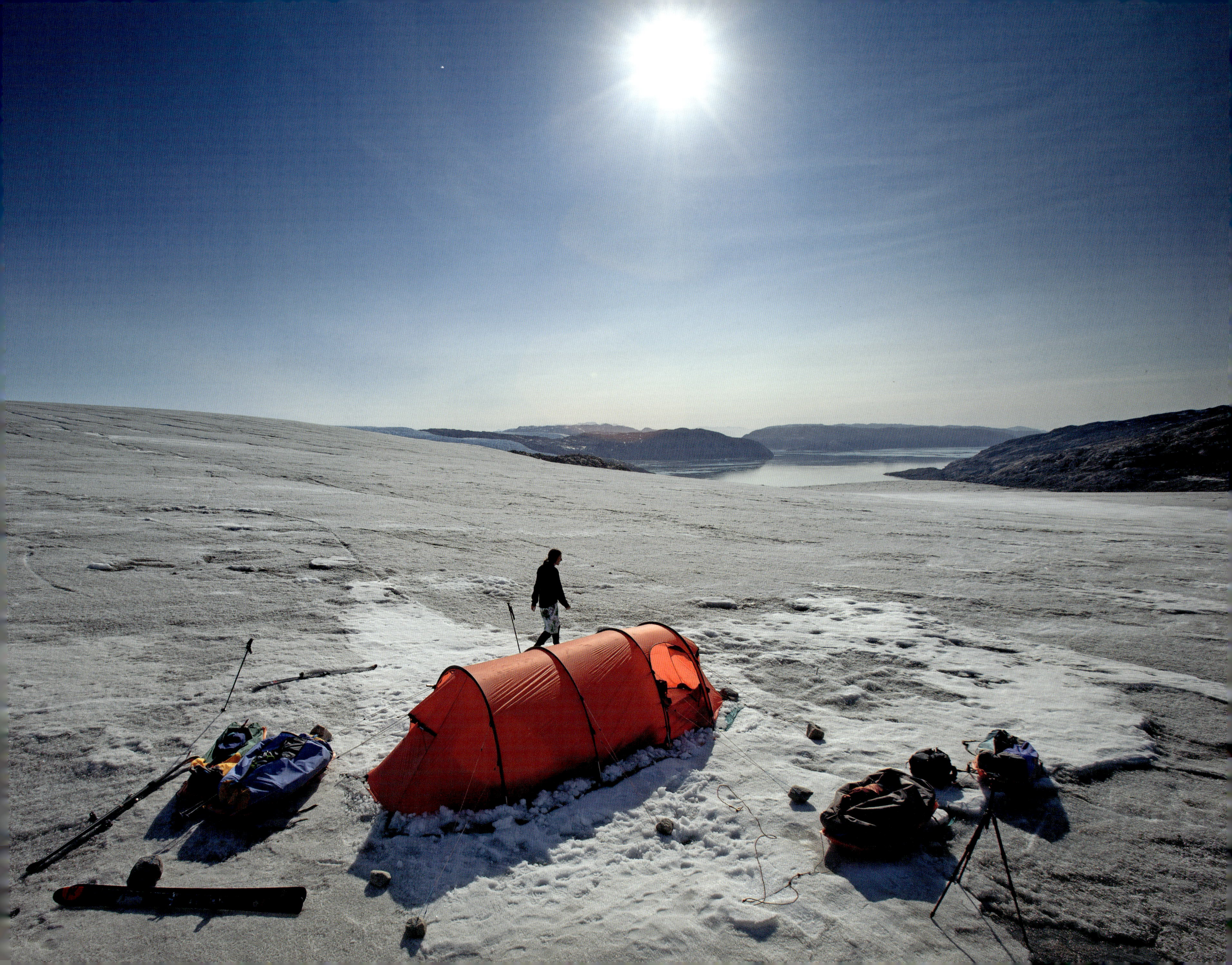

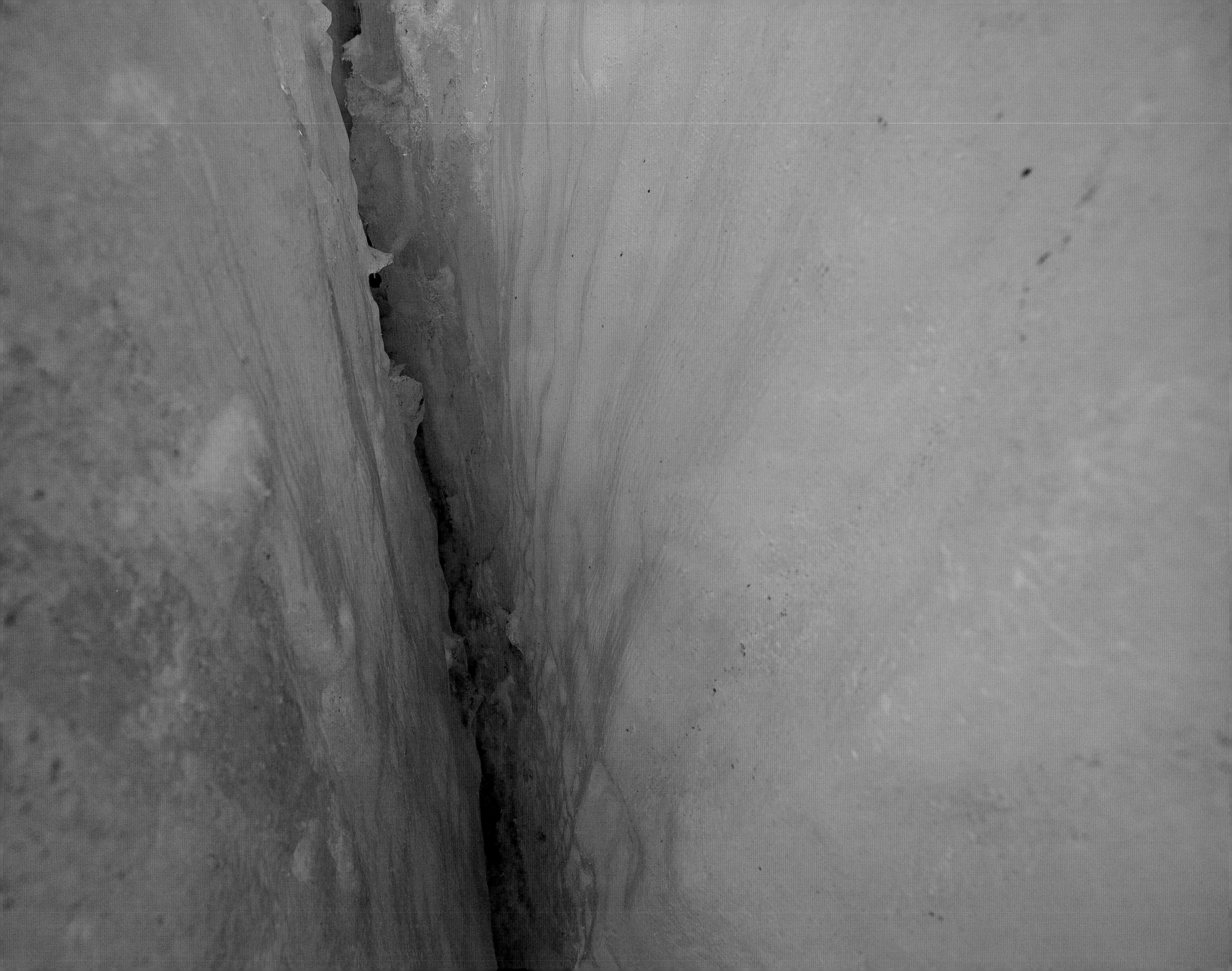

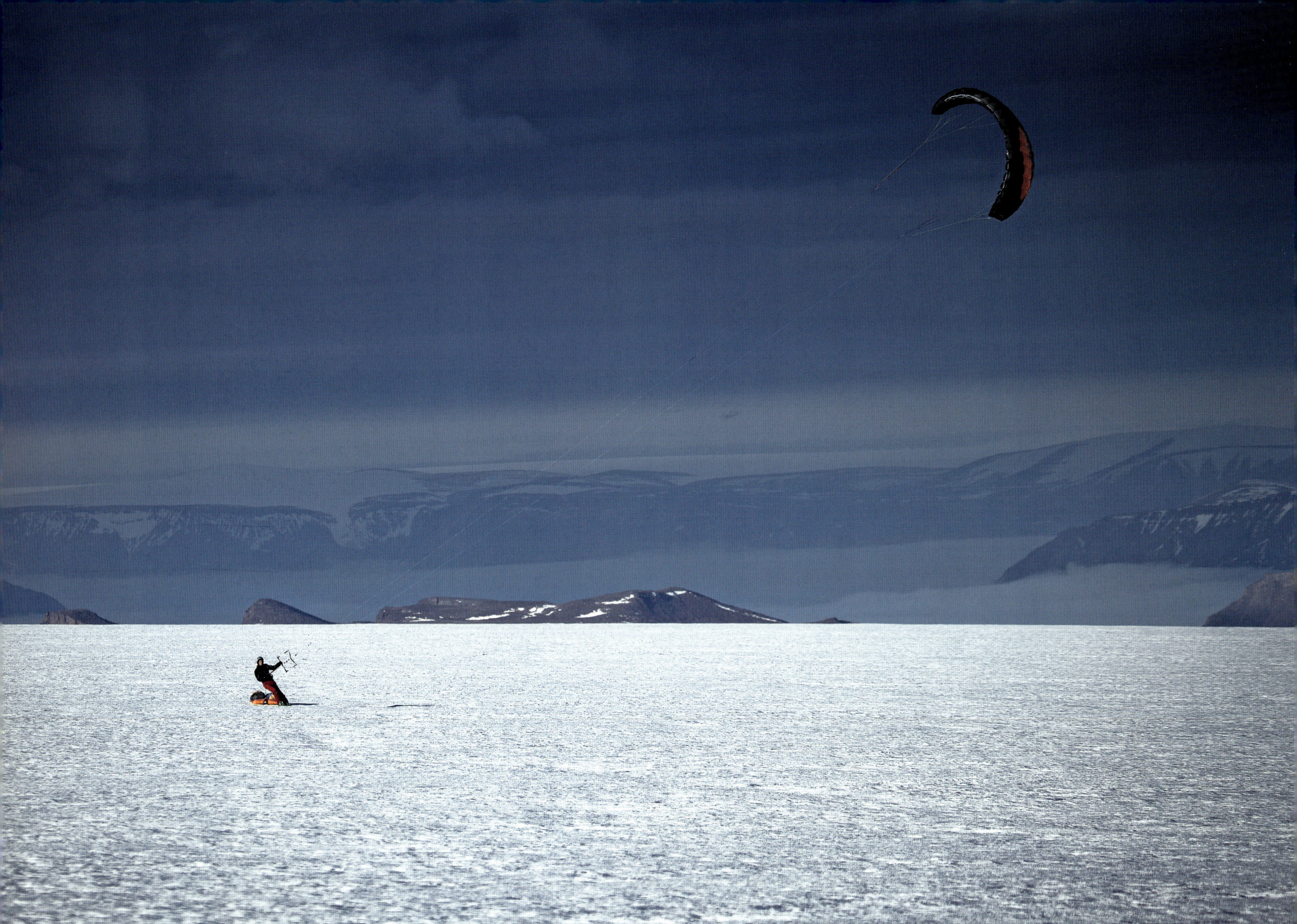

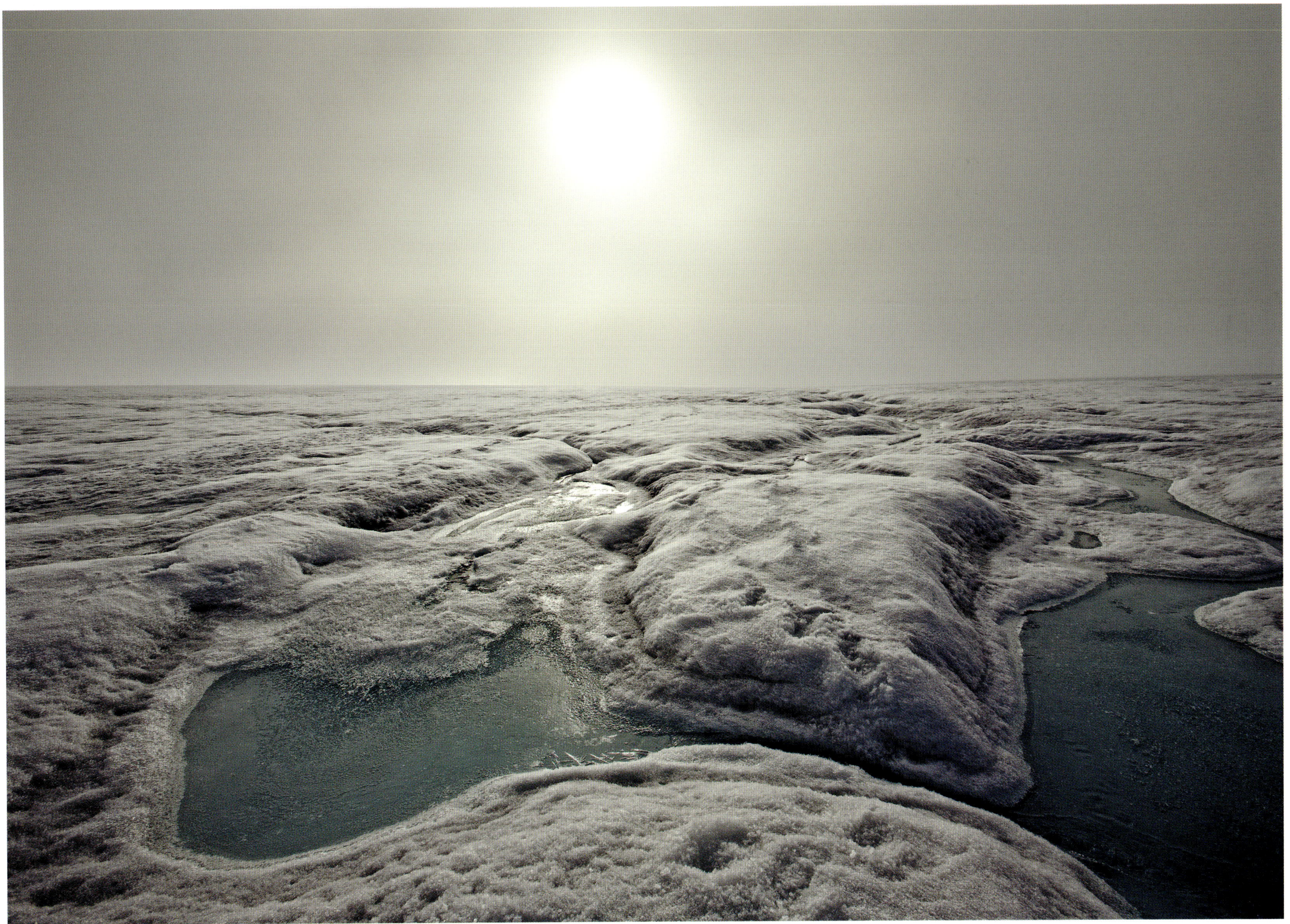

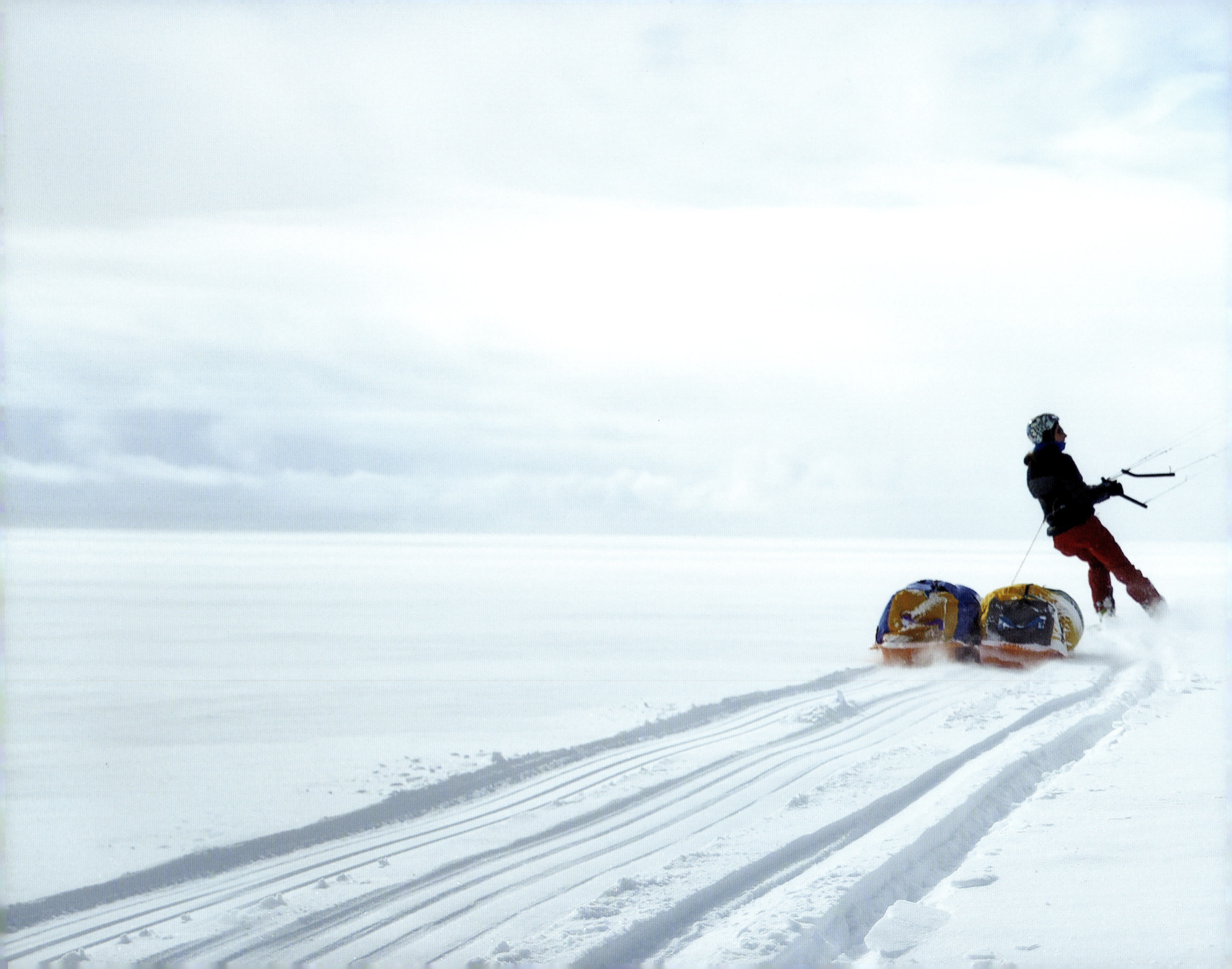

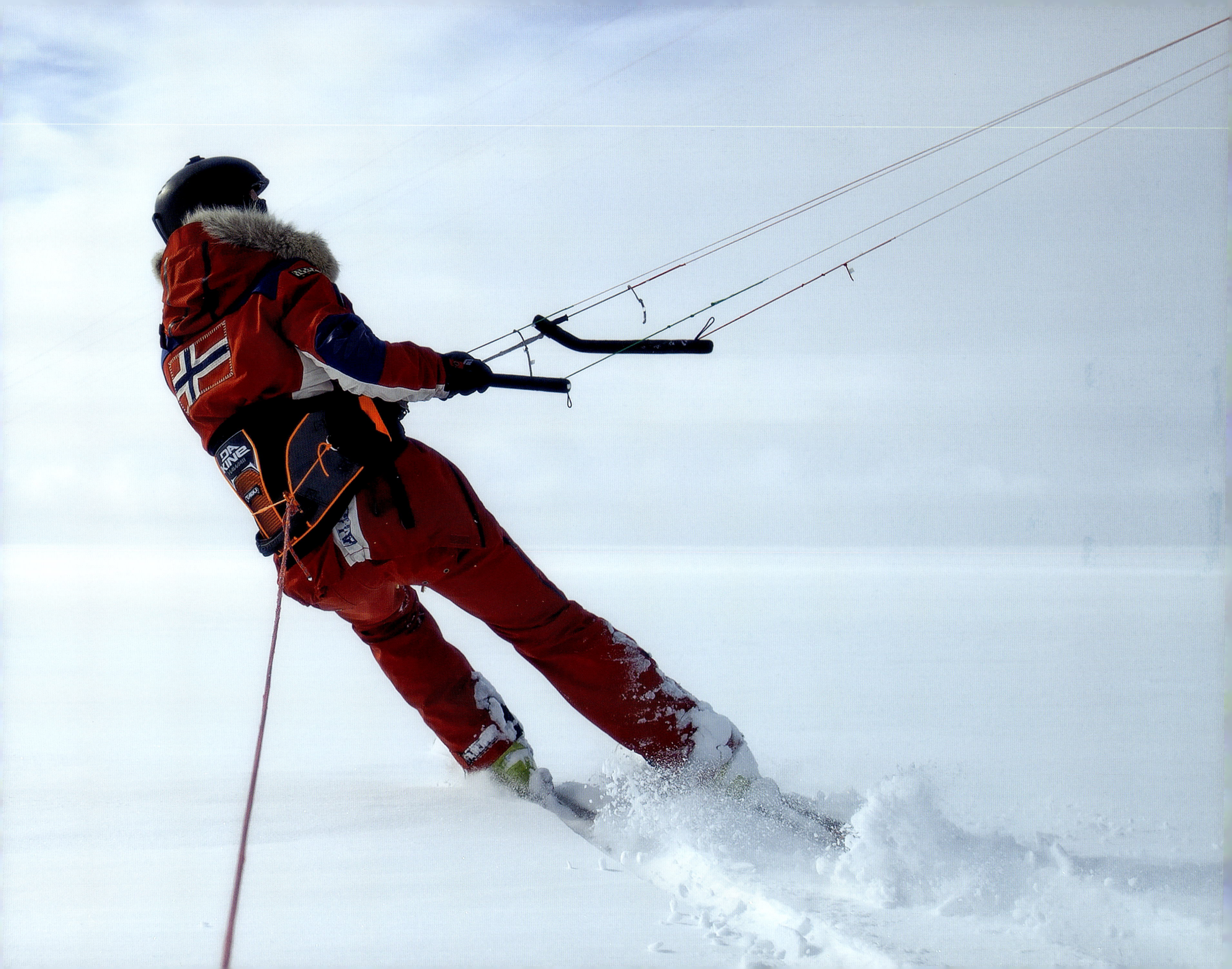

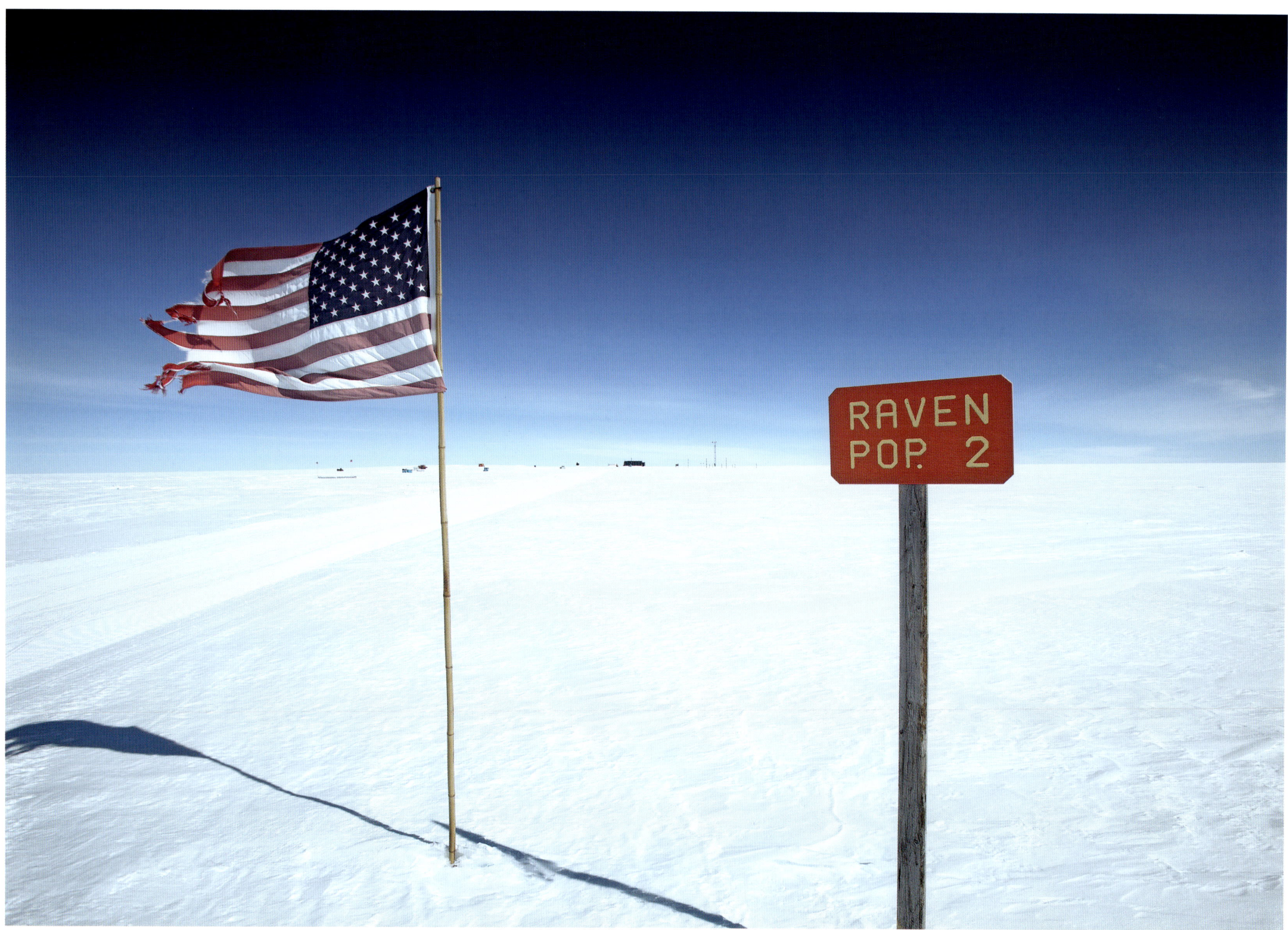
RAVEN
POP. 2

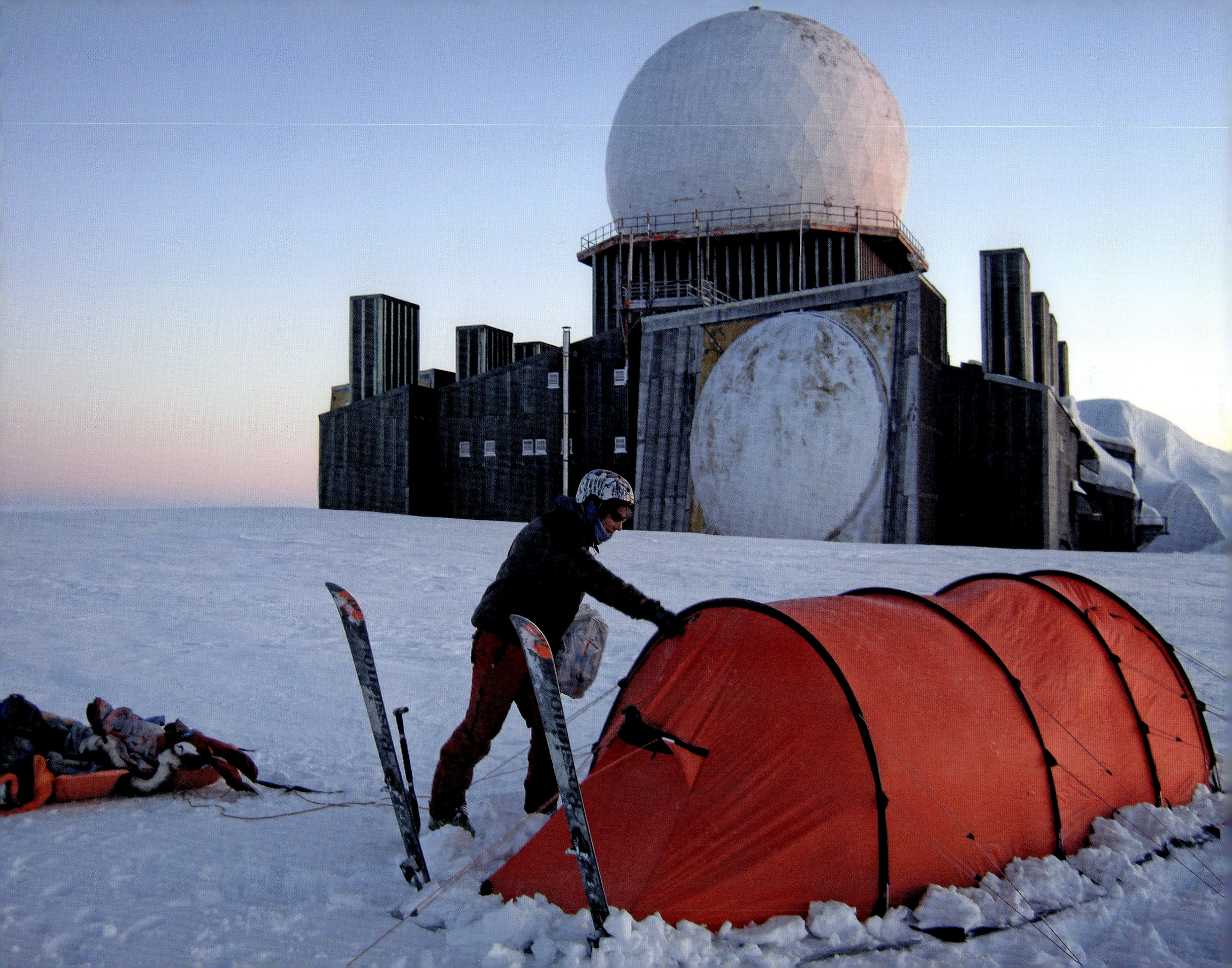

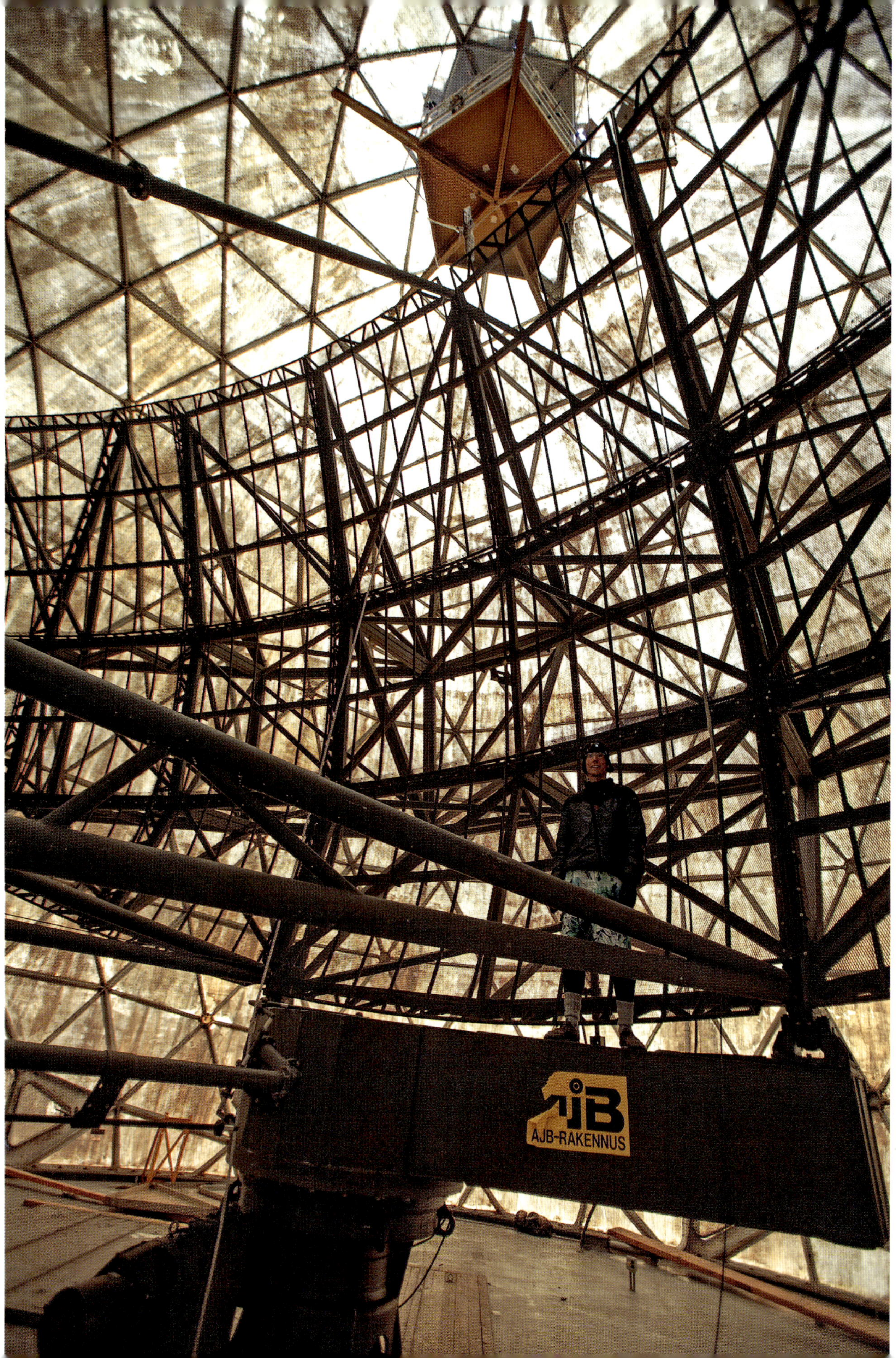

AJB-RAKENNUS

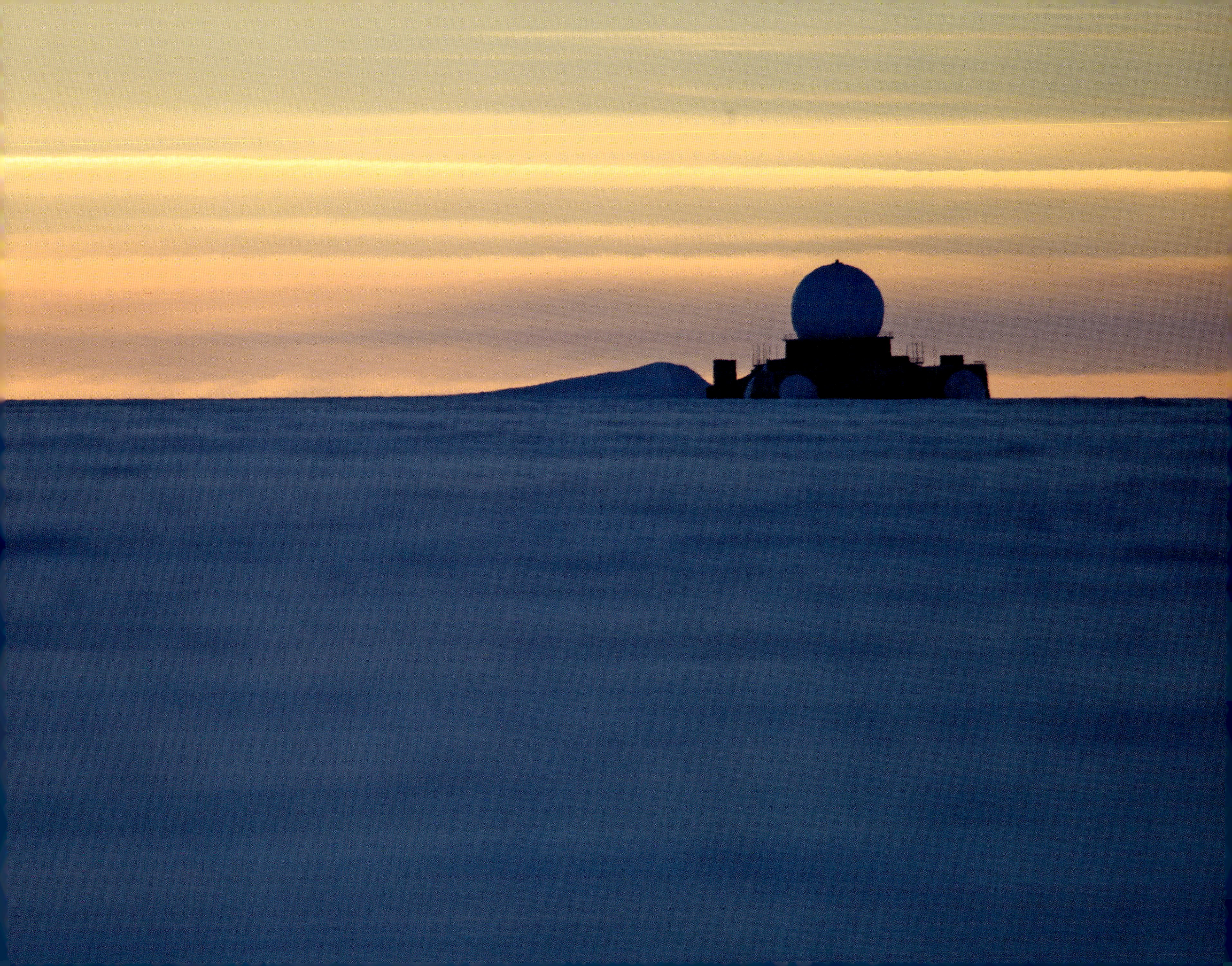

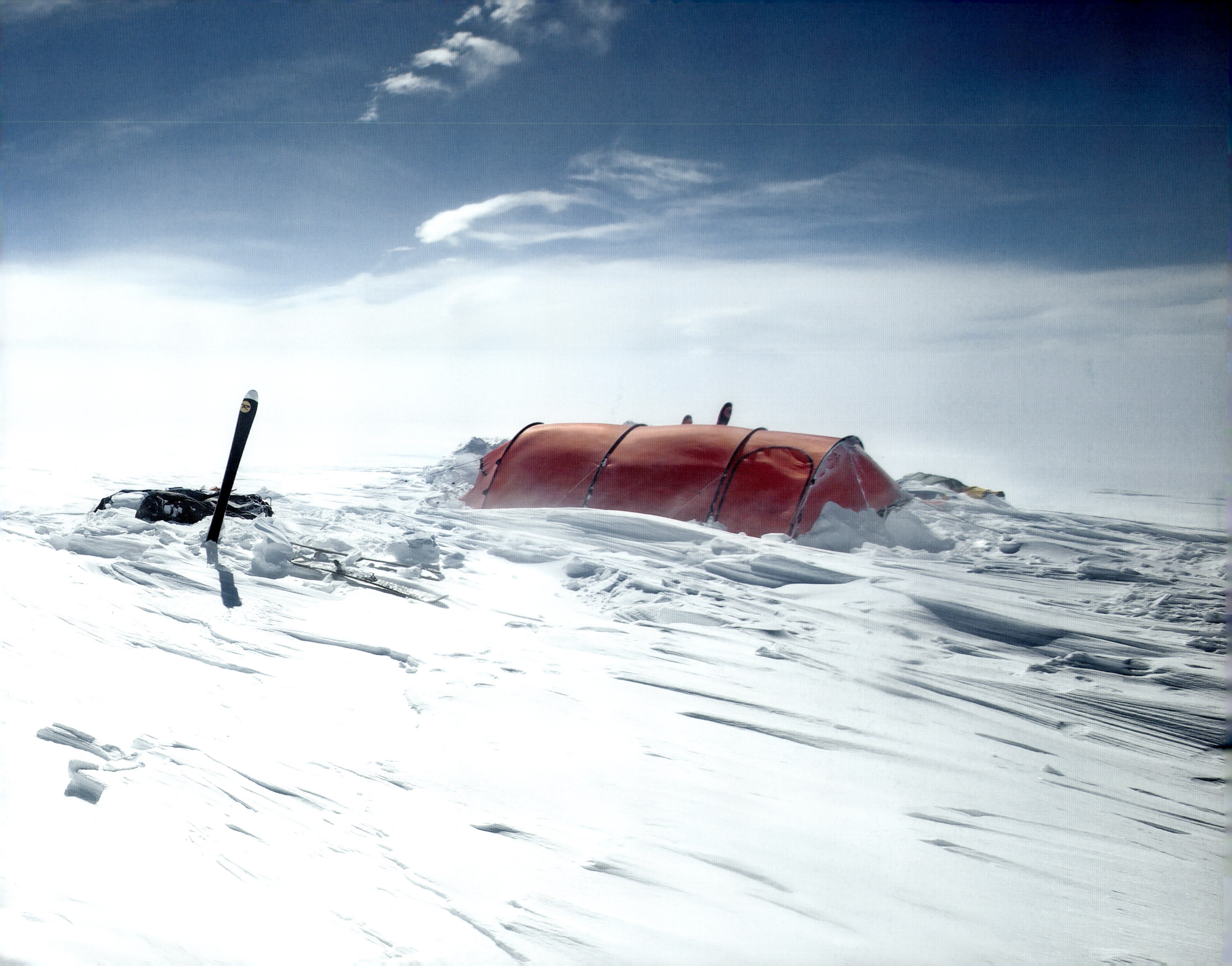

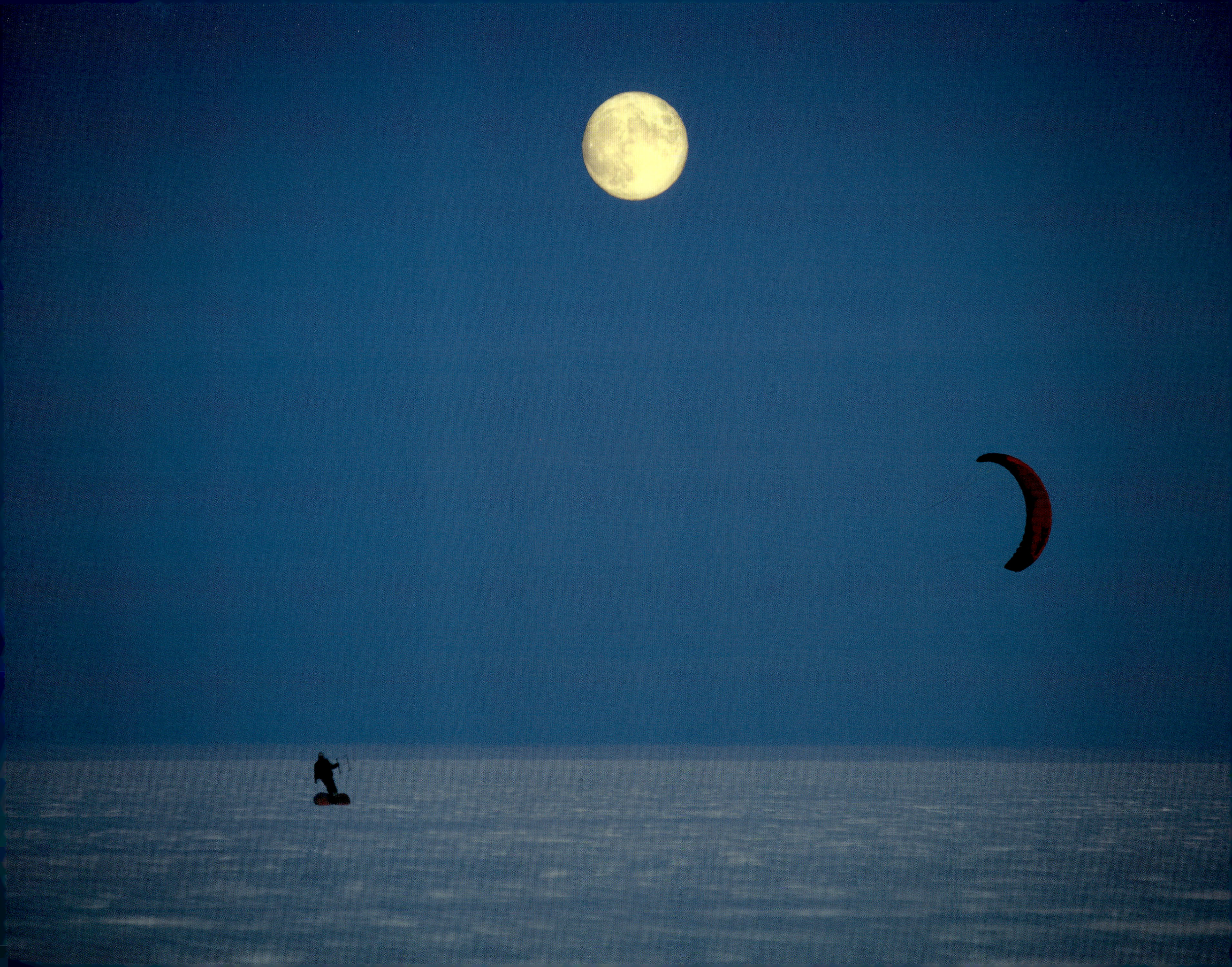

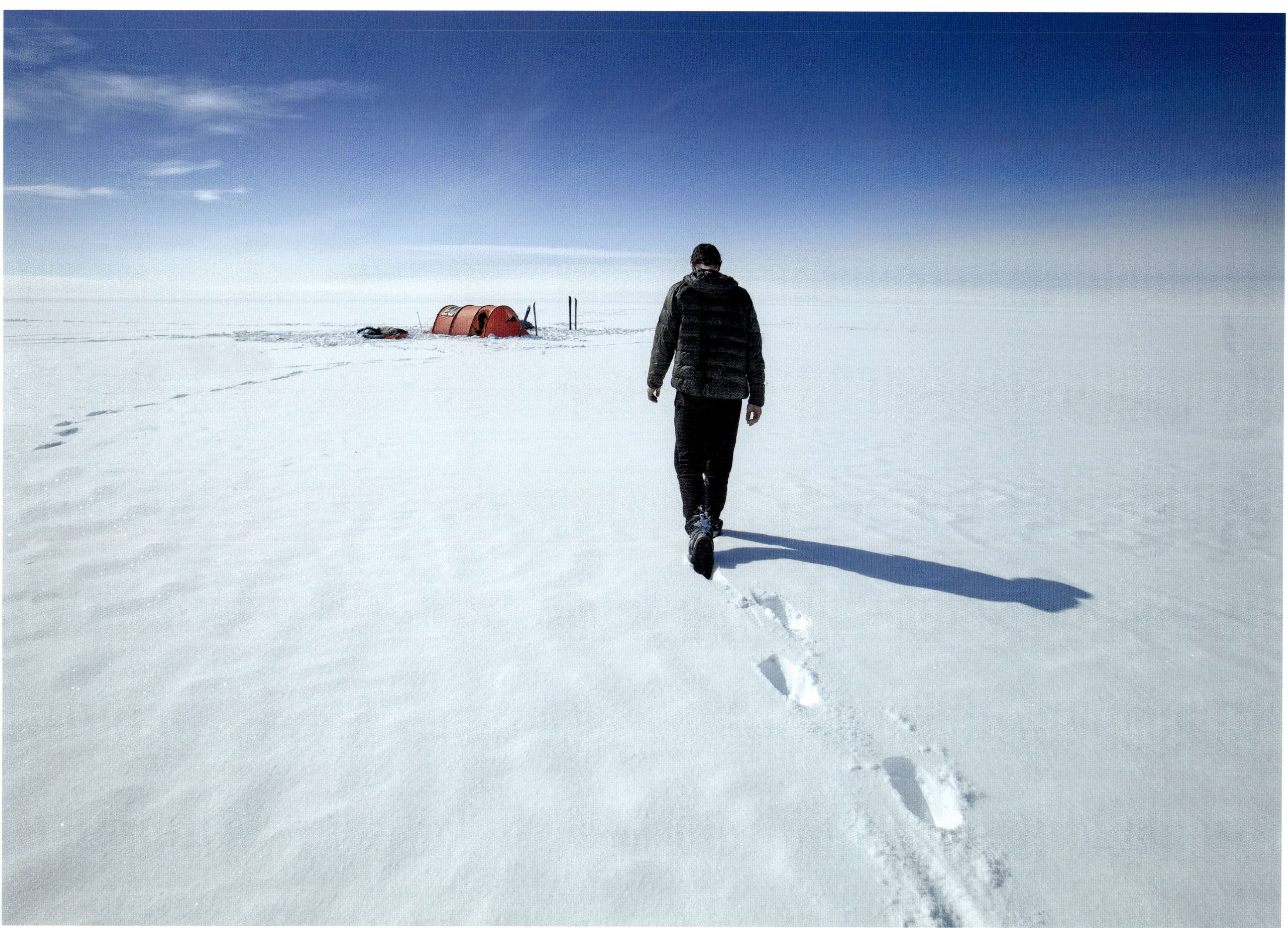

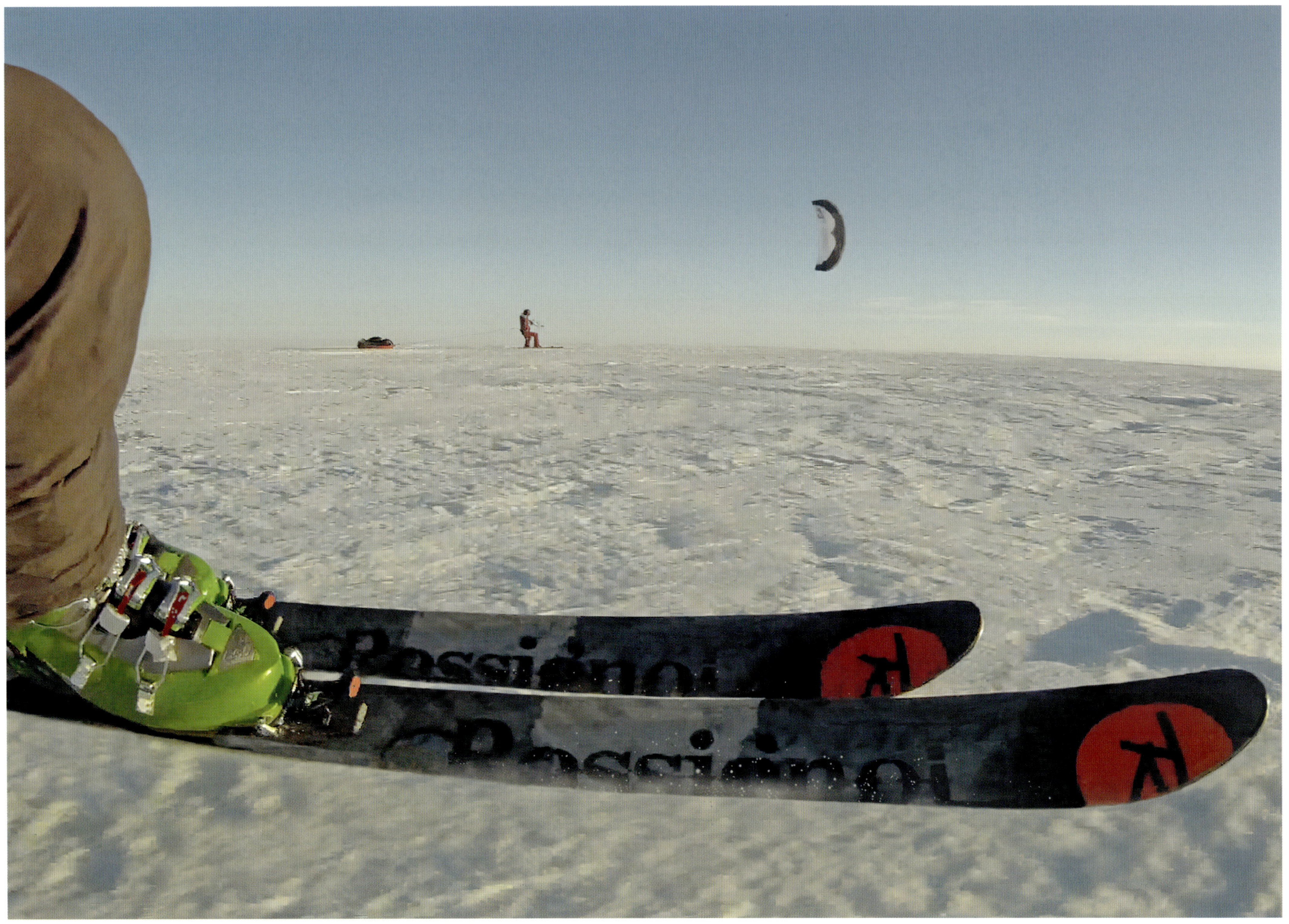

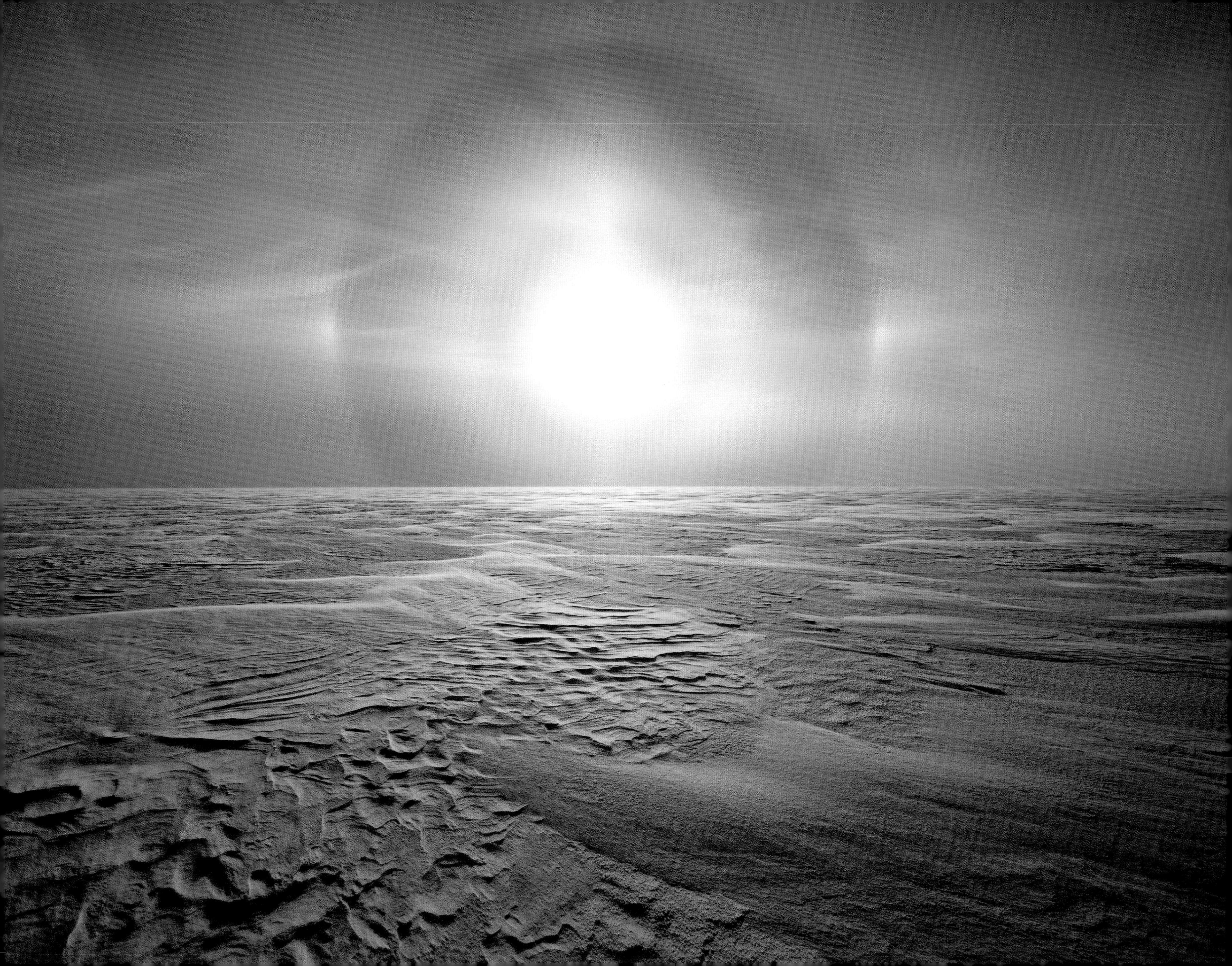

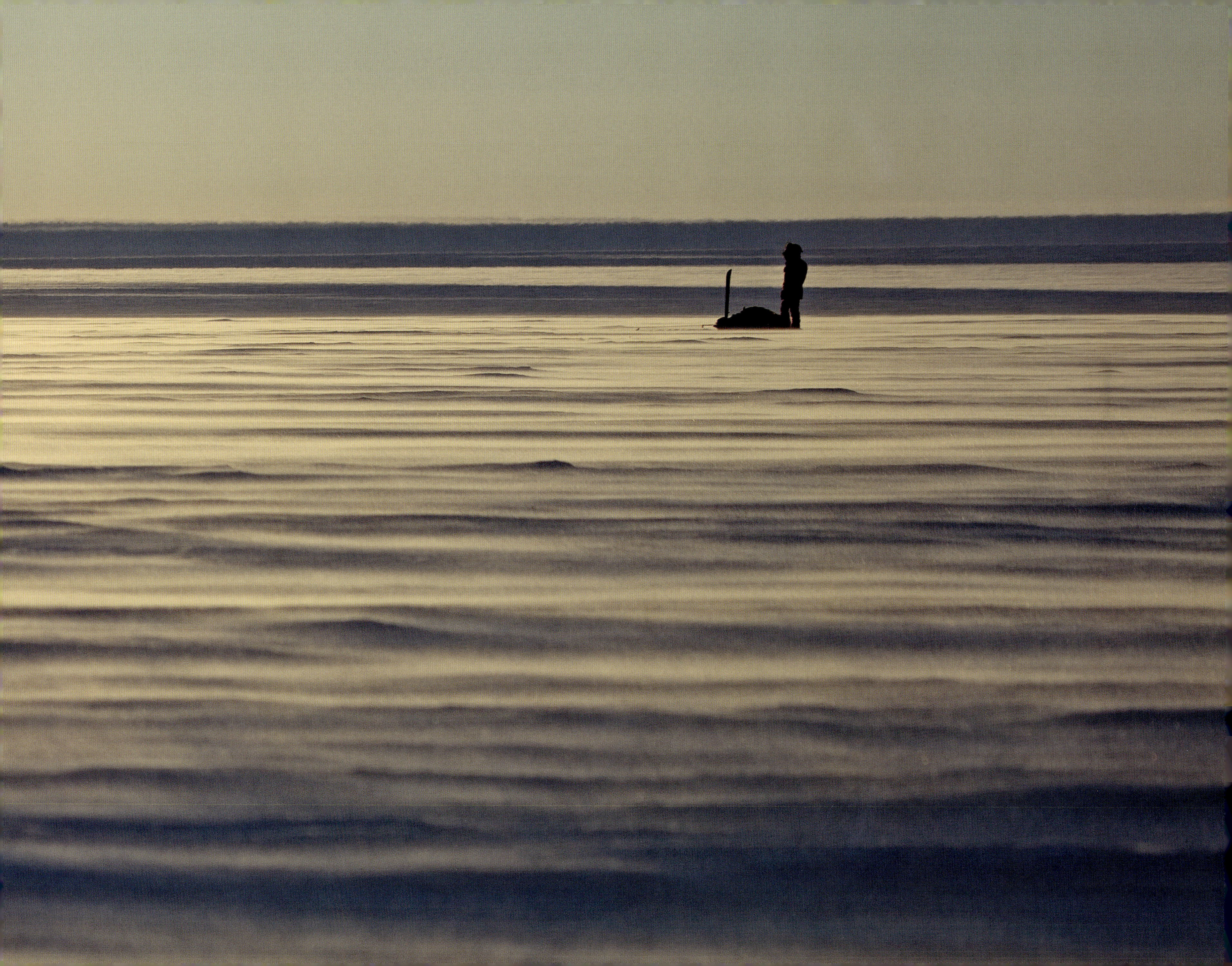

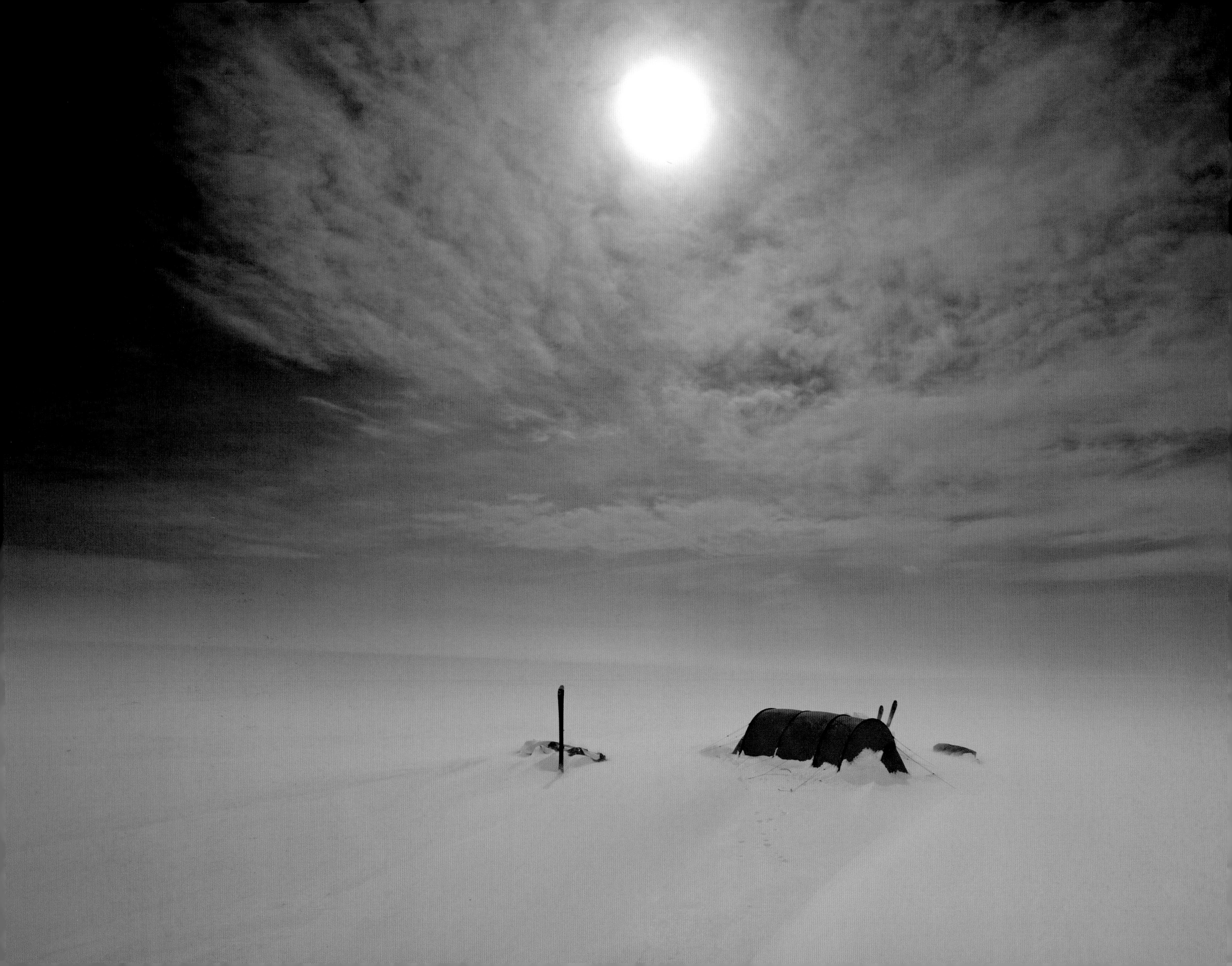

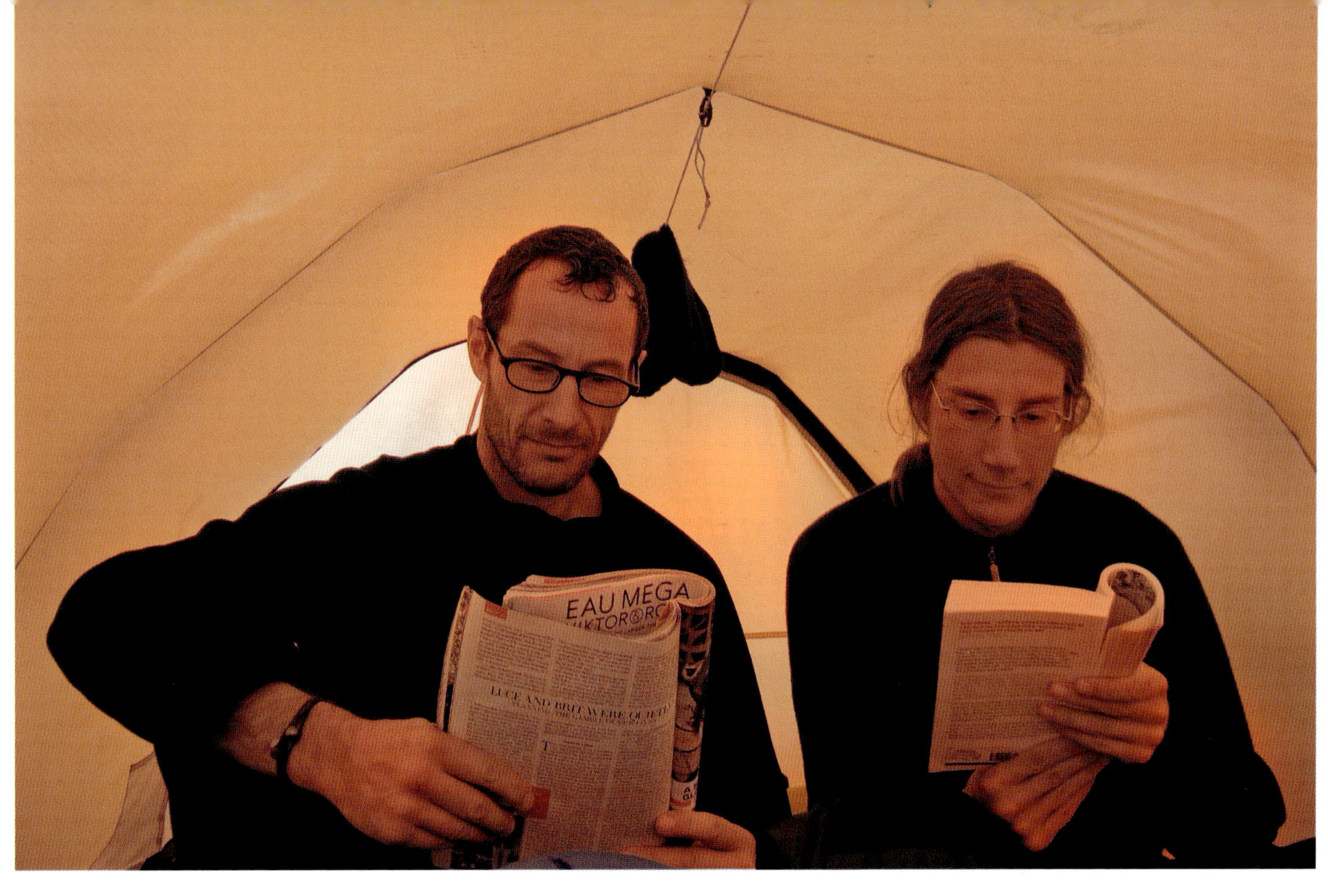

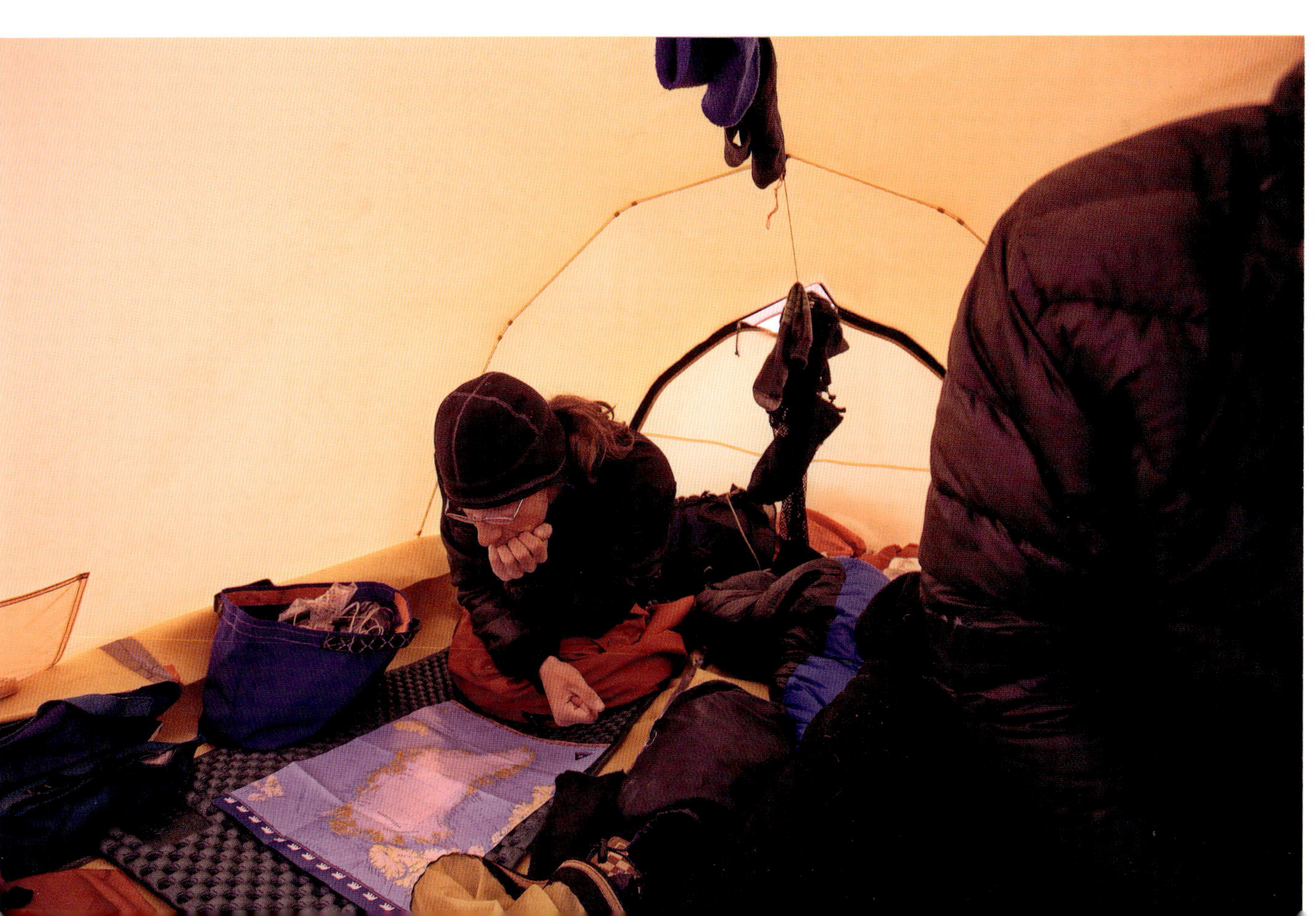

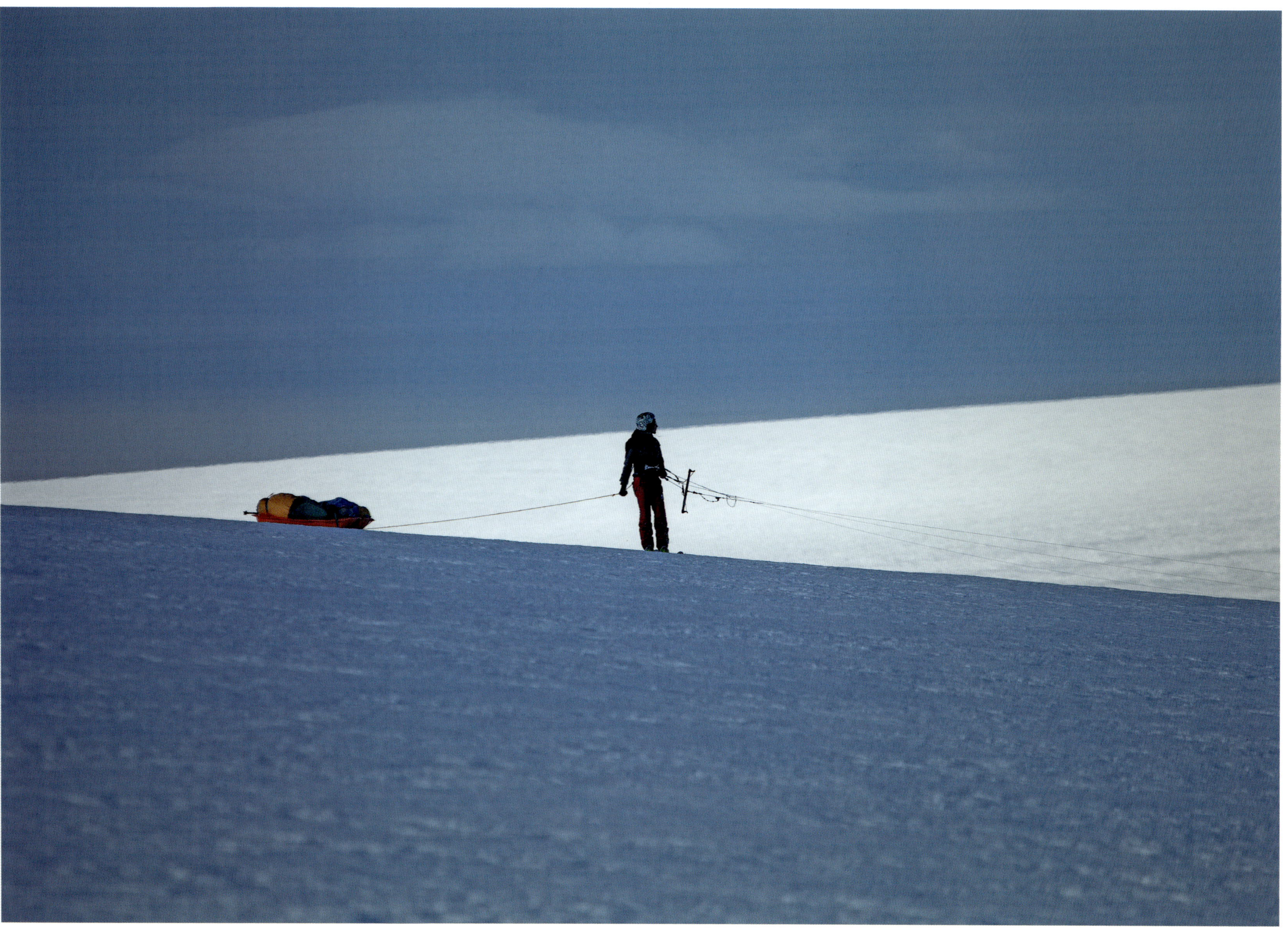

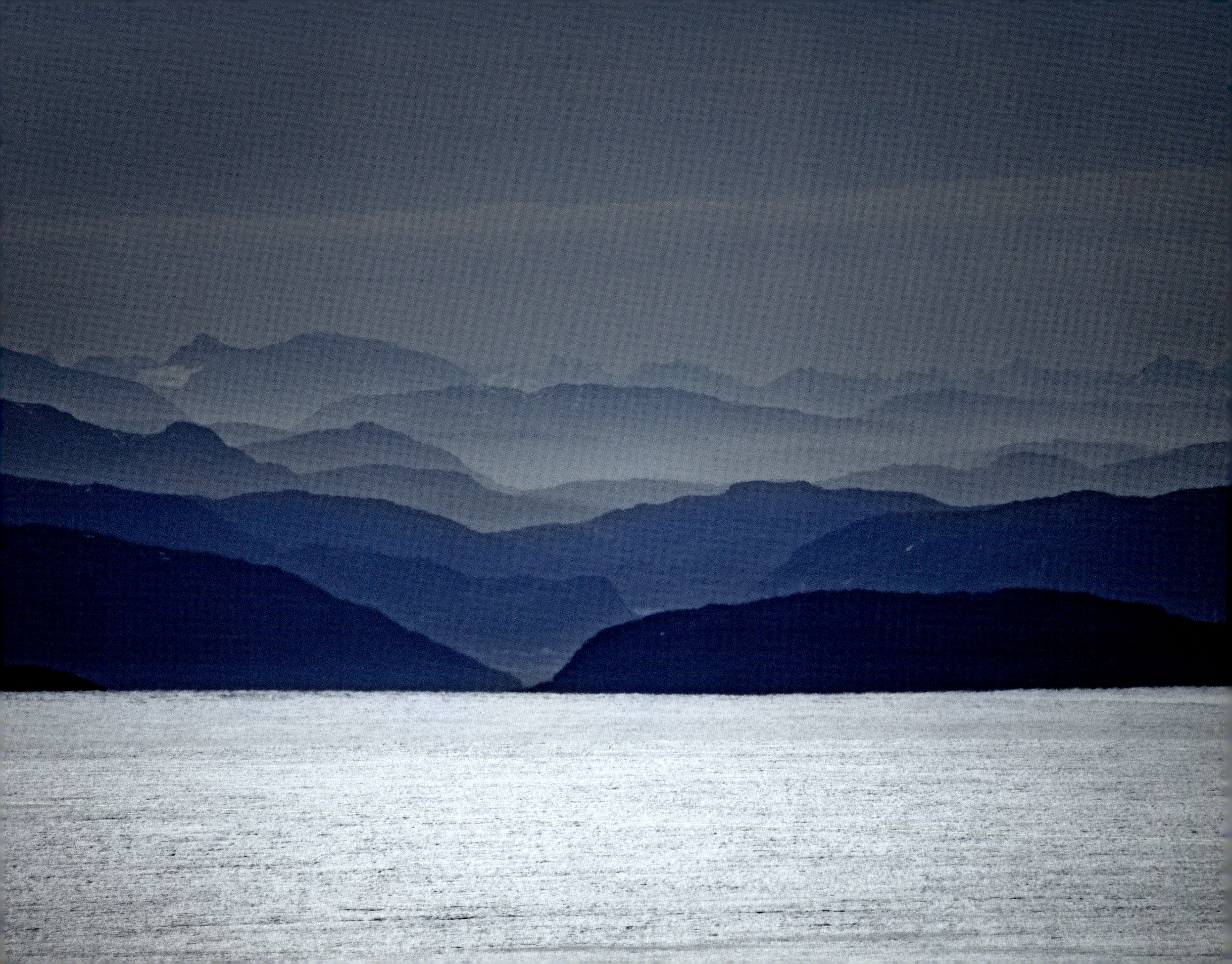

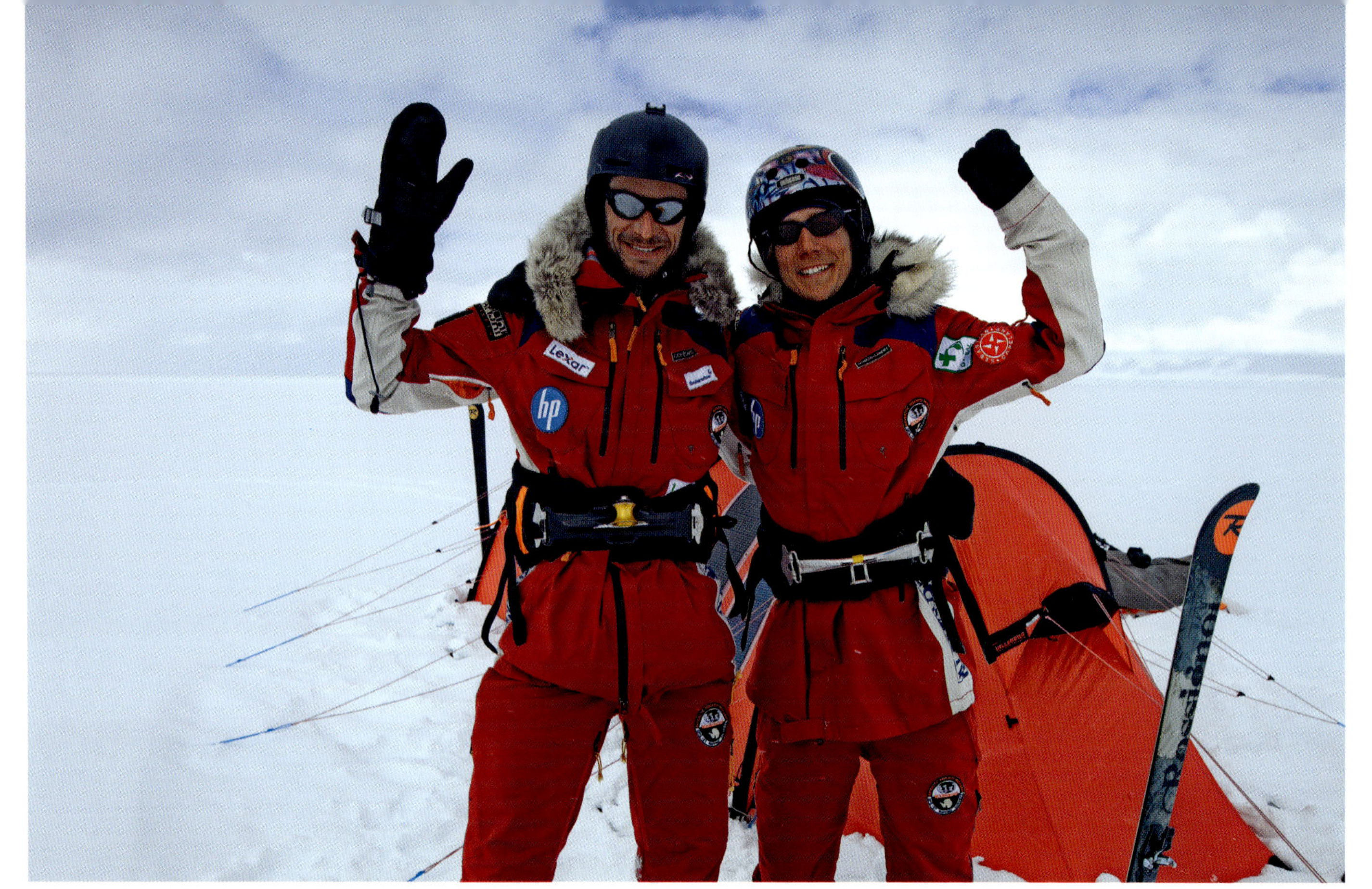
Lexar
hp

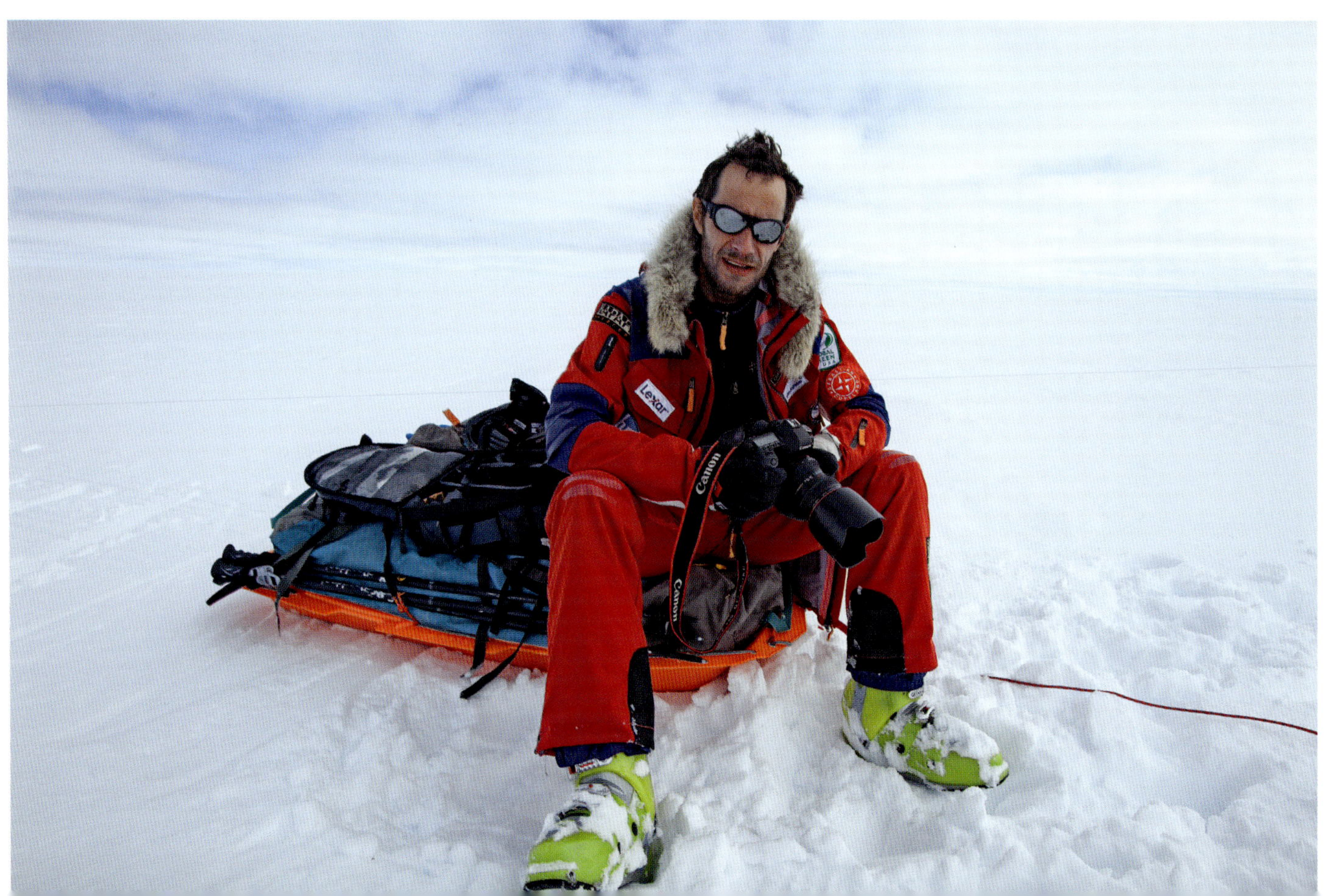
Lexar
Canon

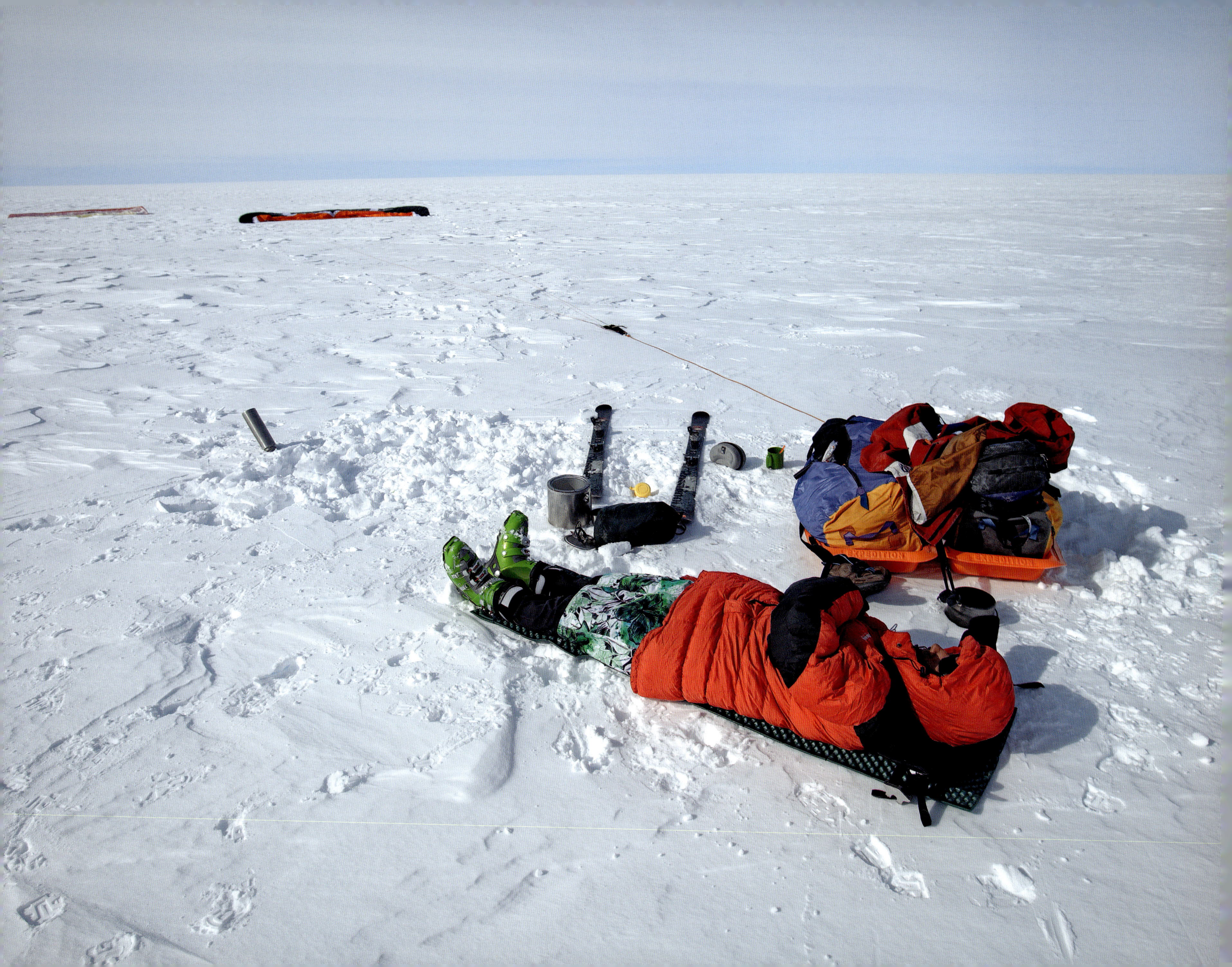

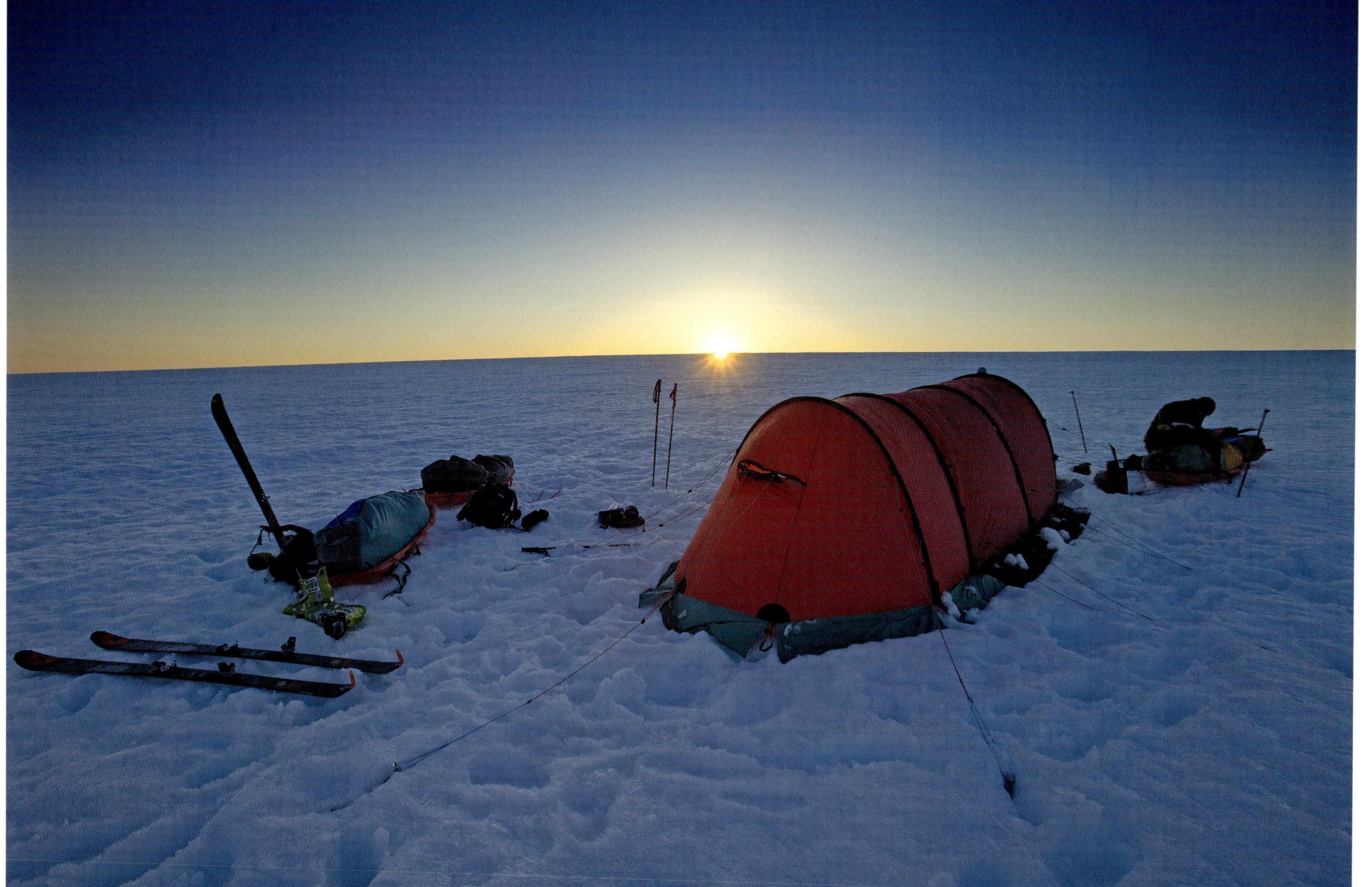

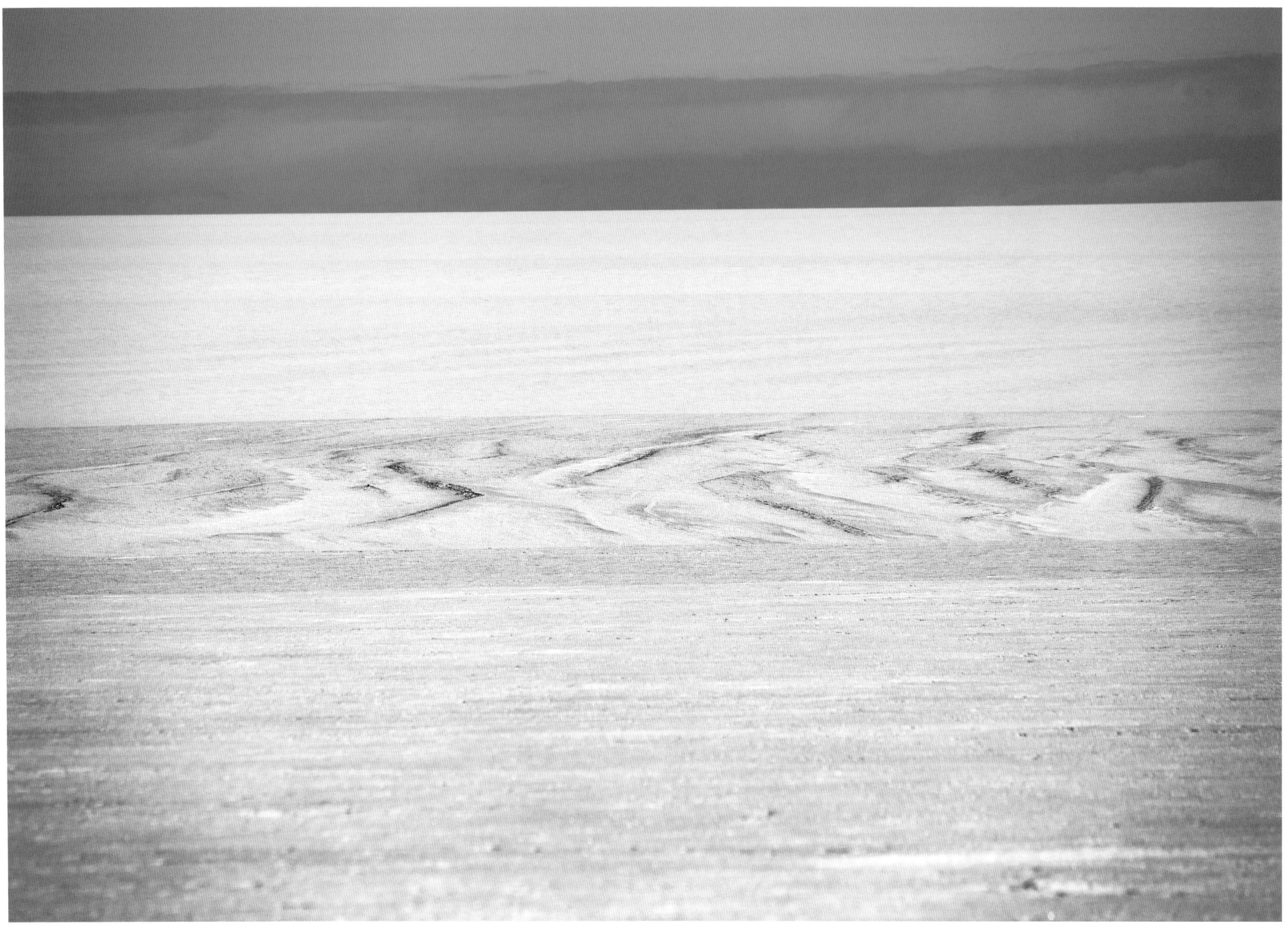

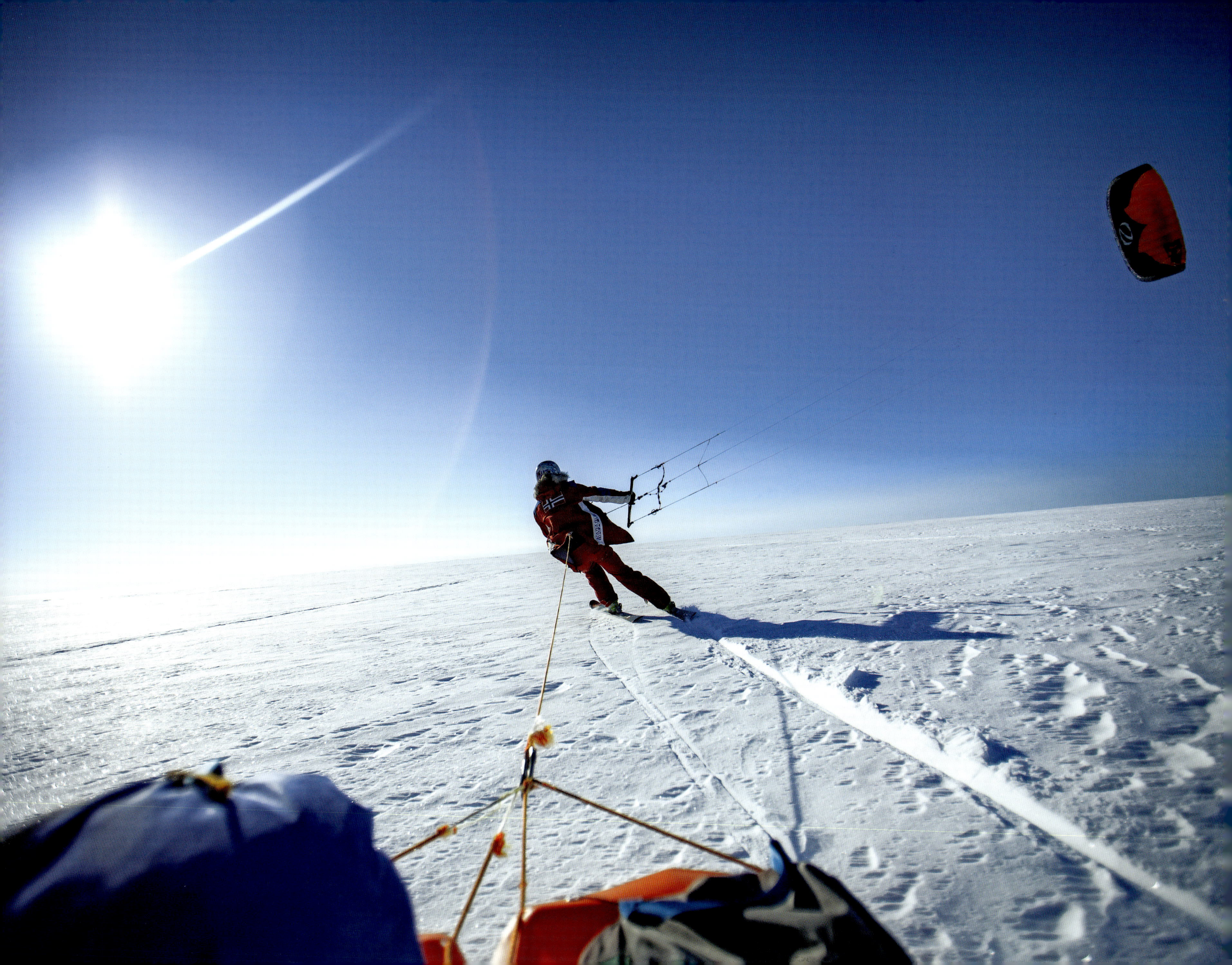

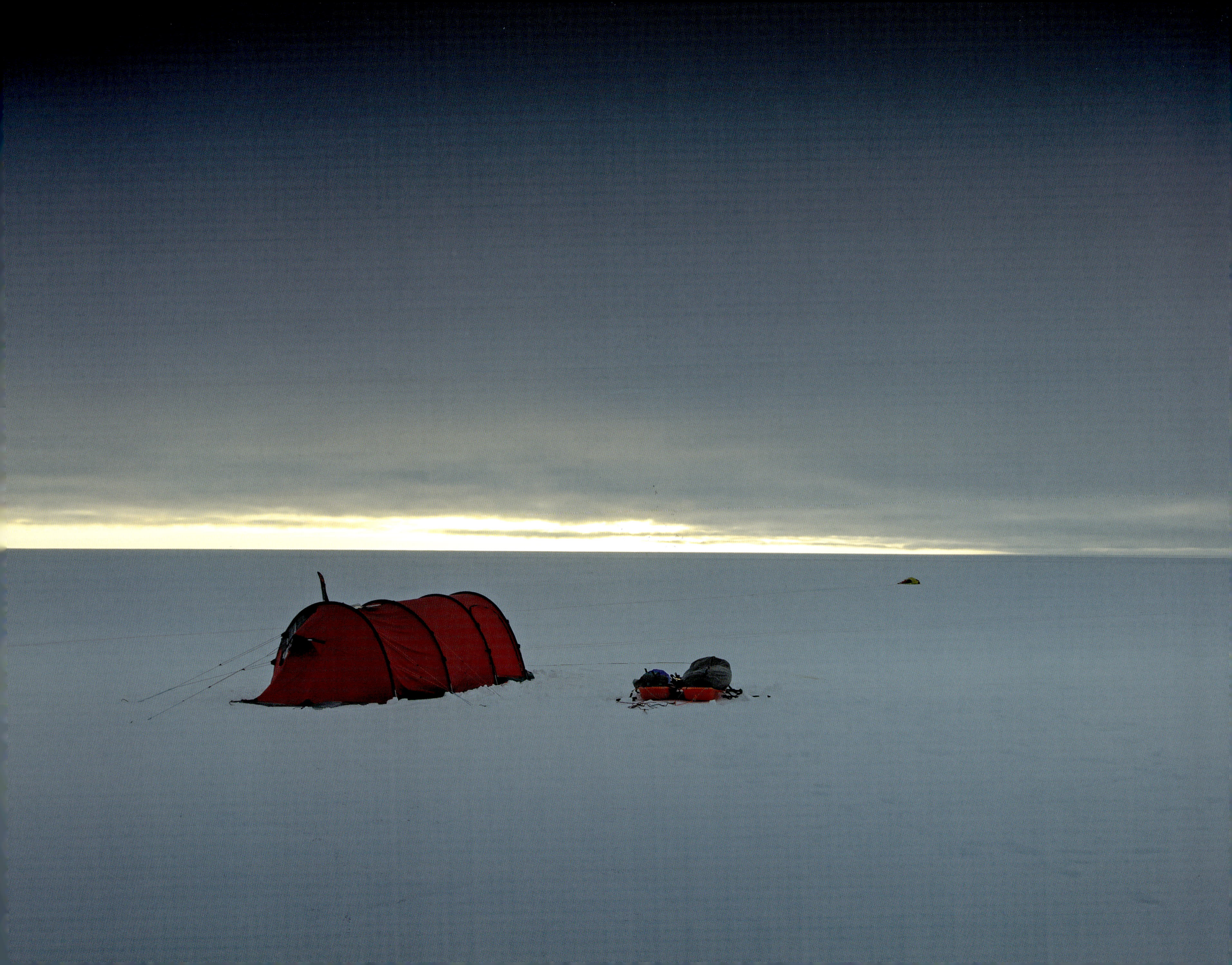

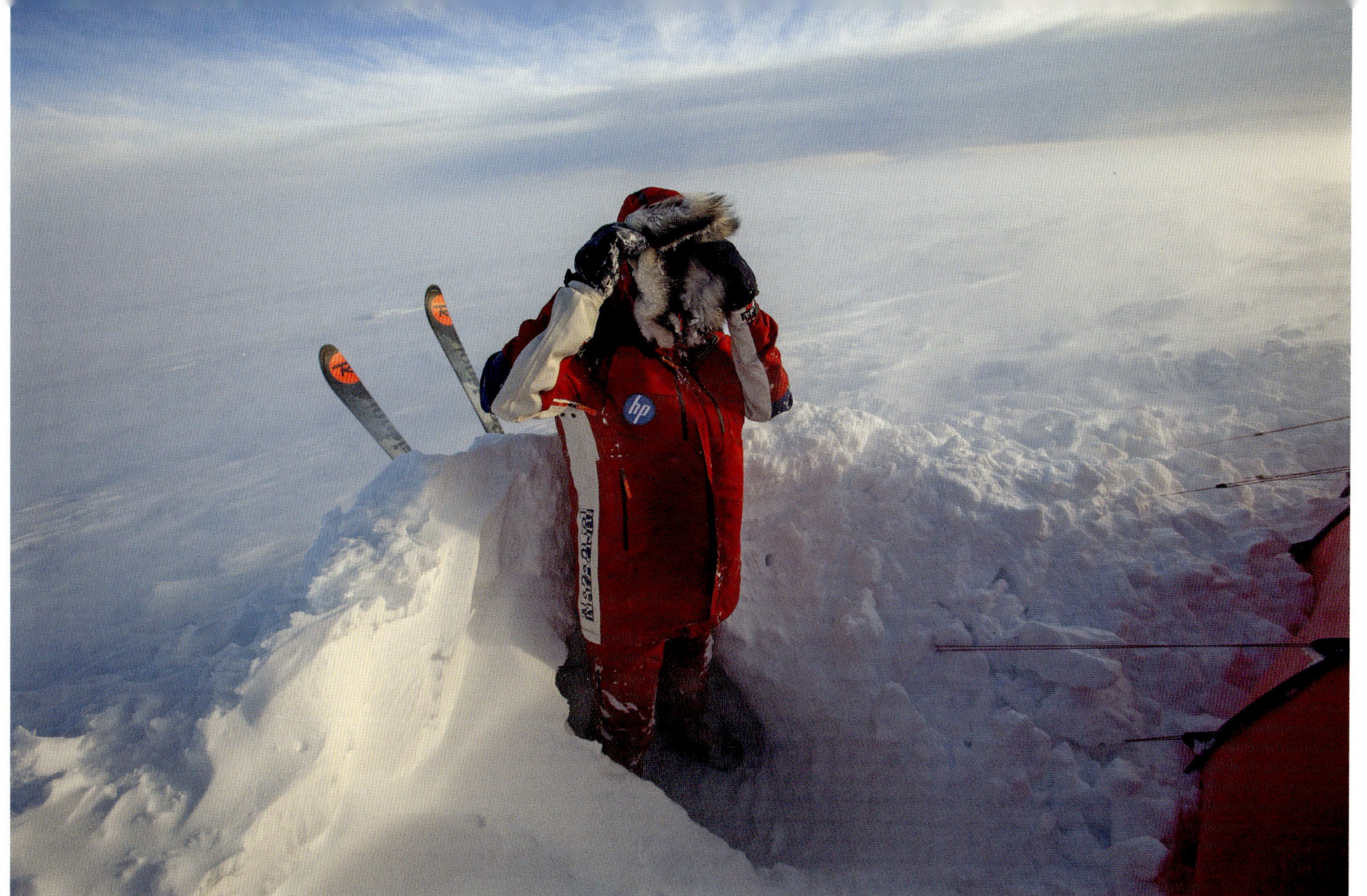
hp

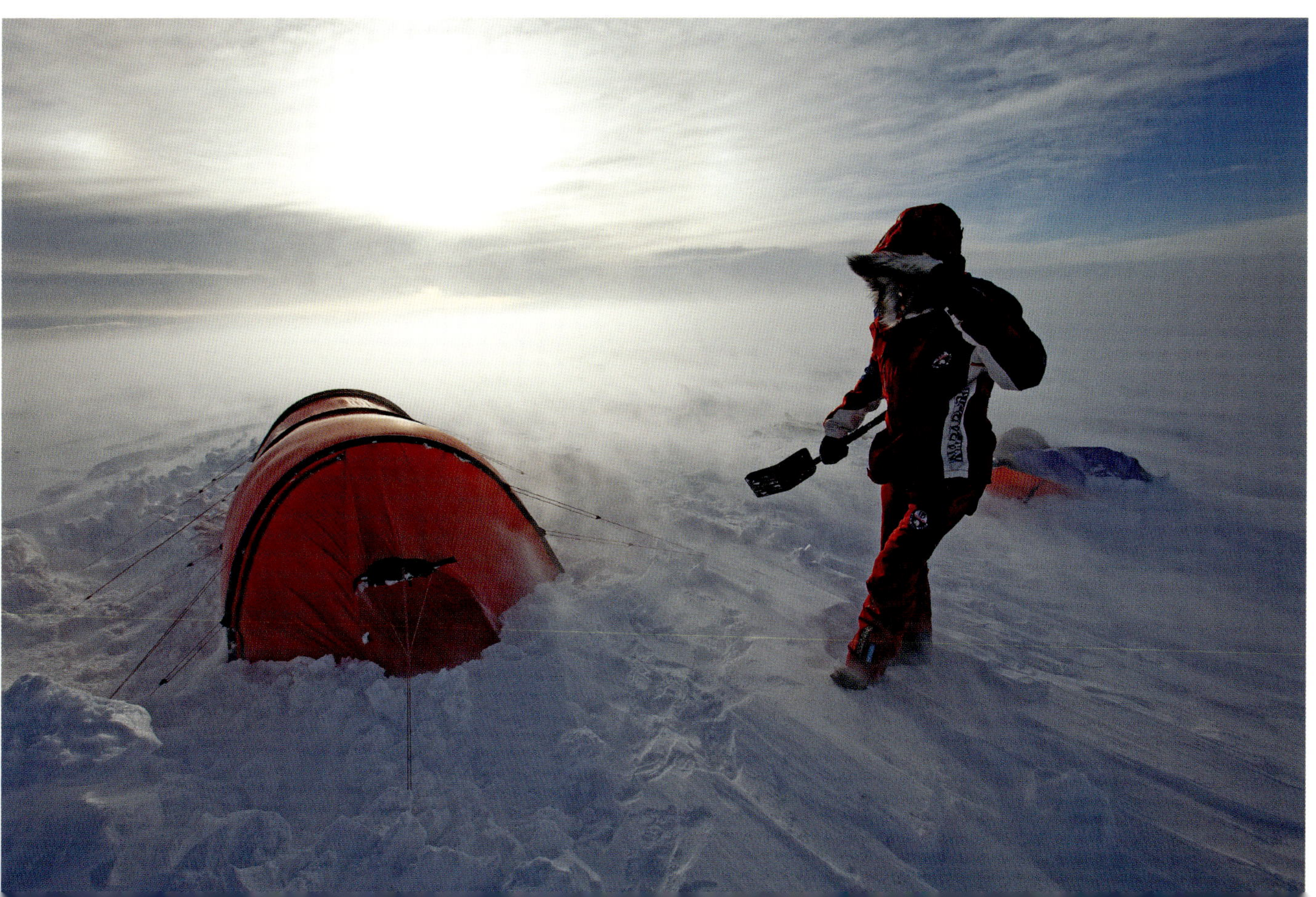

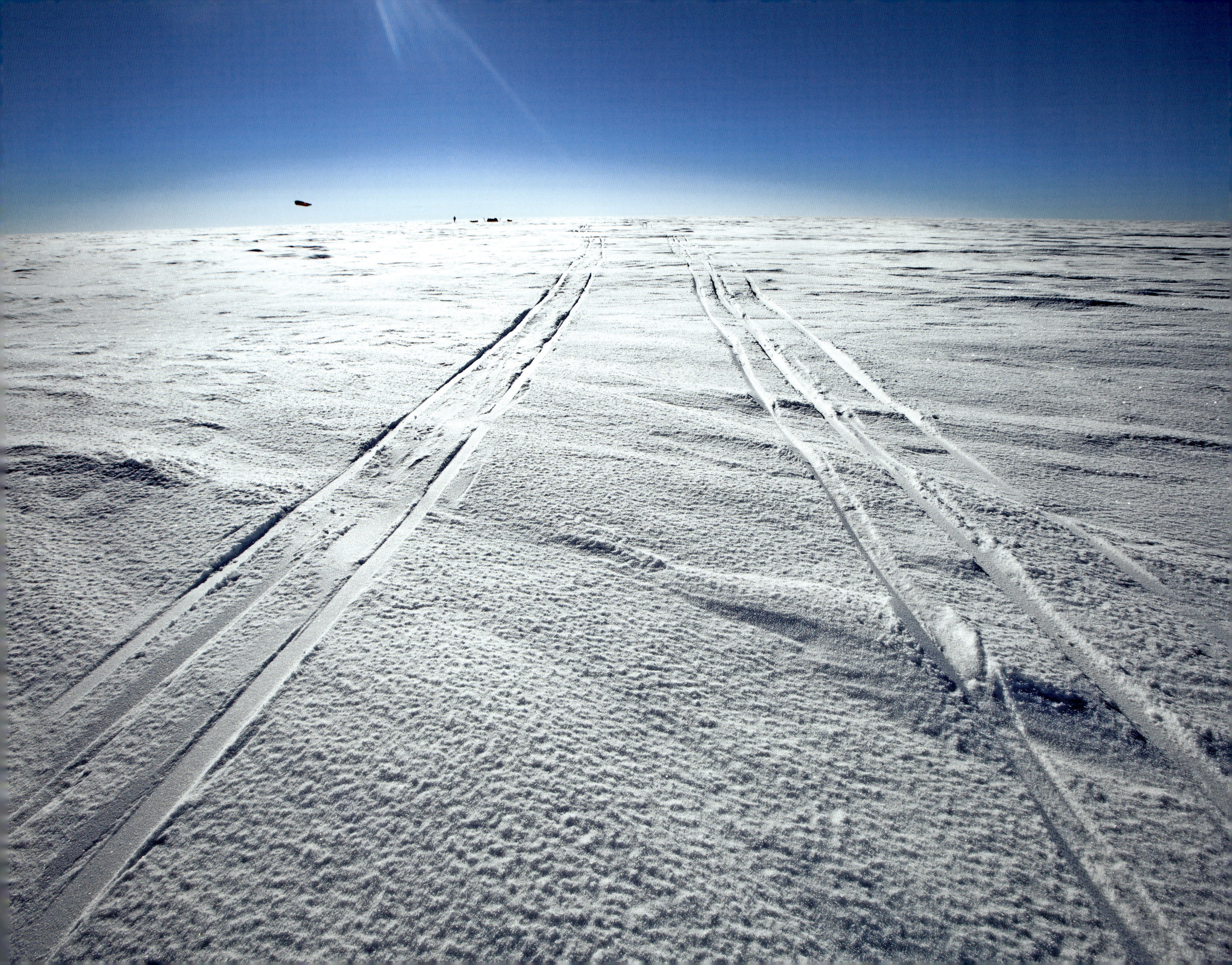

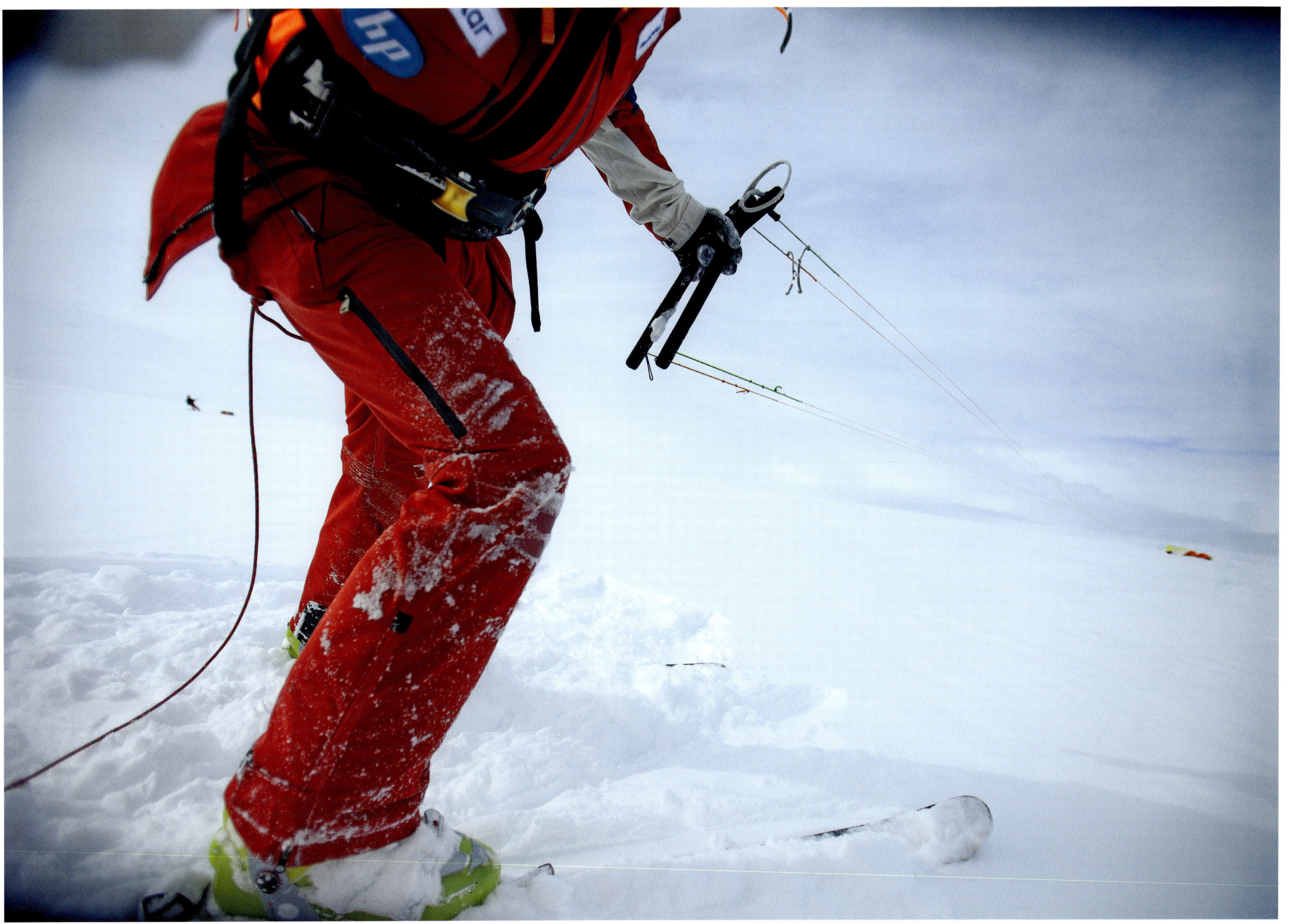

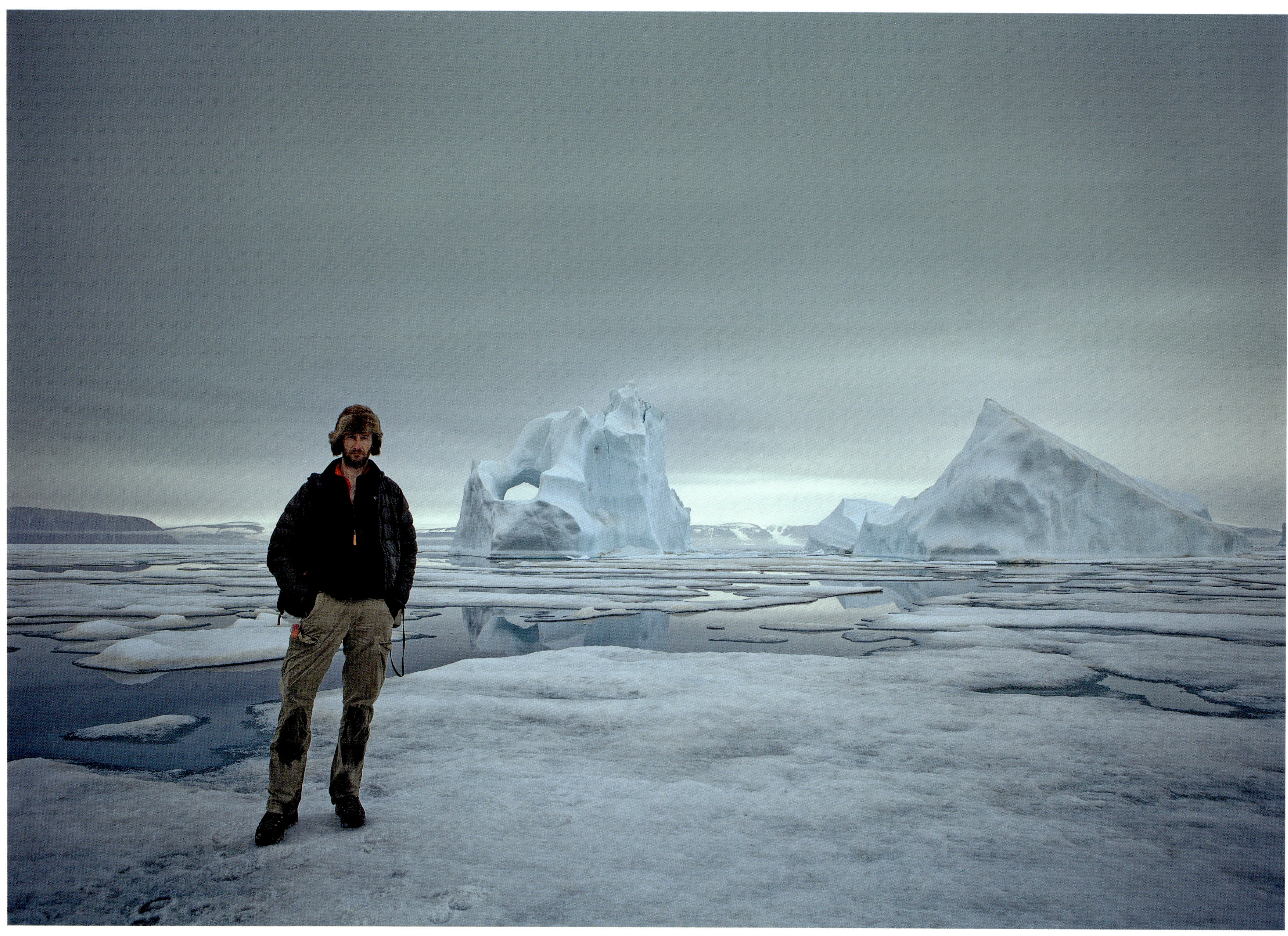

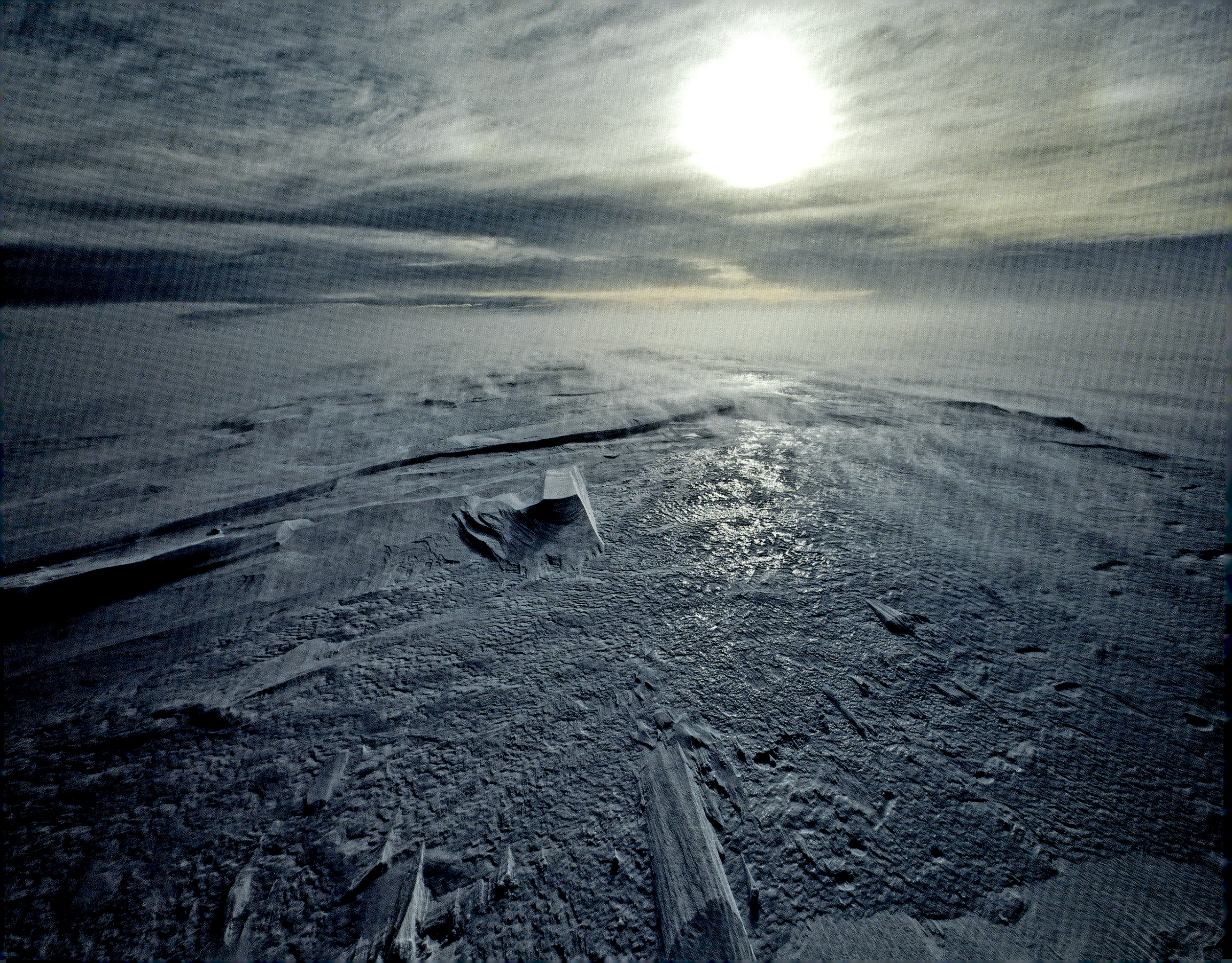

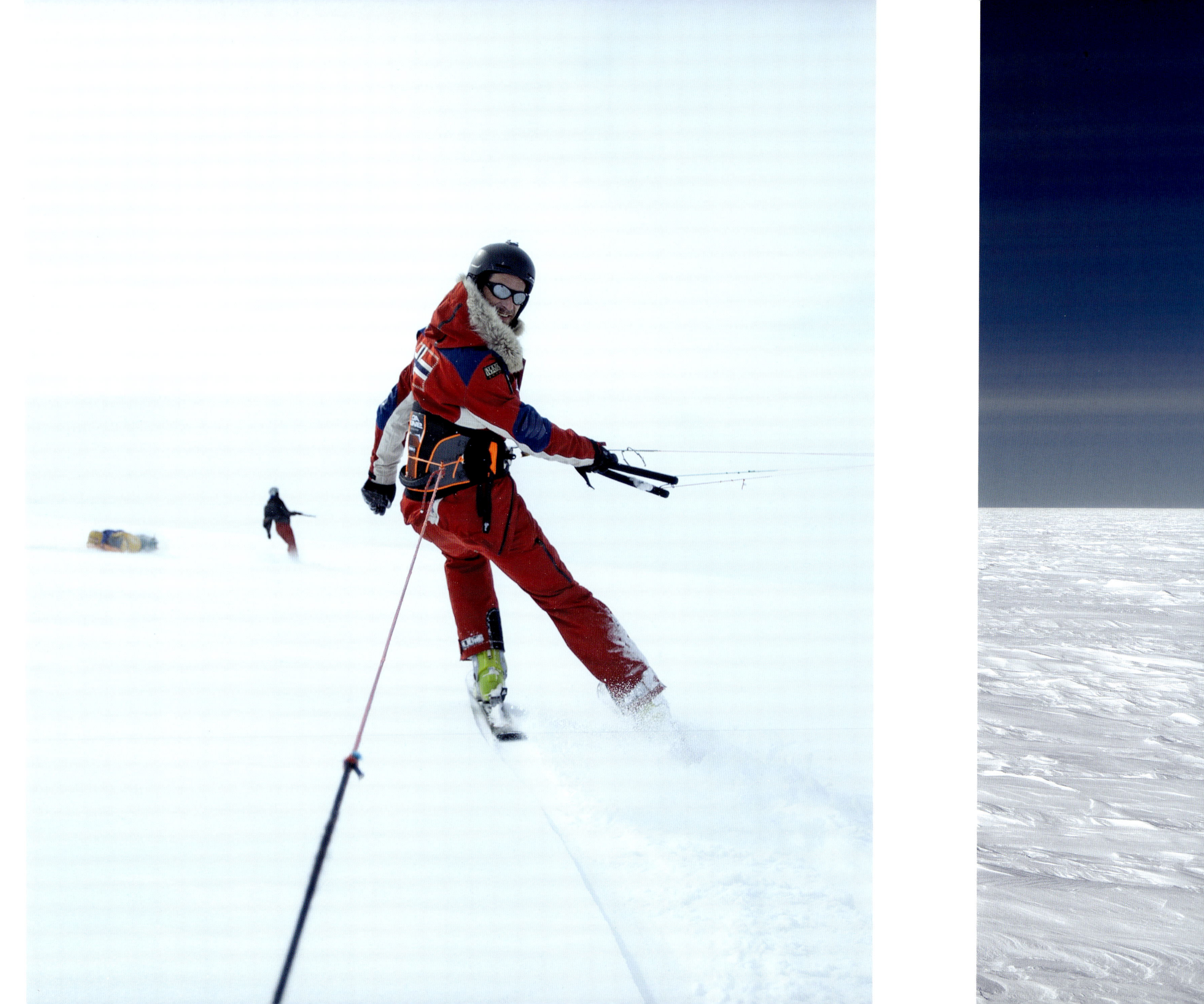

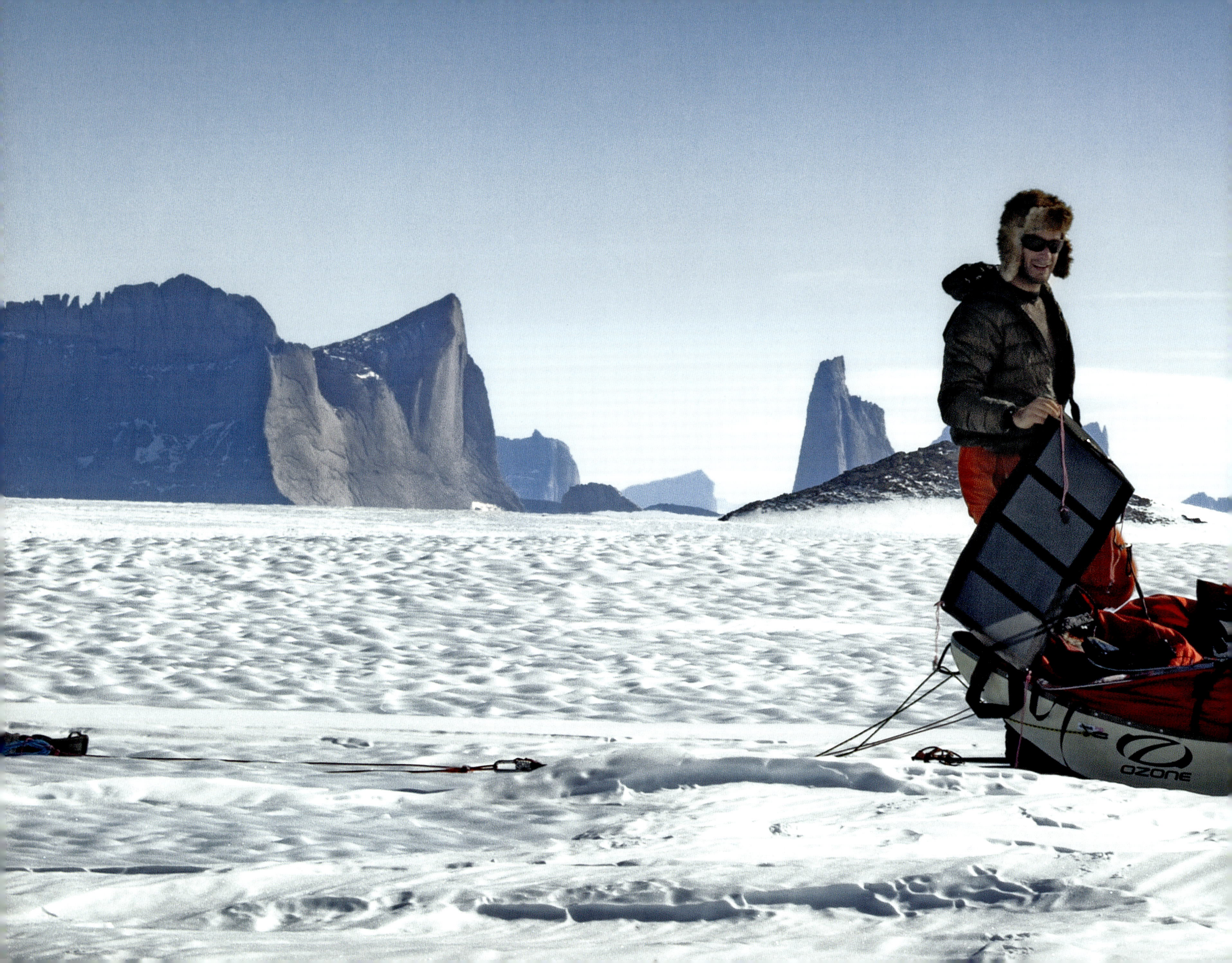
OZONE

ANTARCTICA

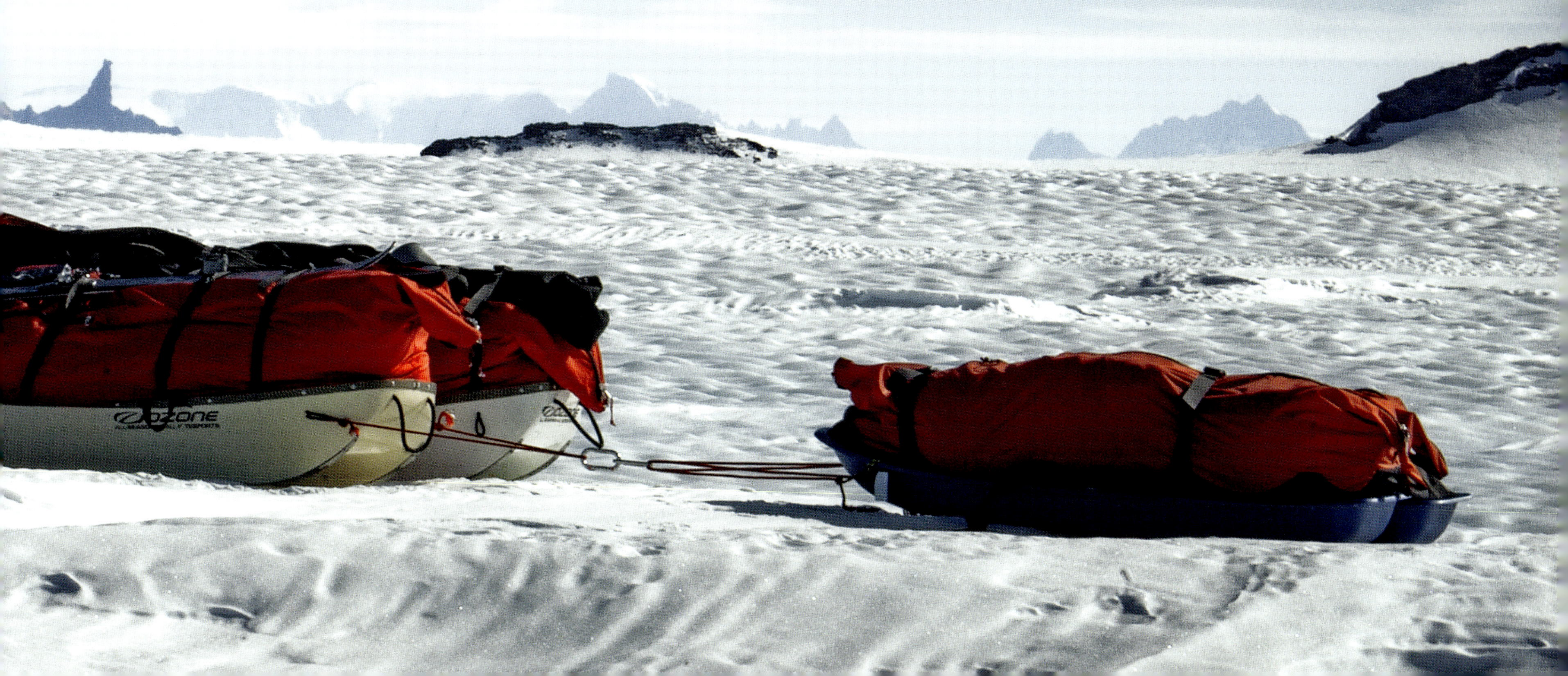

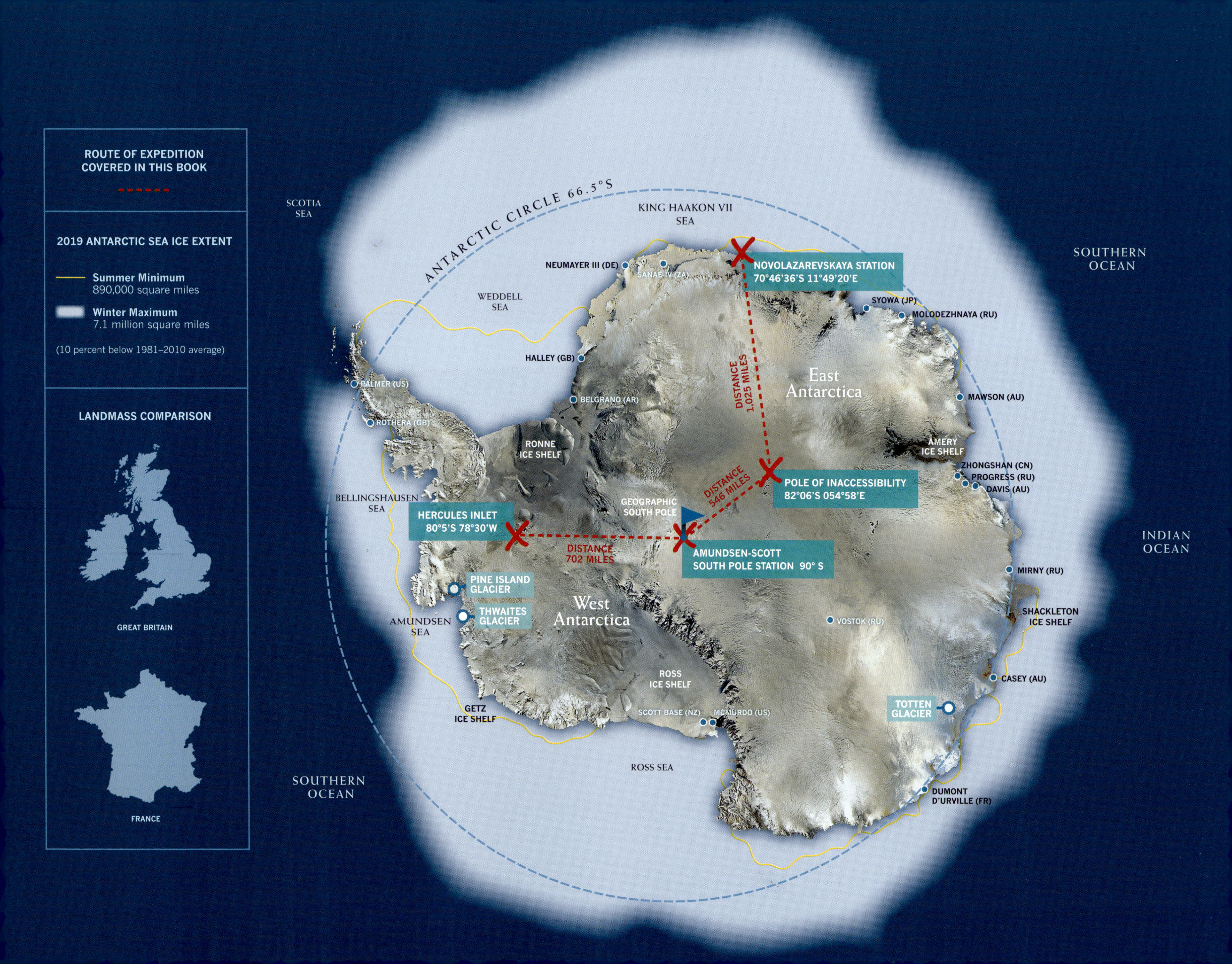

ROUTE OF EXPEDITION COVERED IN THIS BOOK

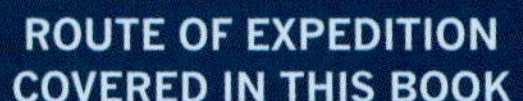

2019 ANTARCTIC SEA ICE EXTENT

Summer Minimum
890,000 square miles

Winter Maximum
7.1 million square miles

(10 percent below 1981–2010 average)

LANDMASS COMPARISON

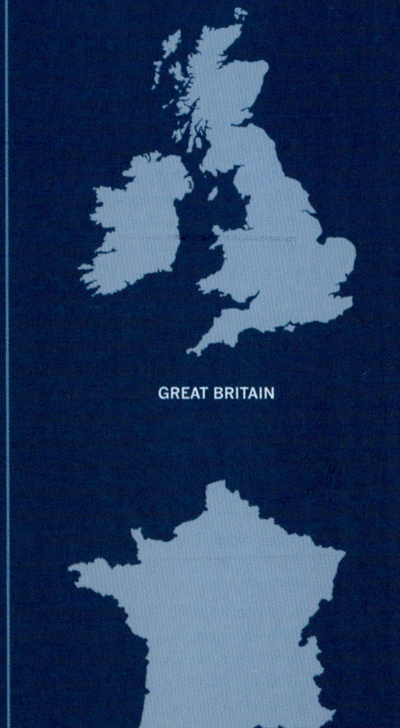

ANTARCTIC CIRCLE 66.5°S

SCOTIA SEA

KING HAAKON VII SEA

WEDDELL SEA

SOUTHERN OCEAN

INDIAN OCEAN

BELLINGSHAUSEN SEA

AMUNDSEN SEA

ROSS SEA

SOUTHERN OCEAN

East Antarctica

West Antarctica

NEUMAYER III (DE)

SANAE IV (ZA)

NOVOLAZAREVSKAYA STATION
70°46'36"S 11°49'20"E

SYOWA (JP)

MOLODEZHNAYA (RU)

HALLEY (GB)

PALMER (US)

ROTHERA (GB)

BELGRANO (AR)

DISTANCE 1,025 MILES

MAWSON (AU)

RONNE ICE SHELF

AMERY ICE SHELF

ZHONGSHAN (CN)

PROGRESS (RU)

DAVIS (AU)

POLE OF INACCESSIBILITY
82°06'S 054°58'E

DISTANCE 546 MILES

GEOGRAPHIC SOUTH POLE

HERCULES INLET
80°5'S 78°30'W

DISTANCE 702 MILES

AMUNDSEN-SCOTT SOUTH POLE STATION 90° S

PINE ISLAND GLACIER

THWAITES GLACIER

MIRNY (RU)

SHACKLETON ICE SHELF

VOSTOK (RU)

ROSS ICE SHELF

CASEY (AU)

GETZ ICE SHELF

SCOTT BASE (NZ)

MCMURDO (US)

TOTTEN GLACIER

DUMONT D'URVILLE (FR)

In the 2011–2012 austral season, my Greenland partner, Eric McNair-Landry, and I endeavored to link the Antarctic continent from east to west via two of its poles—the Pole of Inaccessibility and the South Pole—using nothing but human and wind energy: on skis and kites. At 2,500 miles, this would be a first. The trip threw everything at us—the good, the bad, and the ugly. I lost part of toes to frostbite and gathered wind data from areas of the interior that had never seen a human footprint. After 84 days, we landed our kites one final time at the western edge of the continent, an area called Hercules Inlet. This was the centenary year of Roald Amundsen's and Robert Falcon Scott's discovery of the South Pole. The following excerpts are from my journey during the first part of that trip.

Riders of the Storm

Day 51, December 25, 2011
81°30'193" S, 050°44'931" E
Elevation 12,175 feet

"They're here," I said. Eric responded with a drowsy voice from inside his sleeping bag: "Direction?" "Due north," I replied. "We're good to go." It was 1:30 a.m. We had shut down early, but I did not manage to fall asleep before midnight. At the time, it was dead calm, the kind that screams in your ears. Deep on the Antarctic Plateau, where life has been absent for at least 35 million years, a windless day can be oppressive, its silence deafening. And when your chosen mode of transportation relies on a kite, waiting for wind can feel like water-drop torture. That is especially true when the clock is ticking, as prescribed by the calculus of daily food rations: a day is a day, travel or not.

Winds are ubiquitous on the Antarctic ice, but that doesn't mean they're always there. This is especially true in the austral summer, when sun energy heats up the continent, and high-pressure systems can keep air from descending with force, as they relentlessly do during the winter. With that said, summers see their share of winds too, especially with the help of topography and driven by predictable physics, namely, gravity. Cold wind has mass, which increases as the wind cools further upon descending onto an ice sheet. That wind will then follow the downsloping of terrain, just like water. Antarctica's surface is never entirely flat. Those descending winds are called katabatic, and katabatic winds are vital to kite-skiing missions.

But today, the breeze that was gently flapping the sides of the tent was not katabatic. It was a system. In 24-hour daylight, your body clock adjusts to the conditions: you travel when the winds beckon and sleep when they falter. We were 80 miles from the first stop on our 2,500-mile cross-continental mission, a trek that would cover two poles—the Pole of Inaccessibility (POI) and the South Pole—before reaching the end of the continental mass on the opposite coast at Hercules Inlet. This journey would be done without support, using nothing but human and wind energy. On this Christmas Day, while much of the world gathered around a warm meal, we knew that we faced the head of a storm. The many days lost to dead-calm stillness had left us with little choice but to ride it. By the time we cooked breakfast, melted water, and packed our tent, the wind was blowing snow and still building. The cloud ceiling was low, and the temperature hovered at -22°F, outside of windchill. By 3:30 a.m., we were clipped into our 13-meter kites, and we took off.

On the ice, an oncoming storm brings a new set of variables, and riding the head of one creates a nervous energy that gamblers would know: the uncertainty keeps you alert. The wind came up fast and strong within our first hour. By 4:30 a.m., we switched to our smallest kite, the six meter, which shot up like rockets into the sky. The visibility quickly dropped and within minutes, it was clear that the storm was on us. Gusts grew to 40 knots, and the temperature dropped to -85°F windchill. Visibility was down to 120 feet, and we vigilantly kept each other in sight. Getting separated now could be lethal to at least one of us—the one without the tent. Periodically, a sled would flip after hitting a ridge from a bad angle at speed. This would force one of us to an abrupt stop as the other faded in the blowing snow. One hour of tempting fate in this mayhem and we were done.

We set up the tent while the storm intensified. Eric started digging an ice cave, just in case. But the snowdrift and cold ended that project. Meanwhile, I brought the stove inside and made some tea while getting blood back to my extremities. This was day 51, and I had developed a serious frostbite on my right big toe.

Perennially well below freezing, Antarctica's interior is covered with a thick sheet of ice two miles deep. Its surface is mostly rough and hard, carved by the dominant winds into shapes called sastrugi. In Greenland, my ski boots had worked like a charm during a 1,429-mile crossing of that superb ice sheet. But here in Antarctica, my downwind toe got traumatized by the constant pounding in the toe box, suffering the unrelenting assault of these hard ridges. And skiing with a kite pulling in one direction for months at a time does little in the way of recovery; it's like endlessly edging a ski turn around a mountain. The trauma resulted in swelling and liquid that grew into a cold injury. Necrosis set in, inching its way up the toe. You'd think that would be a reason to quit. But the months of preparation, the pressure of fundraising and sponsor relations, and the blind ambition to succeed had made me gamble a digit and forge ahead with close monitoring and adjustment to my systems. Today, the toe was stable.

While the storm raged outside, the temperature inside the tent rose to a balmy 53.6°F, thanks to the sun's high summer angle beating down on the fabric. It was 7:00 a.m. We hung our clothes to dry and buried ourselves inside our sleeping bags for another long slumber. On this day, we had covered a meager 19.76 miles, but we had finally crossed the 621-mile mark.

Boxing Day Pin Down

Day 52, December 26, 2011
81°30'193" S, 050°44'931" E
Elevation 12,175 feet

In the dream the owl landed next to me and remained close, its big, yellow eyes peering into mine. I was seated and surprised how large a bird it was. More surprising even was our ability to communicate. Eventually, the bird moved closer, and I eased it onto my knees. I asked whether he was territorial and roamed around here, and if we could be friends. He said, "Yes." When I asked him what he liked to eat, he responded, "Noodles." And then I woke up.

We'll be denied our final approach one more time today, as the storm rages outside, displaying the fiercest weather we have yet experienced on this trip. We had hoped to rise at 4:00 a.m. and hit the trail by 6:00 a.m. to close the gap with our first milestone of this 2,500-mile mission, but the conditions held us back. Only 60 miles away, the POI could conservatively be reached in five to six hours with decent weather. But strong winds were shaking the tent violently. At 4:00 a.m., I opened the flap and confirmed that these were not traveling conditions. The sun was in hiding, and blowing snow reduced visibility down to 100 feet or so. The windchill set a morose tone for our advance at about -76°F, especially as the tent remained chilled as well. I did not bother waking Eric.

I checked an hour later, and the wind was only growing stronger. By 7:00 a.m., I gave up and fell asleep for good amid the roaring and violent growl of the building storm. Buried inside my sleeping bag, I did not emerge before noon. Eric was still sleeping. I stepped outside for a few seconds, just enough to stick the wind meter in the air. At 44.8 knots, it had come down some, but this surely was not the strongest gust. Snowbanks had built around the tent, half burying the sleds. We were surrounded by a raging blanket of blowing snow, about five feet high, that swallowed any visibility around us. Within seconds of being out, snow was sticking to my tent clothes and turning me into a Boxing Day snowman. Drift was filling the tent's vestibule. I dove back inside my bag.

From there, I pulled the elastic fastener around my neck, my rabbit-fur hat covering my ears, and watched the steam explode out of my nose toward the dancing socks and gloves hanging from the ceiling's dry line, rocked as they were by the incessant shake. It's almost hypnotic. The displacement of air inside from

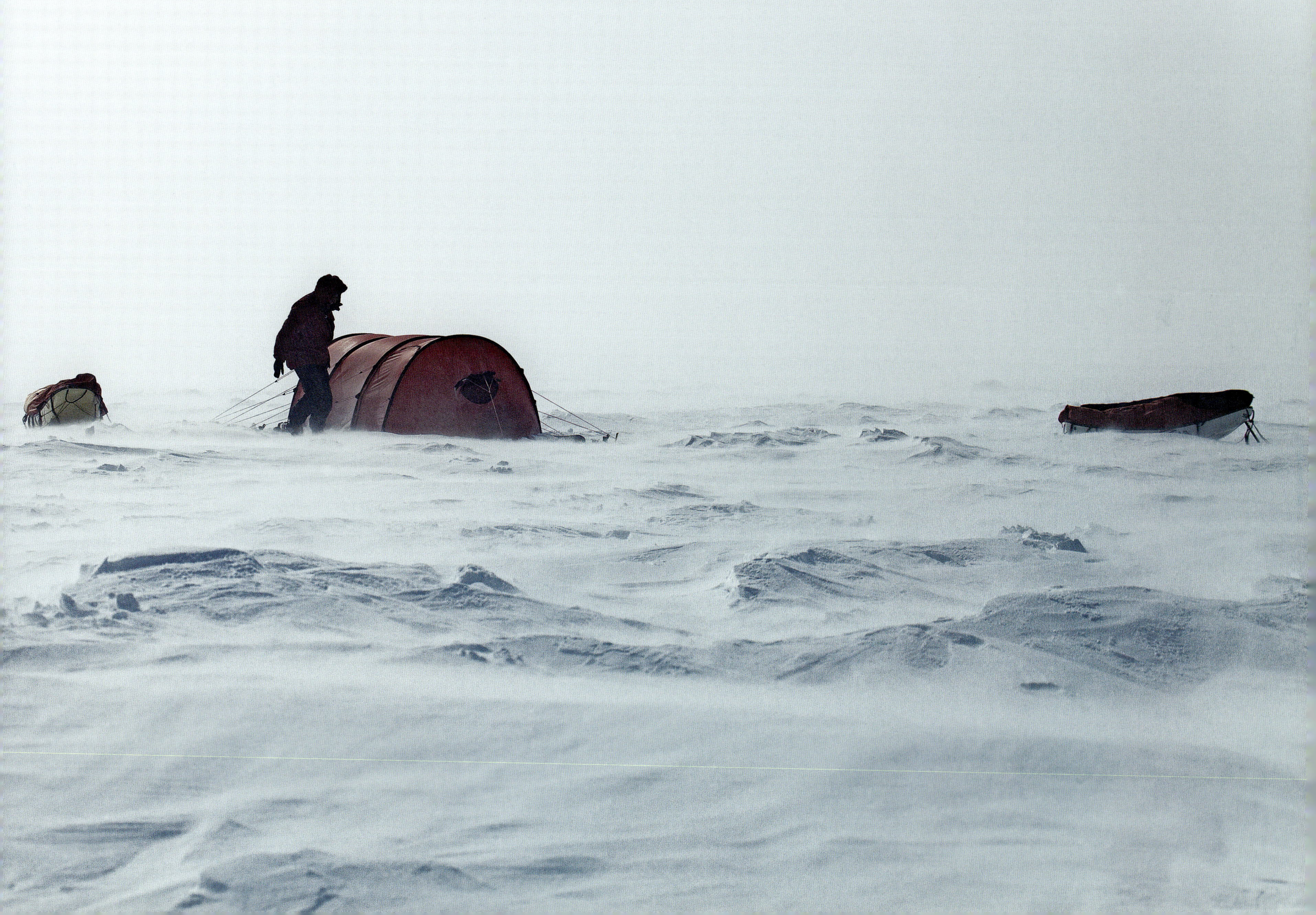

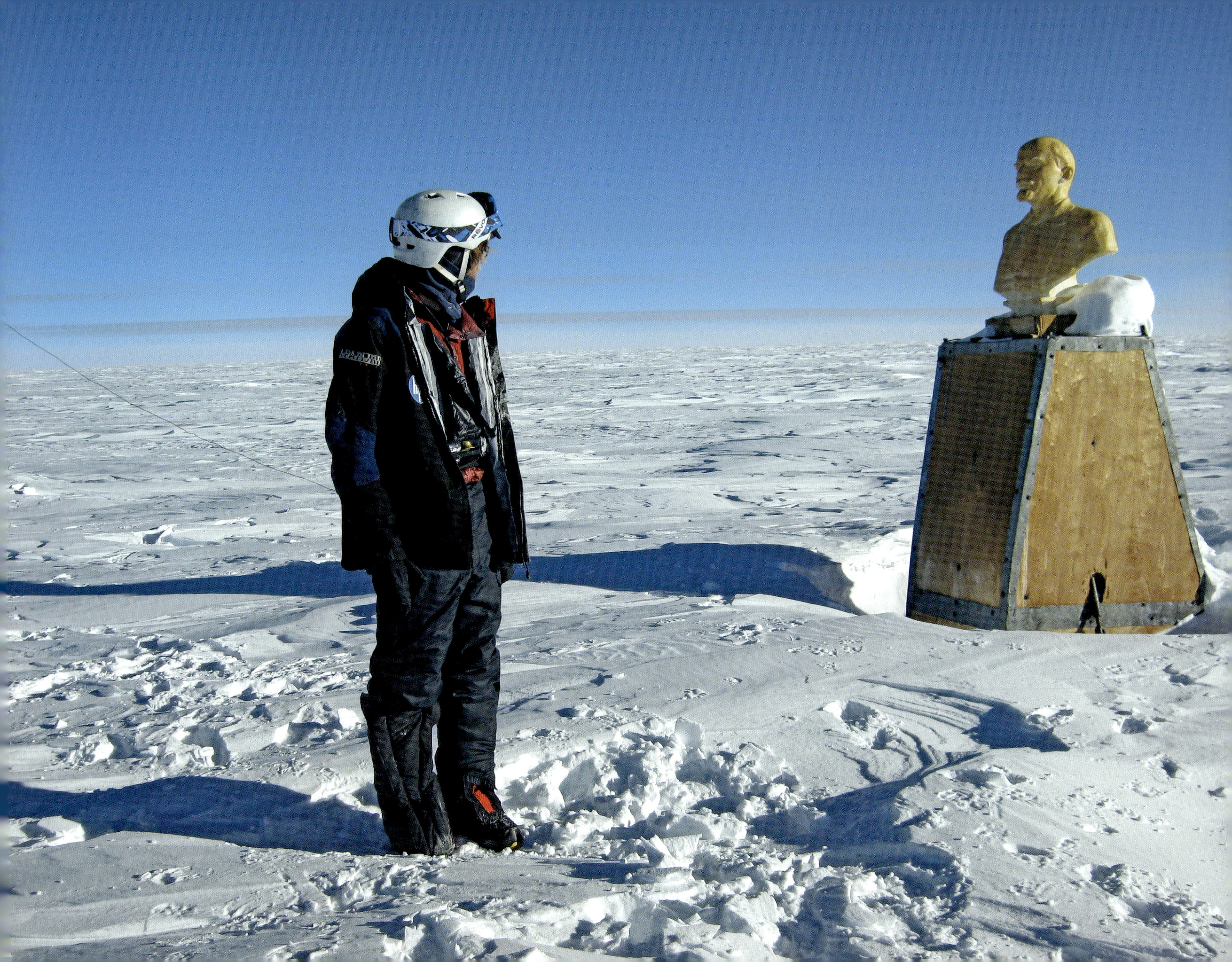

the shaking of the tent's walls makes the steam dodge erratically right and left in strict harmonic unity as it rises. I stared at it for most of the afternoon, making loose and abstract mileage calculations in my head. I am still holding on to the South Pole leg, but the full transcontinental crossing, ending at Hercules Inlet, is beginning to feel compromised. It ain't over until the fat lady sings, but the wind's howl outside hints that she may be warming up. We have just about a month left on the expedition to complete around 1,250 miles. The last 750 miles could be done in 10 to 12 days, given the regularity of the winds in that region. That still does not leave much room for down days, and given how hampered we have been with those, it's easy for the spirit to feel stirred, if not shaken.

Two Days Late, but Santa Delivers

Day 53, December 27, 2011
82°06'696" S, 055°01'951" E
Elevation 12,220 feet

The day started bleak. I woke Eric up at 5:30 a.m., as the wind had dropped considerably, still holding a punch. We were excited to finally get out and make some miles. If conditions held, we could close the 60-mile gap in four, maybe five hours. But during the short time it took to clear the tent of the snowbanks that had accumulated from the storm, the winds were faltering—our hopes along with them. We set off with the big guns, the 14-meter Yakuzas, but within the first hour, our speed kept decreasing. It was disheartening and set the tone for a hardworking day.

Given the pattern, the winds would surely drop, and then what? Additionally, temperatures remained cold at -31°F without windchill. The storm had shredded the ice, and the sastrugi were vicious. My legs were burning; my toes were cold; and the short night was getting to me. The newly fixed binding that had broken last week kept coming undone. I was not having a good day. By 2:00 p.m., I could no longer get the kite up in the air, so weak was the wind. Eric assisted me once by throwing it in the air while I did my best to get the 260-foot lines up to find wind above us. We knew that whatever distance we didn't cover now, we'd likely have to walk. That was motivation enough for Eric to run his own kite and get it in the air; how he managed, I'll never know, but he is a light-air specialist.

Surprisingly, by 4:00 p.m. we were still going. Rather than shutting down, the wind actually built a little. We were now 20 miles from the POI. Would the conditions hold? We blew through our scheduled food break, not wanting to jinx it. This would now be like a summit approach on the mountain: you push until you get there.

By 6:30 p.m., we had been on the trail for 10 hours—our longest stretch yet. Miles had been slow through the day, but they were now picking up. We had nine miles to close the gap! I looked at the ice racing below my feet, and then at the empty vastness ahead of me, scanning the horizon, expecting a marker to appear at any moment. With five miles to go, we set down to check our bearing. Good thing, as we were 45 degrees off. We almost overshot it! We lifted off one last time and rode next to each other in formation. Within minutes, I raised a fist in the air and screamed. I looked over at Eric, who was doing the same. Ahead of us, sticking out faintly from the horizon, was a marker; we sped toward it. The rattling from the tall sastrugi that we were now crossing at a 90-degree angle no longer mattered; the burn in my legs was forgotten; and the adrenaline actually warmed my toes. We were closing in. The distance separating us from what I had so long planned for was fading away. We could now make out two thin, derelict communications towers and the remains of a drilling platform.

At 7:31 p.m., Eric and I closed the gap and reached the distinctive marker of the Antarctic POI. Sticking out from the rising ice sheet were the remaining four feet of a chimney from the buried Soviet-era station that was built there in December 1957. The base was abandoned a few weeks later, but first a bust of Vladimir Lenin was affixed atop the structure. It has remained there to this day, forlorn and frozen, facing Moscow. The rest of the base was somewhere below our skis. We passed the tower, made a slow downwind turn, and simultaneously set down our kites.

The farthest point from any coast, the POI is effectively the heart of Antarctica. It is regarded as the most difficult spot to reach in complete autonomy. We are only the fourth group to reach that point since the Russians left 54 years ago, and the first to do so without resupplies or the help of motorized transportation. Fifty-three days, and we were there. Eleven hours on the trail, and 60 miles later, the Antarctic winds relented and honored our effort by letting us close the gap with our heads held high. We hugged and laughed. My lips were seized by the biting cold, but I mumbled something about accomplishment in life being so fleeting that it must be celebrated. We were giddy. I set up a tripod to freeze the moment in time. Because a photo, you see, is never fleeting.

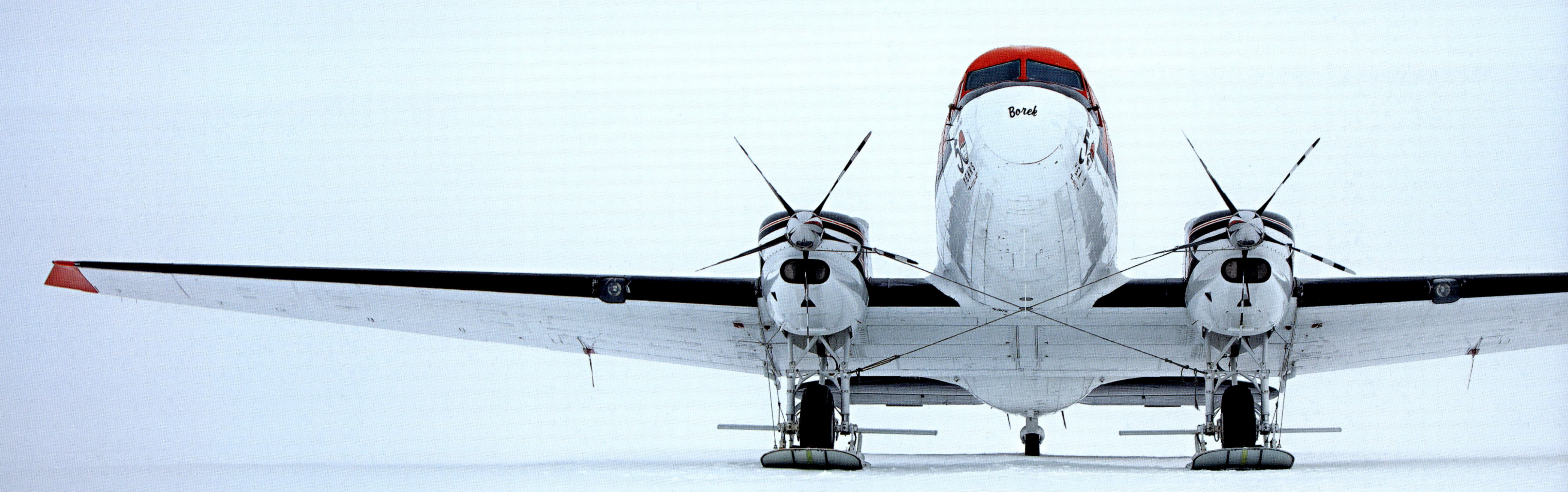
Borek

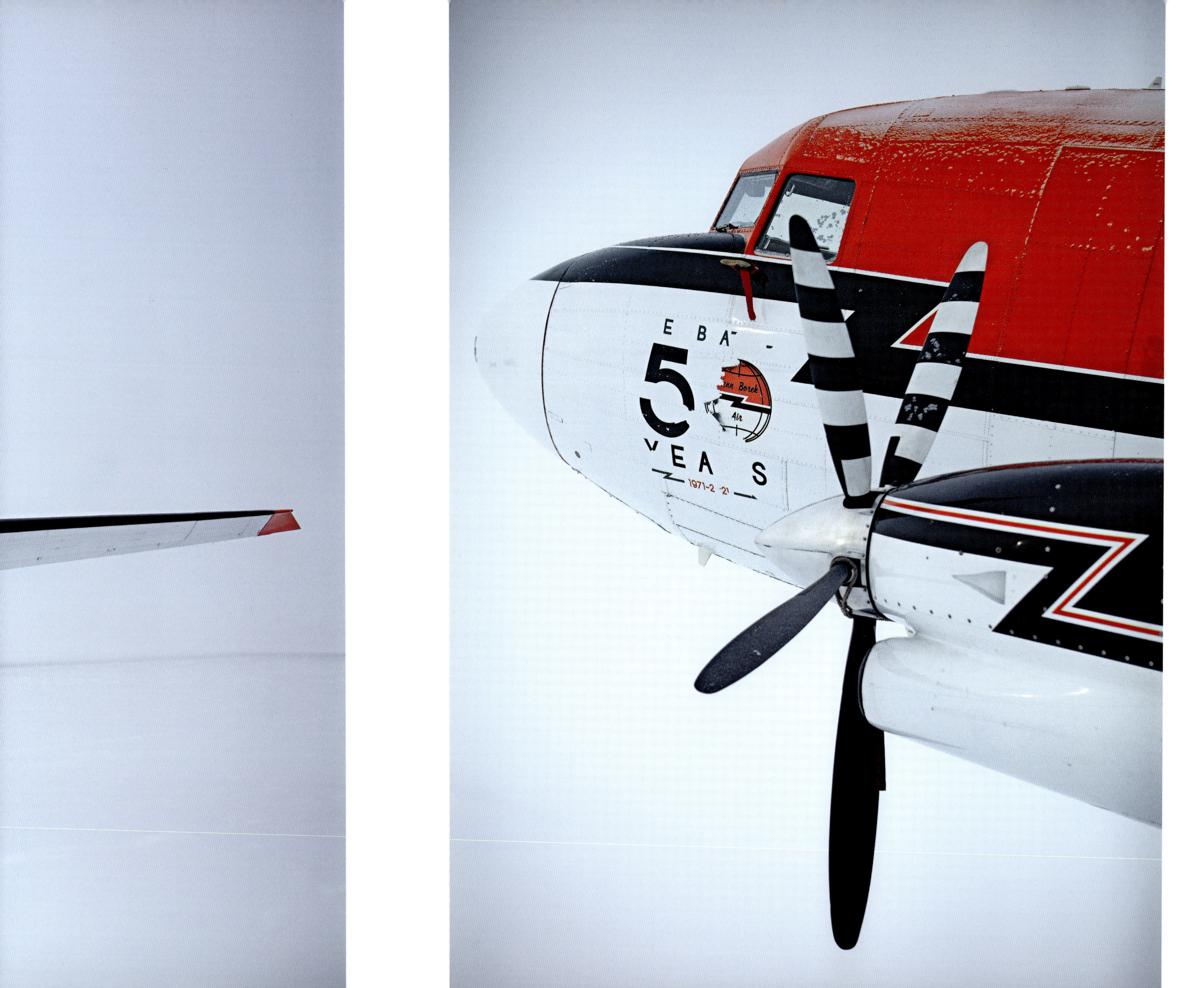
Borek
Air

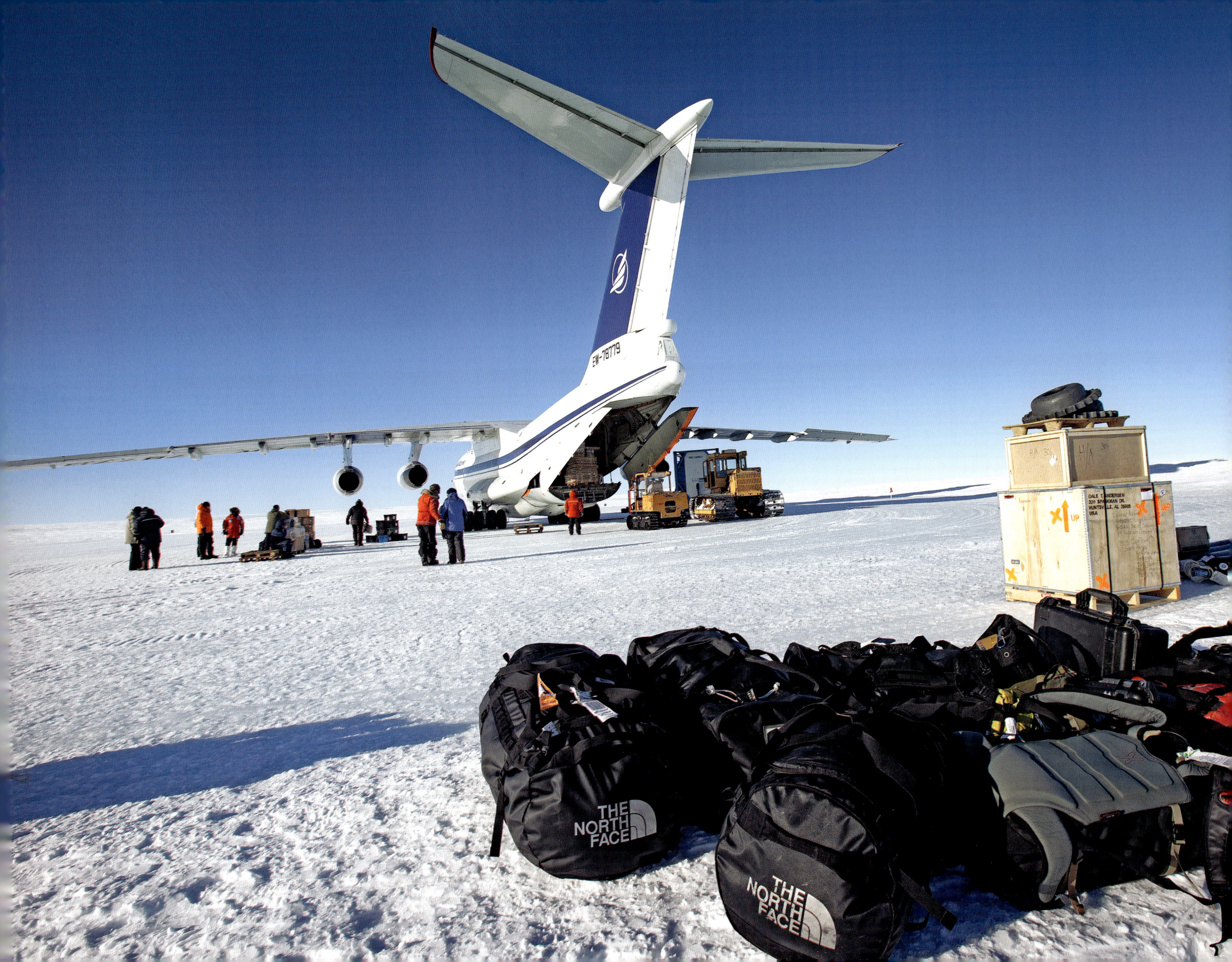
EW-78779
THE NORTH FACE
THE NORTH FACE

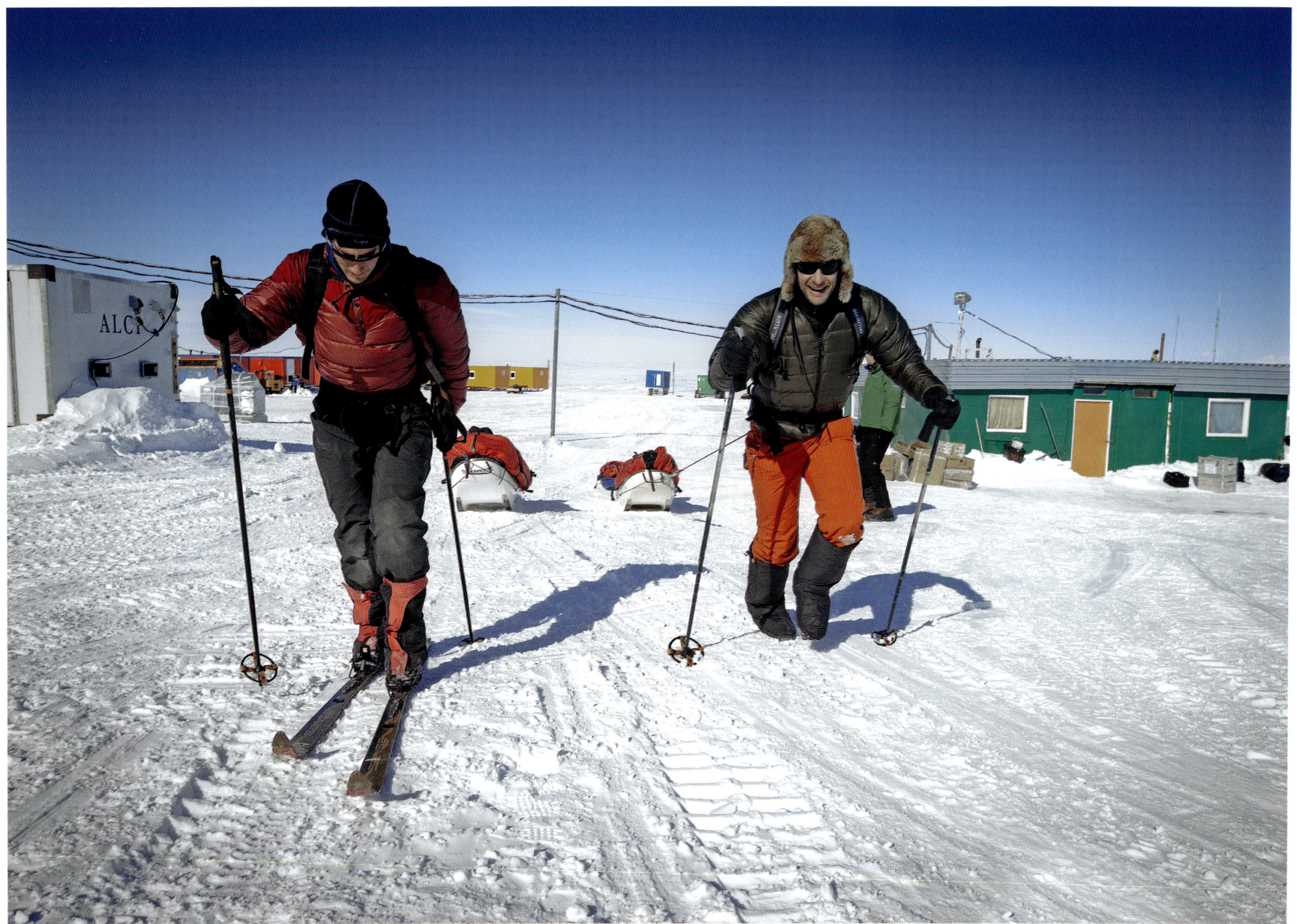
ALCI

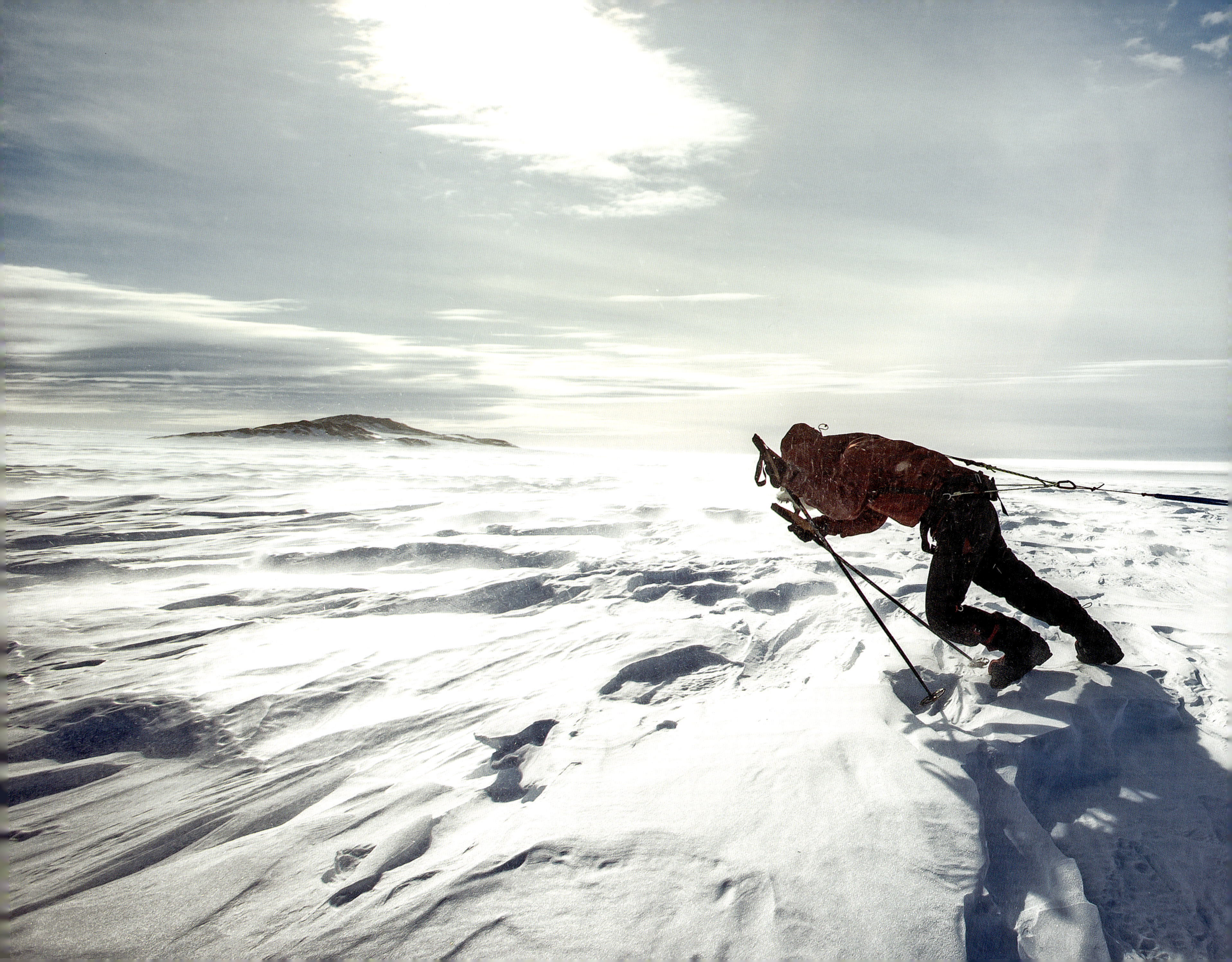

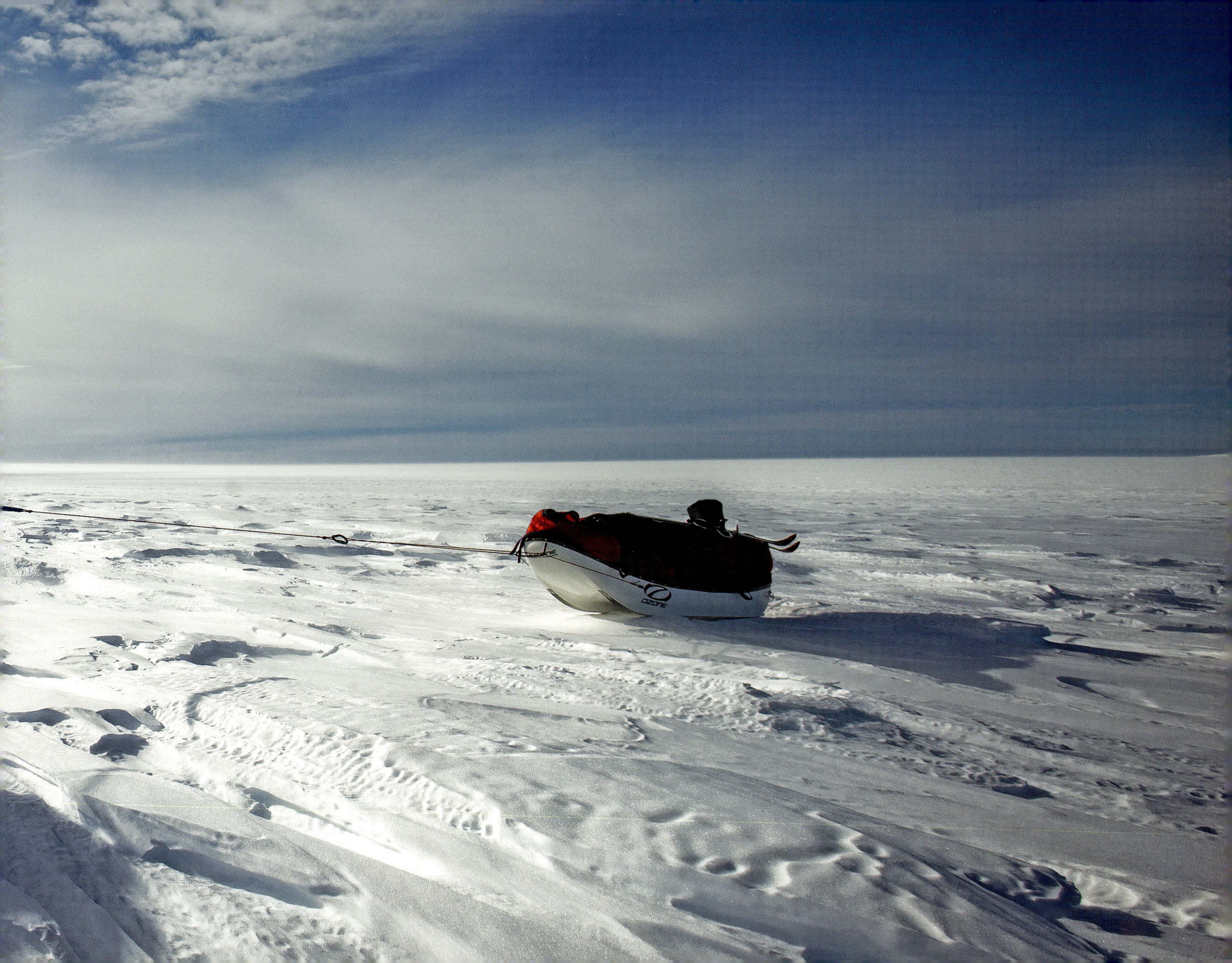
ozone

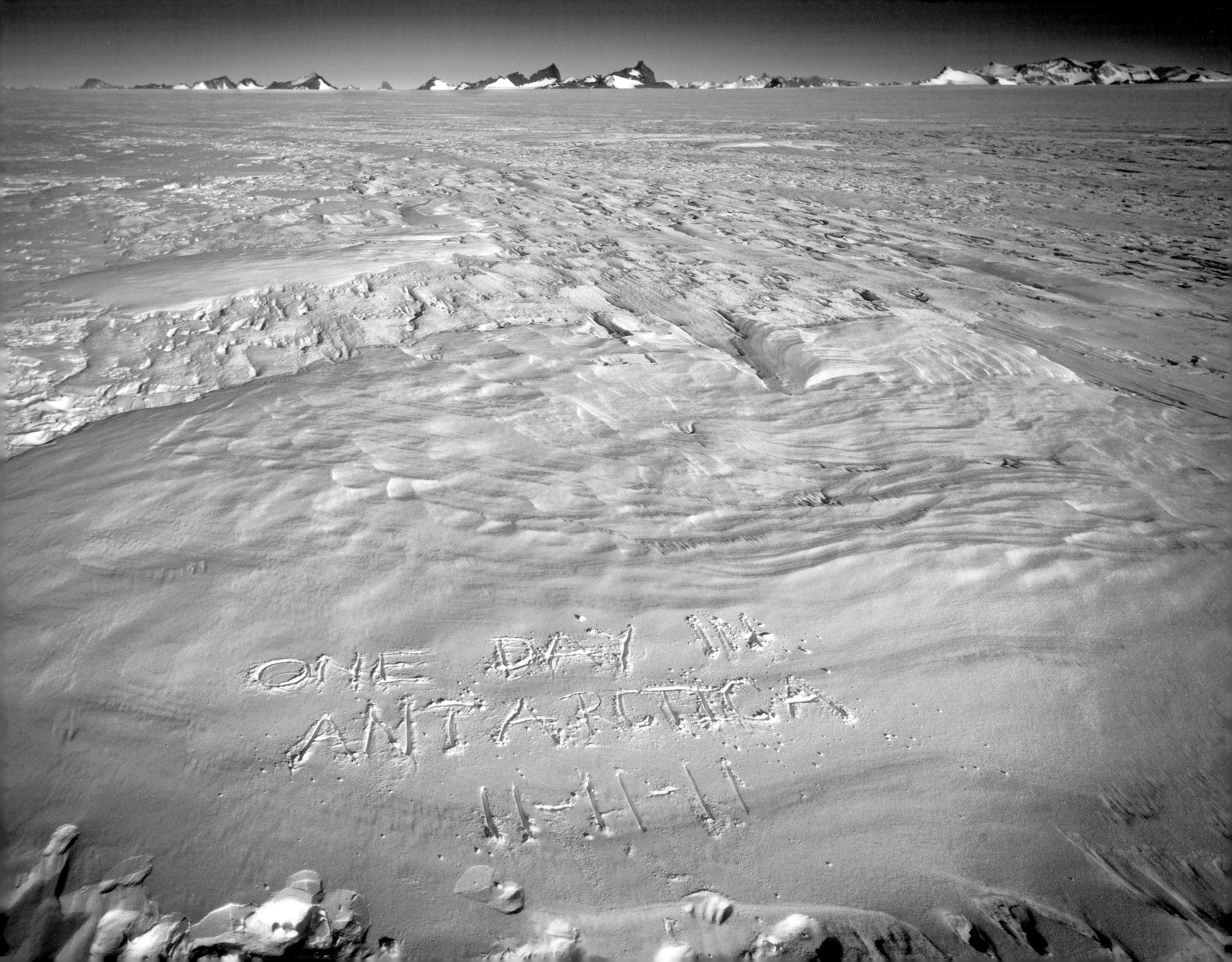
ONE DAY IN
ANTARCTICA
11-11-11

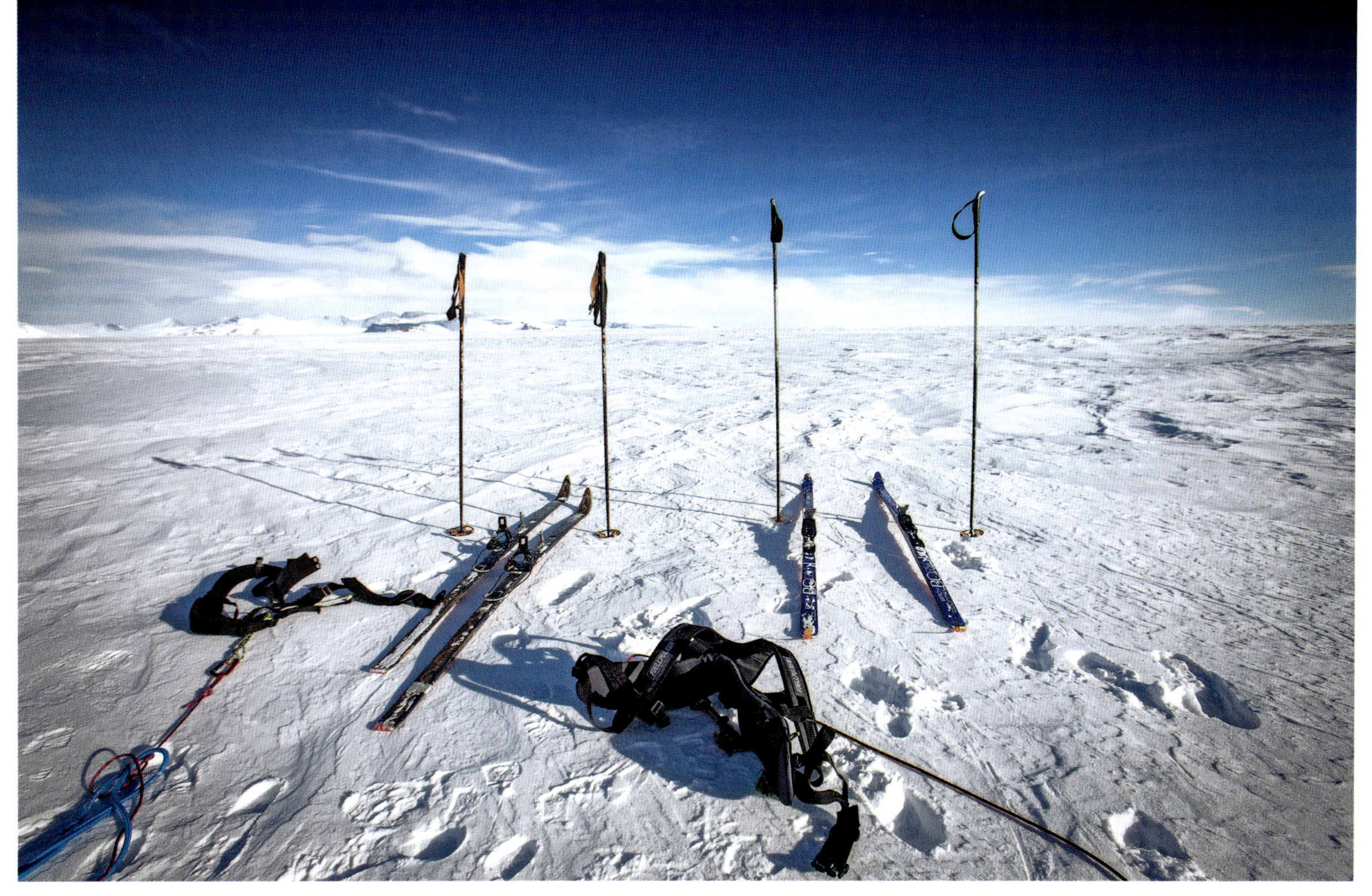

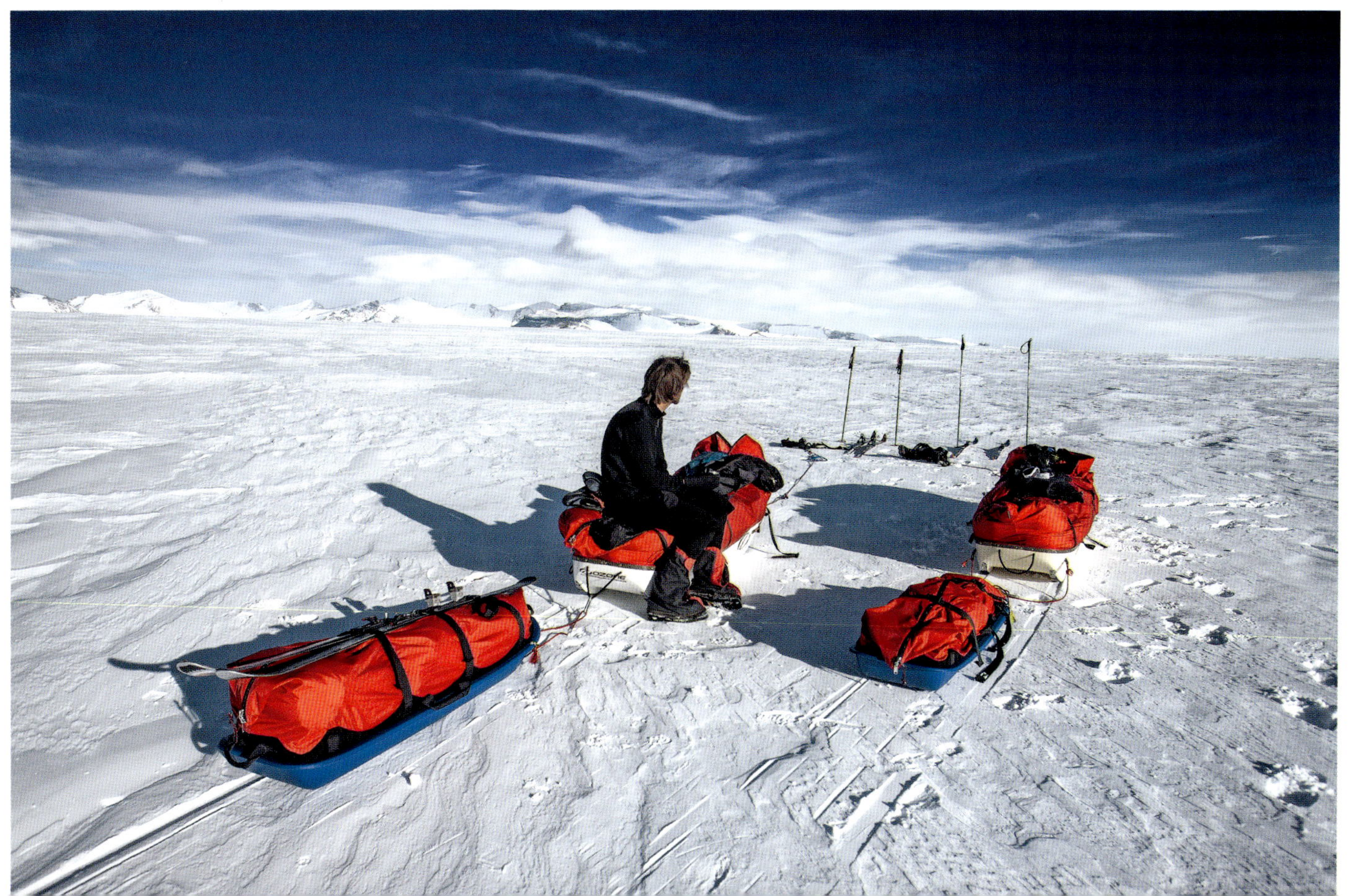

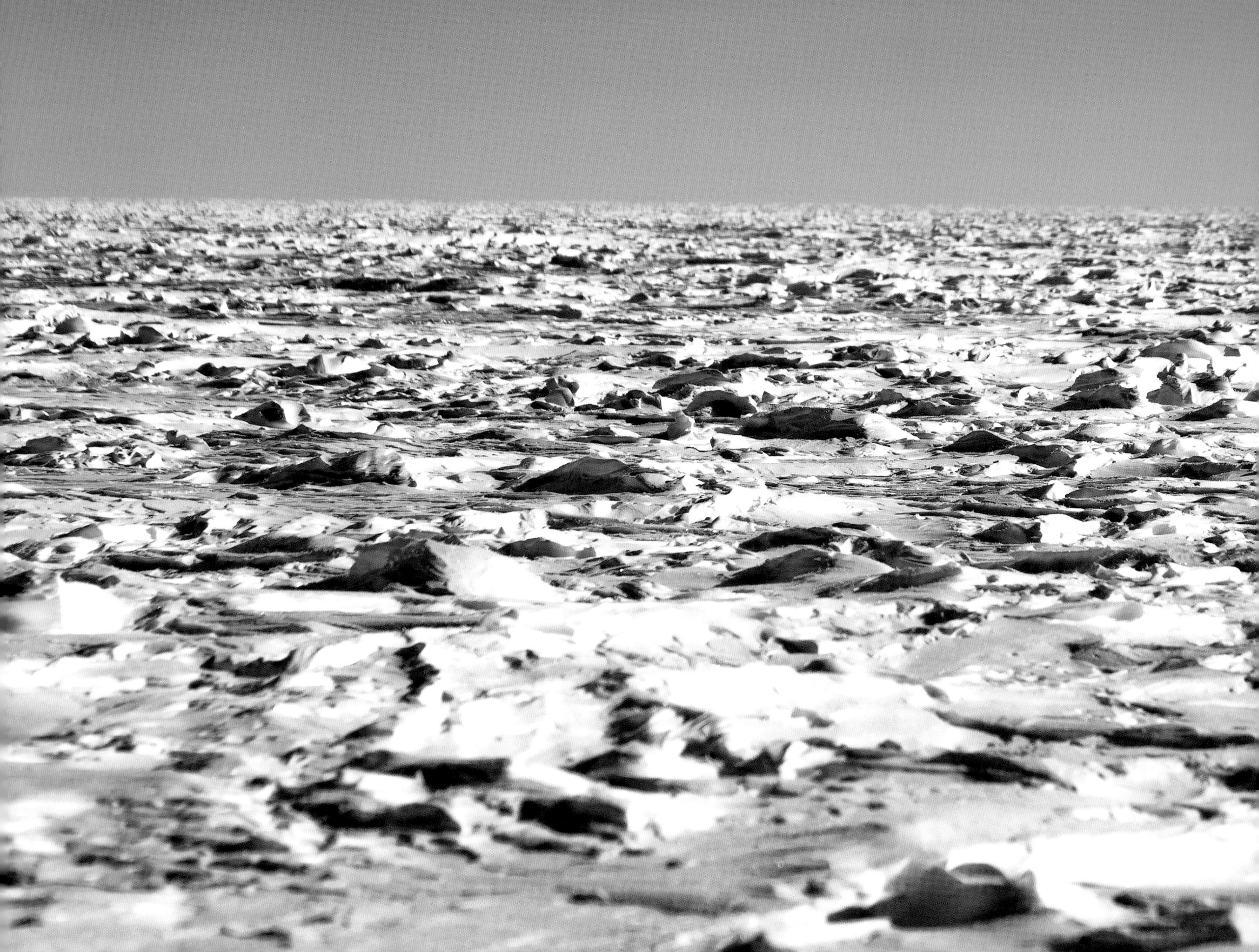

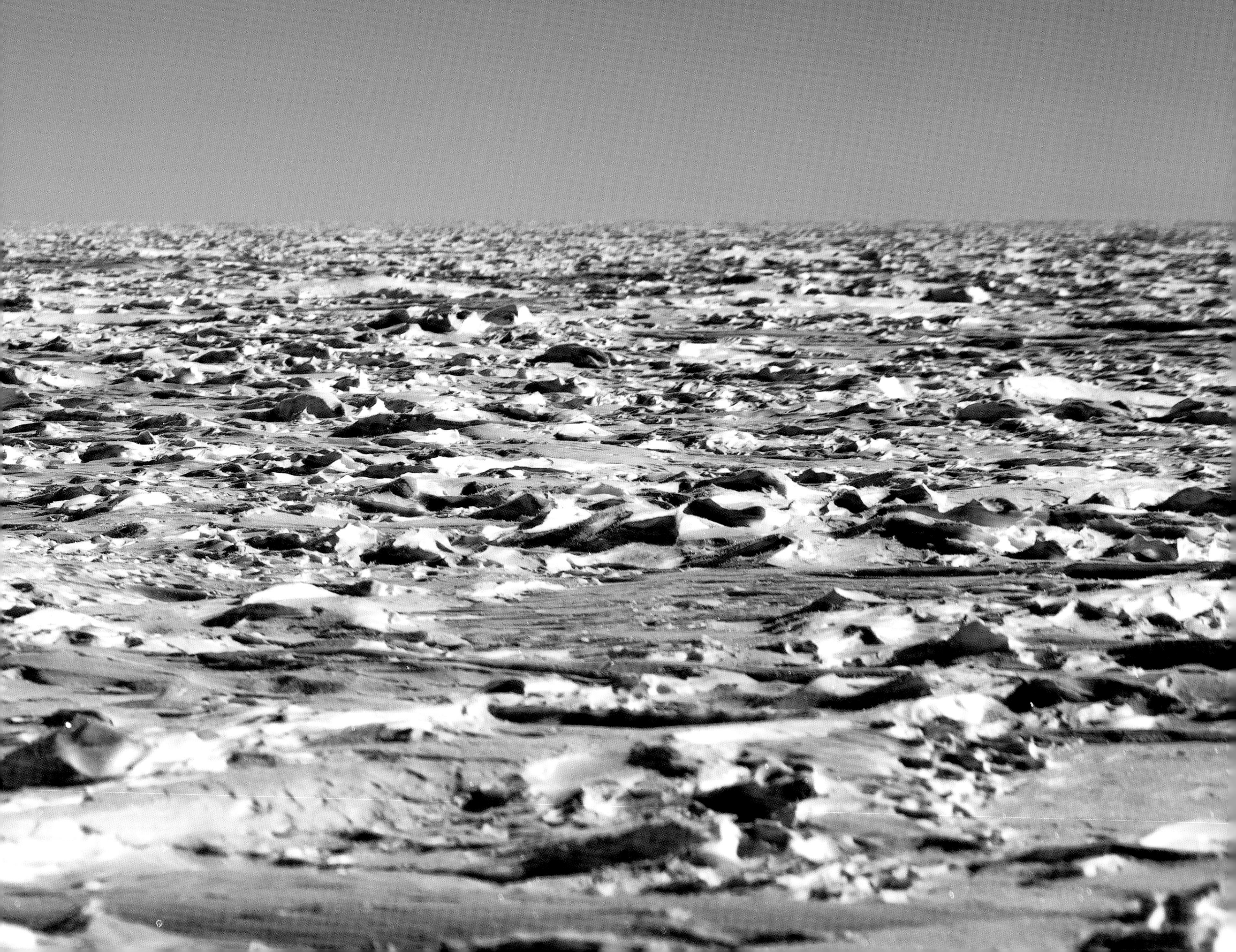

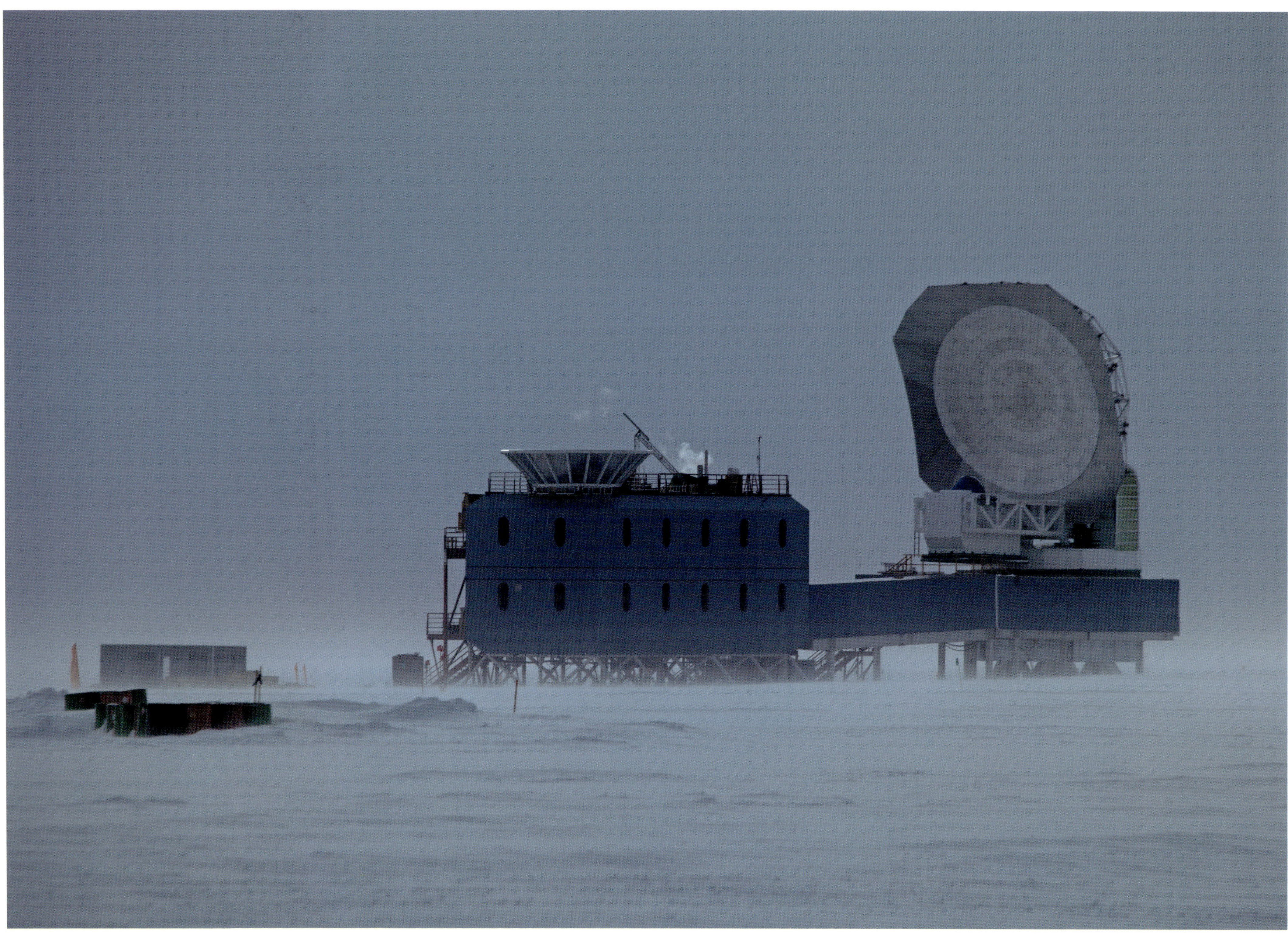

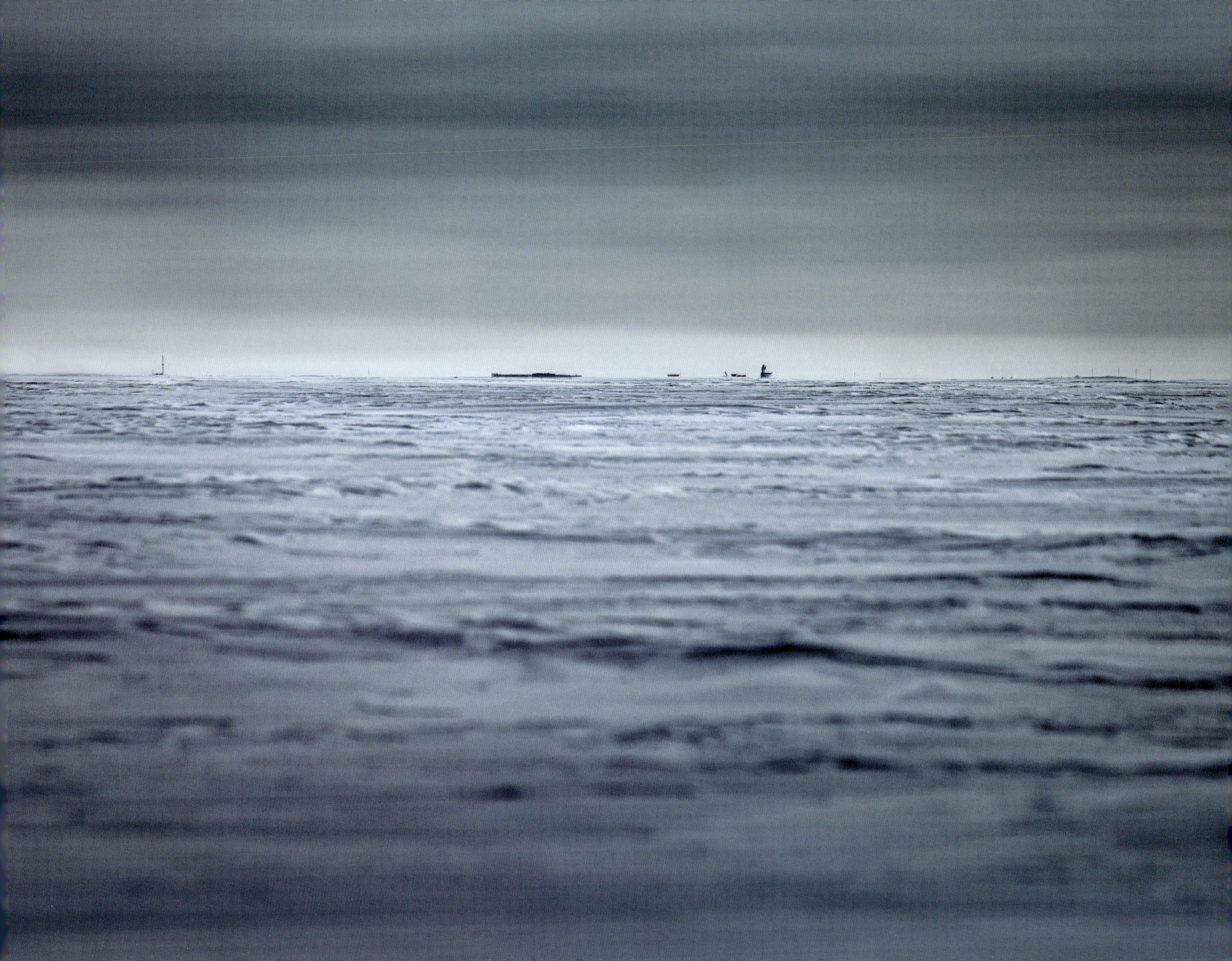

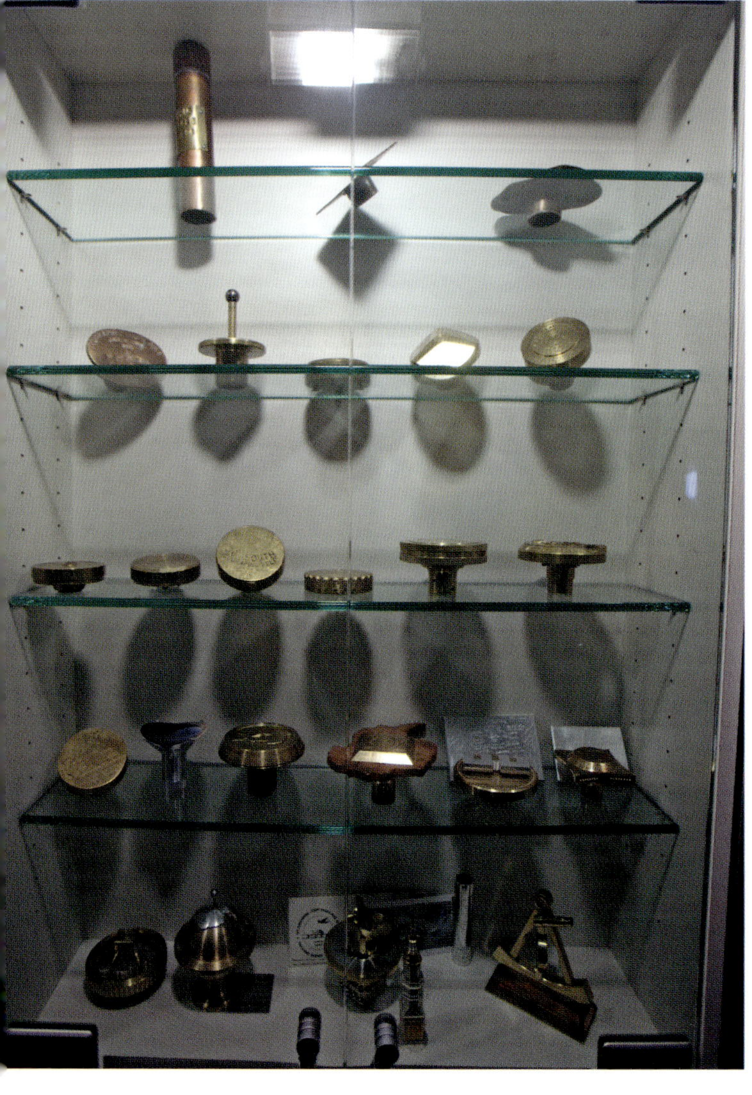

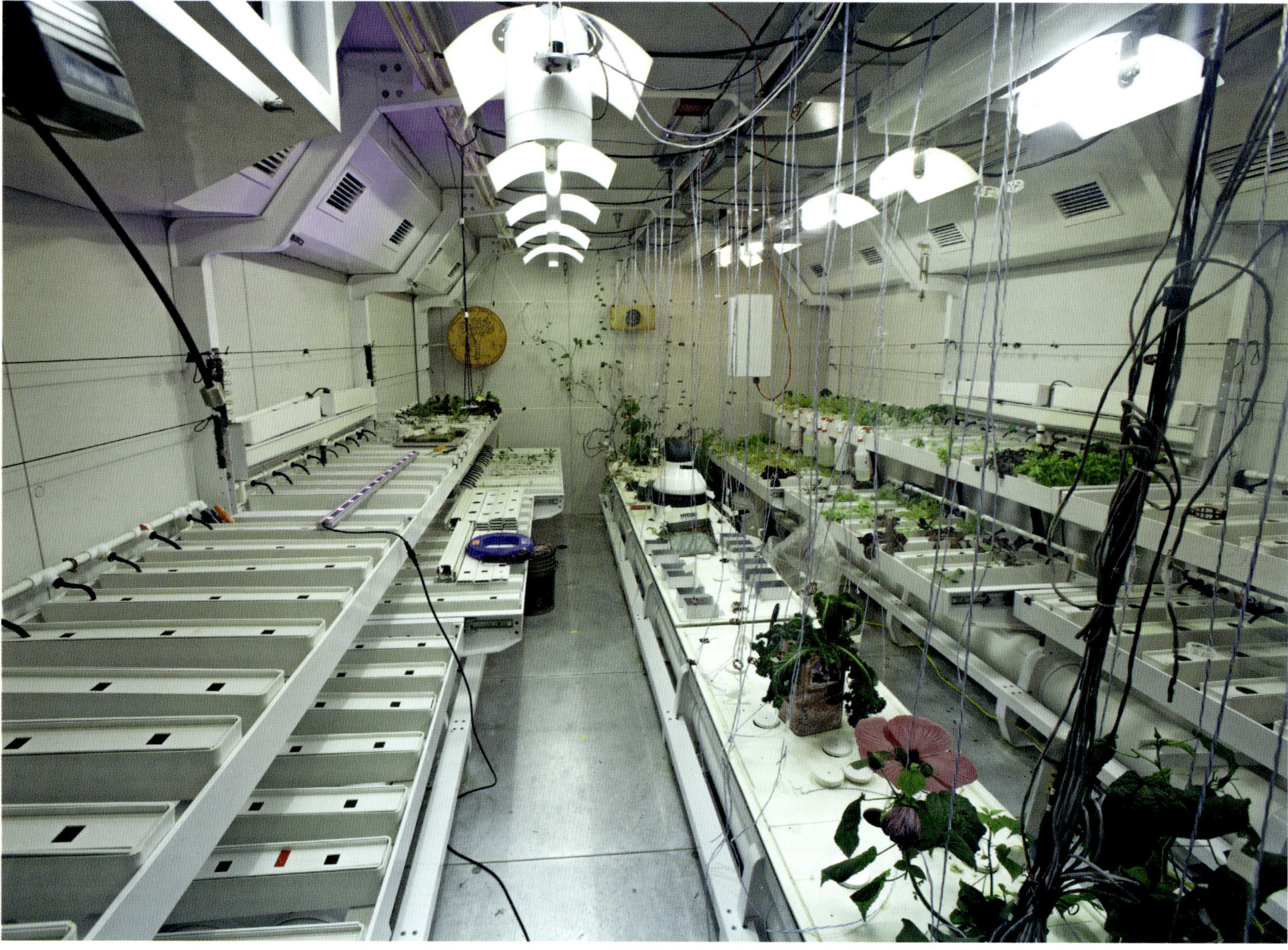

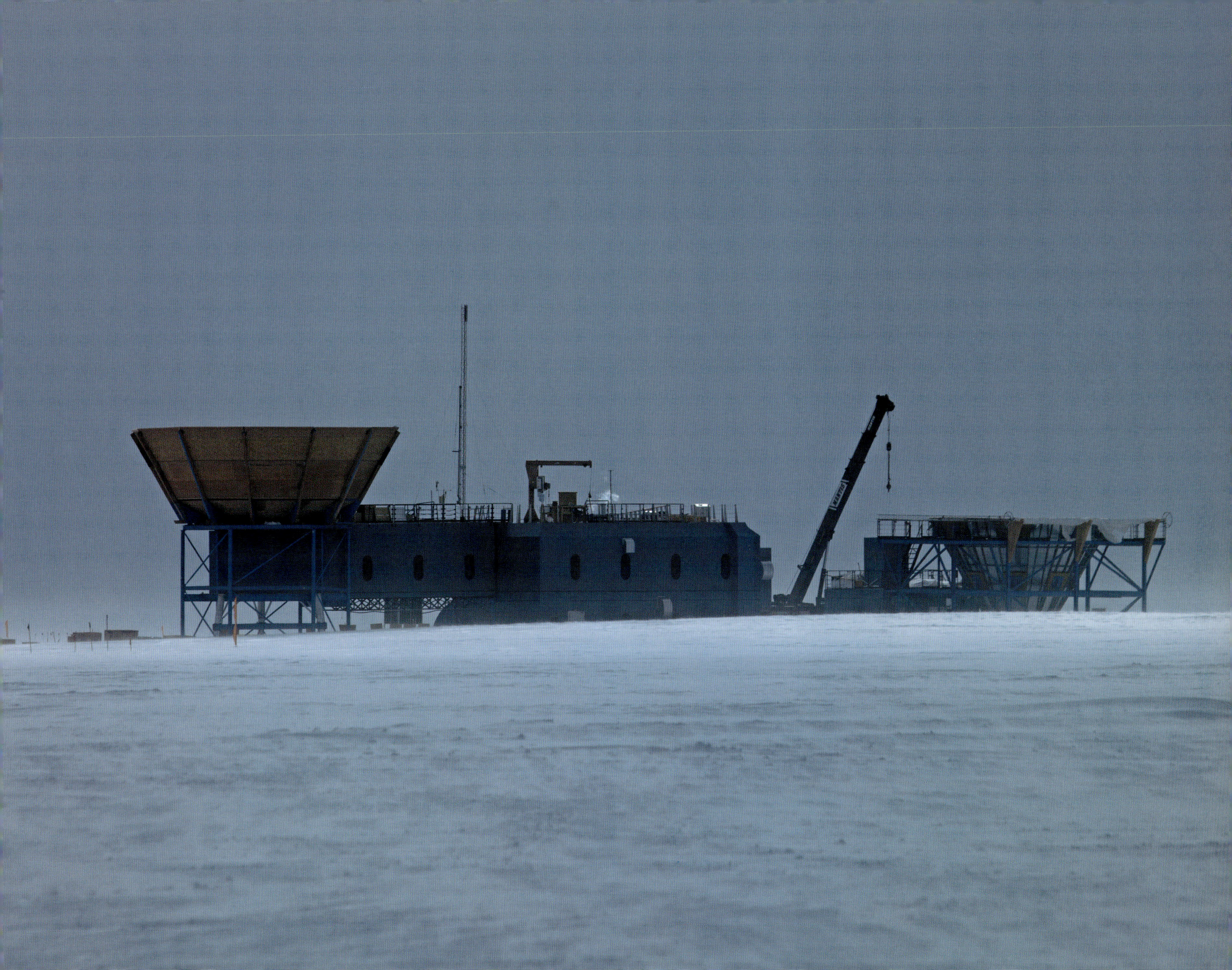

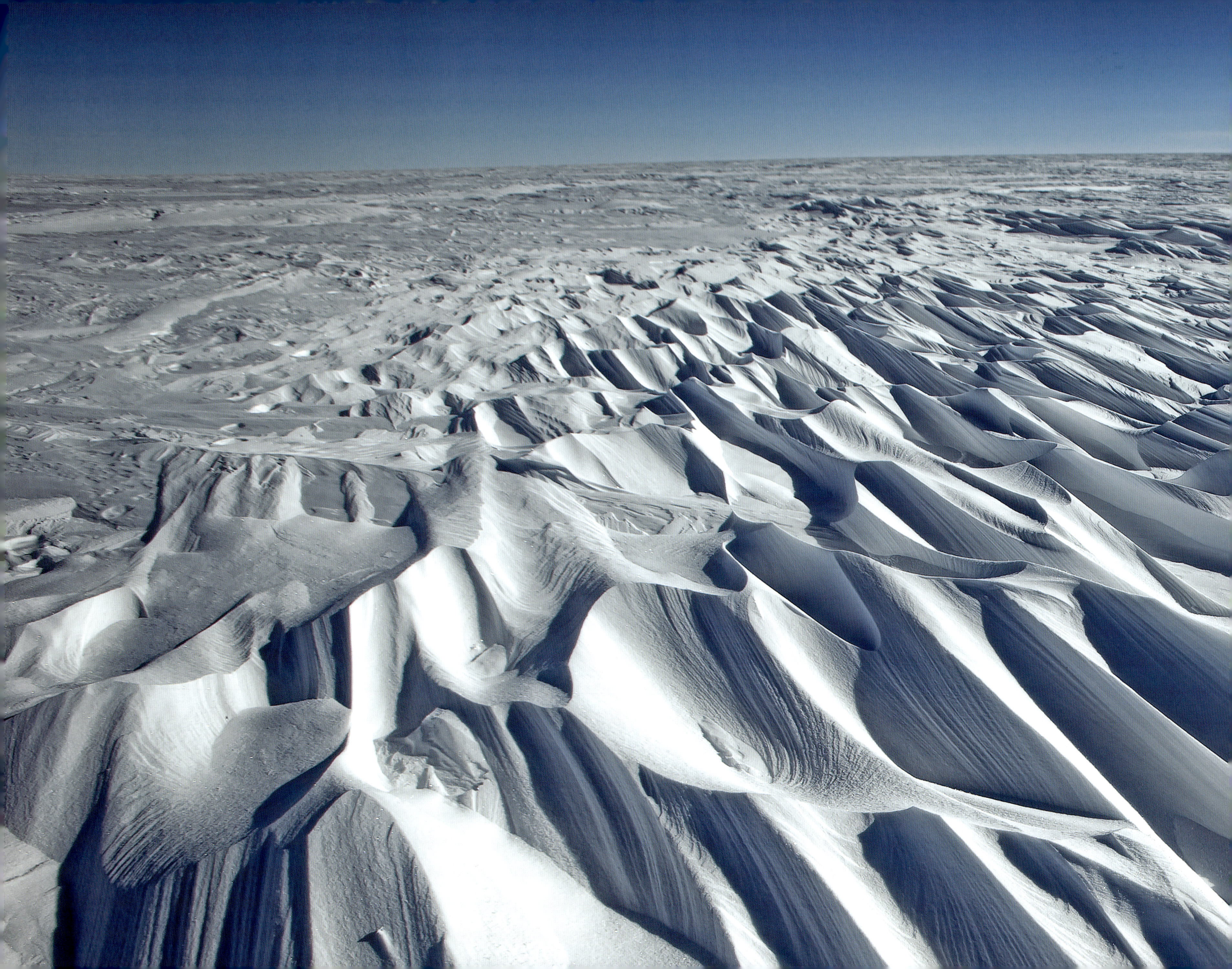

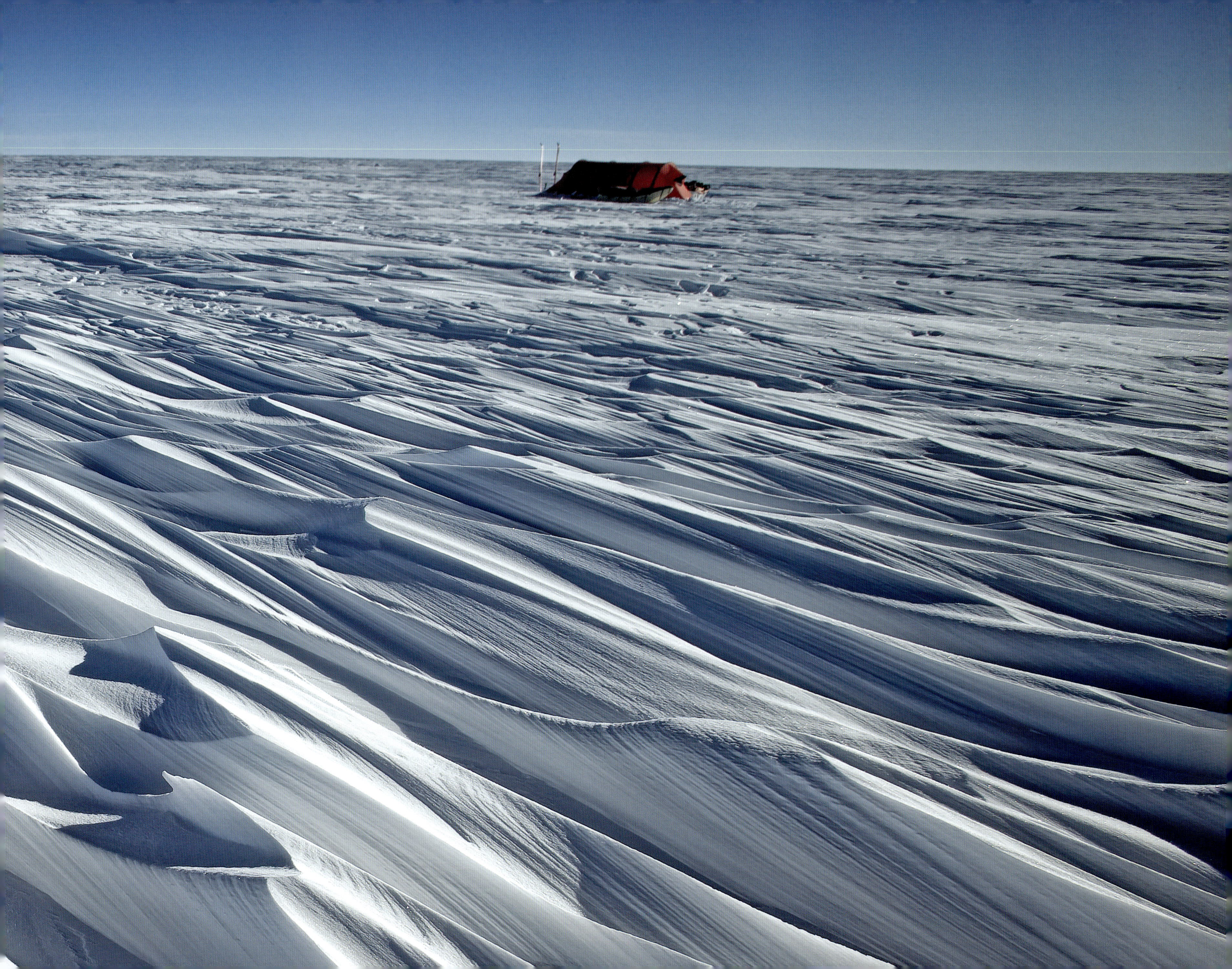

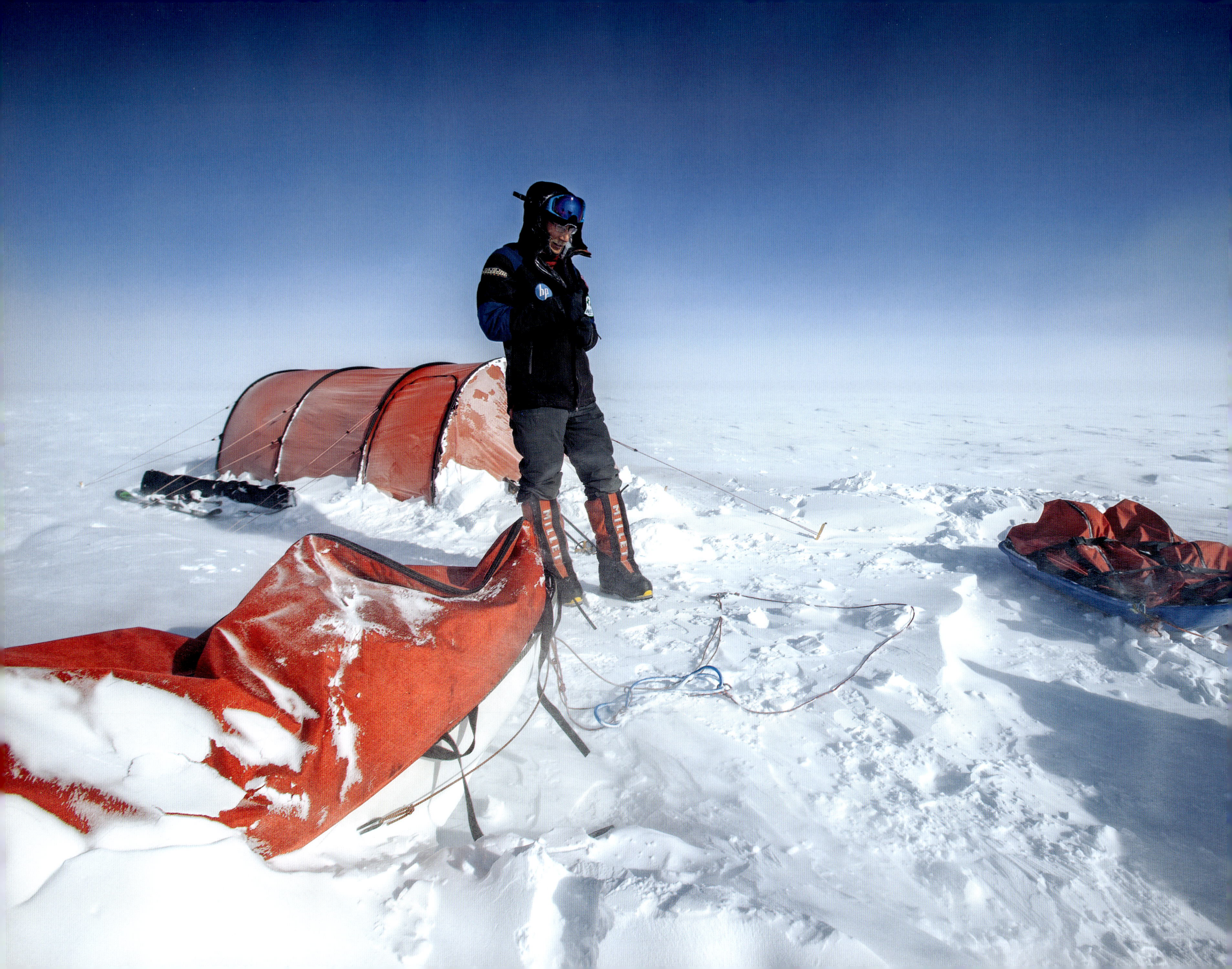
hp
MILLET
MILLET

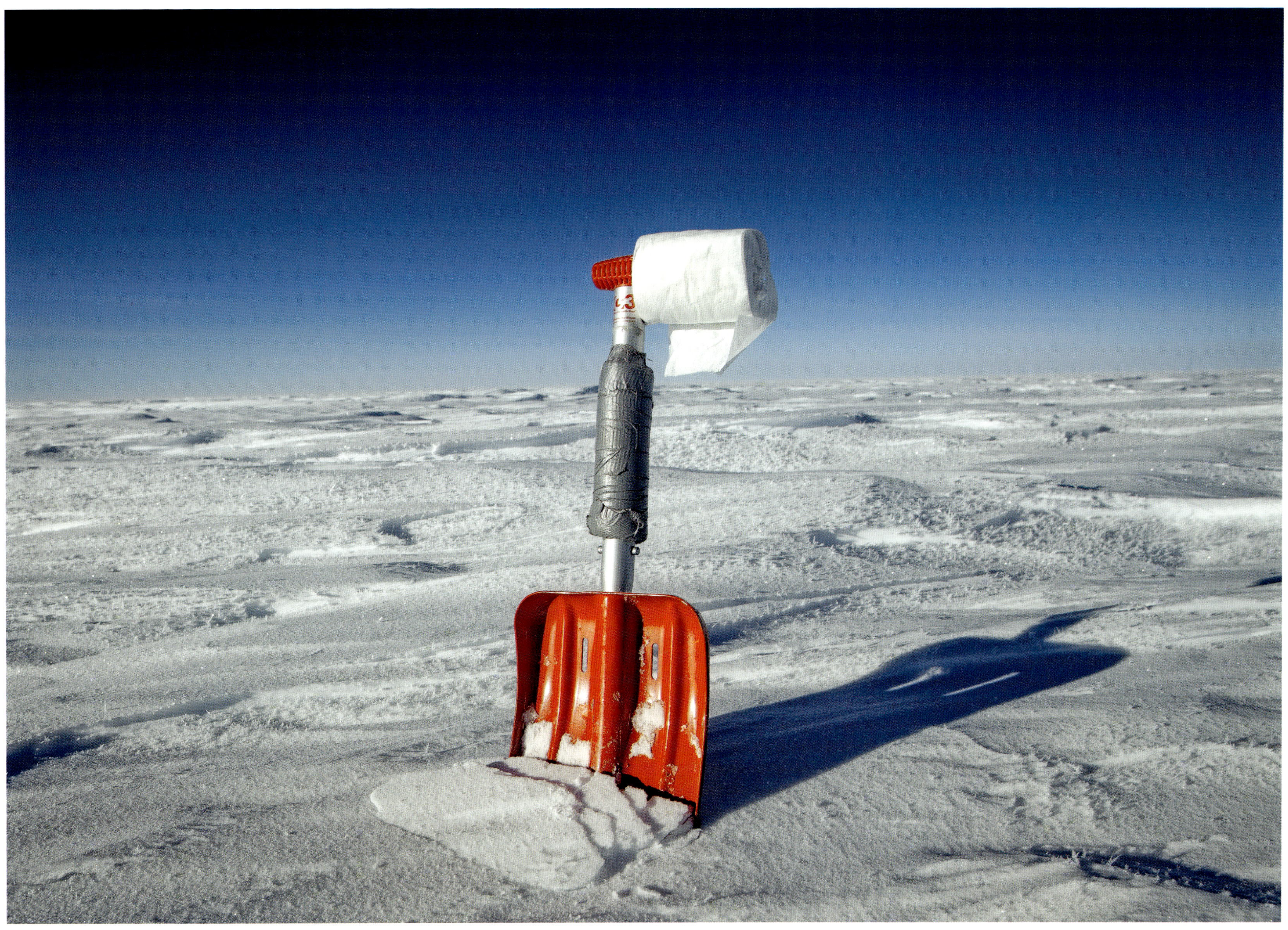

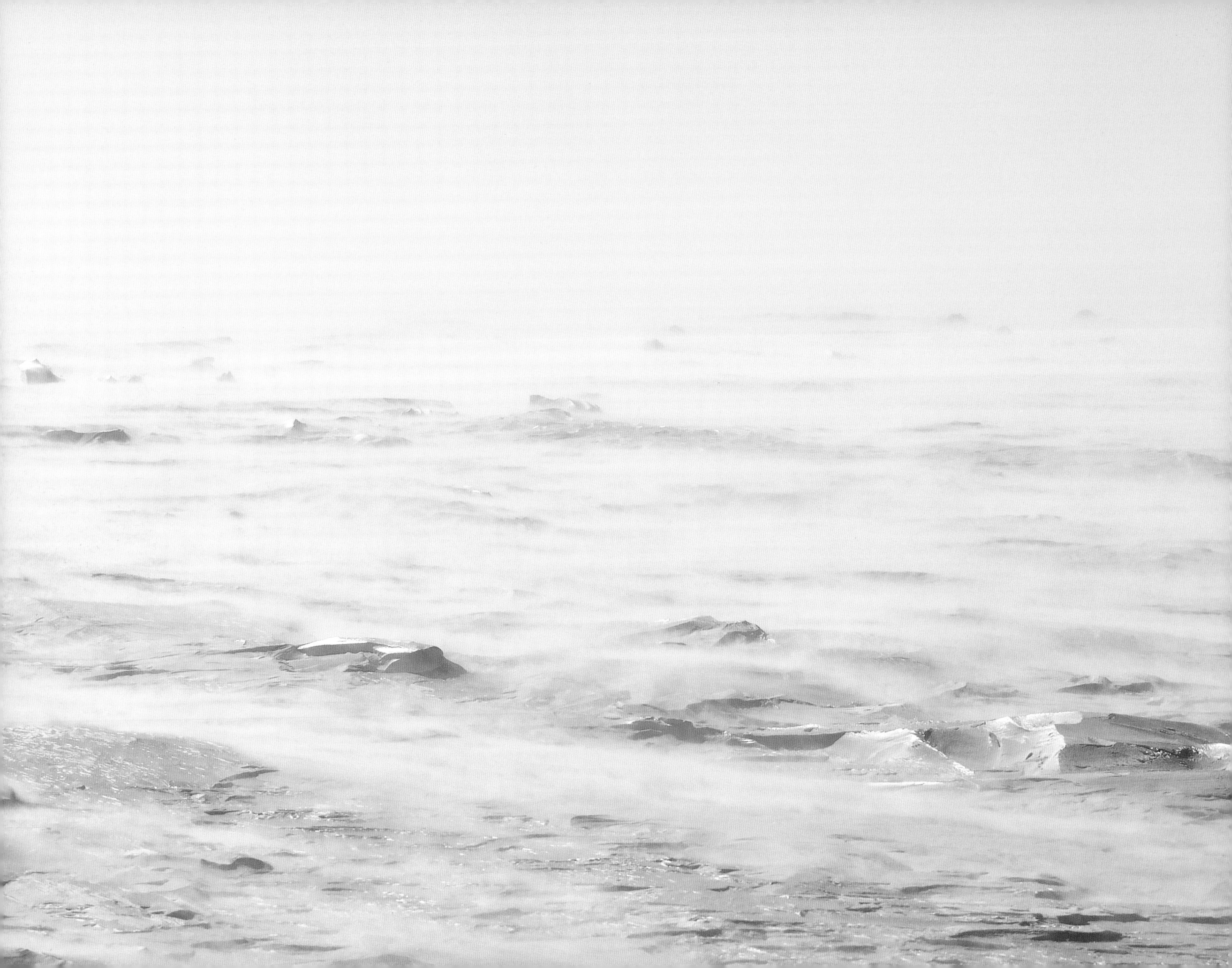

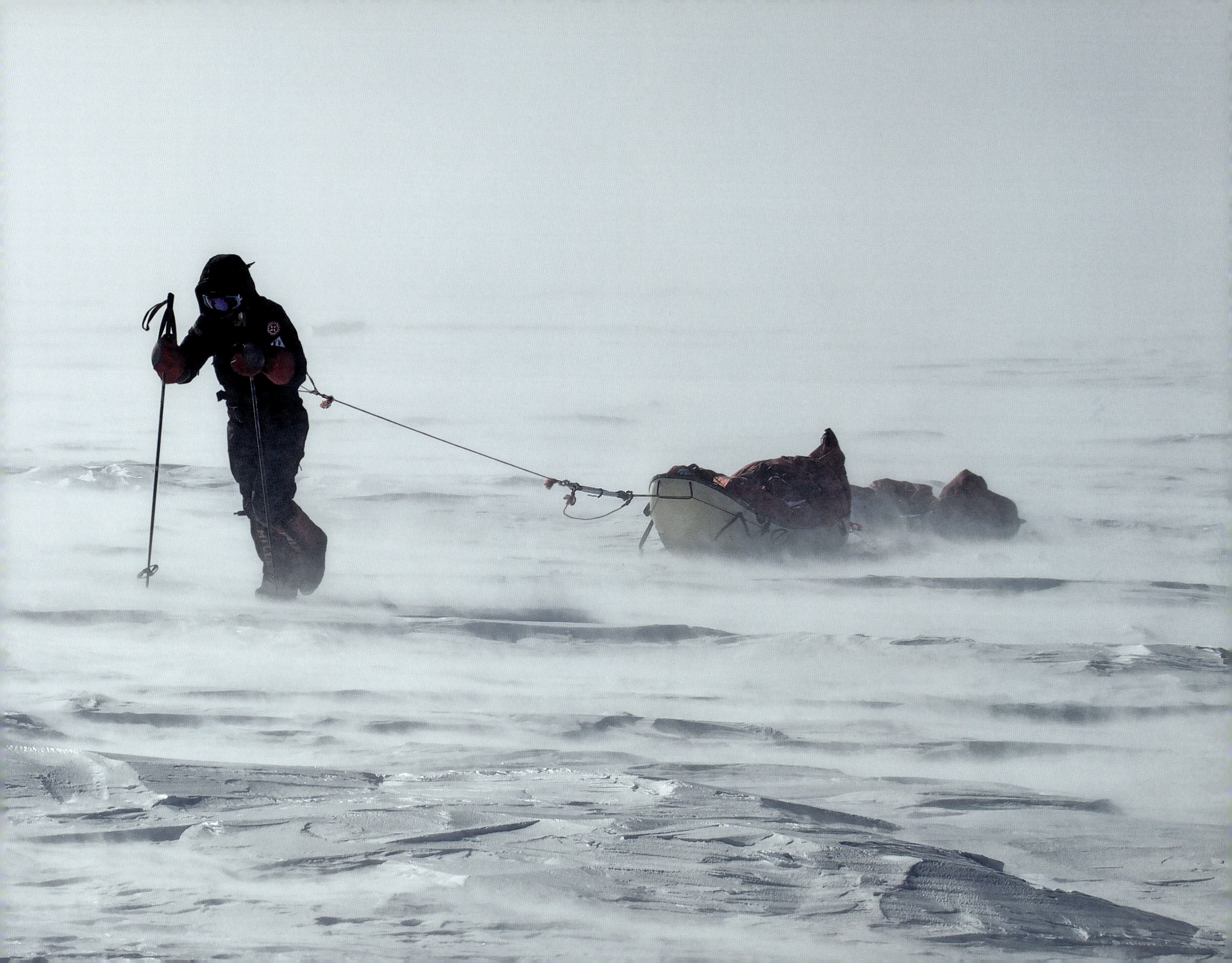

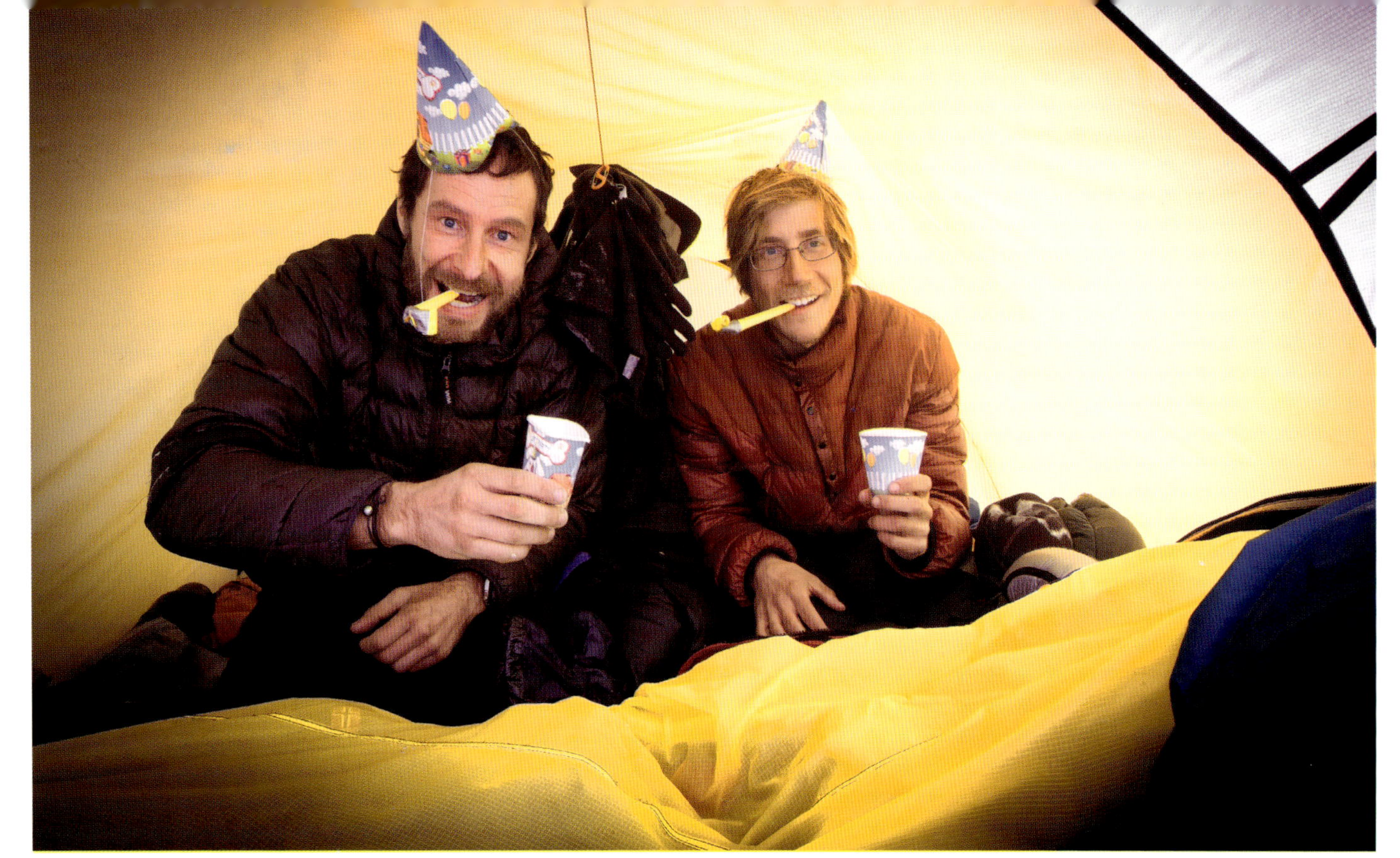

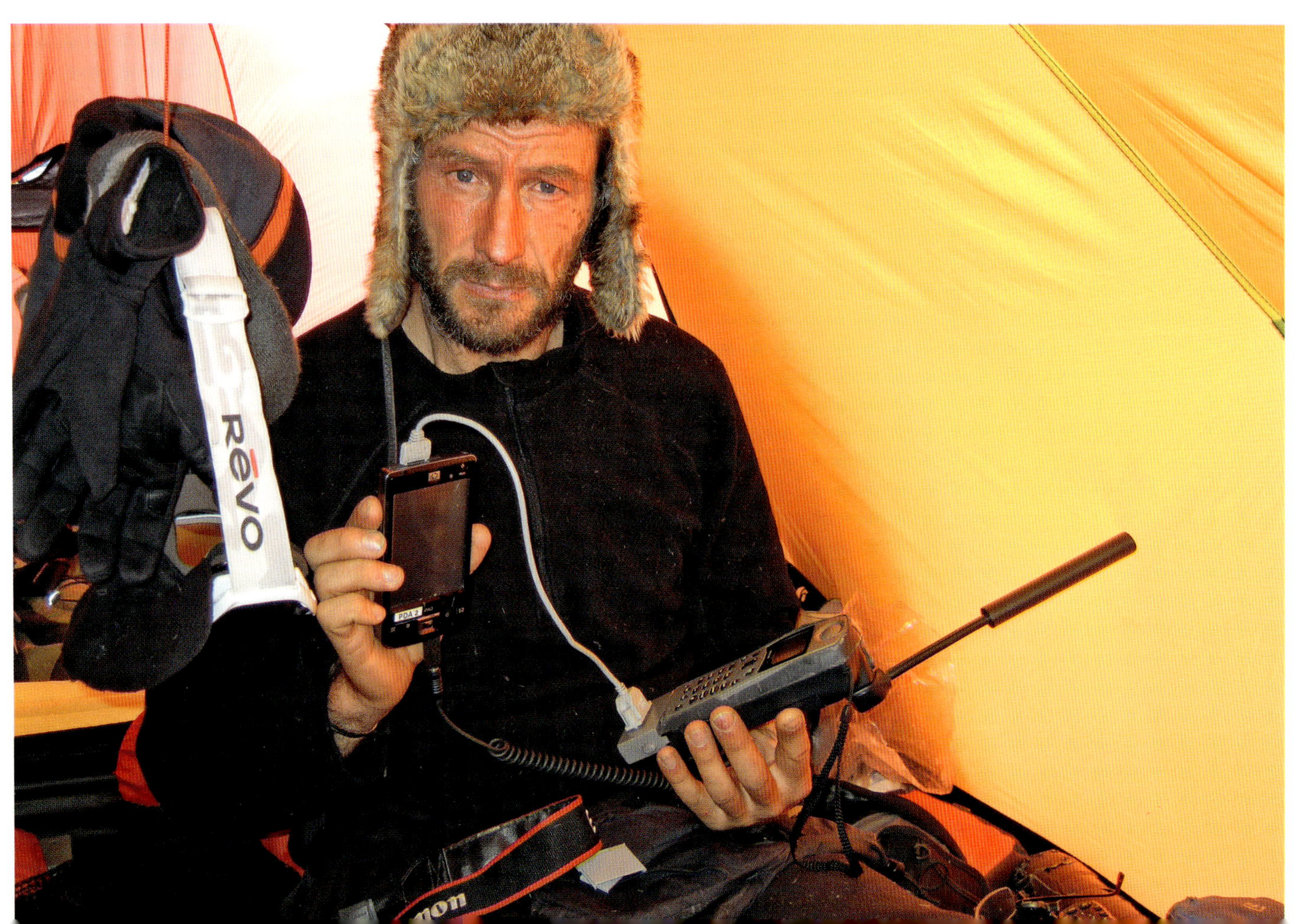
Rēvo

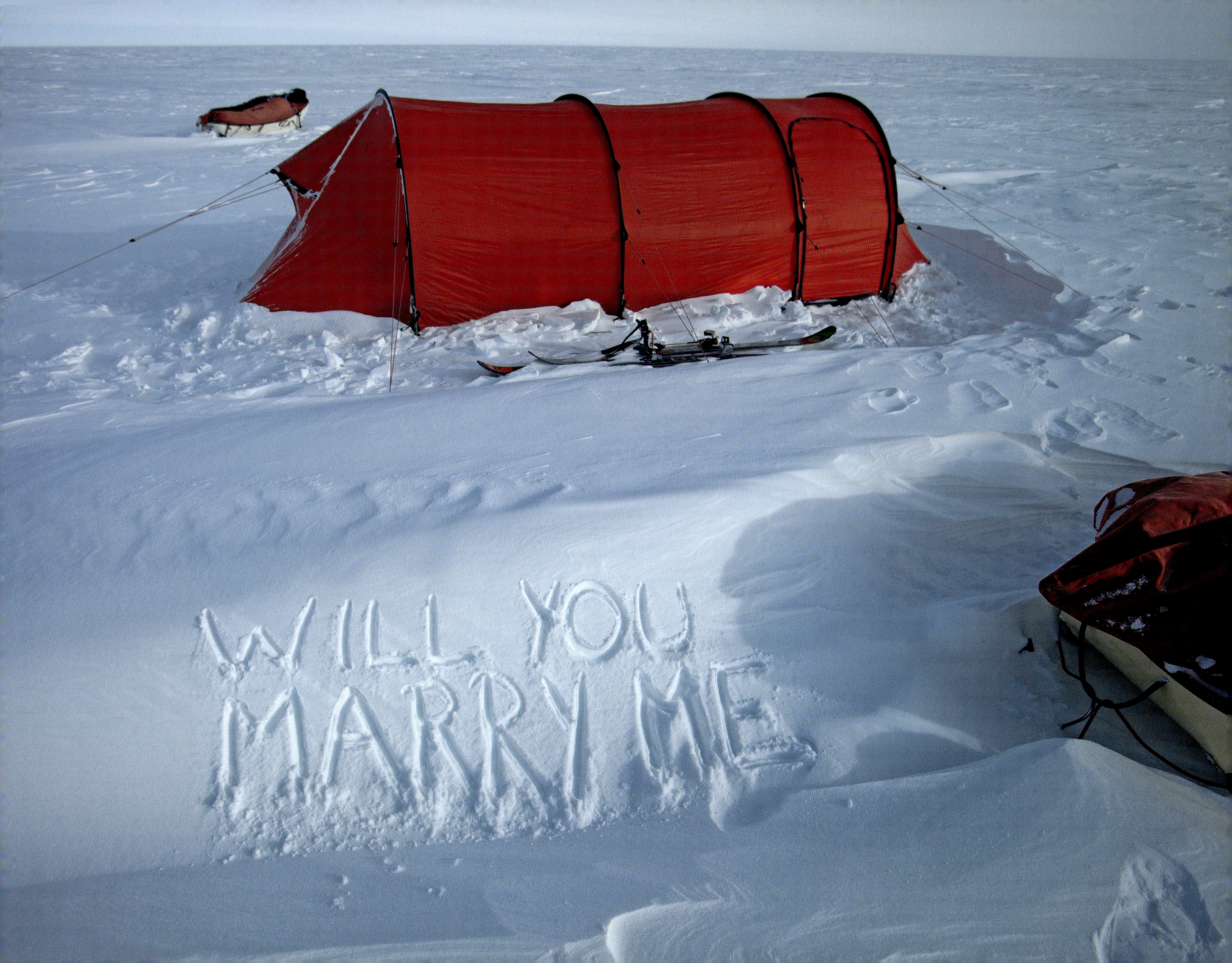
WILL YOU
MARRY ME

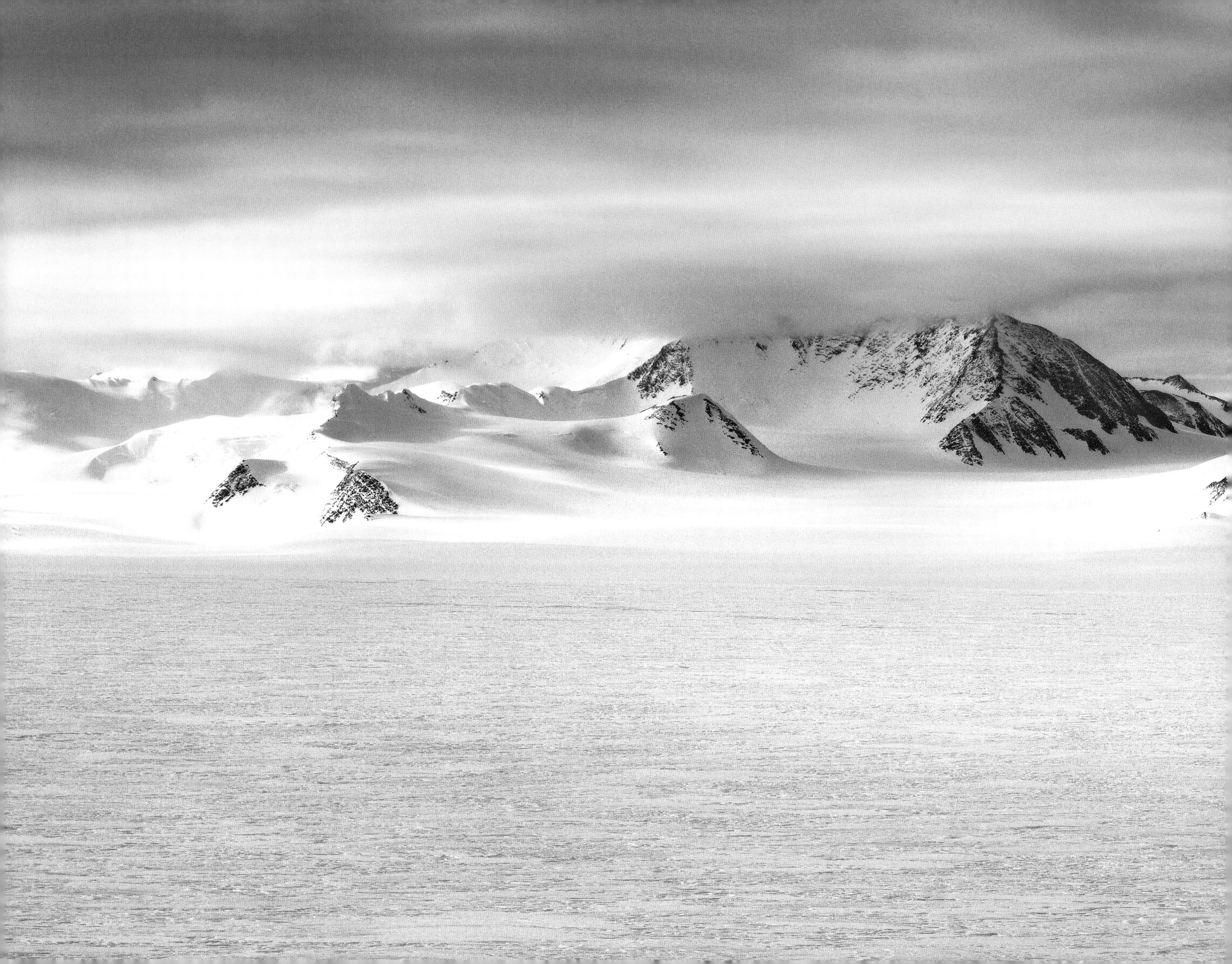

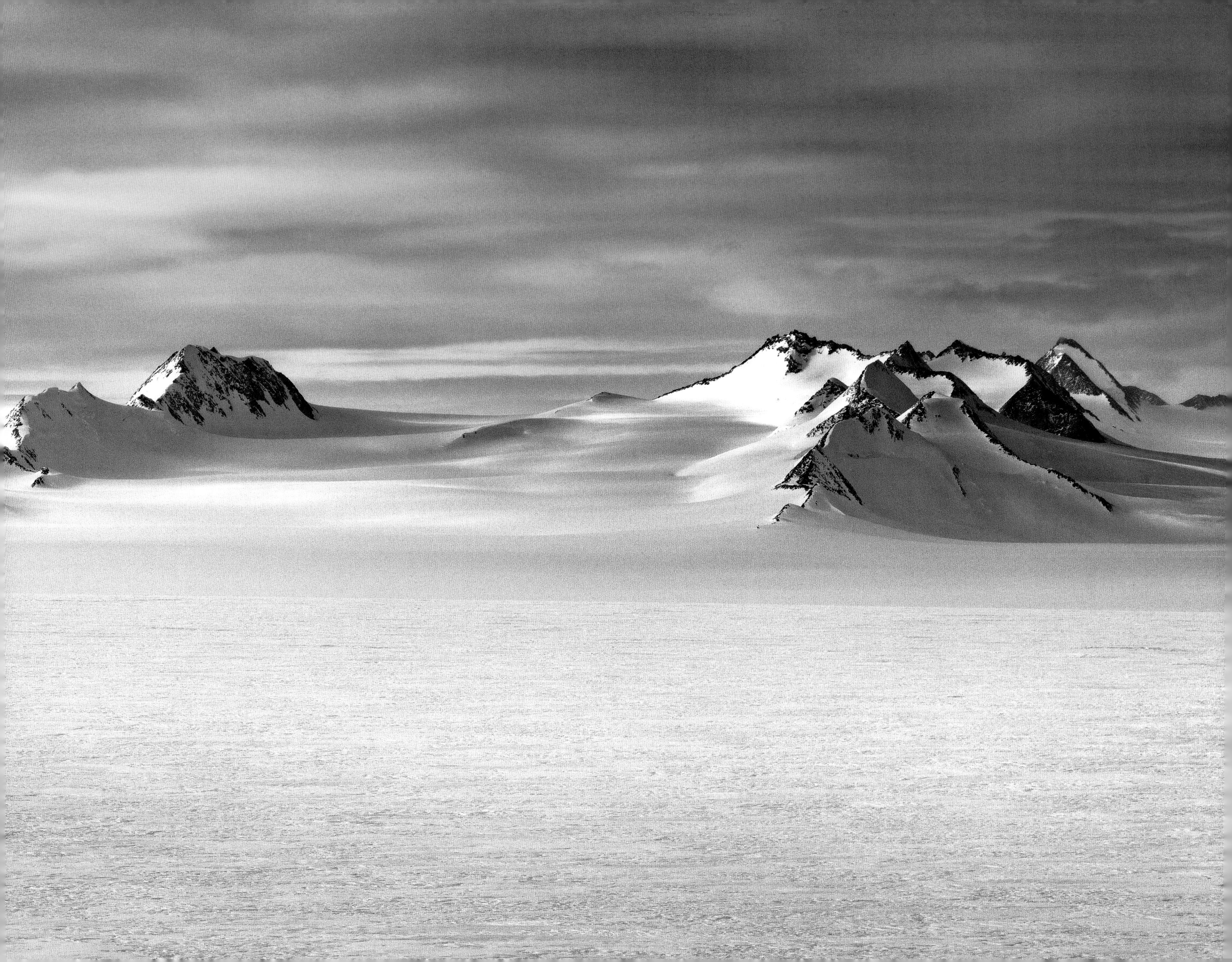

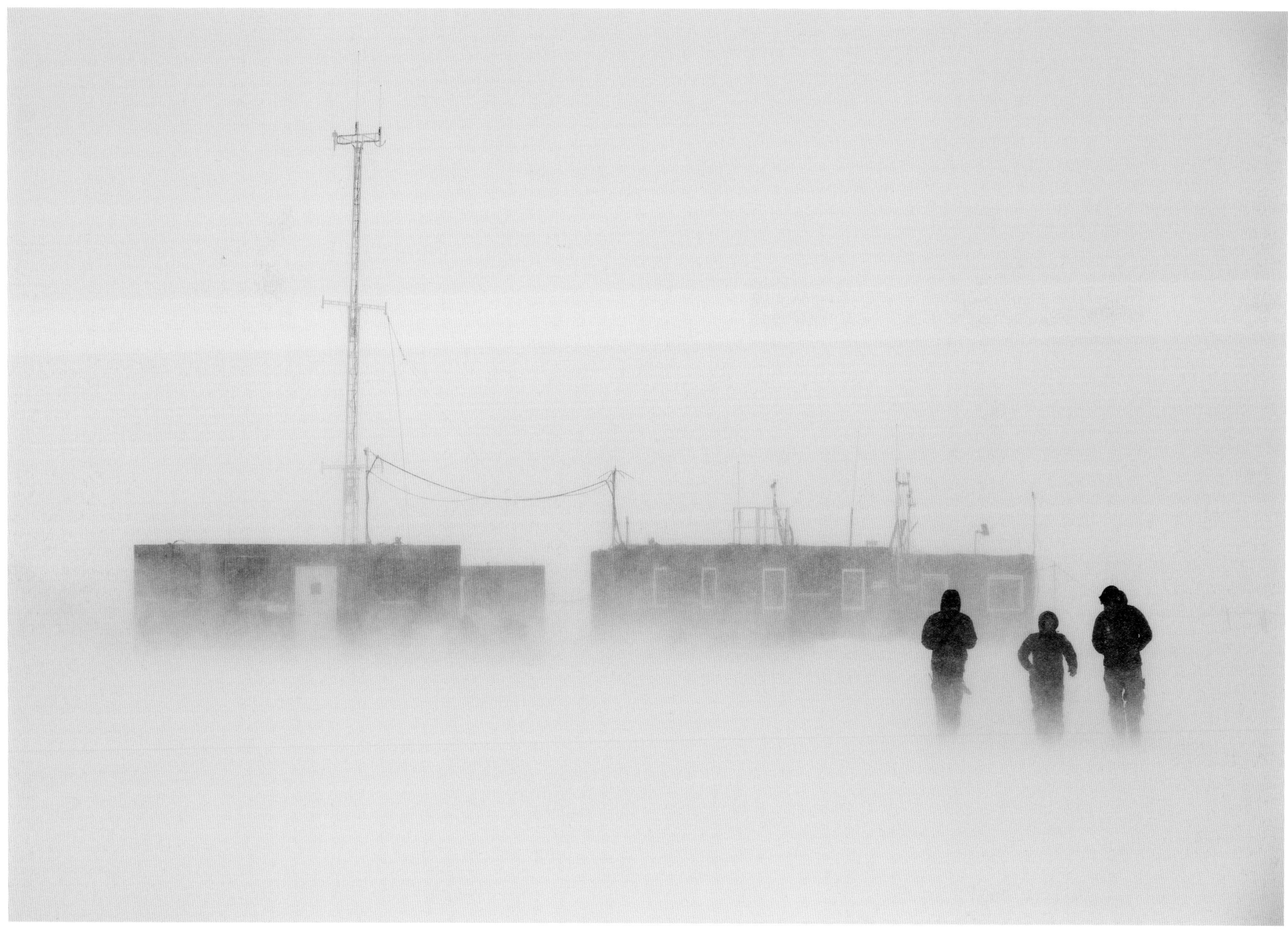

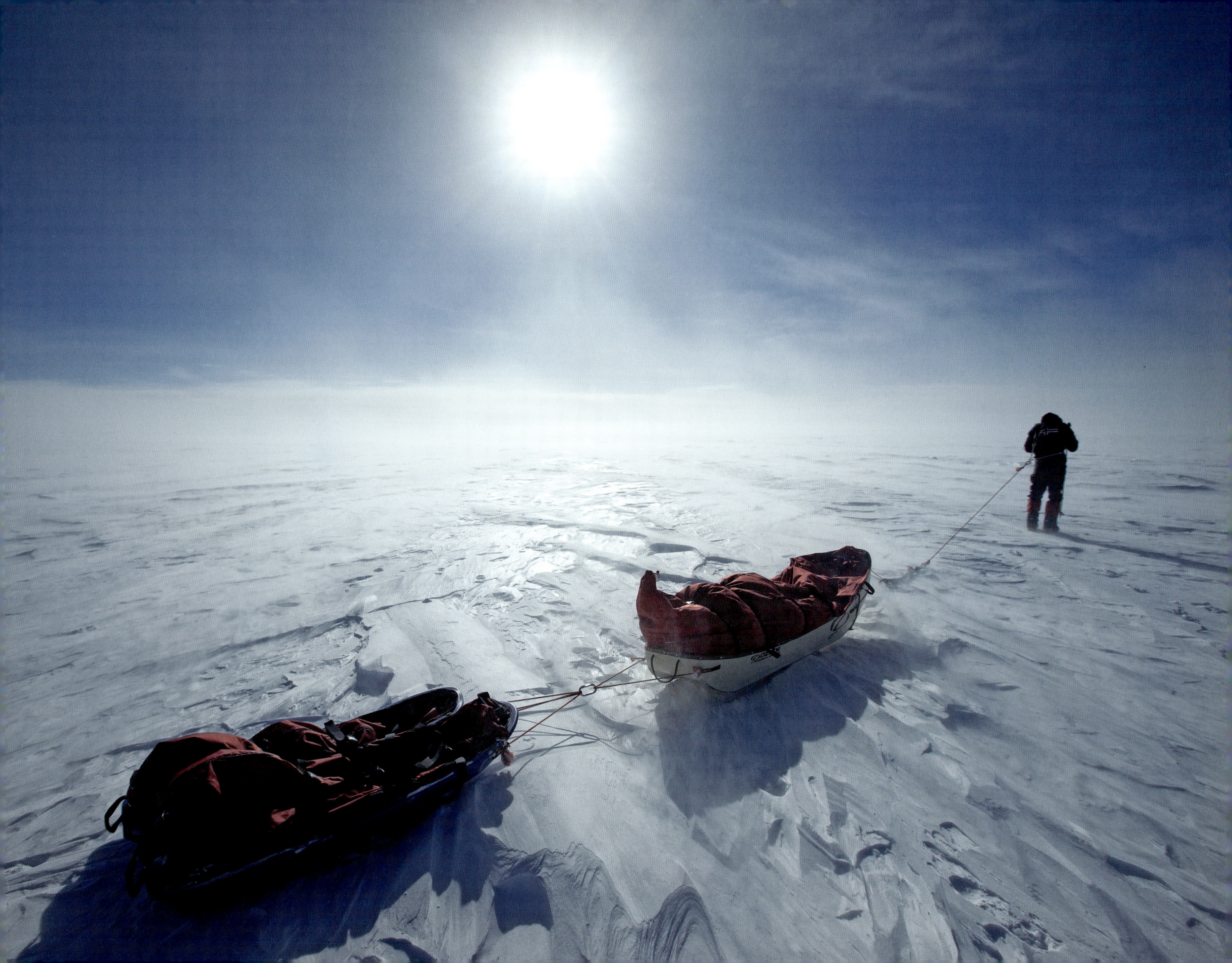

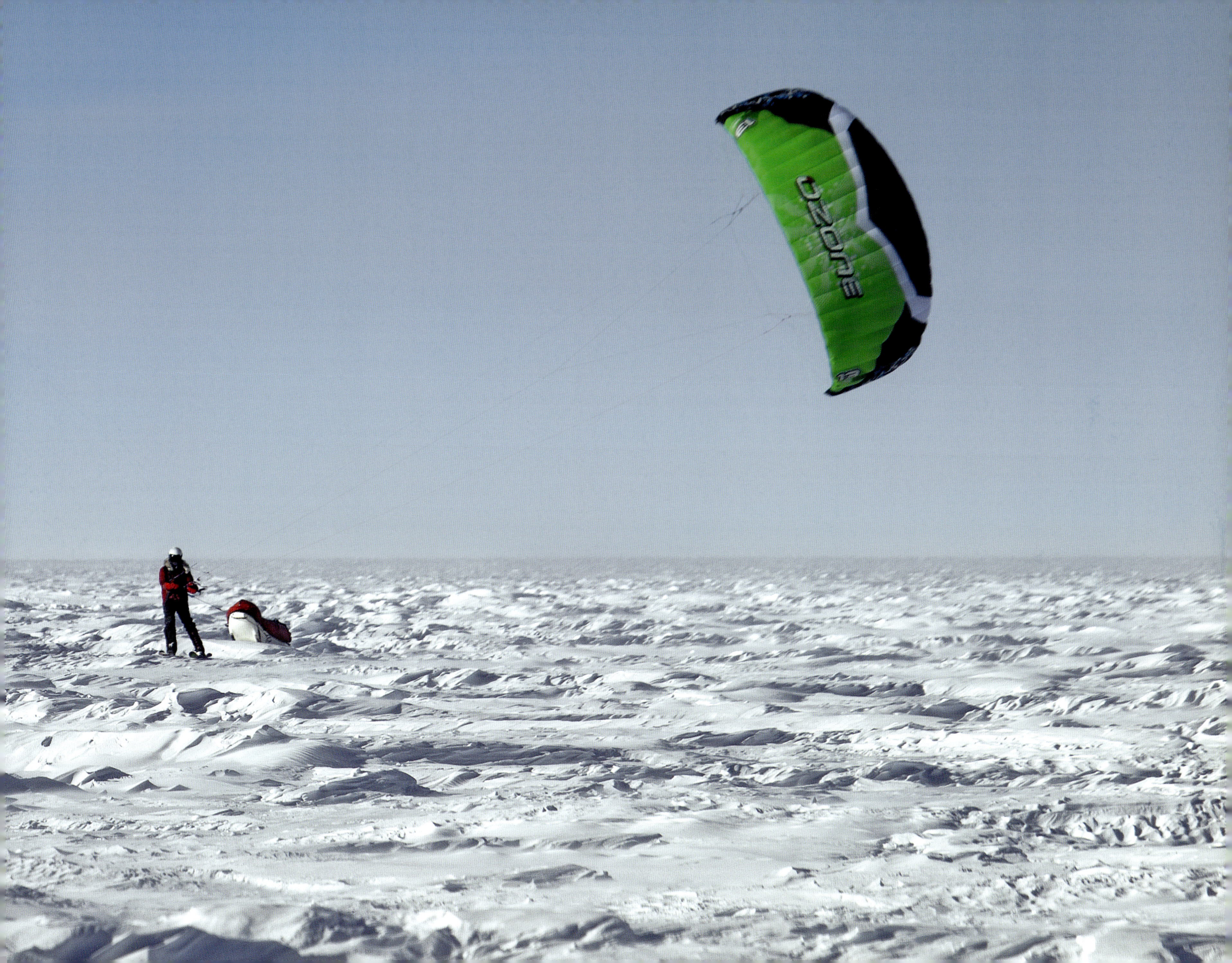
OZONE

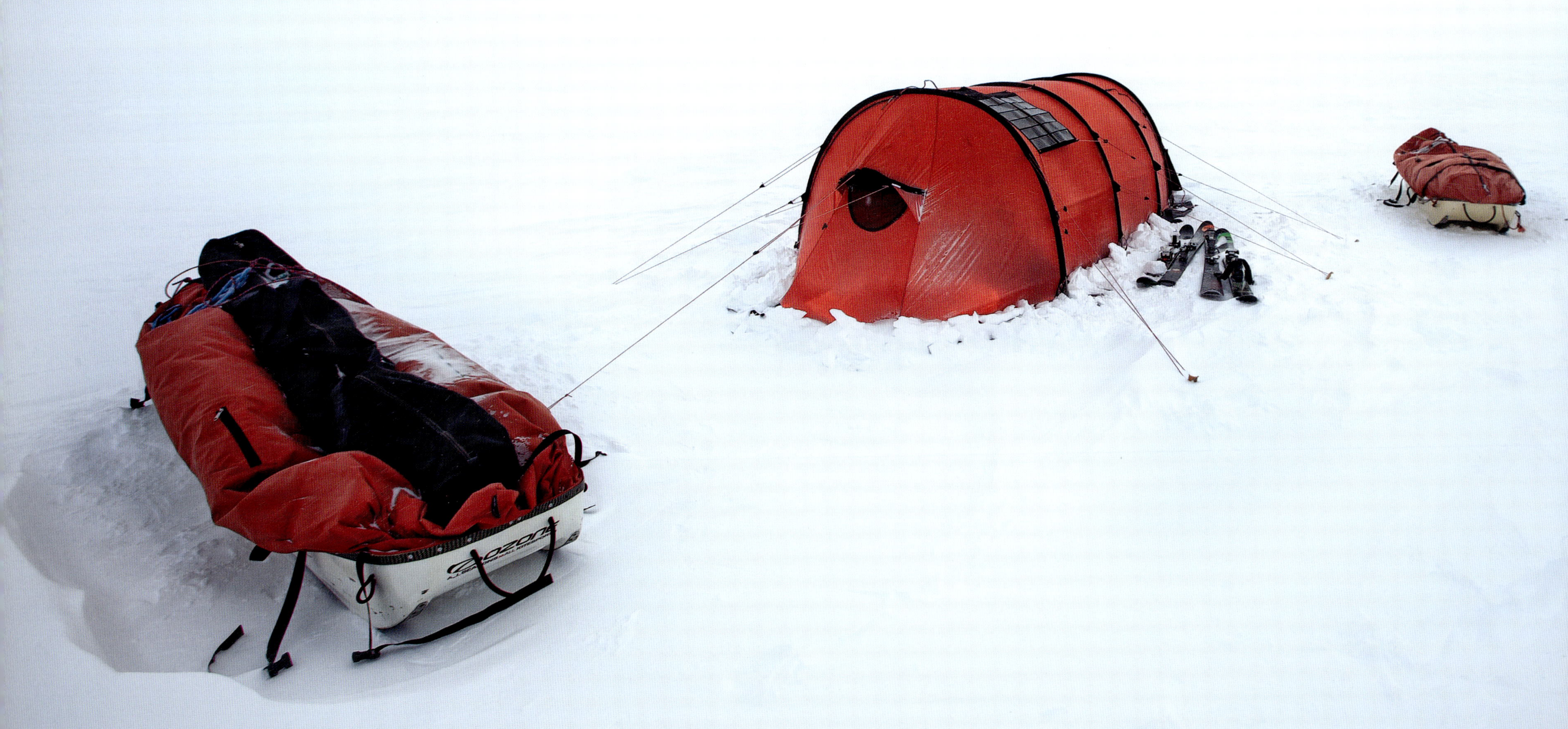
ozone

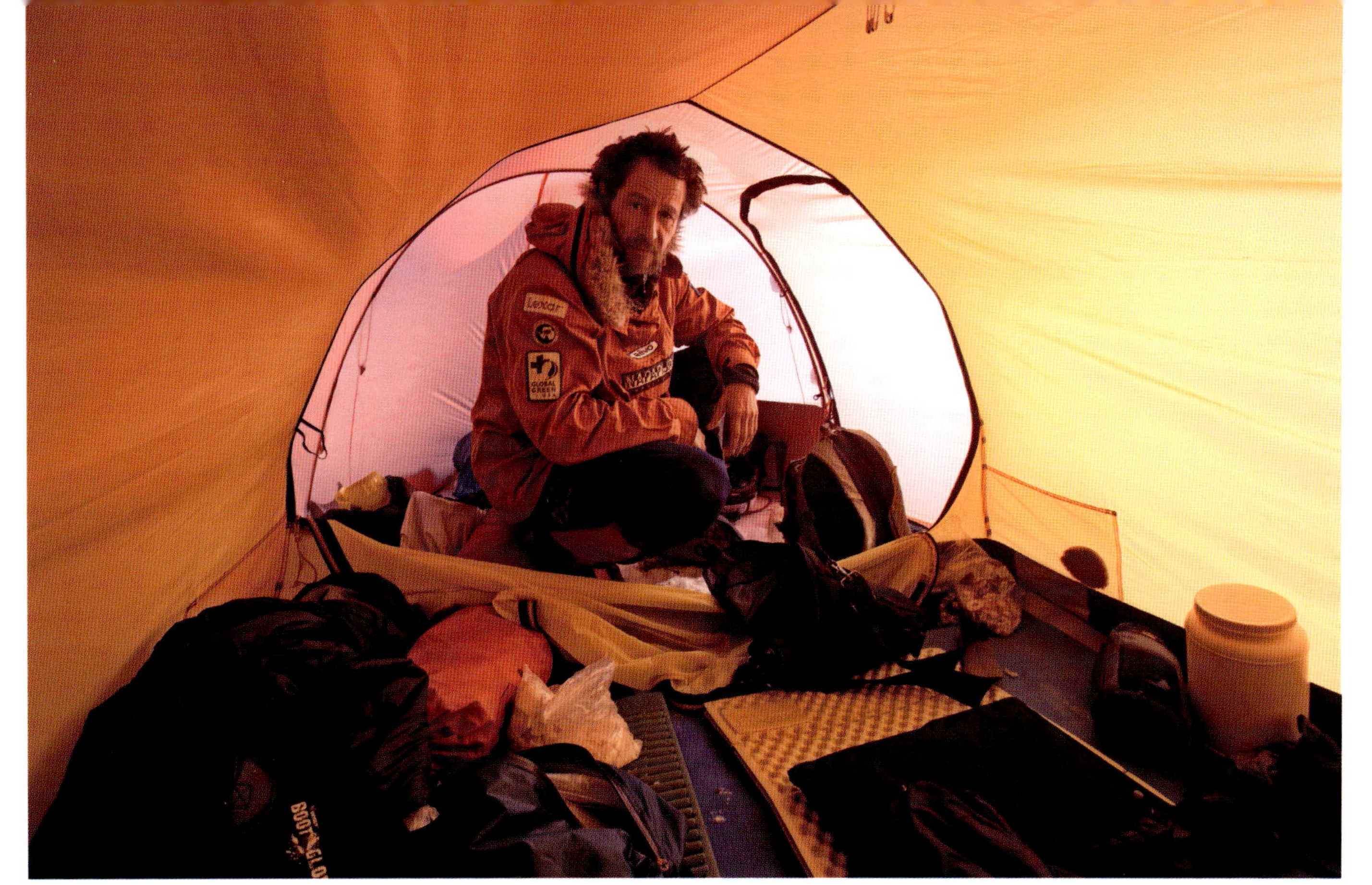

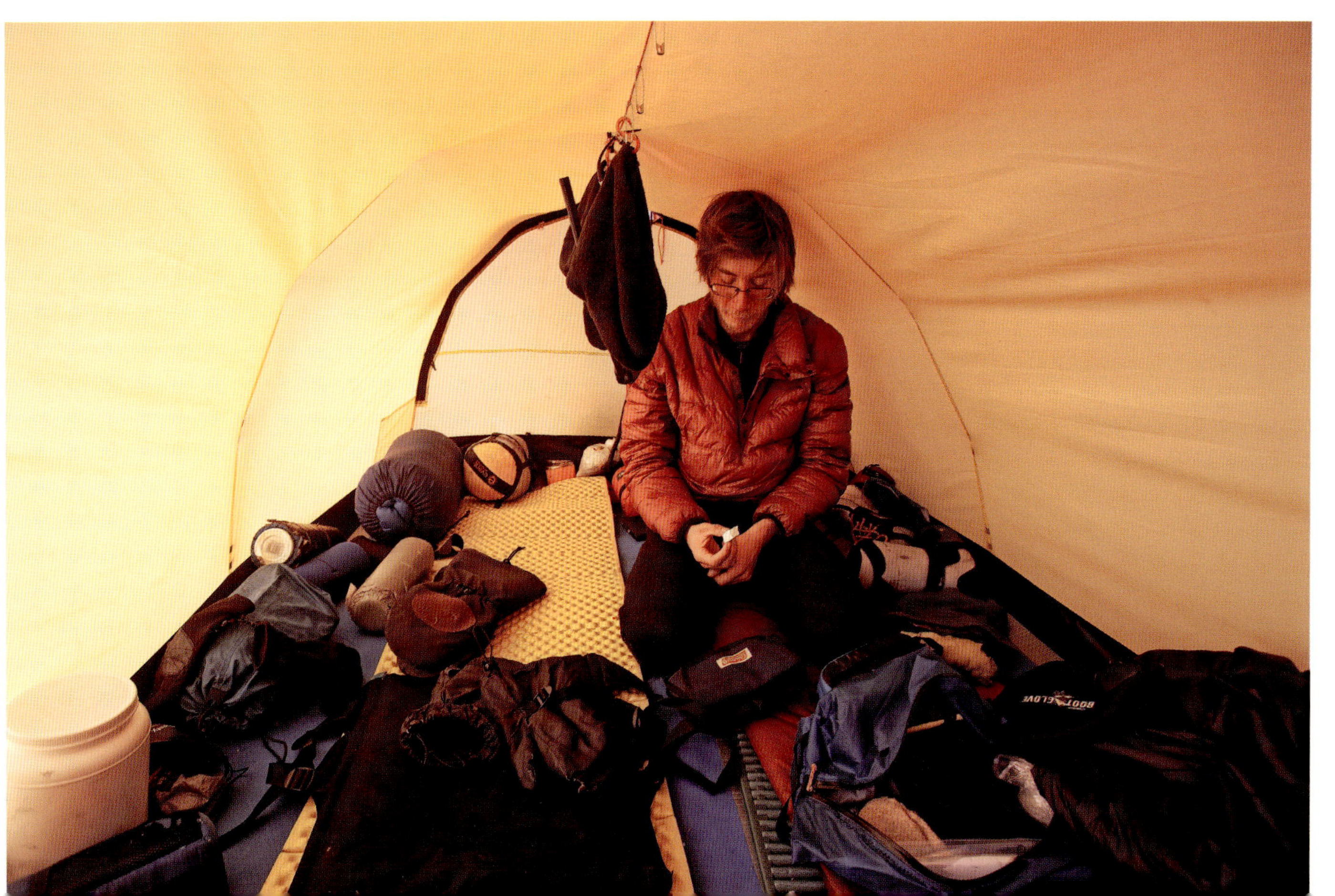

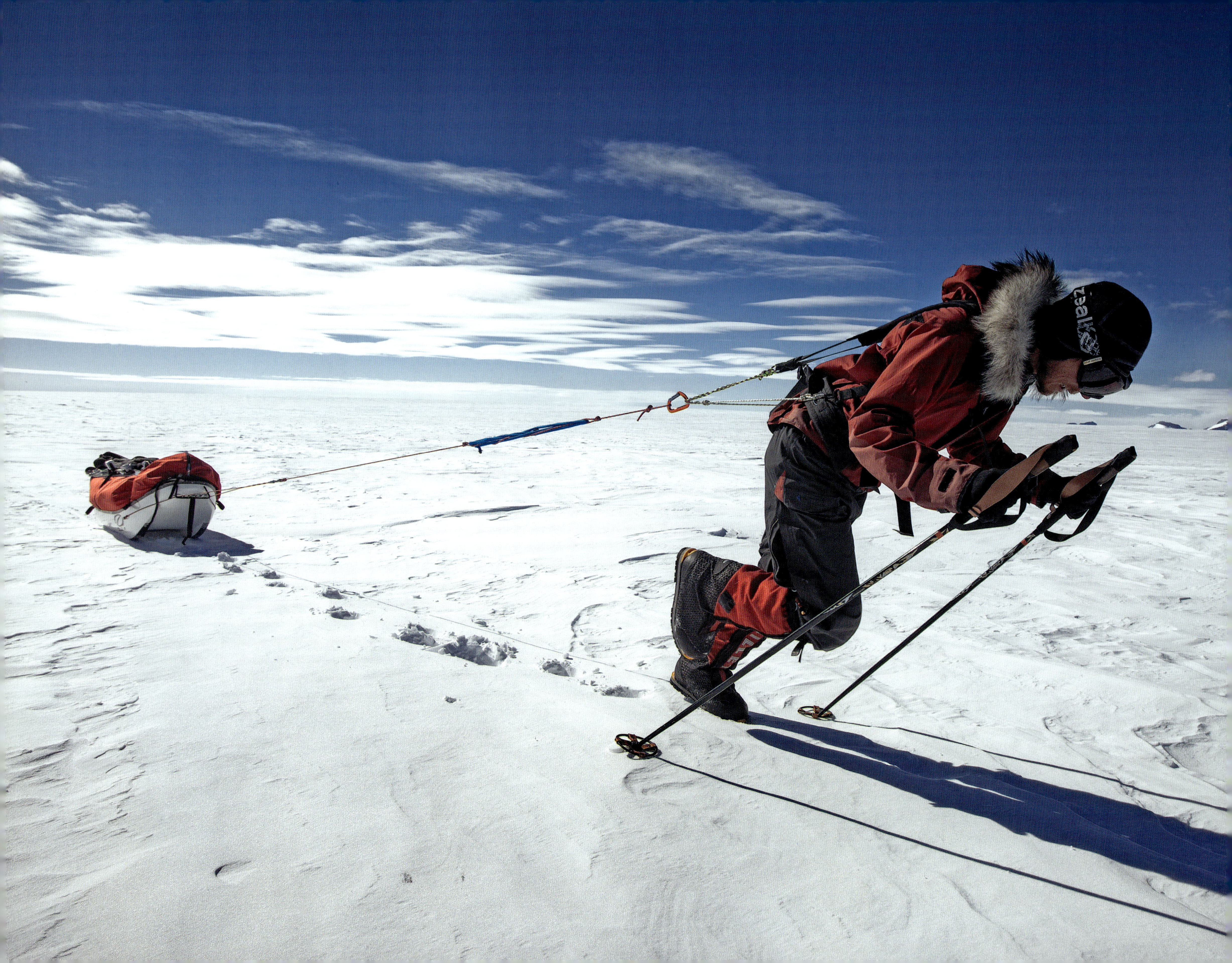

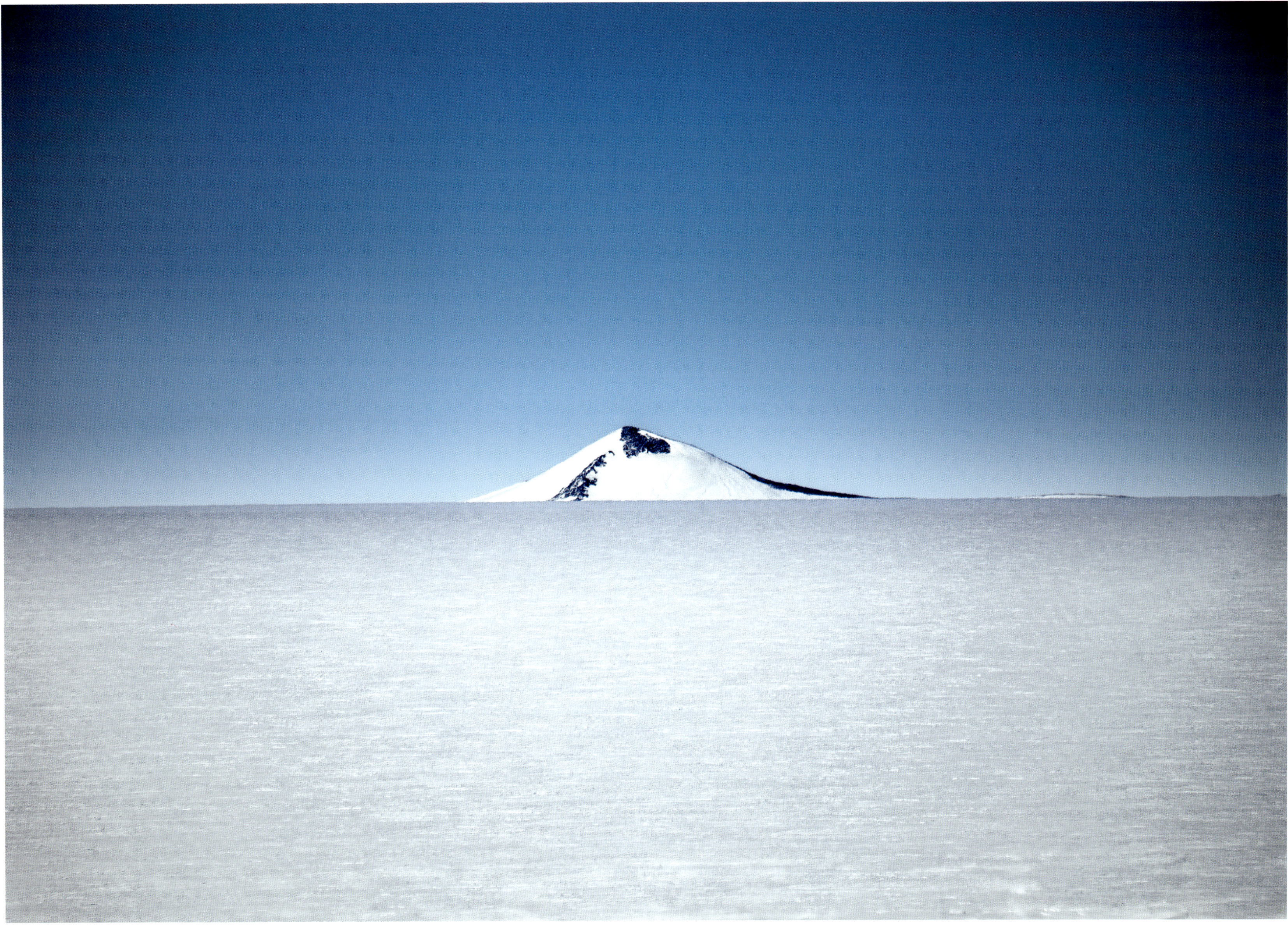

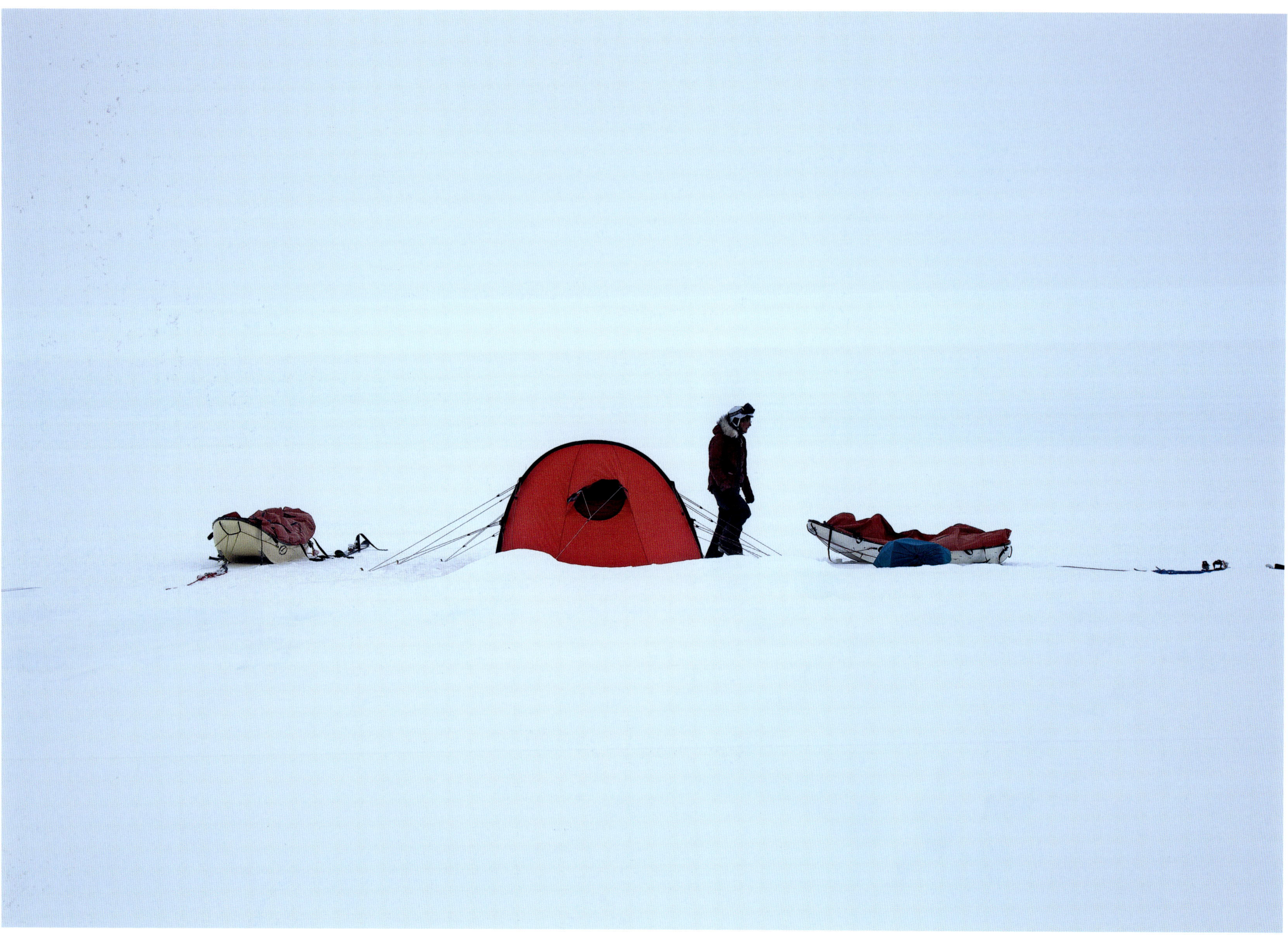

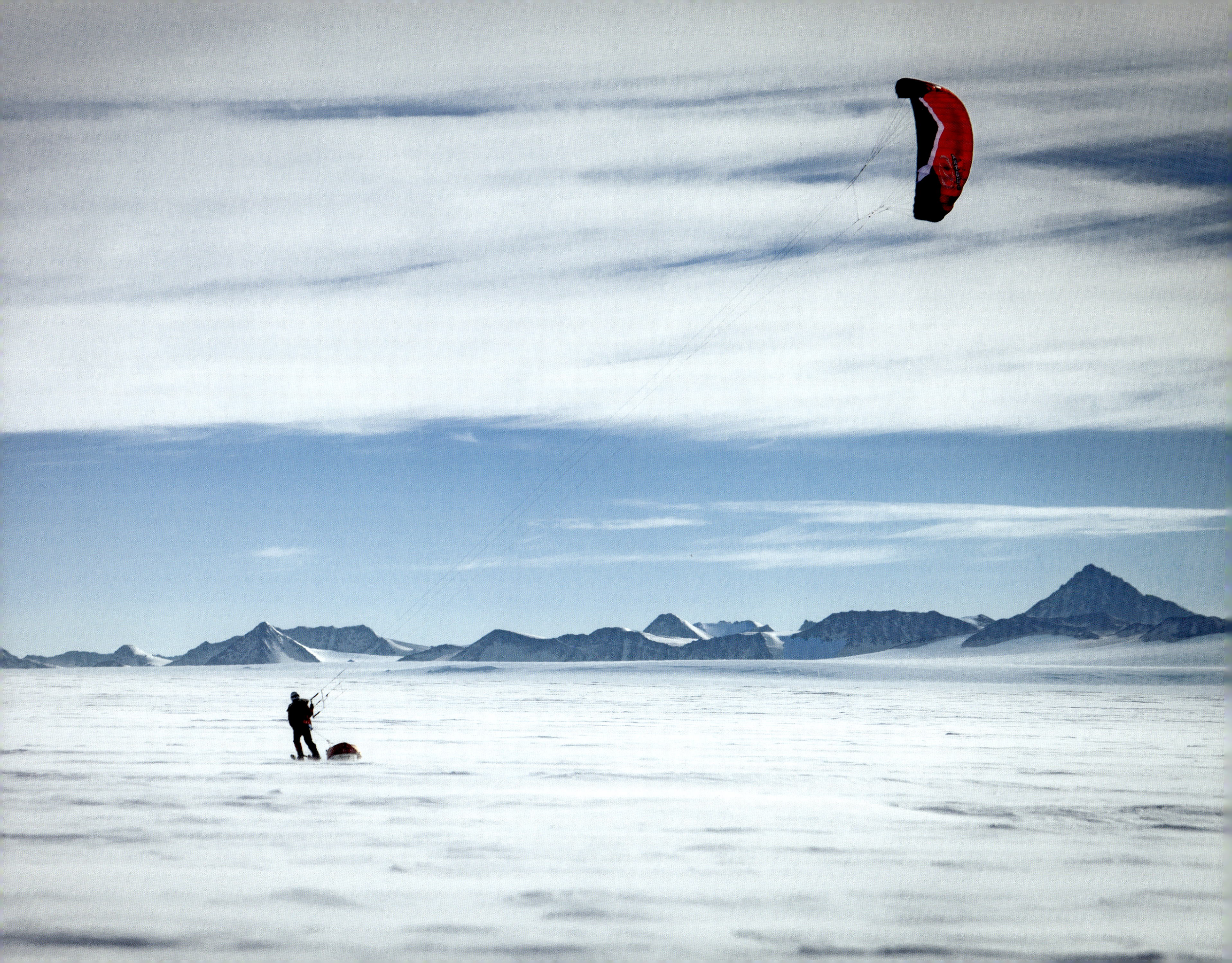

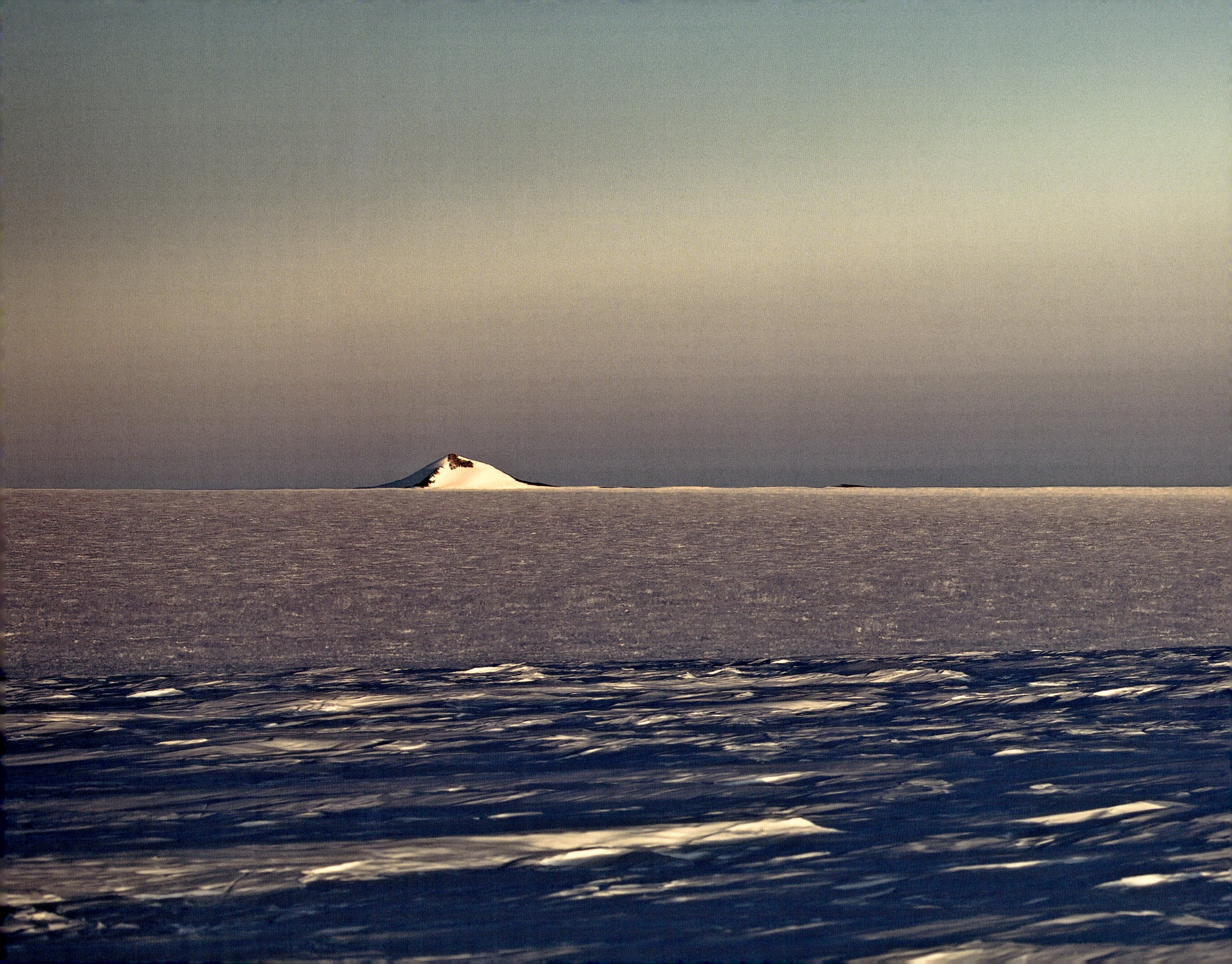

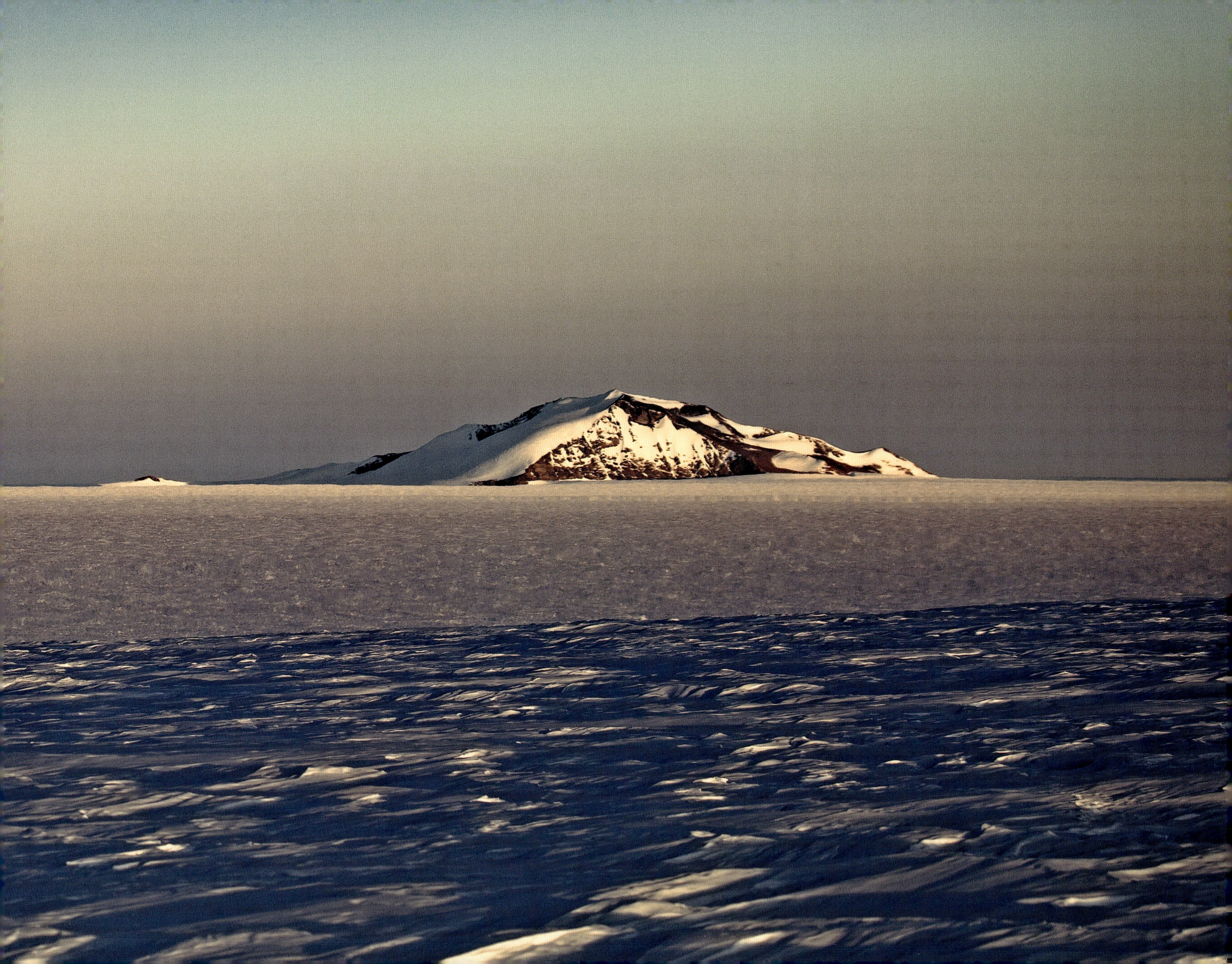

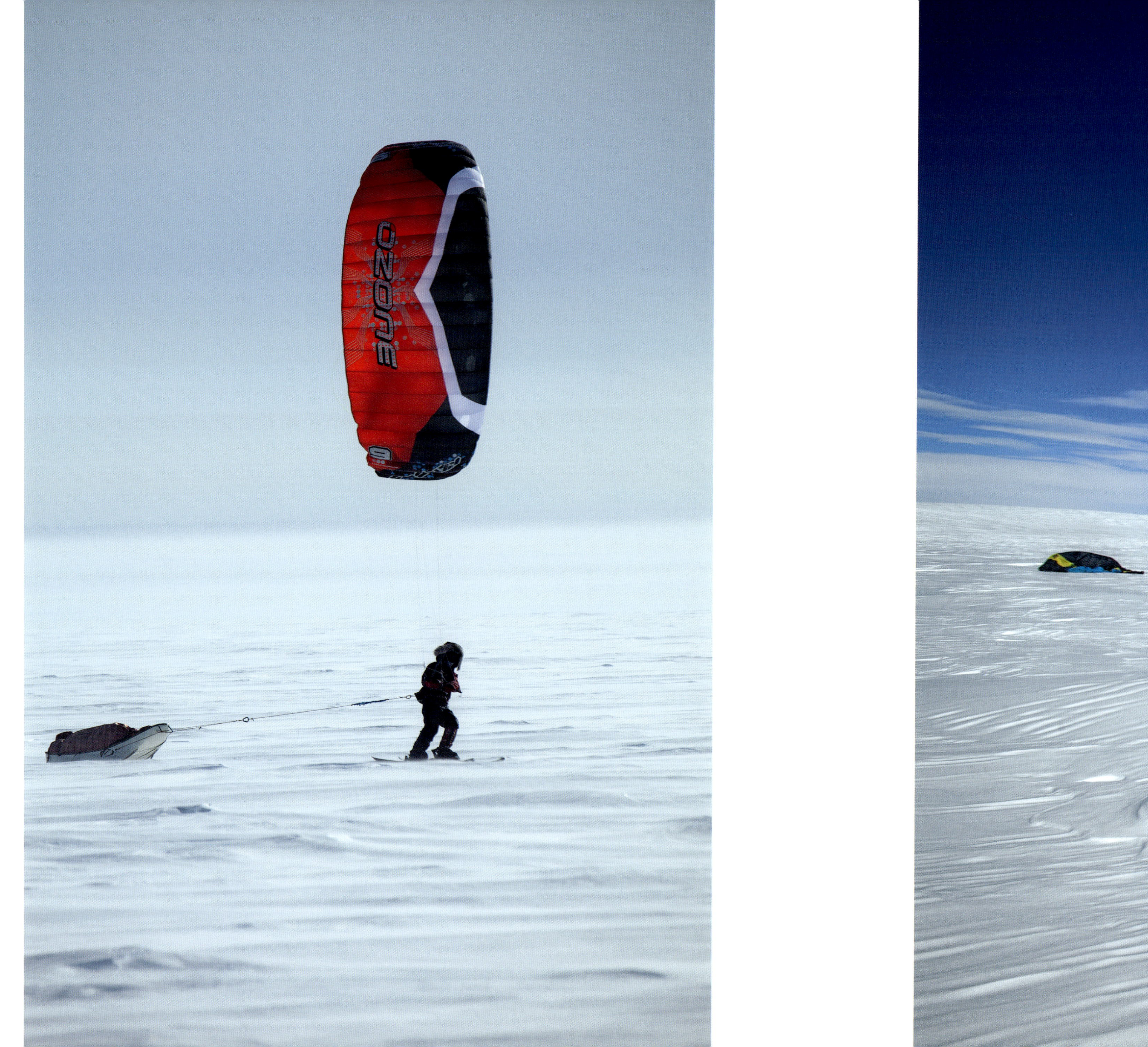
OZONE

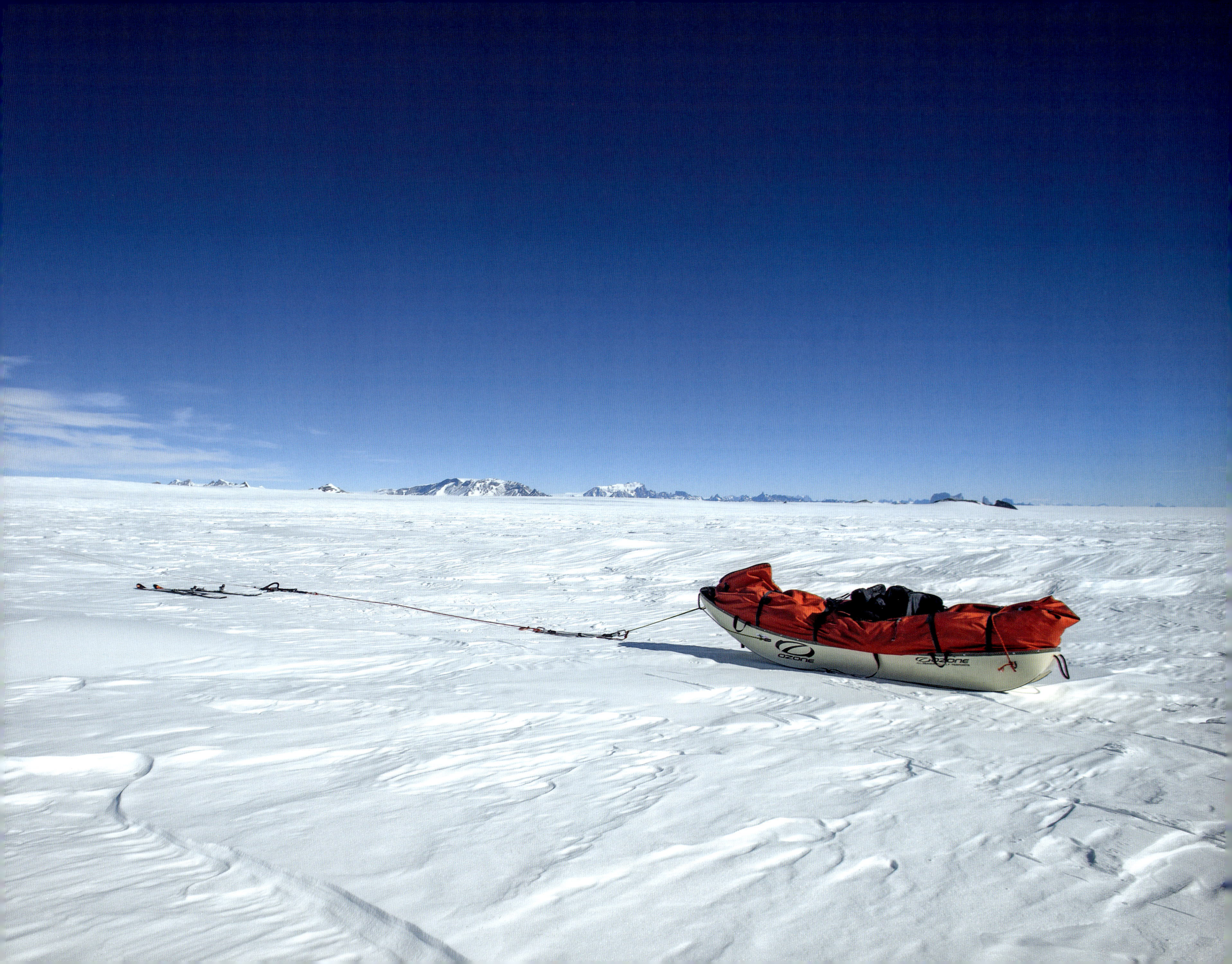
OZONE
OZONE

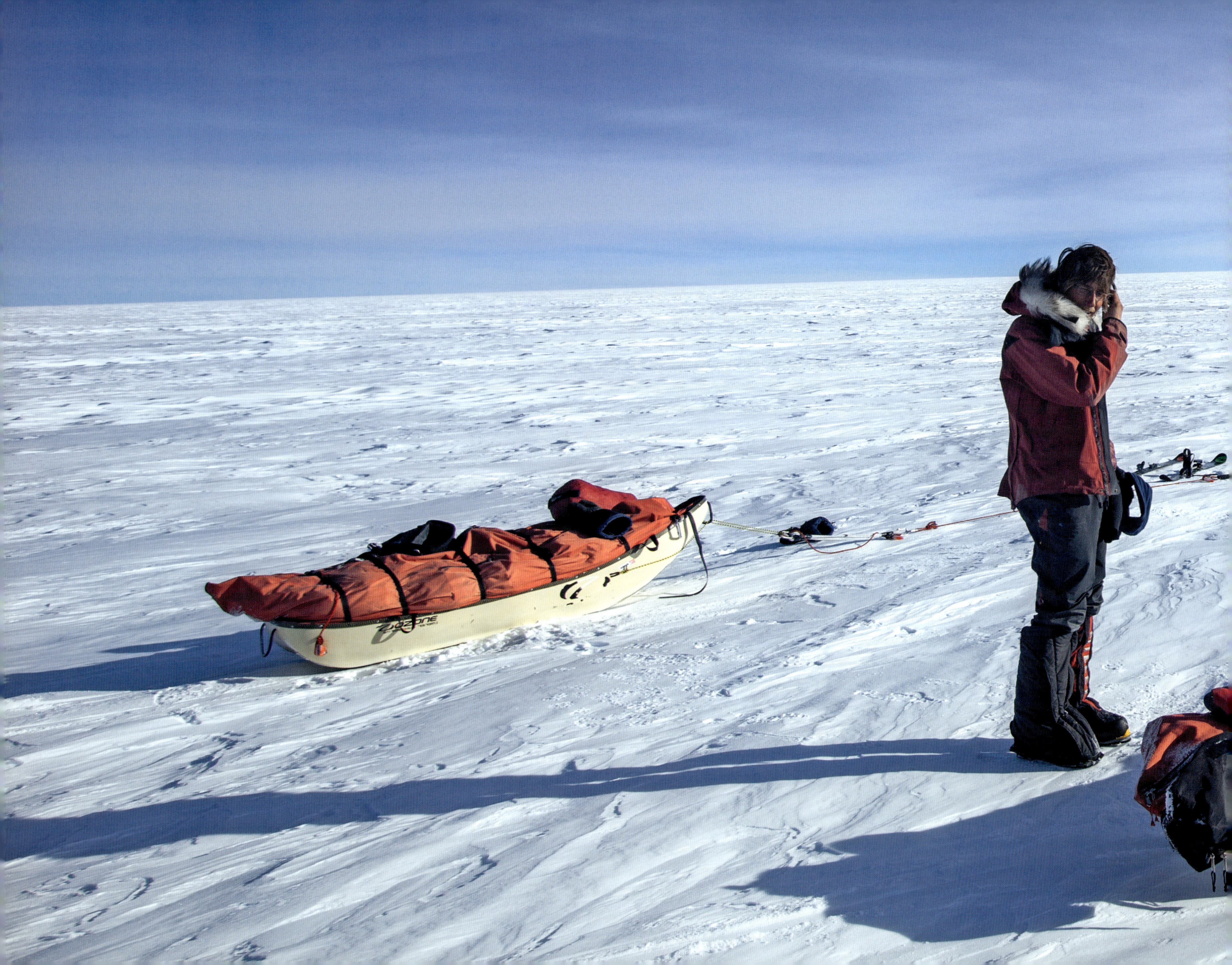

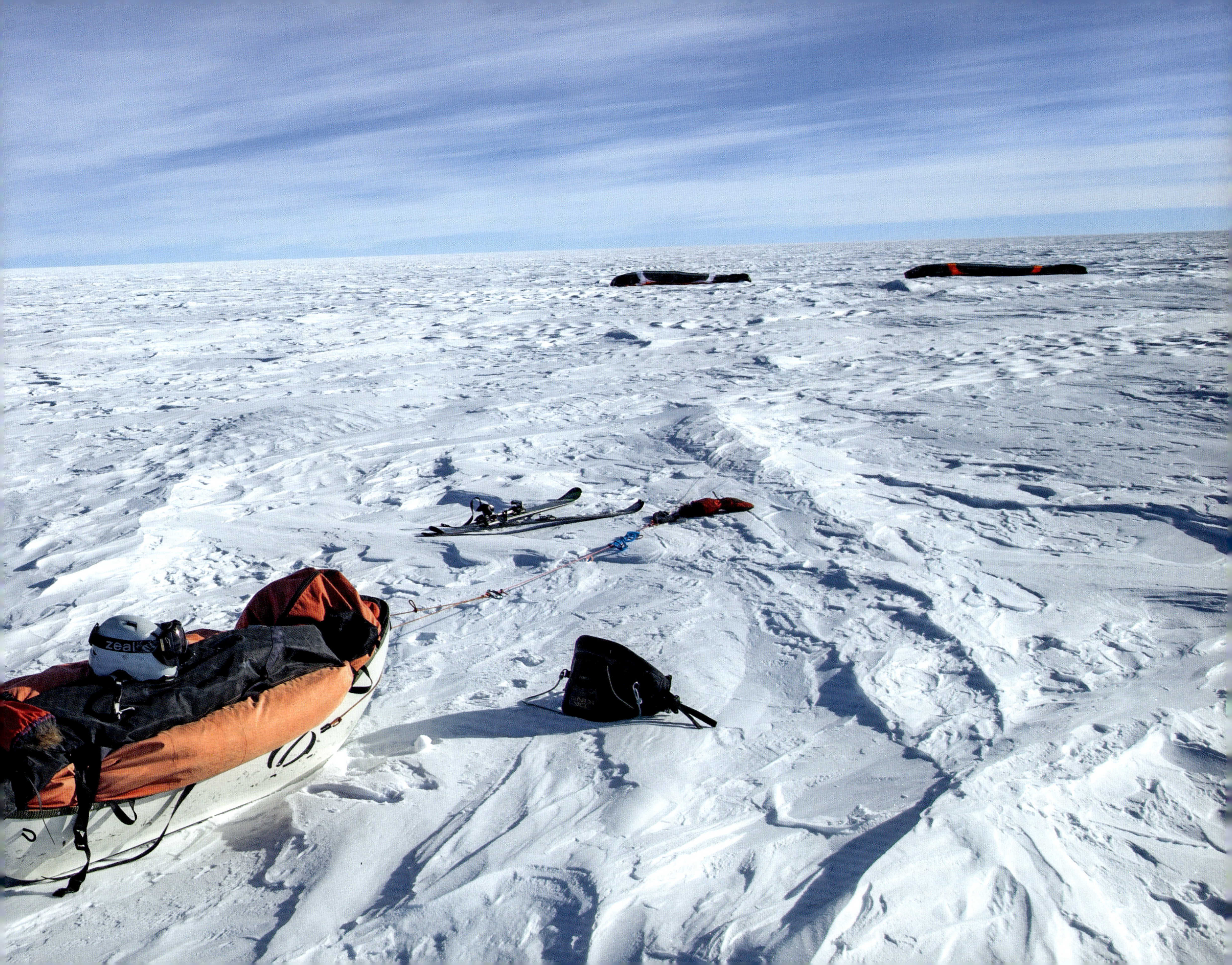
zeal

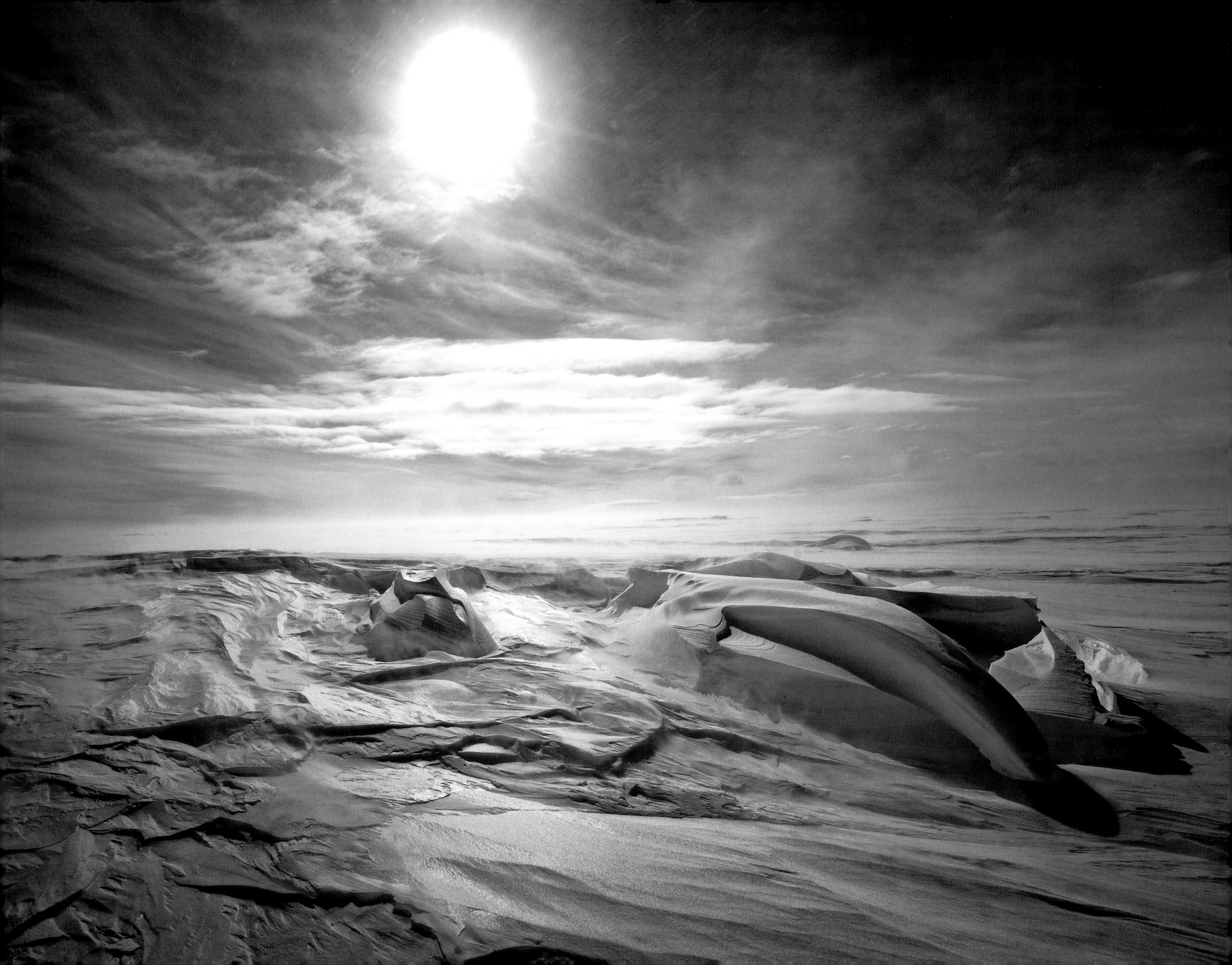

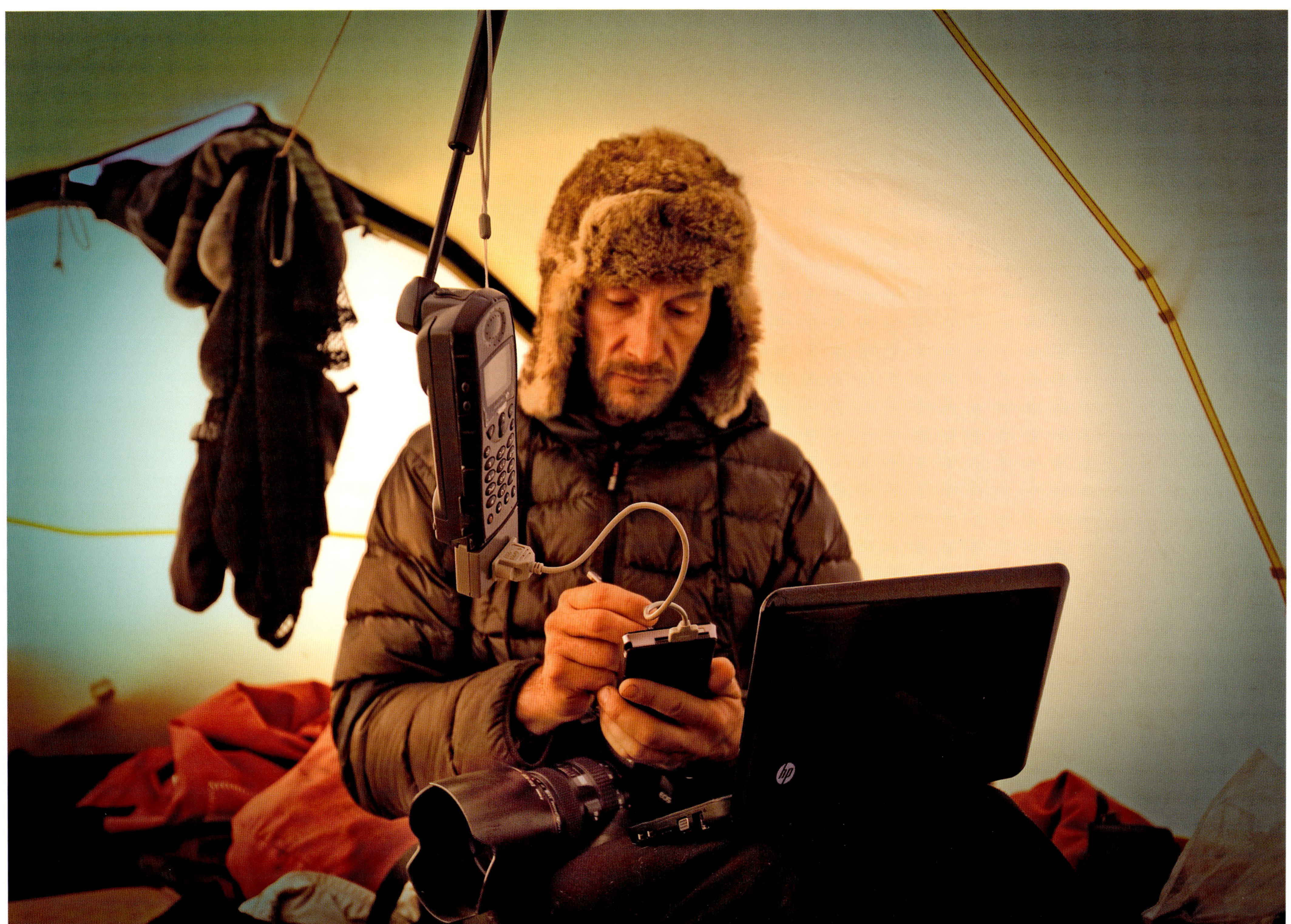

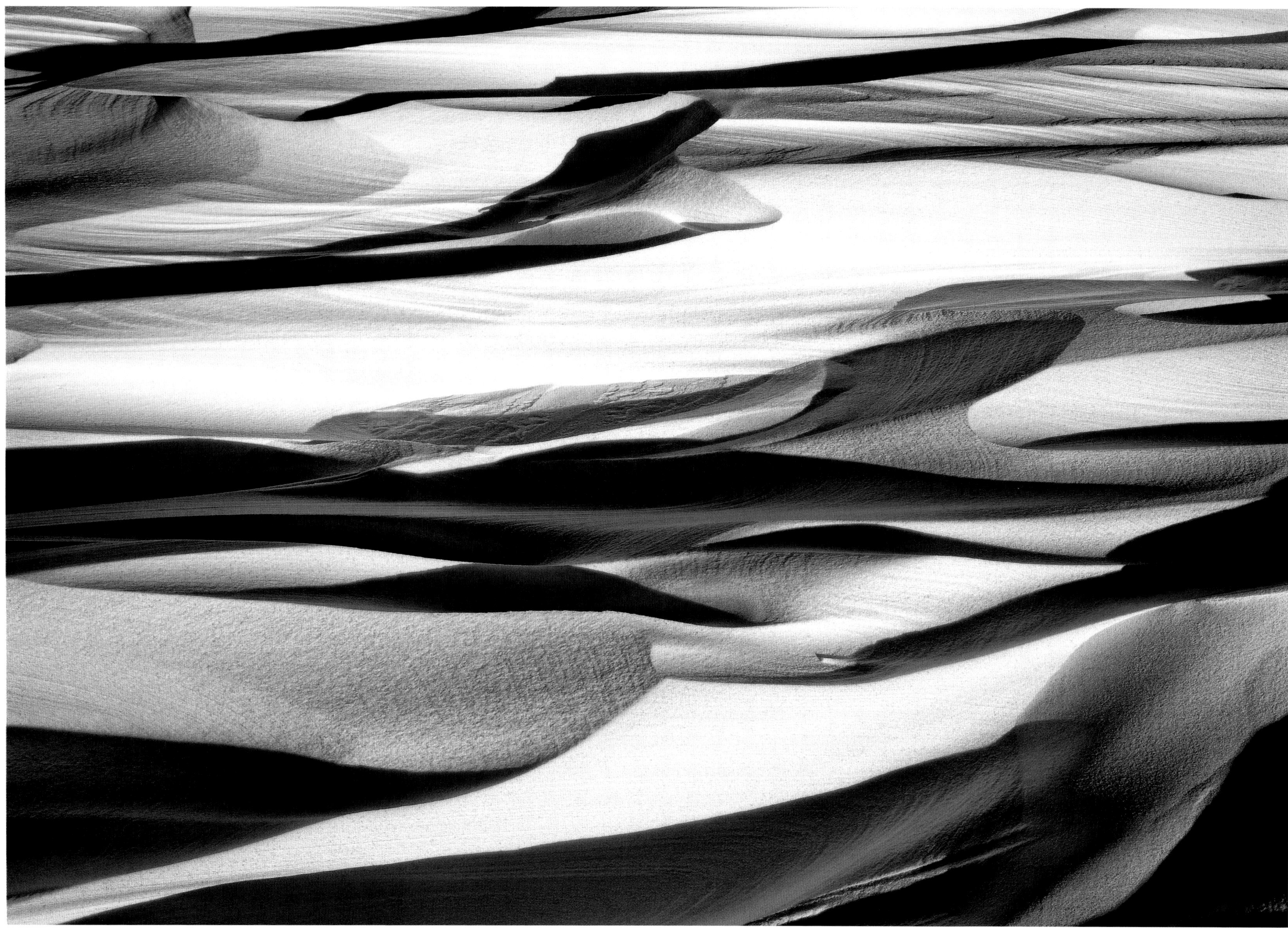

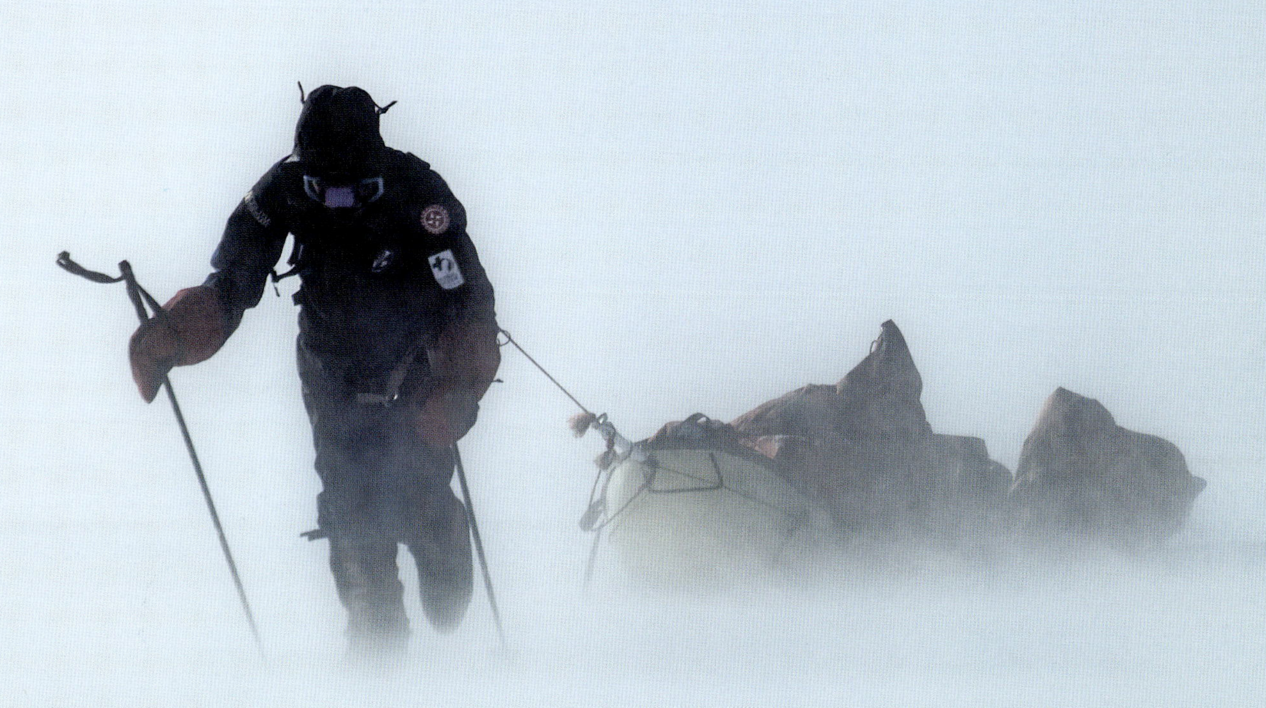

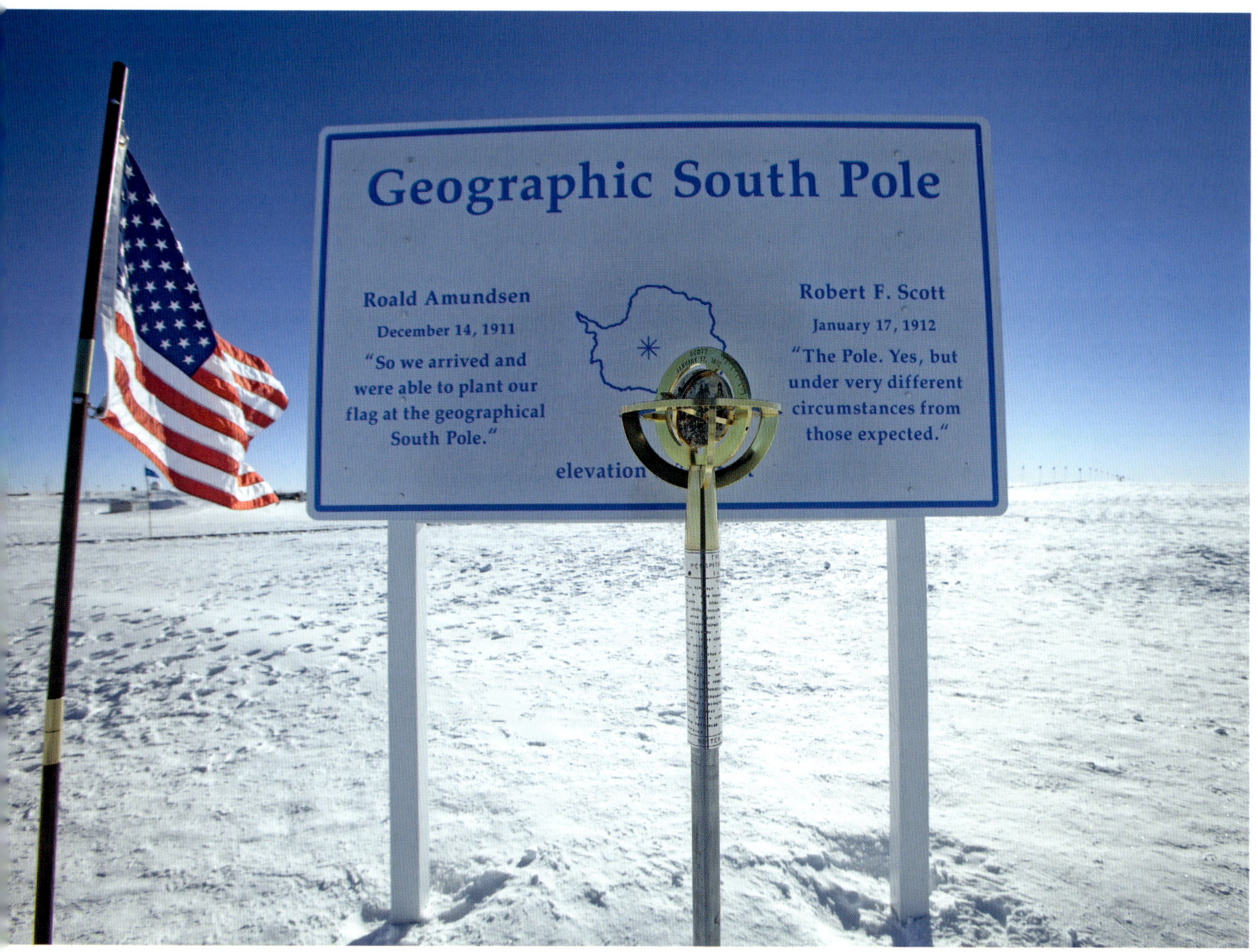
Geographic South Pole
Roald Amundsen
December 14, 1911
"So we arrived and were able to plant our flag at the geographical South Pole."
Robert F. Scott
January 17, 1912
"The Pole. Yes, but under very different circumstances from those expected."
elevation

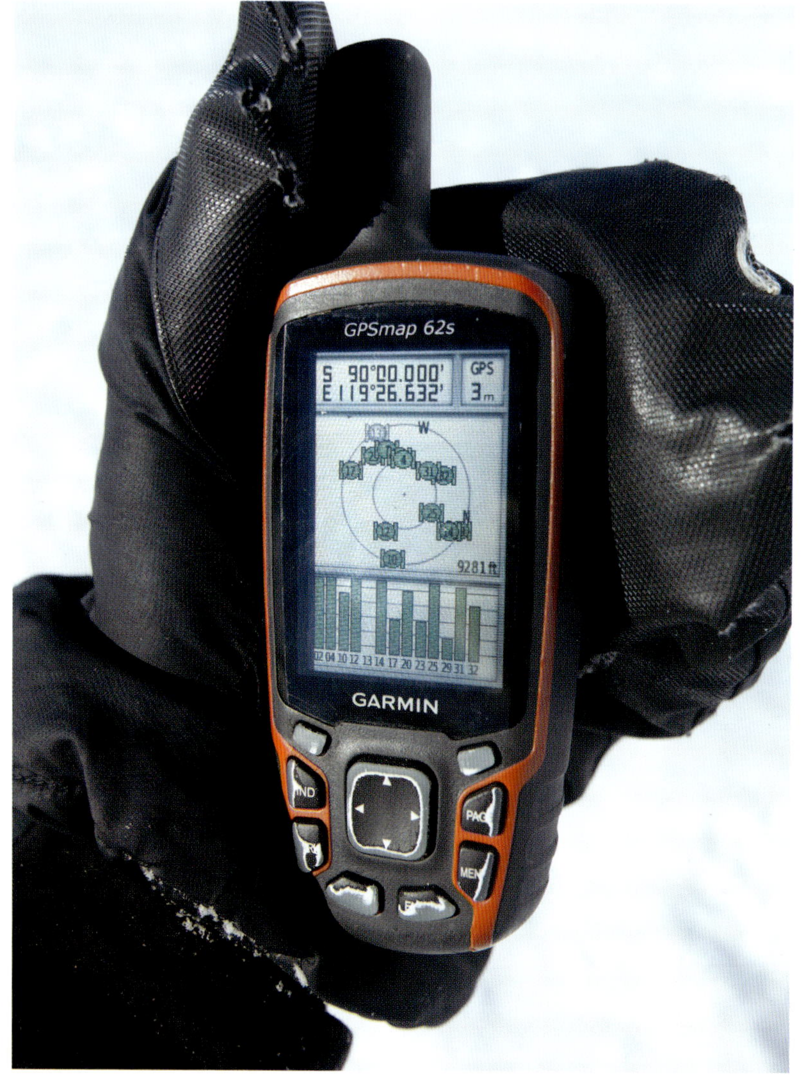
GPSmap 62s
S 90°00.000'
E119°26.632'
GPS
3m
GARMIN

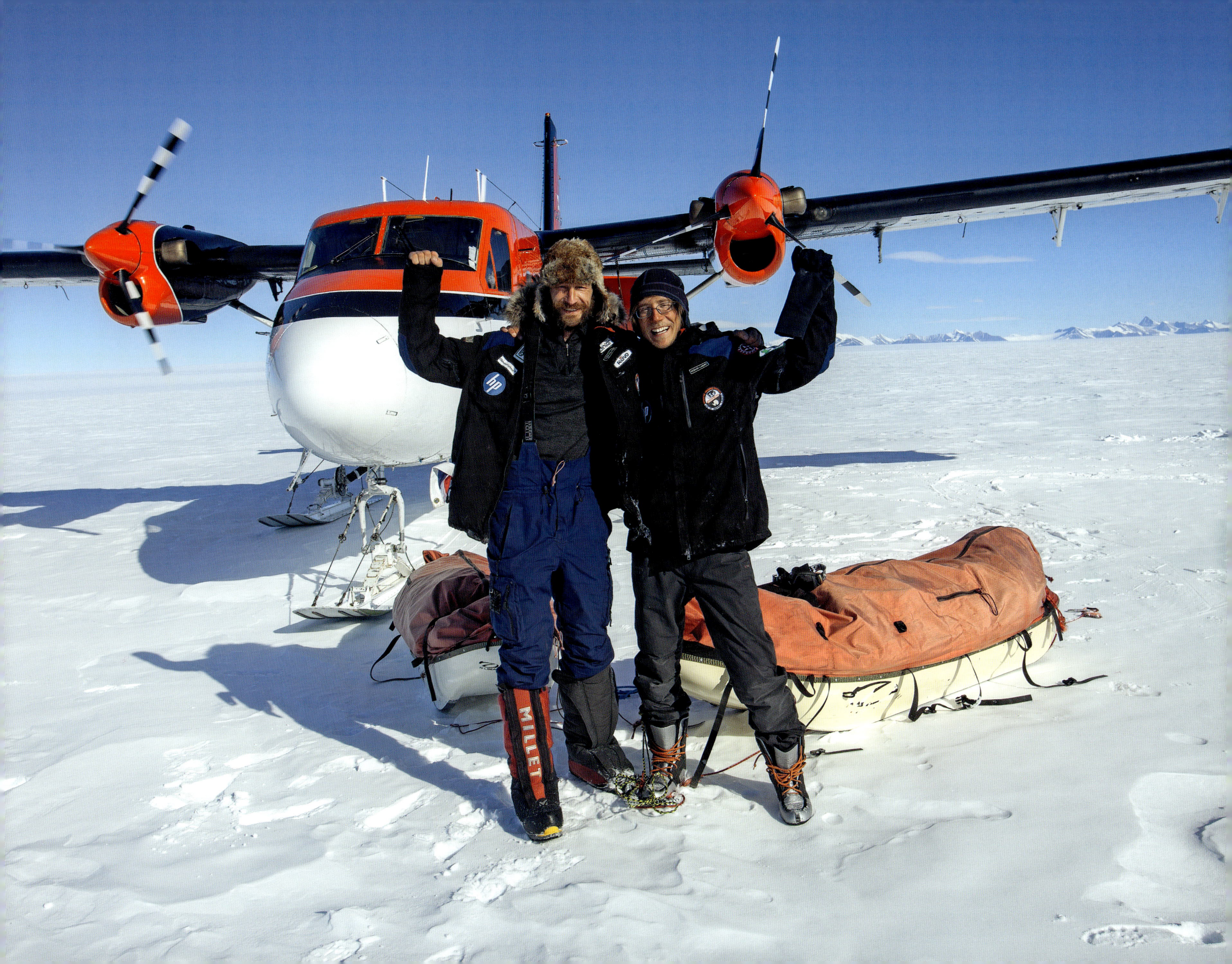
hp
MILLET

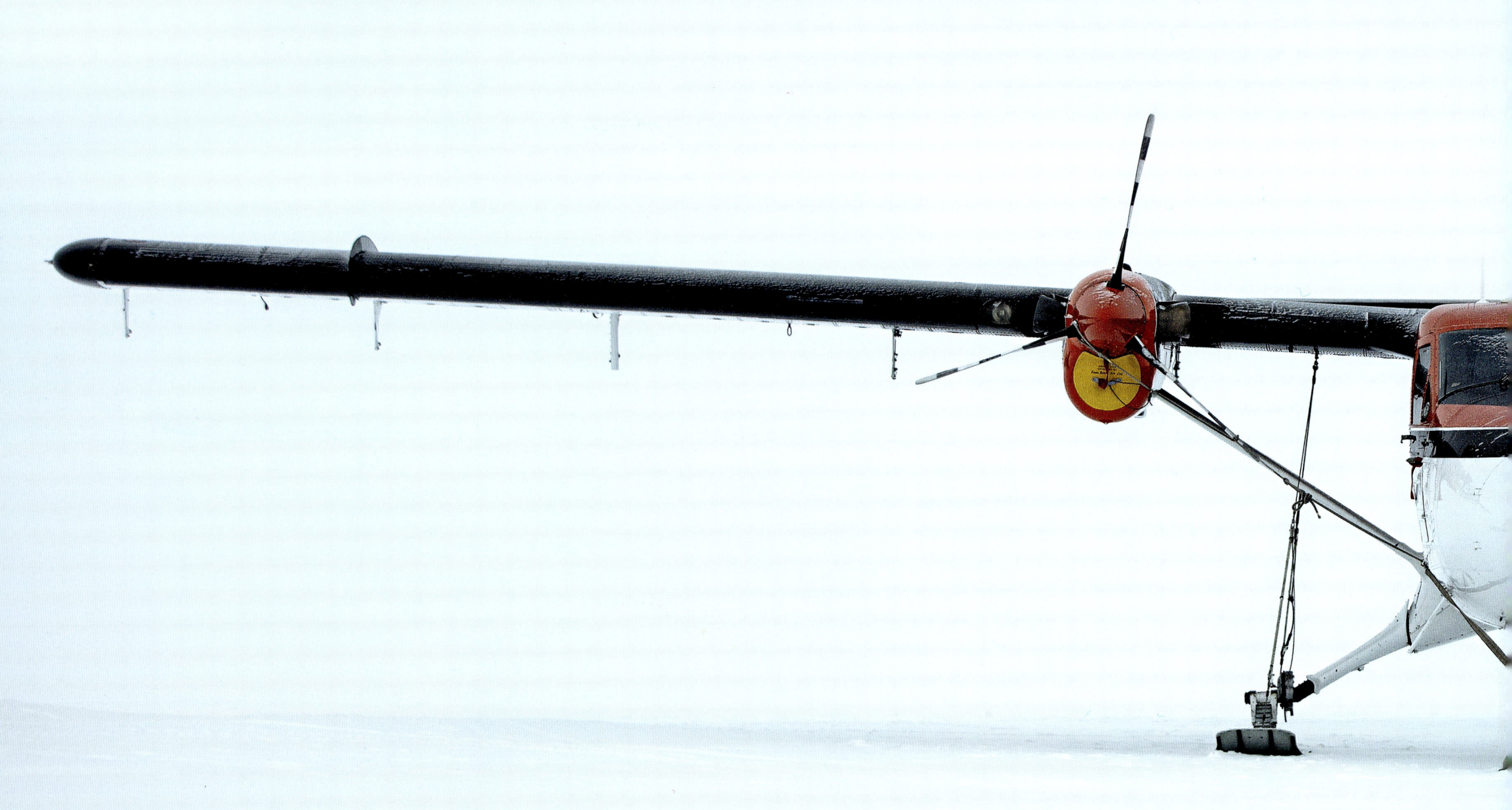

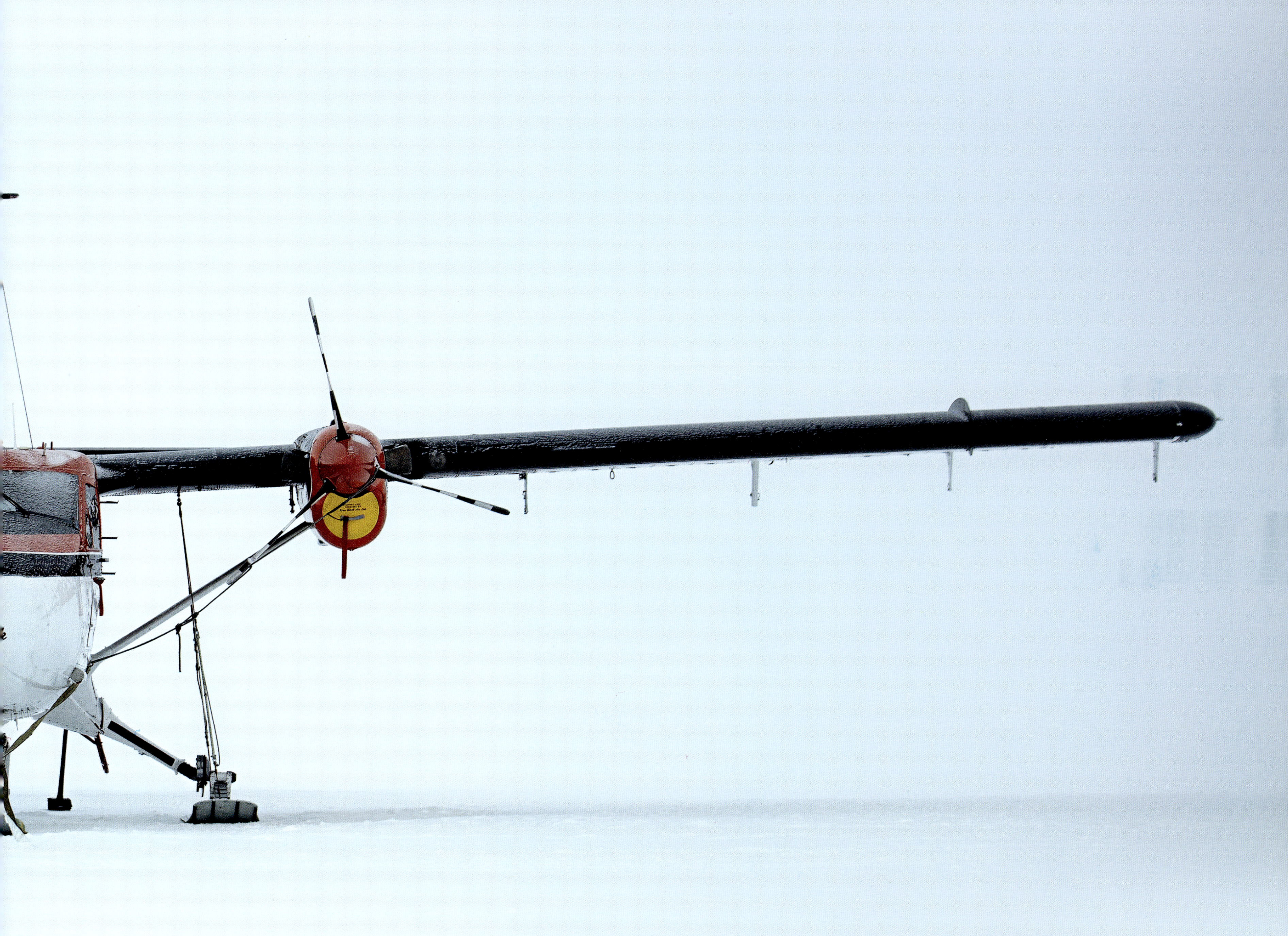

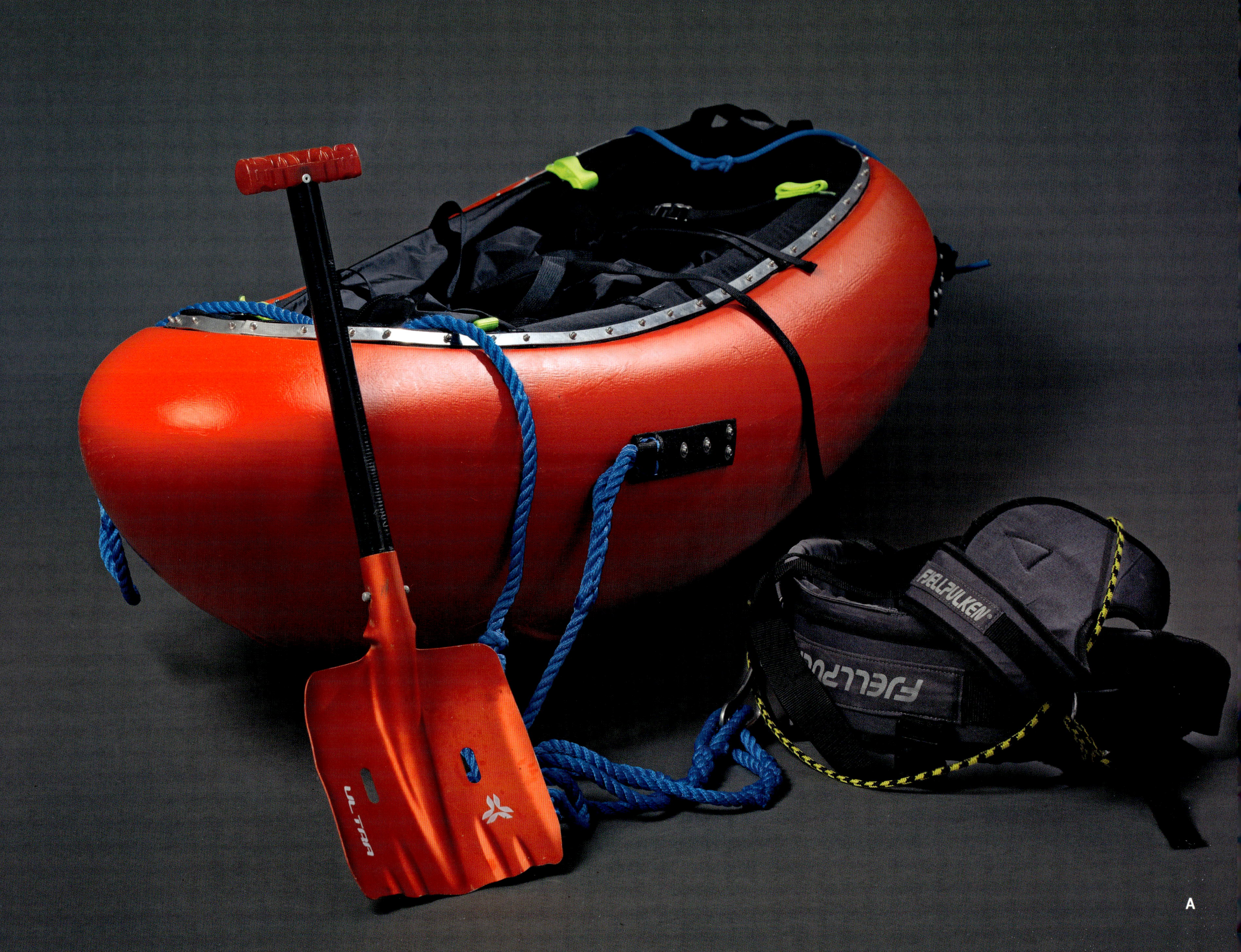

A

THE GEAR

A. The Beluga sled is especially suited for the sea ice because of its roundness (designed by Thomas Ulrich). **B.** Primus stoves, invented in 1892, transformed polar missions with their high heat. **C.** The kitchen: double-walled pot for melting snow, cooking pot with heat exchanger, and aluminum bowls, which don't break! **D.** A carbon base to maximize heat distribution will save a few pounds in fuel over months. **E.** Glove systems can include four layers on kiting expeditions. **F.** Different boots for different trips, but all have double liners; North Pole boots must be partially waterproof. **G.** Technology is, above all, what makes today's trips much easier, thanks to satellites and battery charging. **H.** 2011 Antarctica kiting suit, thick and warm. **I.** 2010 Greenland kiting suit, thinner and good for layering. **J.** Mesh helps keep sweat from soaking the merino wool first layer, which can freeze during stops and lead to hypothermia; the "tongue" sewn on the goggles prevents steam from the breath from freezing on the lens. **K.** Dry suit for North Pole missions. **L.** 2006–2007 Antarctica suit for coastal missions. **M.** 2017 North Pole suit. **N.** 2009 North Pole suit. **O.** 2016 Arctic cold safety suit.

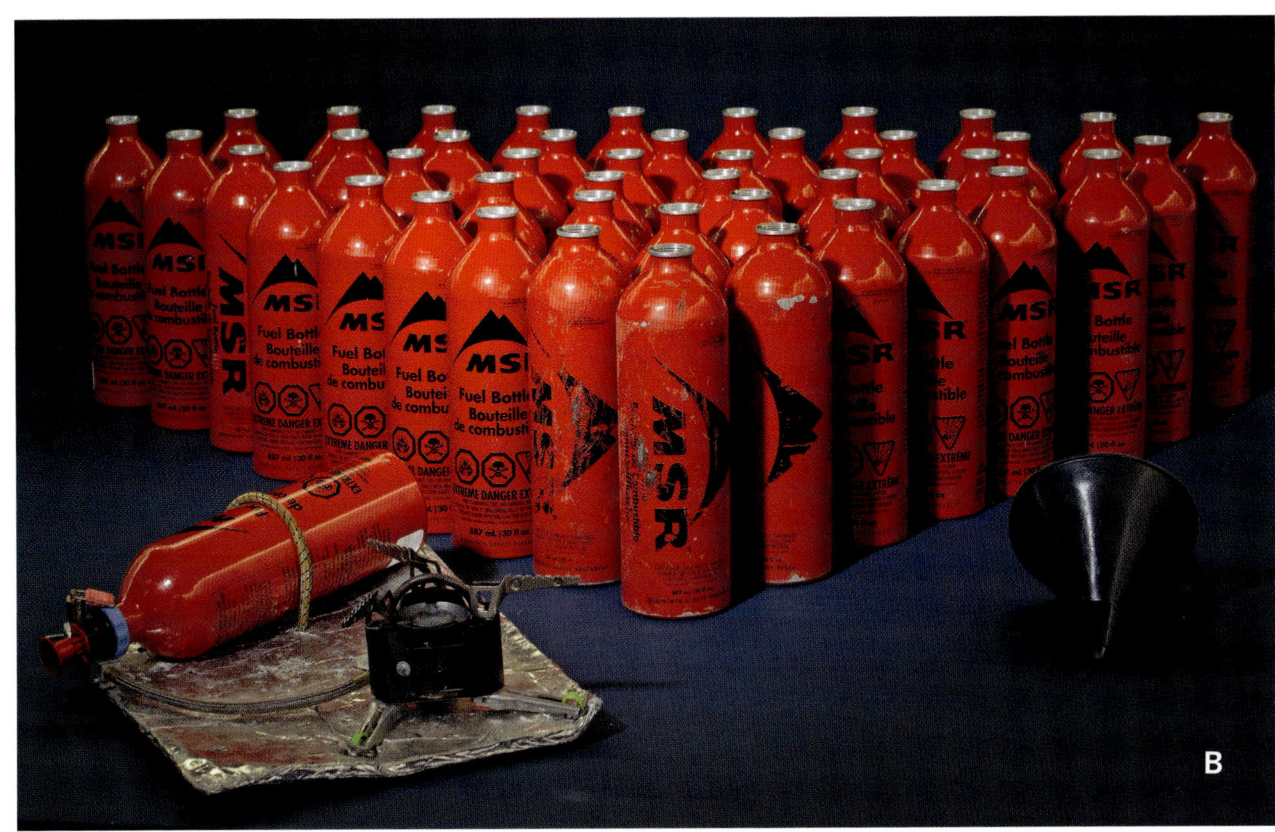

B

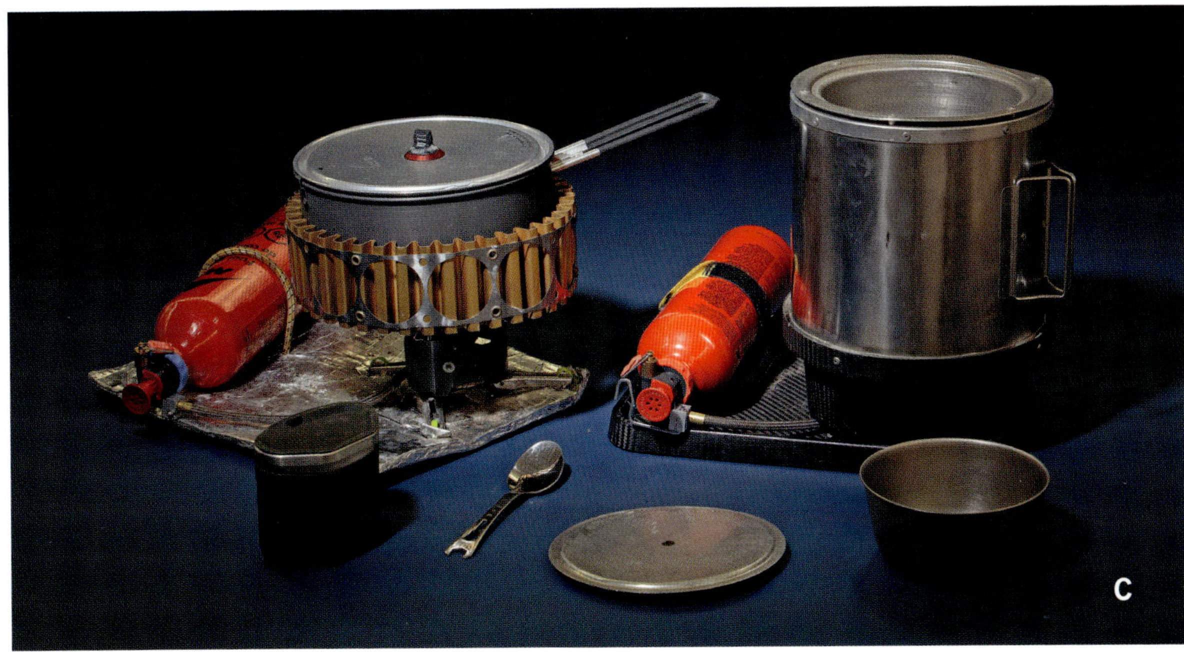

C

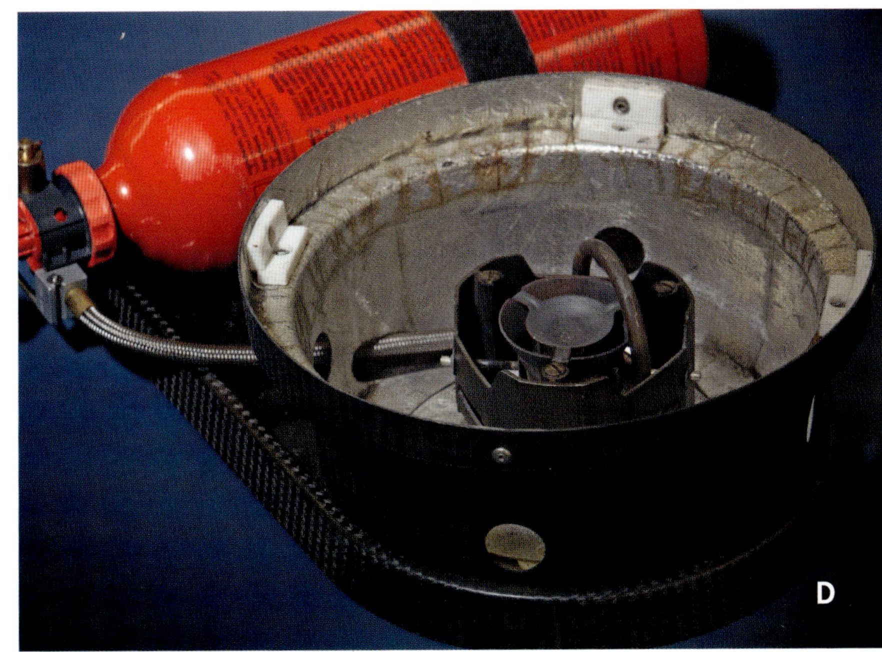

D

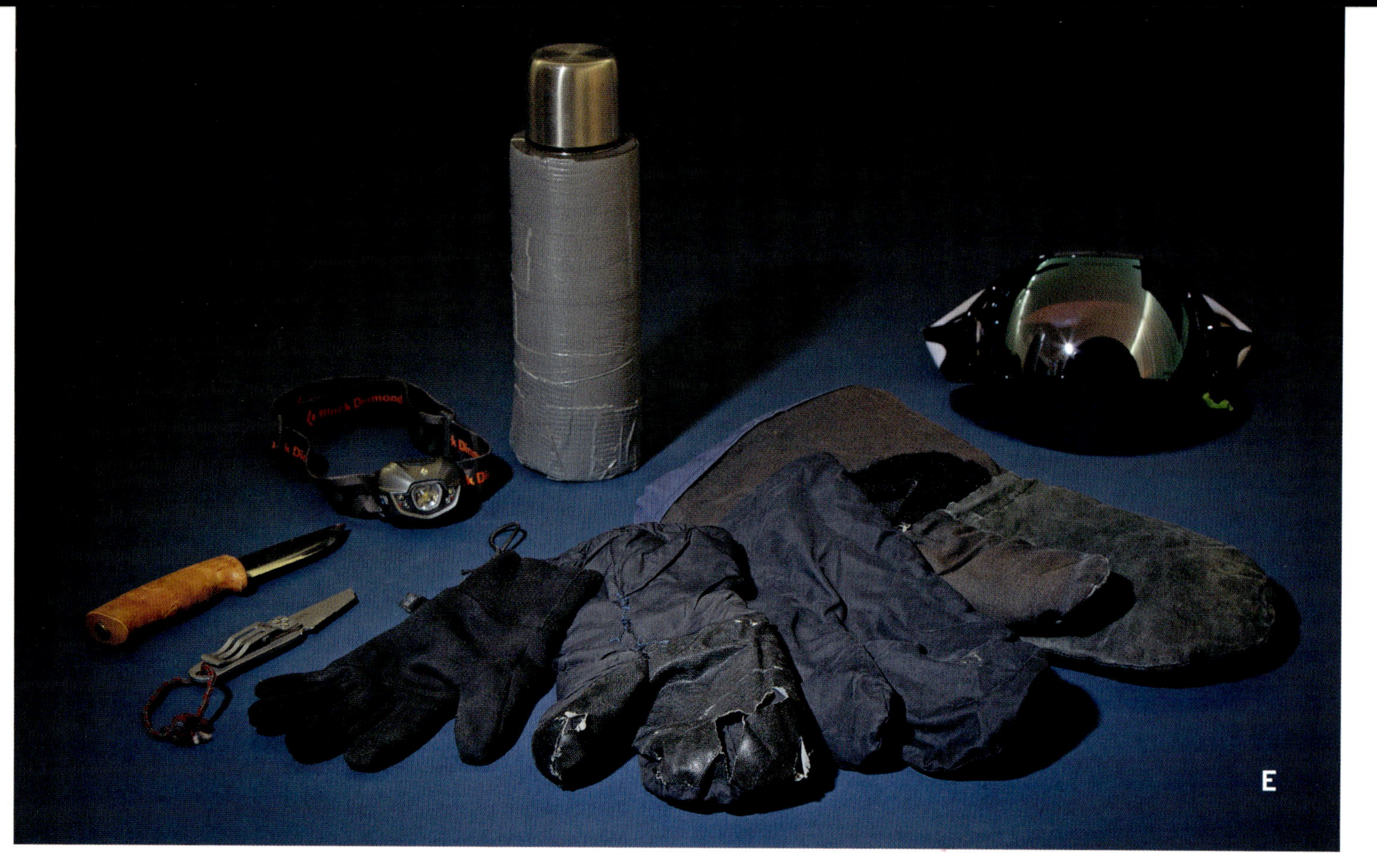
E

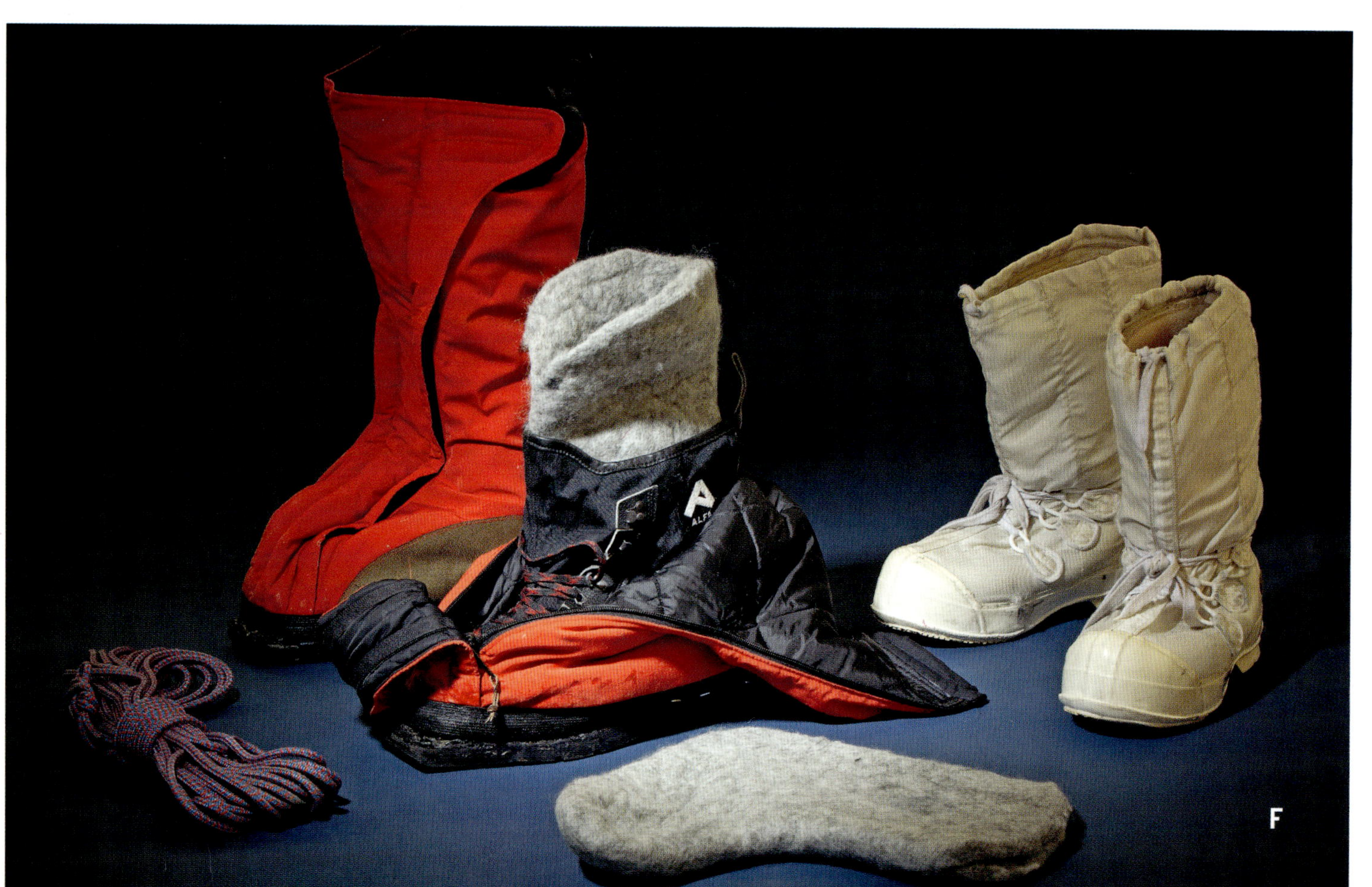
F

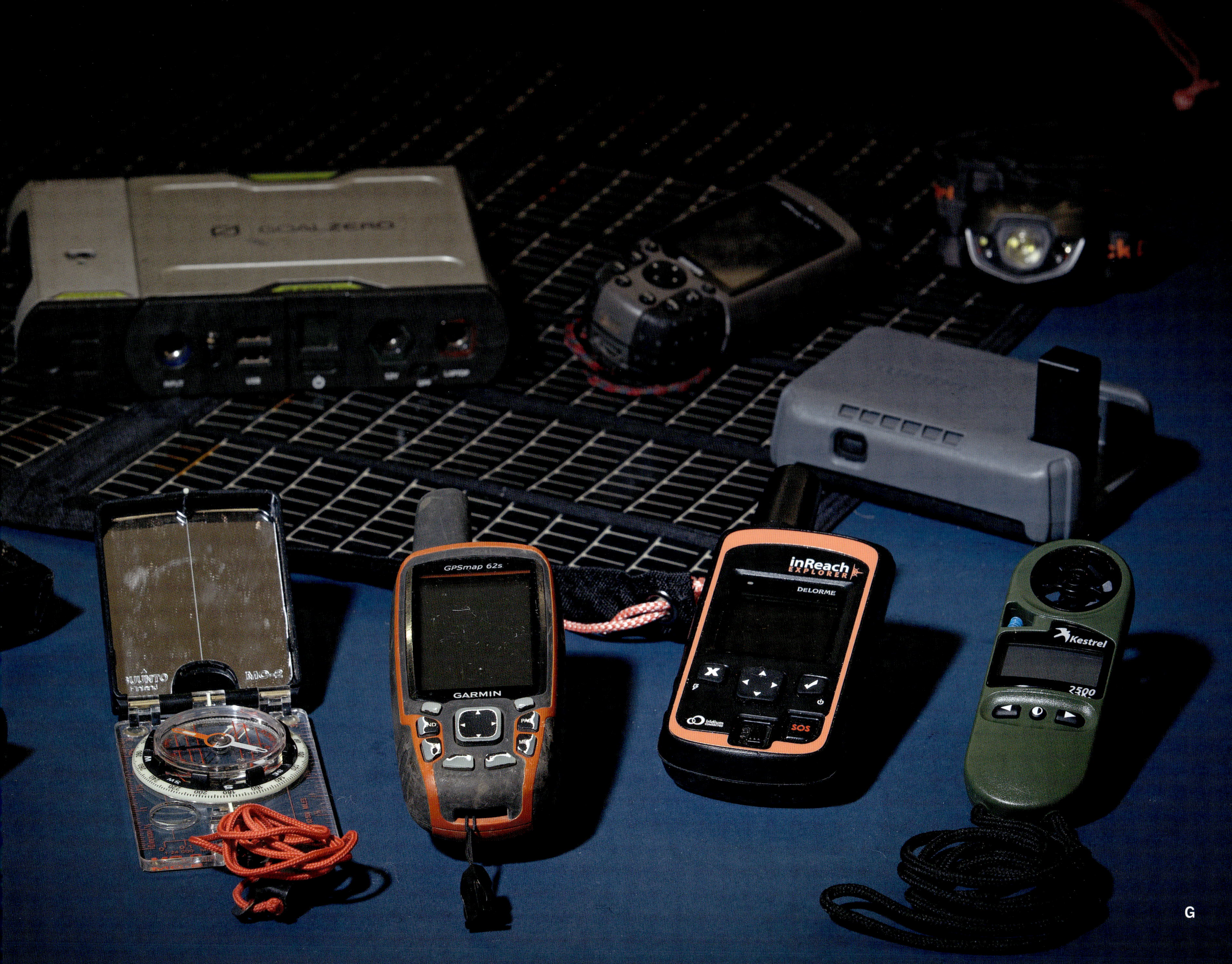
GPSmap 62s
GARMIN
inReach
EXPLORER
DELORME
SOS
Kestrel
2500
MC-2
G

Lexar
COPELAND
Revo
ClimatePartner
hp
Lexar
COPELAND
ClimatePartner
hp
GLOBAL
GREEN
USA

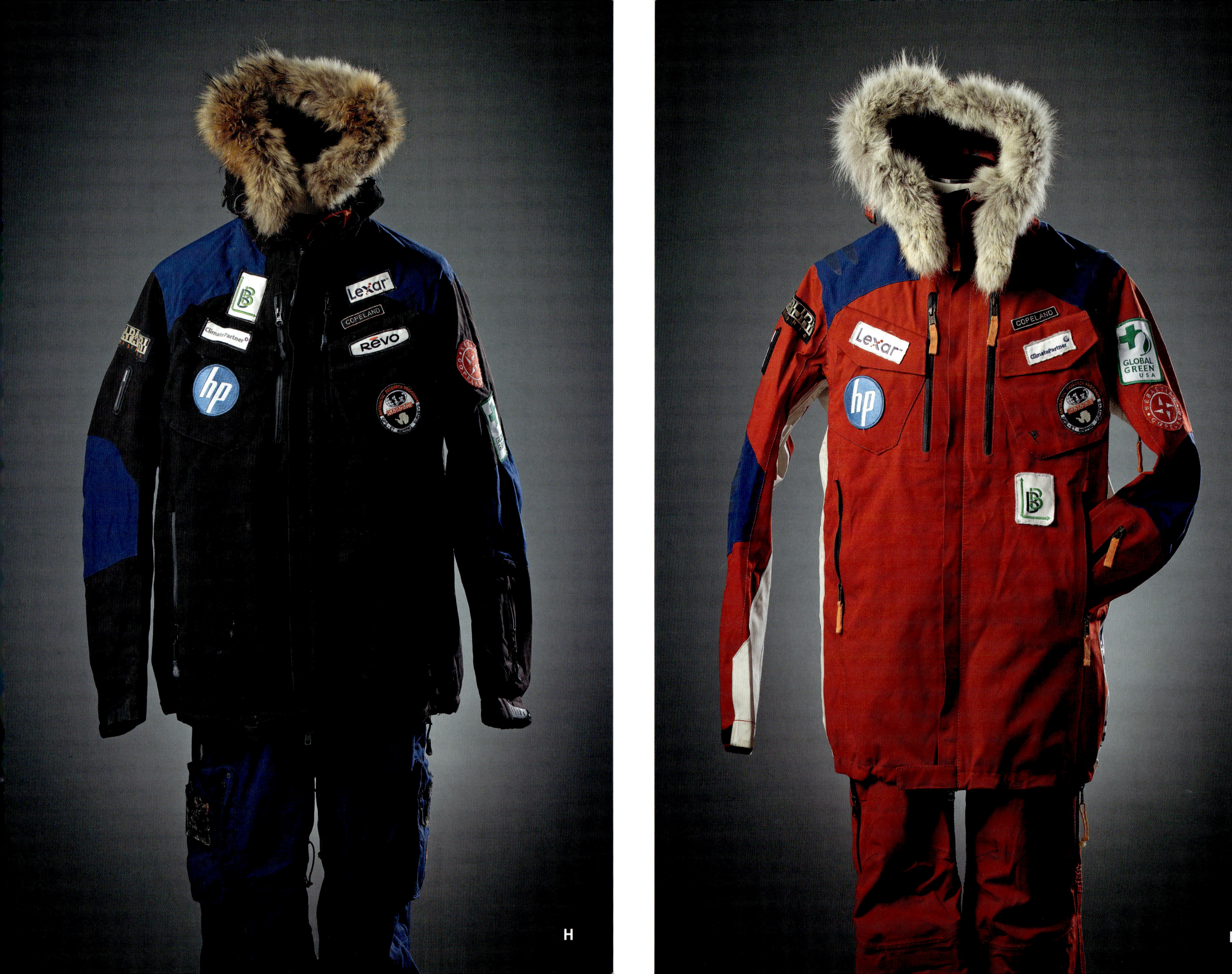

H

I

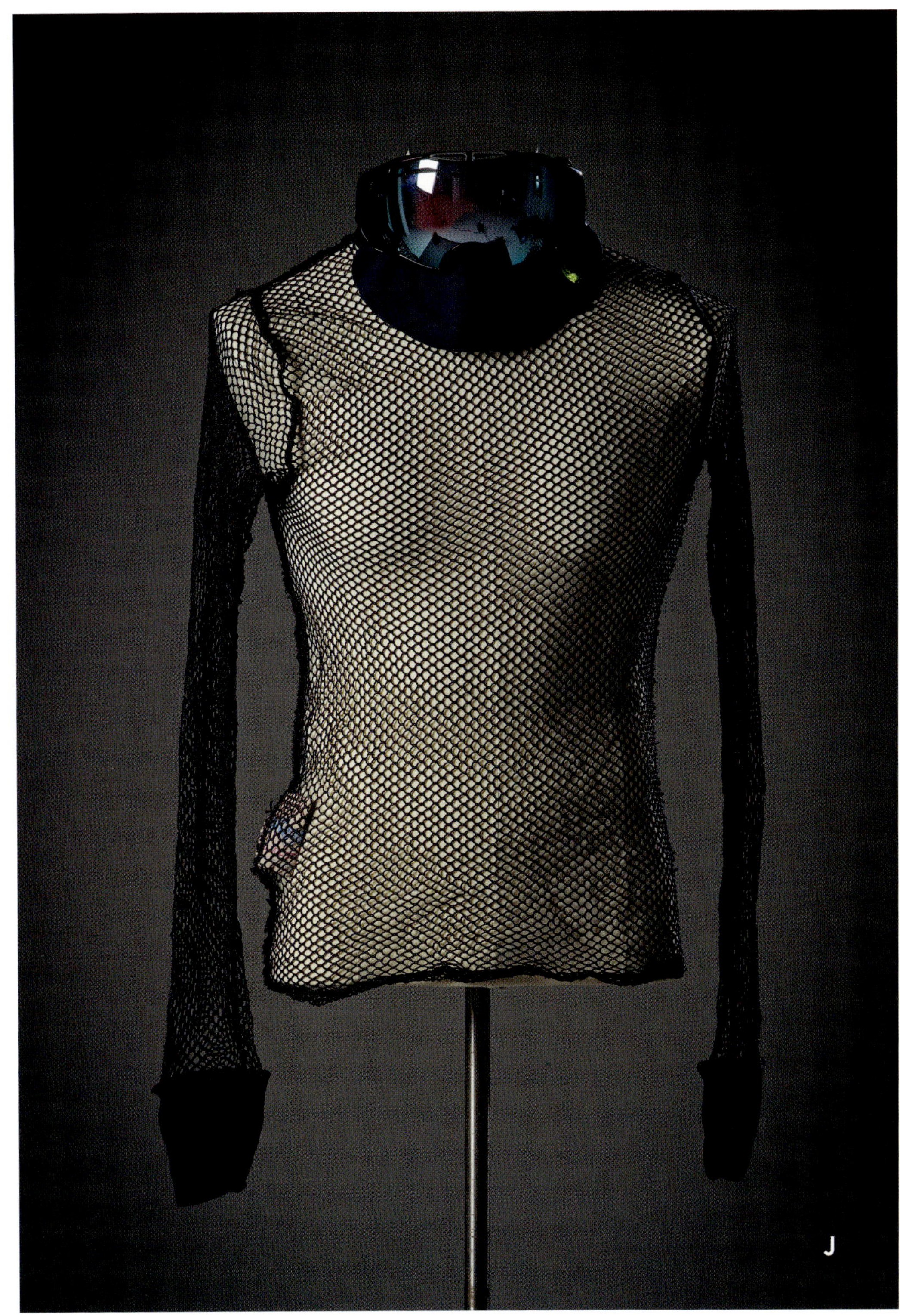
J

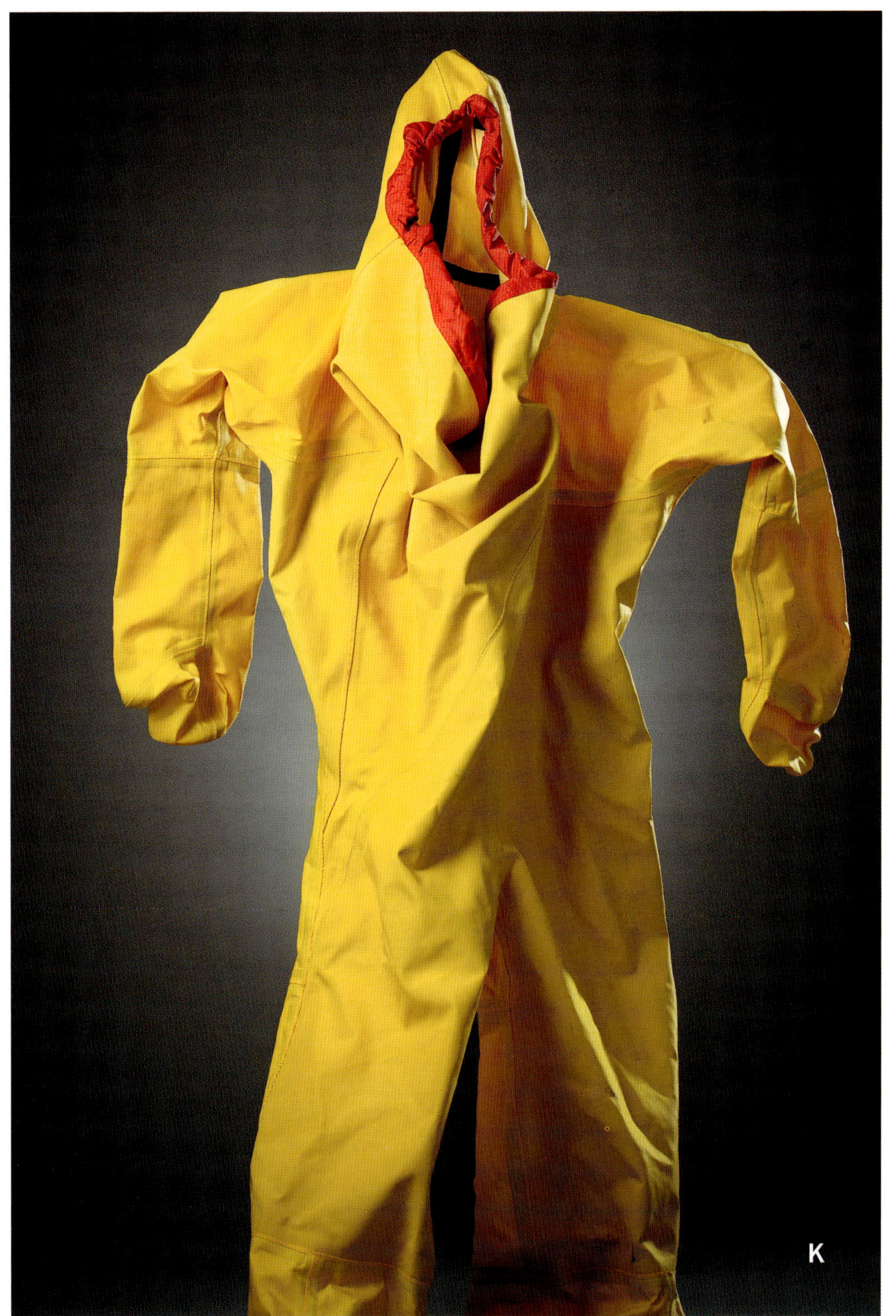
K

hp
ICE LADY PATAGONIA
ARGENTINA
GLOBAL
GREEN
USA

L

GLOBAL
GREEN
USA
ClimatePartner
NAPAPIJRI
geographic
COPELAND
ONE GUN
SEBASTIAN
COPELAND

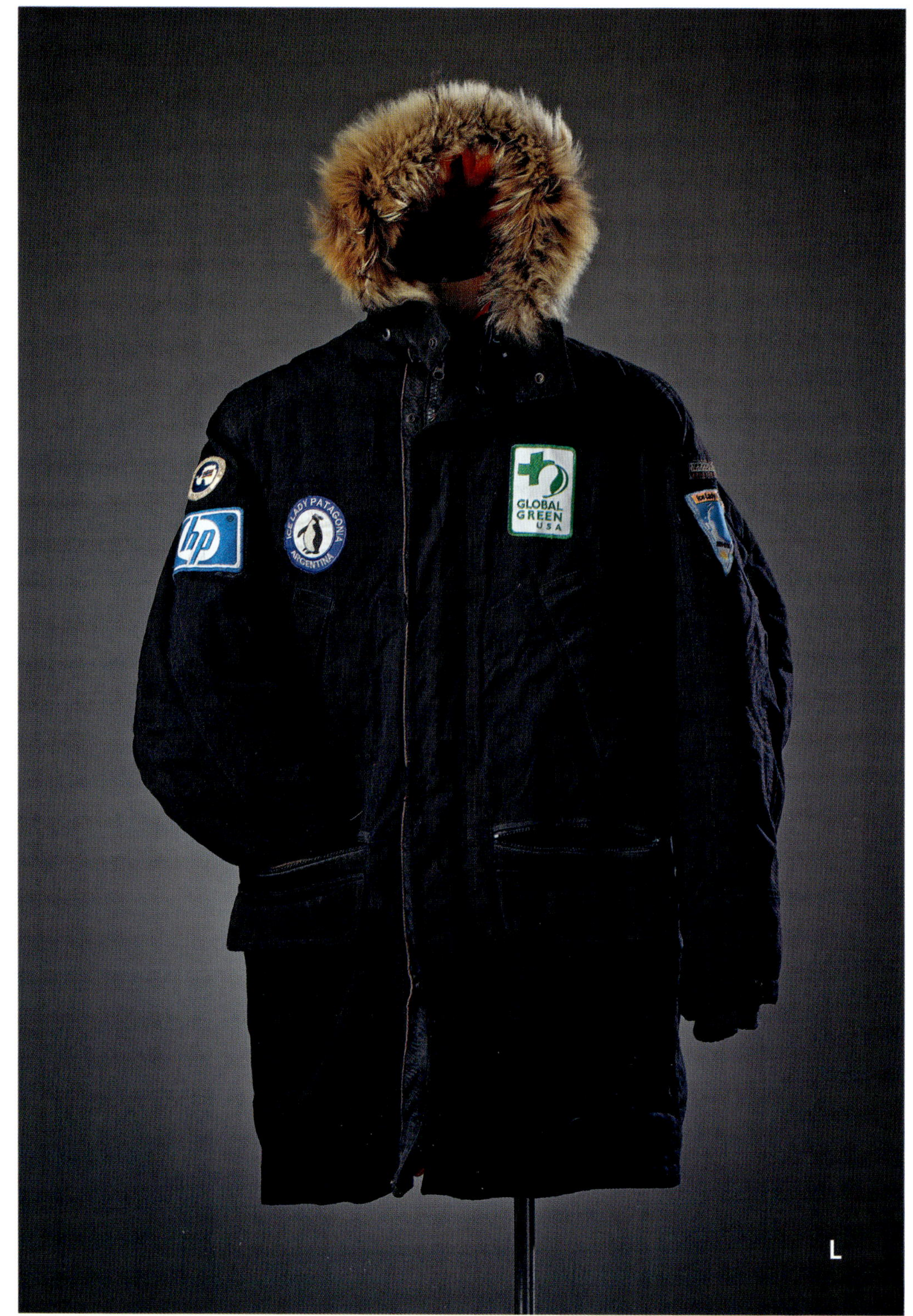

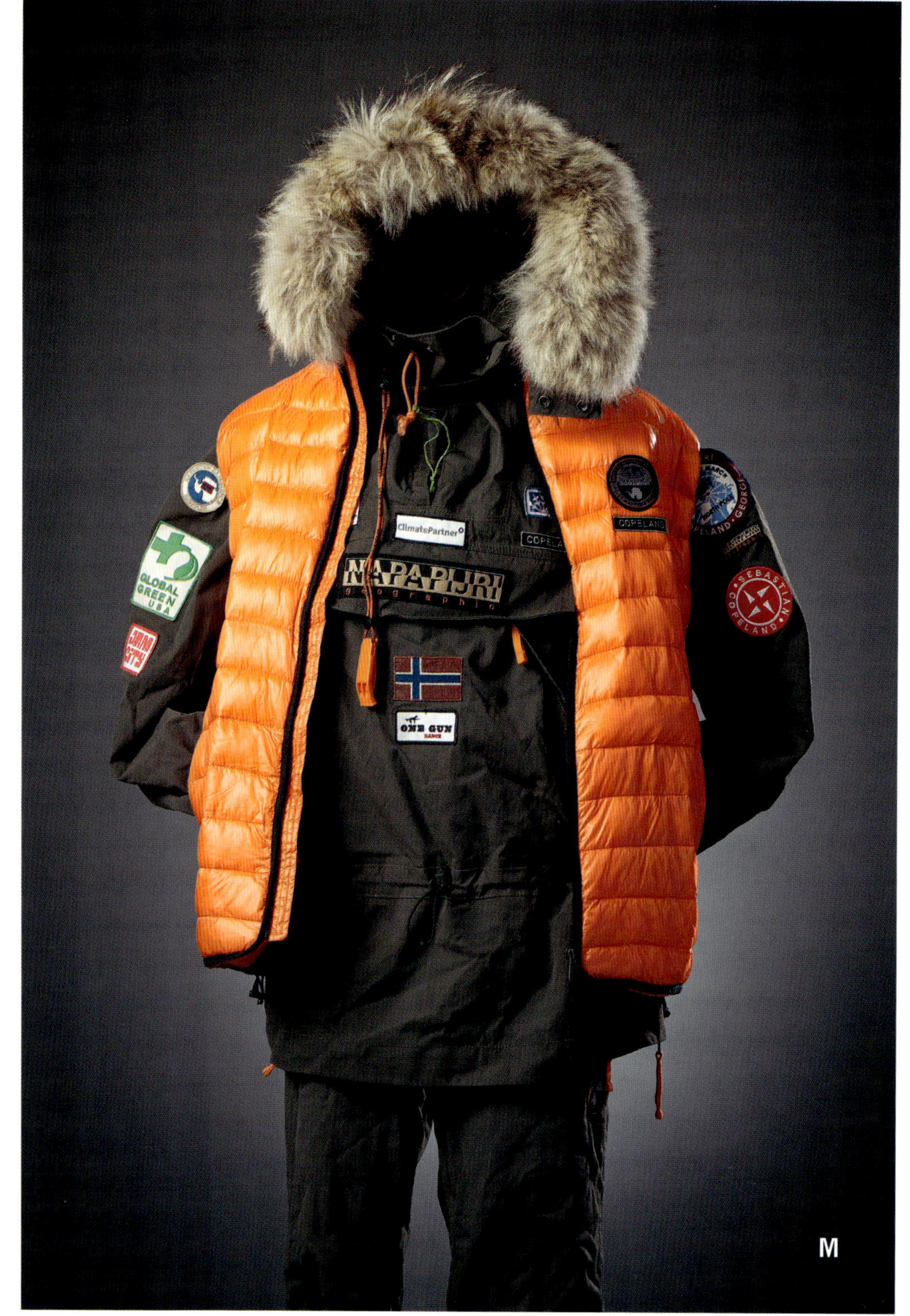

M

Revo
NAPAPIJRI
geographic
ClimatePartner
GLOBAL GREEN USA
hp
NAPAPIJRI
geographic

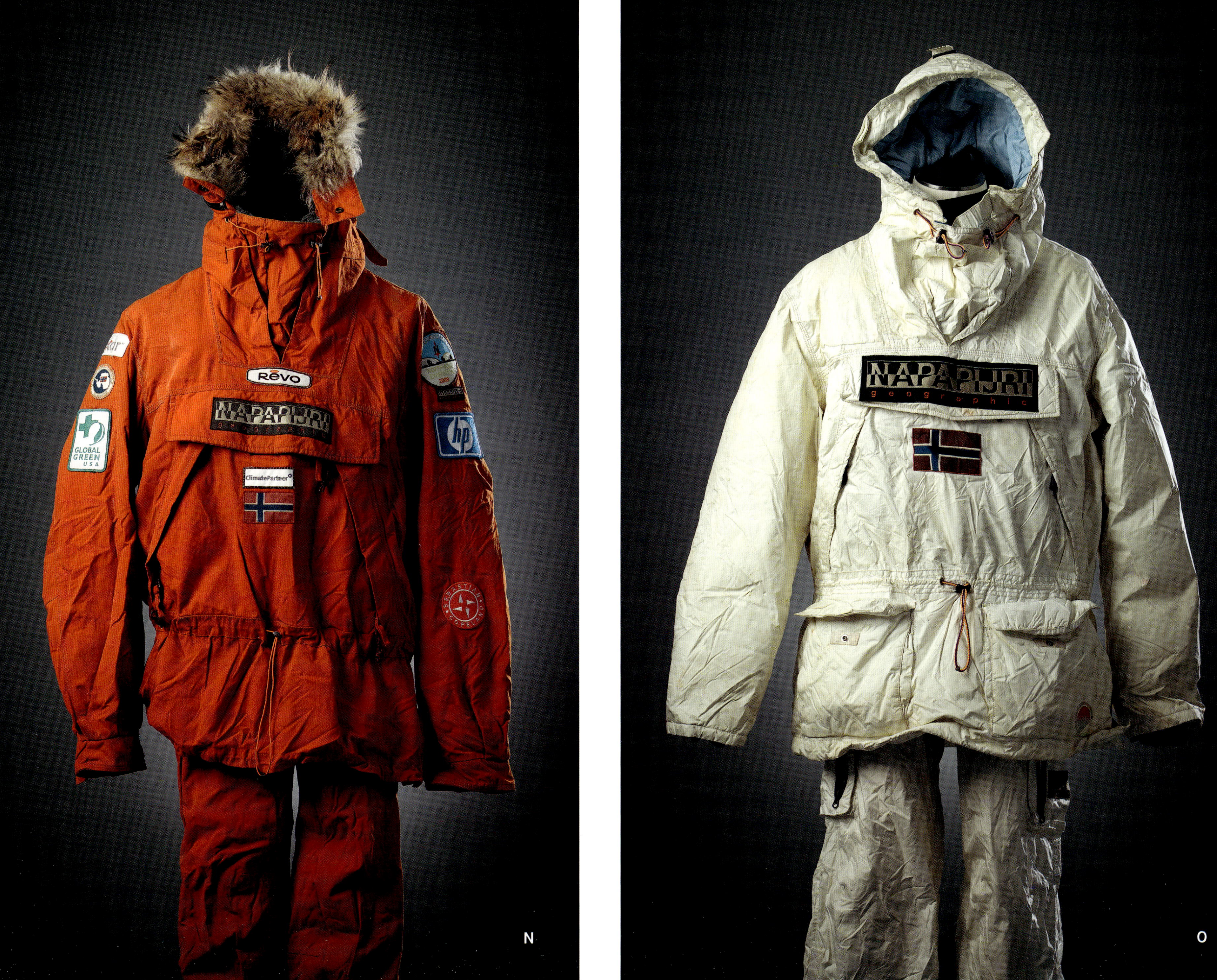

N

O

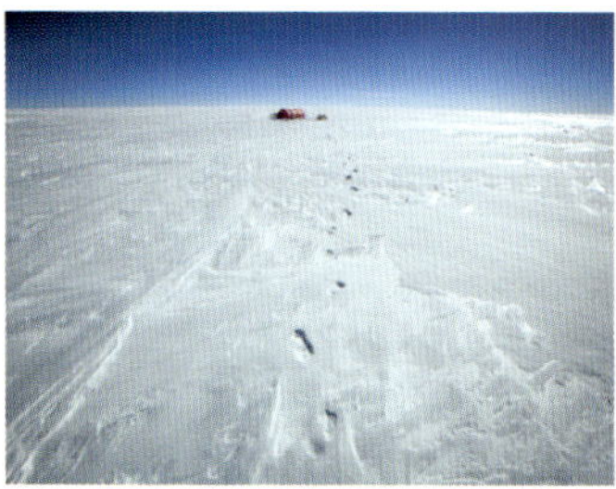

EAST ANTARCTICA, ABOUT LATITUDE 82° SOUTH (Page 2)
Most of the Antarctic ice sheet is mutilated by ferocious winds that shred its surface. Occasionally, the surface can be polished like a stone, with a soft cover of snowdrift. But these surfaces are few and far between. Either way, Antarctica's desolation will make you feel like the last human on Earth—or the first on another planet!

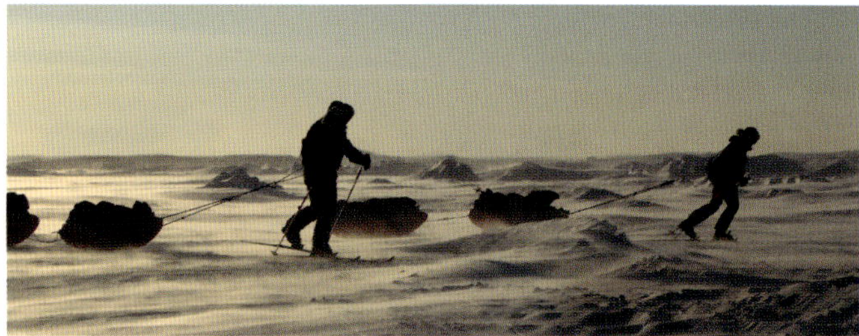

STORM ON THE ARCTIC SEA ICE (Pages 4–5)
The Arctic sea ice is relentless and physically the most depleting of all polar environments. The high humidity gets the freeze into your bones, and the motion of the ice generates obstacles and open water to cross. The drift takes you backward when you sleep, and then come polar bears. North Pole missions will make you cry.

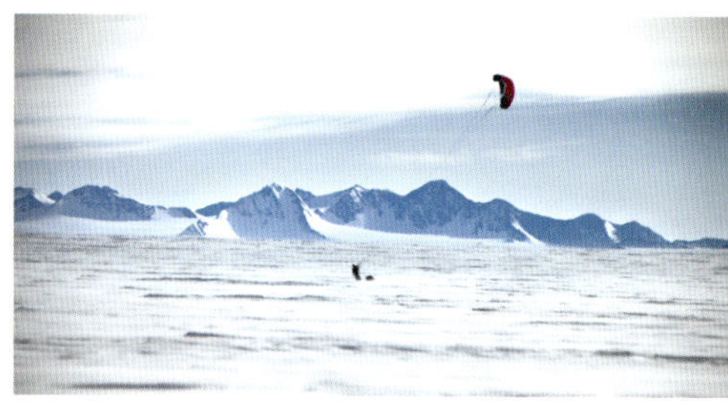

ELLSWORTH MOUNTAINS, ANTARCTICA (Pages 6–7)
The sight of the Ellsworth mountain range in West Antarctica indicates the descending ice sheet on the way to the coast. It is a welcome relief after three months of the featureless ice of the Antarctic Plateau.

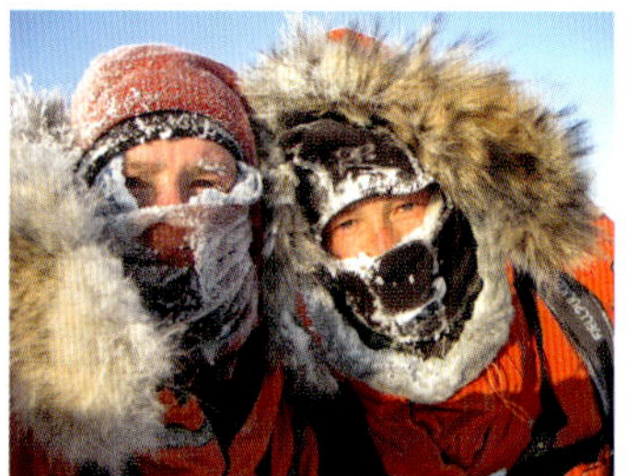

KEITH AND ME ON THE ARCTIC SEA ICE (Page 12)
Keith and I forged bonds sealed in the shared pain of a North Pole expedition. Five days into the two-month mission, facing temperatures below -50°F, we didn't know what hit us. North Pole missions are the hardest of polar journeys and arguably the toughest on Earth.

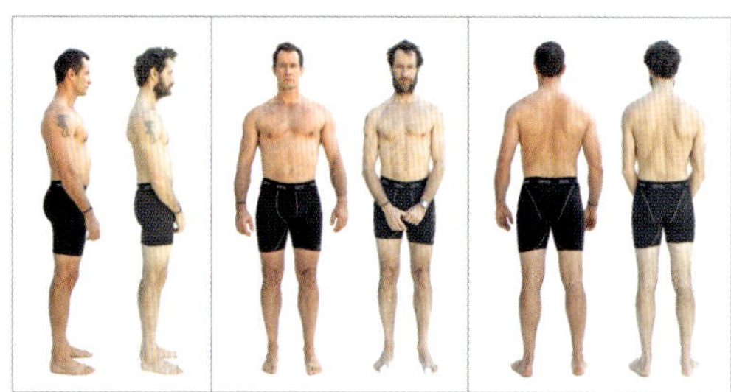

BEFORE-AND-AFTER PHOTOS (Page 13)
These were taken just before my departure and right after reentry from a three-month crossing of Antarctica. I lost 28 pounds on that trip. My body fat was seven percent upon return, making a polar expedition the single best weight-loss program there is. A few pints of ice cream restored my fat reserves in no time.

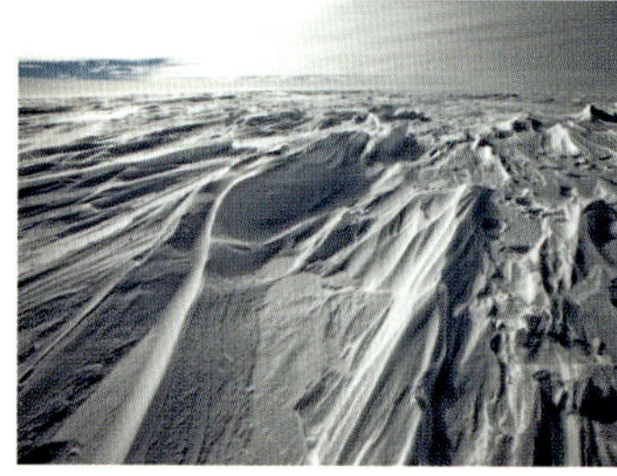

SASTRUGI ON THE EAST ANTARCTIC PLATEAU (Page 15)
If the Antarctic terrain could speak, it would scream in pain. The ice is shredded by winds that reach 200 miles per hour in the austral winter. Kite skiing there means getting thrashed by these tight ridges that are as hard as wood. In whiteout conditions, these features become virtually invisible.

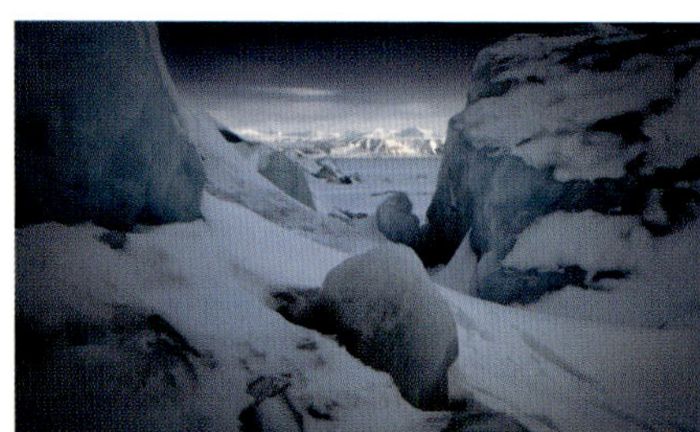

SPITSBERGEN, SVALBARD (Pages 16–17)
Spitsbergen is an island in the Norwegian archipelago of Svalbard inside the Arctic Circle. It was a launching point for many Arctic expeditions. Fridtjof Nansen was reunited with his ship *Fram* on Spitsbergen after spending more than two years on the sea ice. There are more polar bears than people in Svalbard.

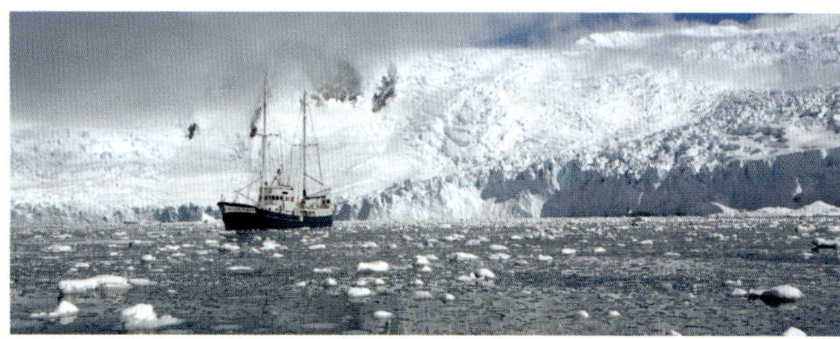

NEAR PAMPA BAY, ANTARCTIC PENINSULA (Pages 18–19)
Sudden drops in temperature can freeze the sea ice without warning. Surface ice will bond and solidify, trapping ships. This is what happened to Ernest Shackleton's ship *Endurance* in 1918, leading to one of the more epic stories of survival in Antarctic history.

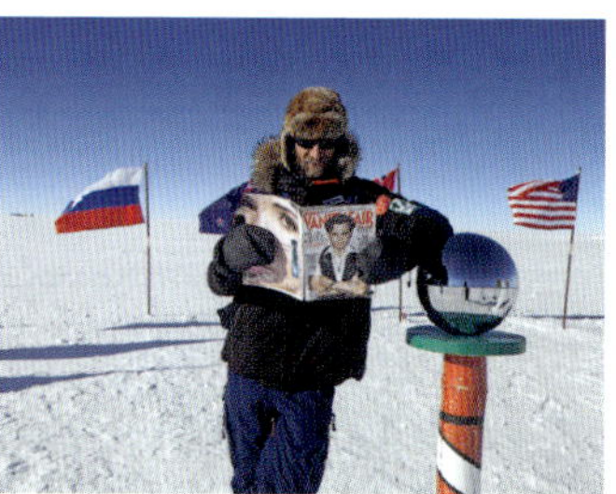

CEREMONIAL POST AT 90° SOUTH (Page 25)
The Geographic South Pole was first reached by Norwegian Roald Amundsen and his team on December 14, 1911. One month later, British Captain Robert Falcon Scott and his team were the second expedition to reach 90° south. In 1957, the United States established the Amundsen-Scott South Pole Station as a permanent scientific base there.

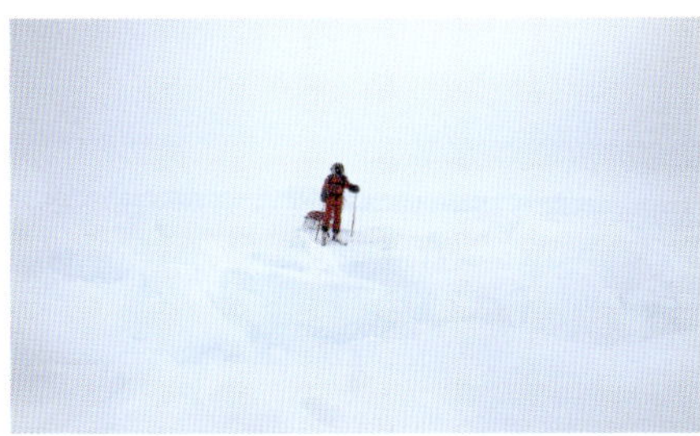

A WHITEOUT ON THE ARCTIC PACK ICE (Pages 30–31)
When the clouds overtake the terrain in a polar environment, all details simply vanish. When the line of the horizon also disappears, it can feel like being lost inside an eggshell. A dusting of snow can cover the dark patches of a thinly refrozen crust covering the ocean's surface, making them almost impossible to discern.

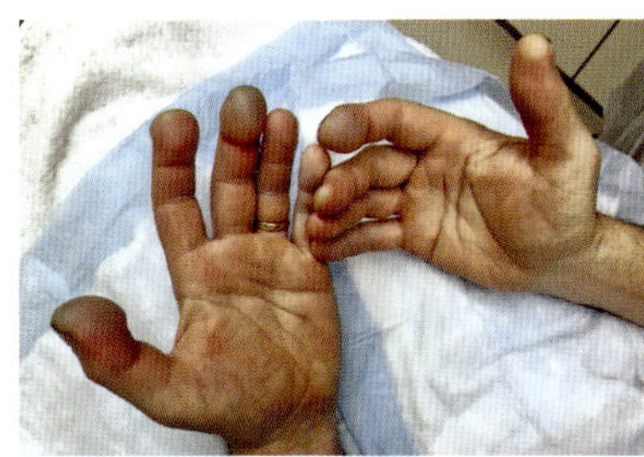

FROSTBITTEN FINGERS (Page 36)
A frostbite is like a burn. The body secretes liquid to protect the next layer of skin. If that liquid freezes, the cold injury will go deeper until it reaches the flesh and kills cells, nerves, and blood vessels. A digit may need to be amputated to the next phalanx to prevent both spread and the possibility of infection.

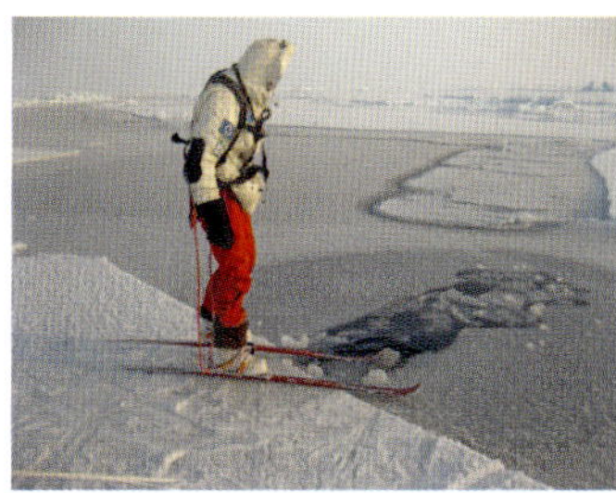

FRESHLY REFROZEN LEAD ON THE PACK ICE (Page 37)
Crossing open or refrozen leads is the trade's currency. Young ice that is less than three inches thick is called nilas. That thin crust can be strong enough to carry a human, but it can also break, leading to scary moments. The open water in this image shows the shape of my body after I went through.

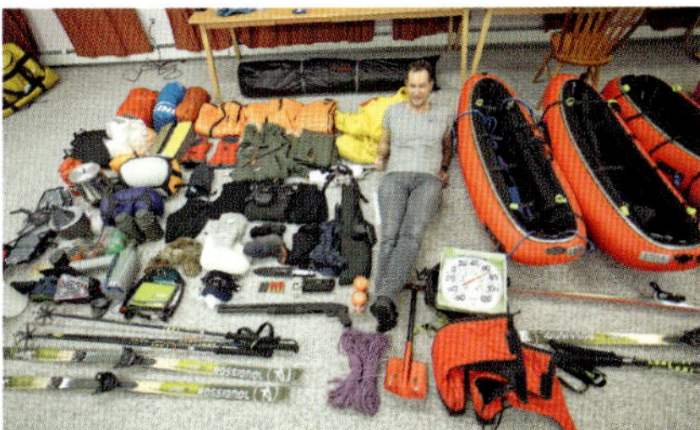

NORTH POLE EXPEDITION PACK (Page 38, Top)
The weapon in this picture means this is an Arctic equipment pack. There are no dangerous predators in Antarctica, but polar bears in the Arctic are a constant danger. A weapon is a last resort. Pepper spray or bear bangers will often suffice. Missing from this photo are food and fuel, which bring the total weight to 370 pounds.

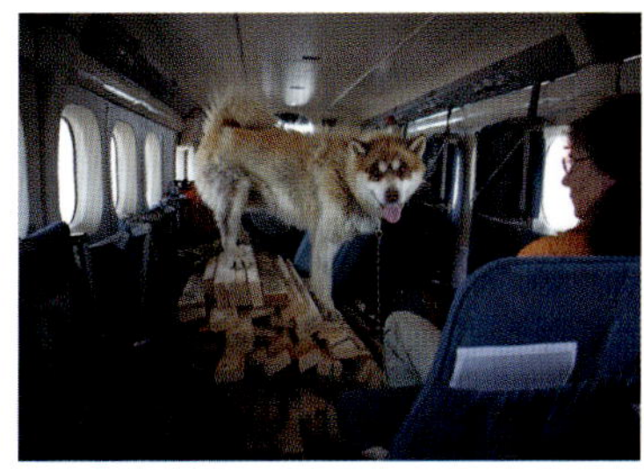

ZEPHYR (Page 41)
Huskies or sled dogs can be good companions when traveling alone in the Arctic. They provide an early warning for polar bears, especially when sleeping in the tent. Dogs have been known to play with polar bears, but they can also get killed and eaten if a bear is hungry and aggressive. Dogs are not allowed in Antarctica.

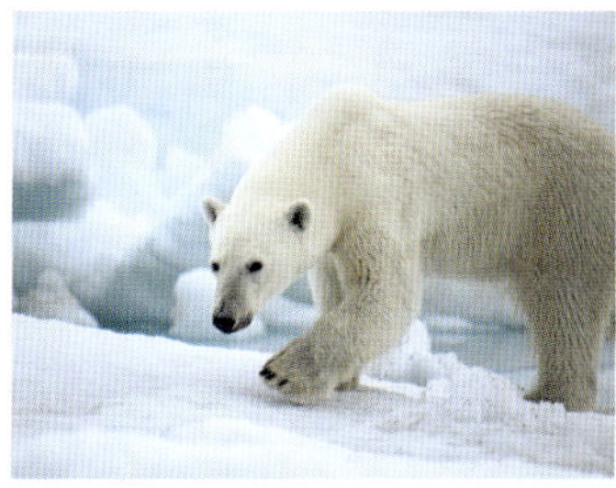

POLAR BEAR (*URSUS MARITIMUS*) (Page 43)
There are about 26,000 polar bears in the Arctic. A bear has no business on the winter sea ice given the absence of food, but they are nonetheless present. Bears are strategic hunters that will stalk their prey and use the ice's features to hide. They are also inquisitive and bold, fearing no predators of their own.

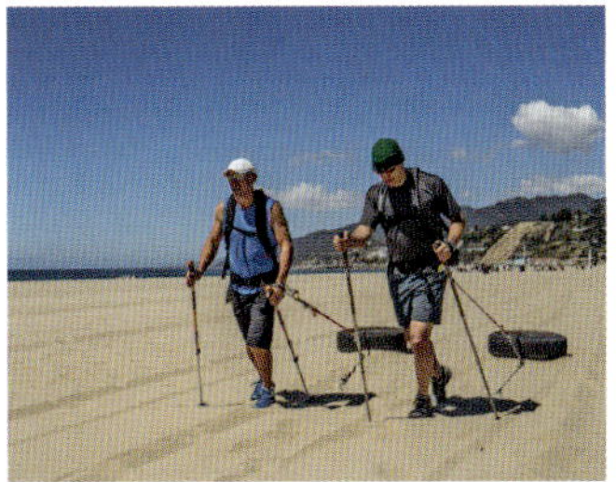

PULLING TIRES (Page 44, Right)
There is no substitution for pulling a heavy sled over the rubble fields of Arctic pack ice. With close to 400 pounds in tow, the uneven terrain makes for taxing and sometimes hazardous work. But pulling tires filled with sand or bundling multiple tires can get you close while providing a serious workout.

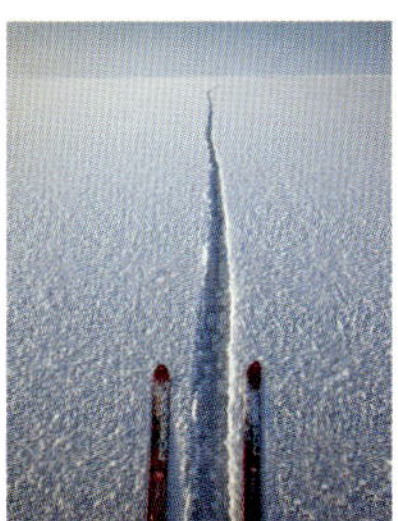

ARCTIC SEA ICE NEAR THE NORTH POLE (Page 48)
This is a freshly refrozen pan barely a few inches thick. In the 1980s, 57 percent of the Arctic sea ice was thick and survived the summer melt. Today, only seven percent of multiyear ice remains, hastening the demise of the ice cover in summer. The thin ice is also crippling to expeditions from land to the North Pole.

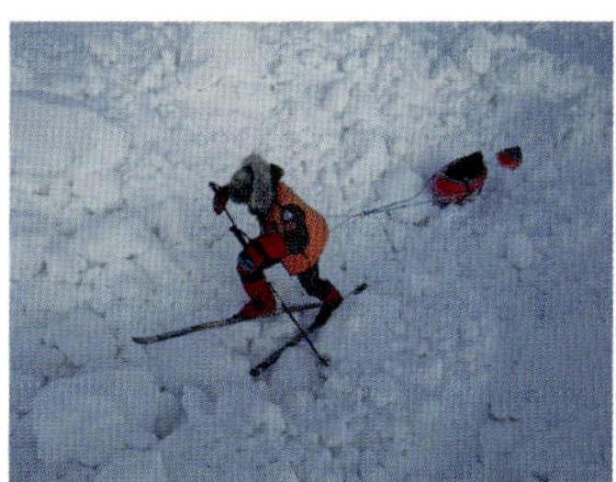

ARCTIC CRUMB CAKE (Page 55)
The Arctic pack ice moves at the mercy of currents and tides, cracking and crushing the crust into open channels and fragmented clusters. These can range from the size of fists to two-story buildings. At times, it can feel like traveling on a giant crumb cake.

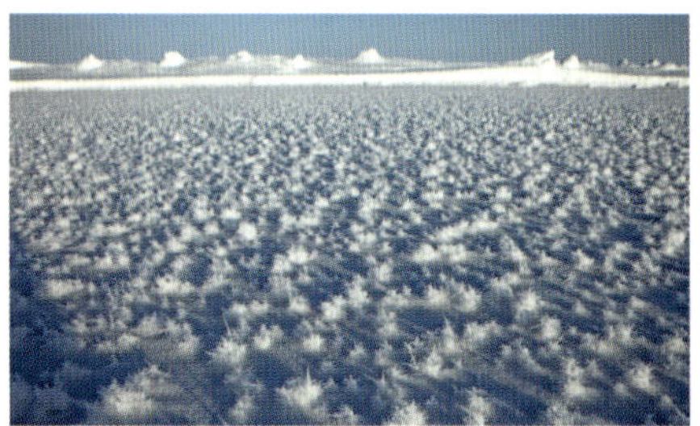

FROST FLOWERS (Pages 60–61)
Frost flowers form on the young sea ice when the air temperature is much colder than the underlying ice. The extreme cold rapidly freezes the ocean water, pushing the salt up, while gravity pulls it back down. This results in saline crystals. Pulling a sled through these crystals feels like pulling it through syrup.

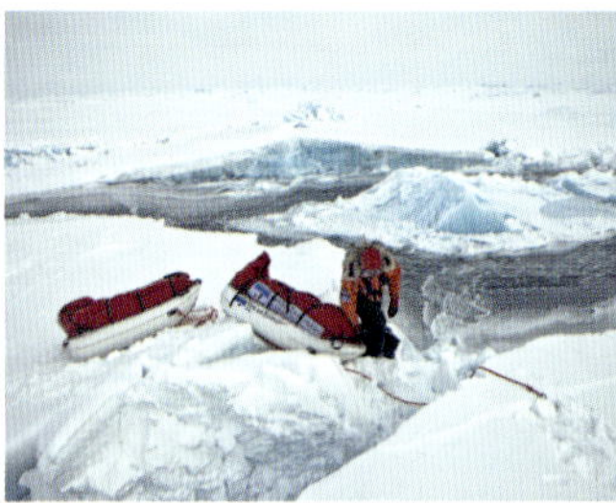

NILAS AND OPEN LEADS (Page 66)
Keith is negotiating a tricky uplift from the crushed pans of ice. The background section is a multiyear ice pan, probably about eight feet thick. That thickness is now extremely rare in the Arctic, where ice that is 10 years or older accounts for about seven percent of the surface, compared to 57 percent 30 years ago.

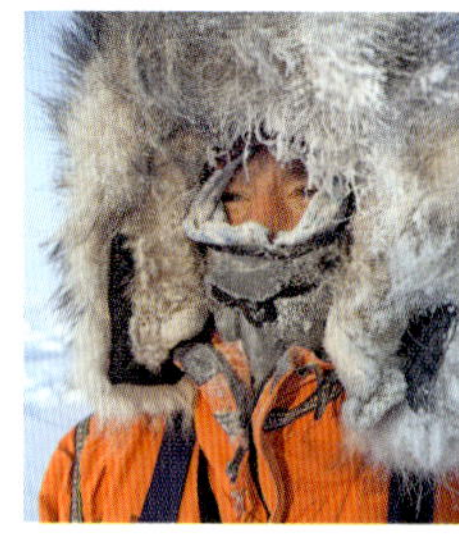

KEITH TRAPPED IN FROST (Page 75)
Midwinter on the Arctic Ocean means temperatures that can plunge below -60°F. A fur ruff helps trap humidity in its thin strands of hair, creating a microclimate around the face. Clothing layers are minimal at full exertion to avoid overheating. Sweating is deadly; a soaked fabric can rapidly freeze on the skin, leading to hypothermia.

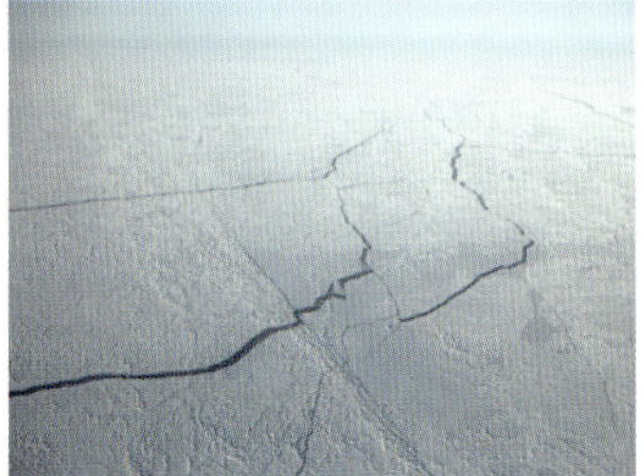

OPEN LEADS ON THE PACK ICE (Page 79)
Currents, winds, and tides fracture the pack ice in winter in the Arctic, resulting in leads and pressure ridges. Pressure ridges develop when pans of ice collide with slow but enormous force and crush the ice surface into walls reaching nearly 10 feet high. The ice also breaks into open leads, revealing the polar ocean below your feet.

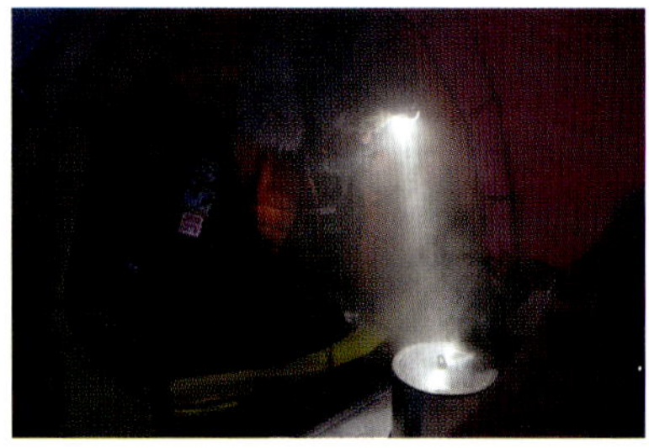

THE DAILY RITUAL OF MELTING SNOW (Page 84, Top)
Ice expeditions have one clear benefit: endless access to water in frozen form. This shuns the need to carry H_2O and replaces it with the daily task of melting snow, which is slow in the cold environment. Consequently, melting duties are the first priority of tent life.

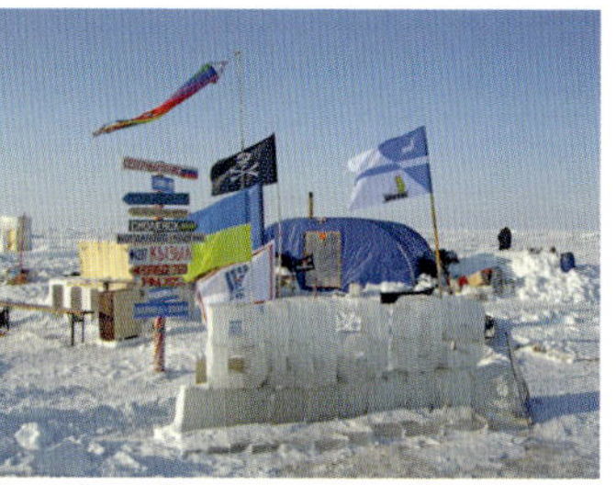

BARNEO, NEAR THE NORTH POLE (Page 87)
Barneo, a floating station about 30 miles from the North Pole, is set up to service expeditions and research on the Arctic sea ice. It is open for about three weeks in April. Started by the Russians in 2002, it was once maintained for an additional two weeks, until the faster spring melt forced a shortening of its operation.

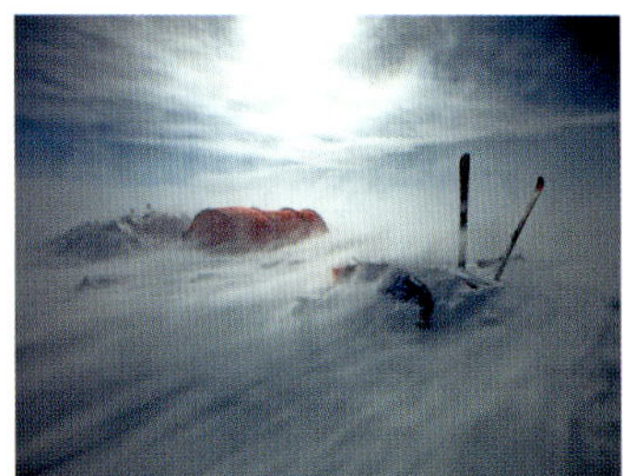

STORM IN GREENLAND (Page 93)
Southern Greenland is known for its powerful storms. The winds build suddenly on the ice sheet and transform a dead-calm environment into a fierce natural theater. This one lashed 80-mile-per-hour winds for seven consecutive days at the tent's thin nylon walls. Living through these storms is a testament to human engineering.

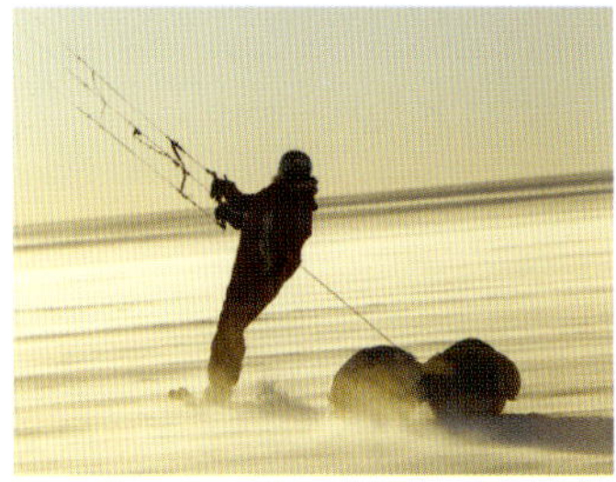

ERIC IN THE MIDNIGHT SUN (Page 98)
Kite skiing is well suited for travel on an ice sheet, especially in Greenland. Katabatic winds follow gravity, and a north-south bearing can easily be set. The big advantage is the considerable distance that is made possible. Eric and I posted 370 miles during our 24-hour run in 2010. The record still holds today.

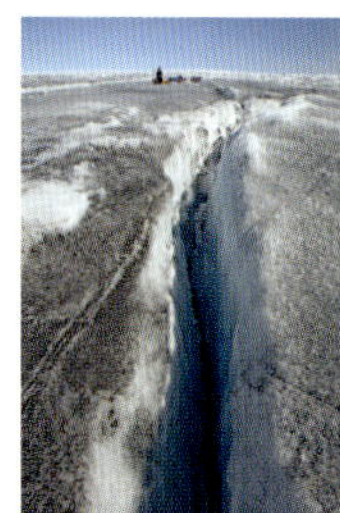

CREVASSES IN GREENLAND (Page 100)
Crevasses are formed by gravity, as the descending glacier pulls to the sea. Transported by the jet stream as a result of forest fires and pollution, soot covers this ice in southern Greenland. The dark color absorbs solar energy, accelerating the melt process and neutralizing the reflectivity from its white color, also known as its albedo.

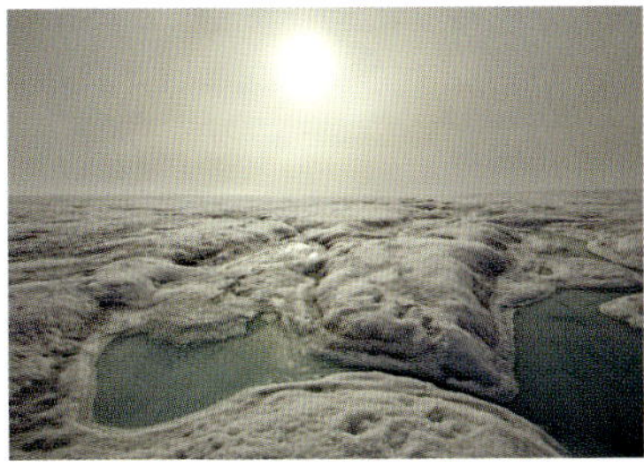

MELTWATER RIVERS IN GREENLAND (Page 103)
When the ice melts on an ice sheet, it gathers in rivers and disappears in holes called moulins that reach the bedrock, sometimes 6,500 feet below. In 2012, for the first time since satellite observation began in 1979, Greenland experienced 98 percent surface melt. Ice expeditions had to be emergency airlifted out.

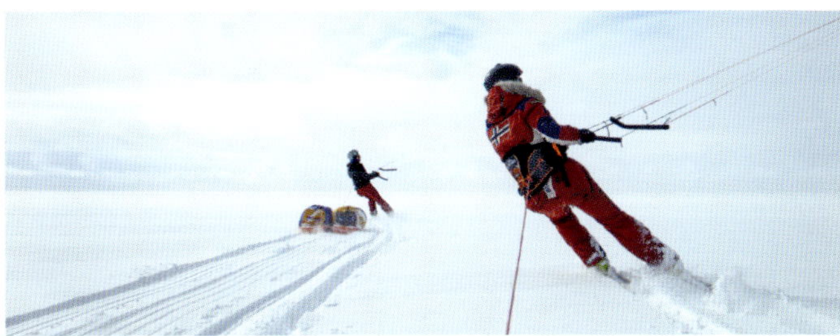

KITE SKIING IN GREENLAND (Pages 104–105)
Greenland is the second-largest ice sheet after Antarctica, but conditions there are considerably milder. With an average elevation almost 2,500 feet lower, it is also latitudinally farther from the pole and therefore warmer. This translates to surface ice conditions that are much softer on the knees when kite skiing.

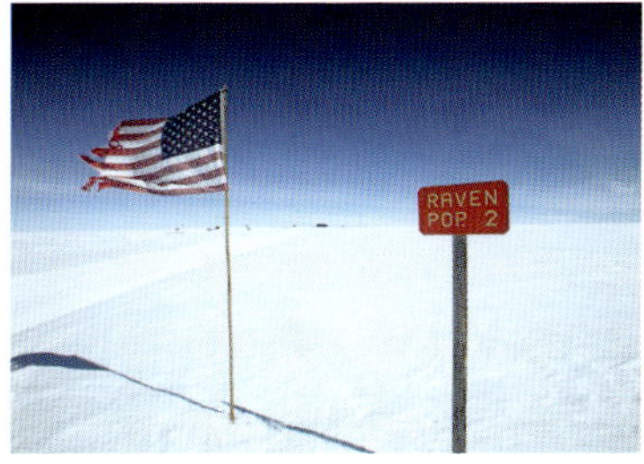

RAVEN CAMP, GREENLAND (Page 106)
Raven Camp is the only populated area on the Greenland ice sheet. It consists of a seasonal camp populated by two people whose mission is to maintain the runway next to the DYE-2 radar station. That runway is used to practice takeoffs and landings for the Antarctic season. The couple generally stays stationed there for five months.

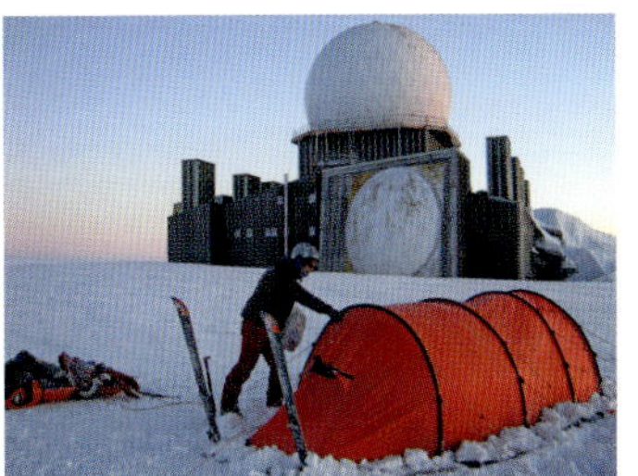

ERIC AT DYE-2 (Page 107)
The DEW (Distant Early Warning) Line was a system devised by the United States during the Cold War. It linked Alaska to Iceland with radar stations spaced every 100 miles. DYE-2 is one of two stations on the Greenland ice sheet. Rendered obsolete by satellite monitoring and the end of the Cold War, the station was abandoned in 1988.

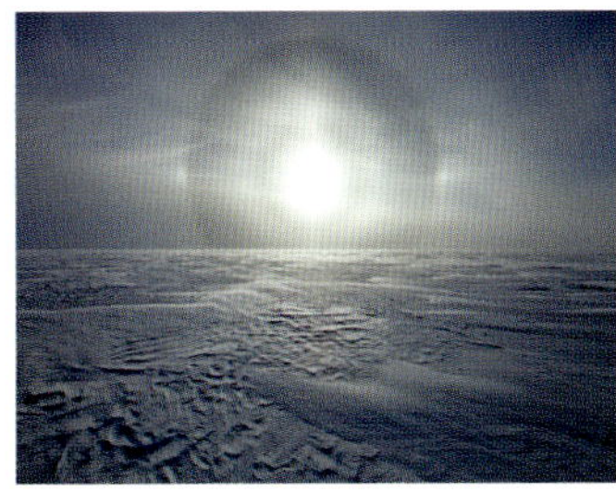

ICE SHEET, CENTRAL GREENLAND (Page 115)
A sun dog (parhelion) forms on the Greenland ice sheet. While these can be seen in any climate, they are most spectacular in cold climates. Sun dogs are concentric halos of refracted light around the sun, filtering through ice crystals in the air.

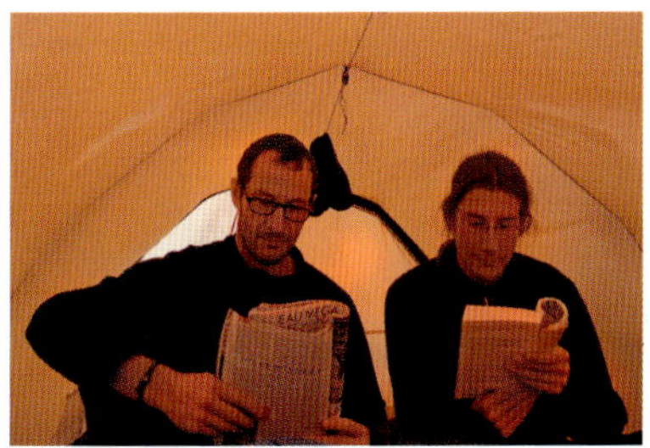

PASSING TIME IN A STORM (Page 119, Top)
When the sun reaches its spring zenith, the angle is high enough in the sky to heat the tent, enabling a greenhouse effect. The dry cold allows for the temperature inside the tent to be up to 50°F warmer than outside. When pinned down by a hurricane-strength storm, passing time means reading, playing chess, and sleeping.

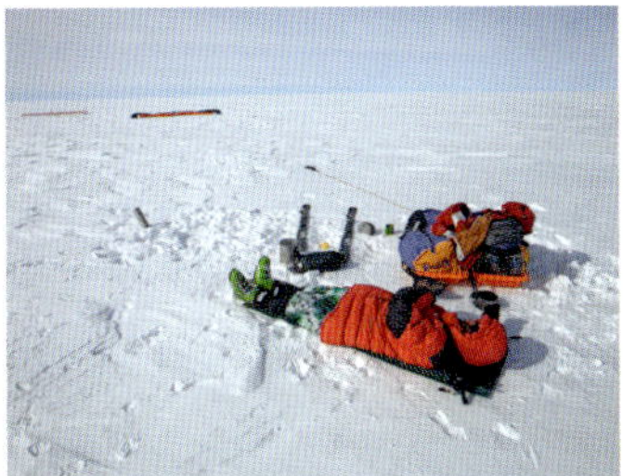

ERIC WAITING FOR WIND (Page 123)
Kite-skiing missions rely on wind for propulsion. The wind can shut down unceremoniously, dropping the kite from the sky. Given kiting speeds that can top 40 miles per hour, there is little incentive to the walking alternative that clocks at one mile per hour. In dead-calm conditions, sometimes the best thing to do is simply nap.

A GREENLAND WHITEOUT (Page 124)
When the clouds overtake the sky, the absence of shadows in a white environment makes every feature disappear. The binary dimensions of air and water in frozen form blend with little distinction. It is especially disorienting when the horizon vanishes, wreaking havoc on our sense of balance. This can lead to random falls from the warped perceptions.

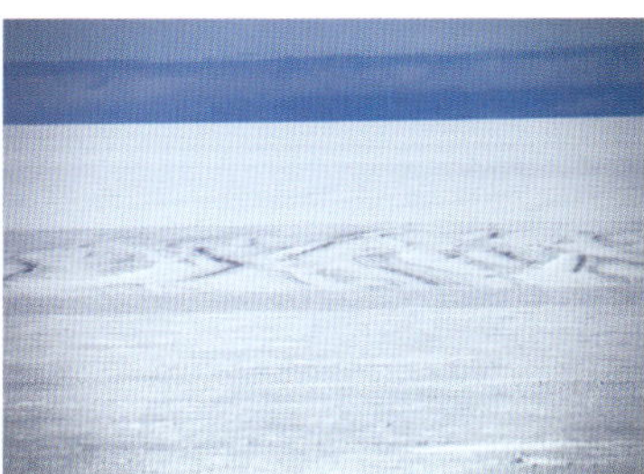

CREVASSE FIELD, NORTHERN GREENLAND (Page 126)
When a slope of a glacier reaches a breaking point, crevasses begin to form. Snowdrift and wind can form bridges that eventually cover the cracks. With enough thickness and cold temperatures, the bridge can hold a human's weight, especially when distributed on skis. But not always.

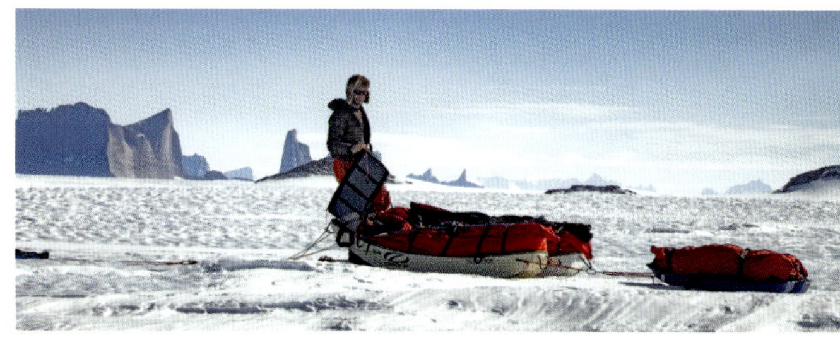

QUEEN MAUD LAND, EAST ANTARCTICA (Pages 136–137)
Queen Maud Land offers some of the most scenic polar landscapes anywhere. Crystalline and granite rock emerge from the ice as far as 124 miles from the coast, where sheer 2,000-foot faces are commonplace. The view from the ice sheet is unique to that part of the world.

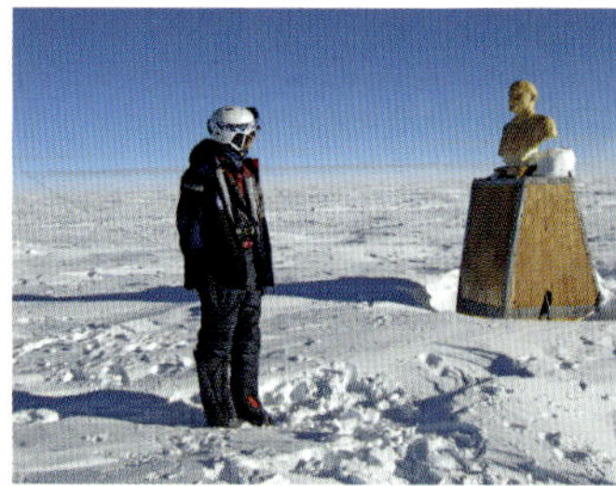

ERIC STARING DOWN LENIN (Page 142)
The Pole of Inaccessibility (POI) station was established by the Soviets in 1958. It was abandoned a few weeks later, but first a bust of Vladimir Lenin was placed atop the now-buried station. The POI is the farthest point from any coast, arguably the toughest point to reach in Antarctica.

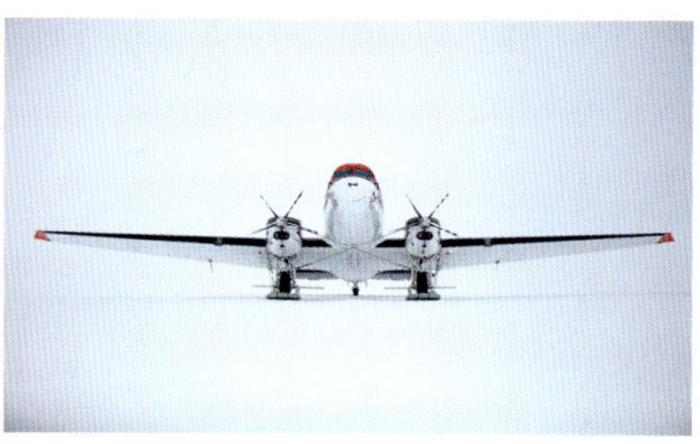

BASLER BT-67 (Pages 144–145)
The Basler BT-67 is a modified DC-3 with turboprop engines and a lengthened fuselage. Along with the Twin Otter, it is one of the favored air transports on the Antarctic ice sheet. The Basler's range can be extended to more than 2,000 nautical miles and can service missions from the coast to the South Pole.

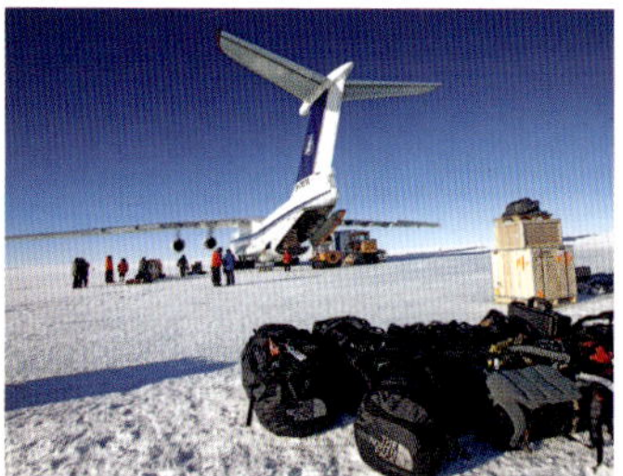

NOVOLAZAREVSKAYA, EAST ANTARCTICA (Page 146)
The Russian Novolazarevskaya (Novo) Station on the eastern coast of Antarctica services missions to Queen Maud Land and the eastern sector all the way to the South Pole. Novo is accessible from Cape Town, South Africa, with an Ilyushin Il-76 cargo aircraft that lands on an ice runway.

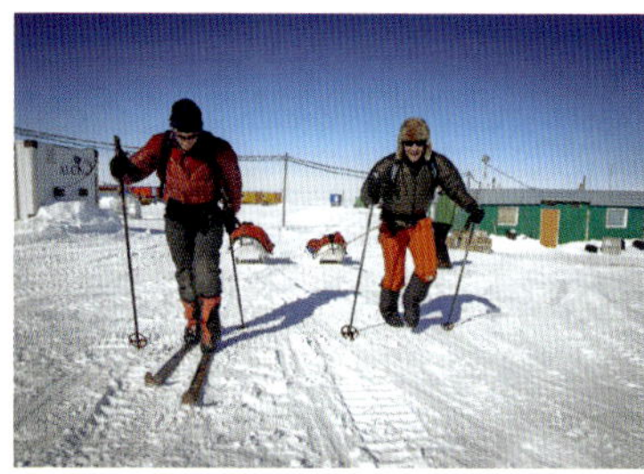

LEAVING NOVOLAZAREVSKAYA (Page 147)
The start of an expedition is always exciting. Months or years of preparations finally get you to the starting line. The beginning also means the heaviest pulling loads. Within days, the cold and enormous effort sows doubt over the plan that took so long to formulate. The goal becomes making it to the end of the next day.

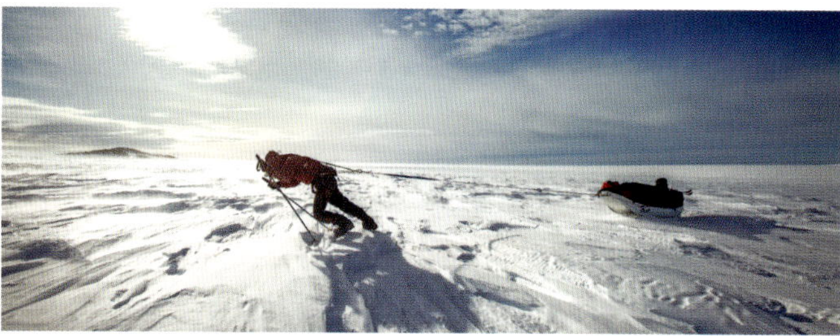

EAST ANTARCTICA (Pages 148–149)
Ascending a glacier means challenging gravity. The outcrop in the background is a nunatak. These mountain peaks will disappear under the rising mammoth ice sheet, which stretches virtually uninterrupted from one end of the continent to the other. Soon, the plateau's ice will flatten. There is nothing here but cold, wind, and desolation.

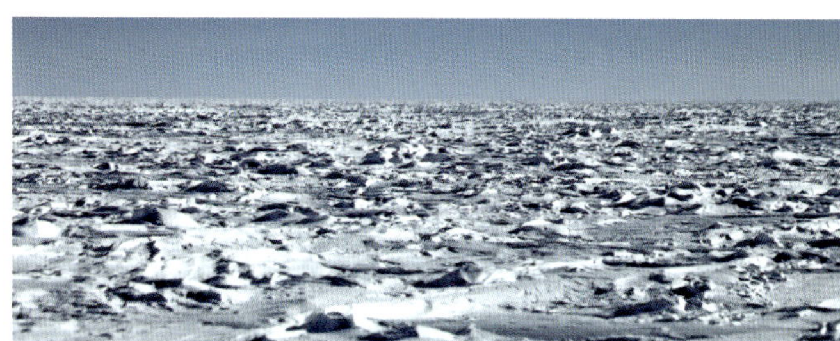

SASTRUGI, EAST ANTARCTIC PLATEAU (Pages 152–153)
With an average elevation of 8,200 feet, Antarctica is the highest continent on Earth. Due to powerful winds, most of the interior's surface gets scarred from the high velocity of tiny flying ice particles. Kiting at speed over this shredded terrain will give your brain's right and left hemispheres a chance to meet.

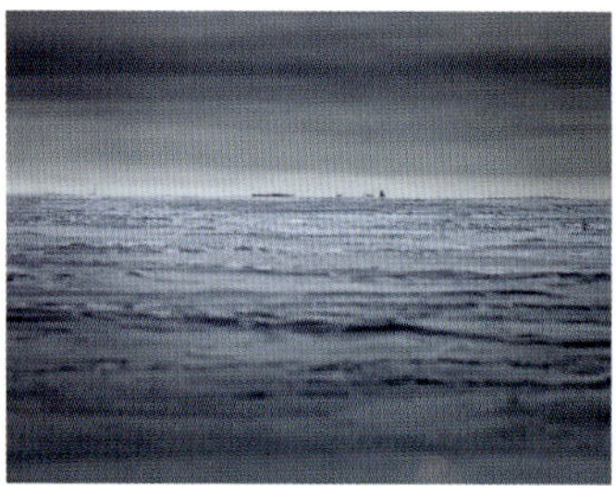

AMUNDSEN-SCOTT SOUTH POLE STATION (Page 155)
When approaching from the east, the South Pole Station is the first feature to stick out of the ice from the coast, which is 1,330 miles to the north. The South Pole Station is populated by about 46 people who stay over the winter. In summer, the station hosts around 220 scientists and maintenance personnel.

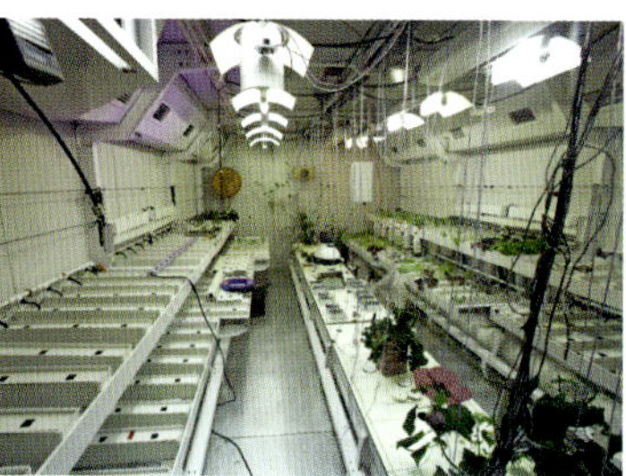

SOUTH POLE STATION HORTICULTURE (Page 156, Right)
The South Pole is plunged into six months of darkness. It is then cut off from the world until the return of the austral spring. Not even planes can resupply the station in the winter darkness. Hydroponics are used to grow fresh produce with daylight lamps.

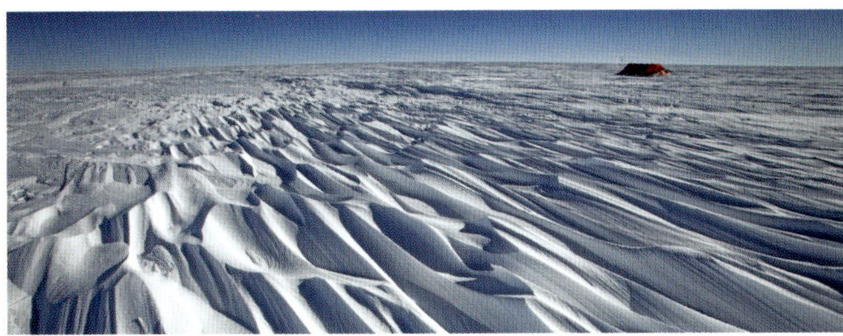

SASTRUGI, ANTARCTIC PLATEAU (Pages 158–159)
High on the plateau, the sastrugi take on systematic patterns aligned with the dominant winds. Barely a few inches tall, these shapes will form in ways not found anywhere else on the globe. To witness them requires a commitment to traveling this vast and lifeless frozen world.

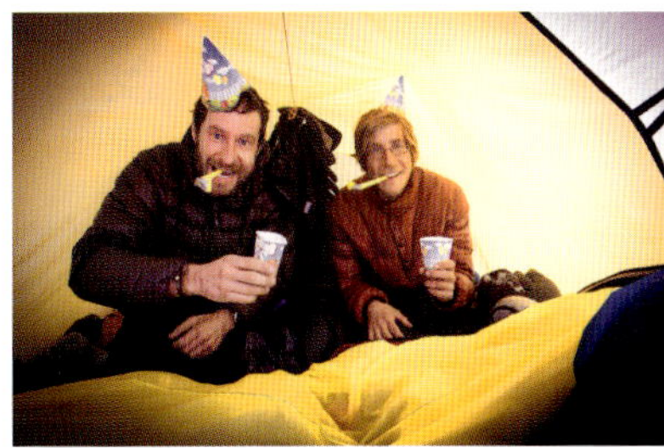

CHRISTMAS IN ANTARCTICA (Page 164, Top)
Days blend into one another on expeditions. The isolation lends itself to meditation. Still, expeditioners are tethered to the outside by daily communications to report their location. In the event of interrupted communication, a plane would be dispatched to the last reported location in less than 24 hours, initiating a search-and-rescue mission.

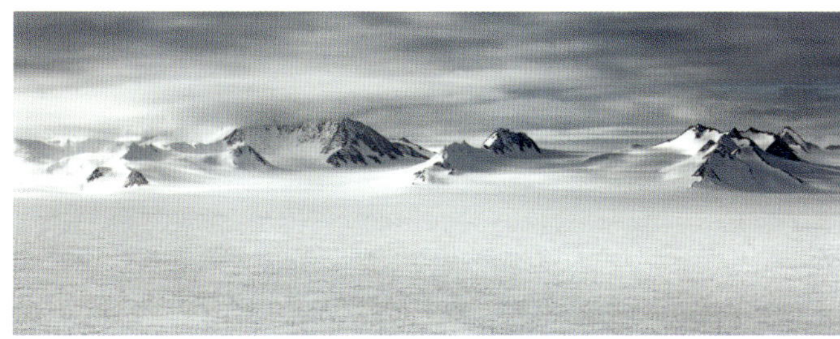

HERITAGE RANGE, WEST ANTARCTICA (Pages 166–167)
The Heritage Range stands at the northern end of the Ellsworth Mountains. Union Glacier, in the foreground, is a river of ice that flows to the Weddell Sea, where it eventually releases in the form of ice shelves and eventually icebergs. It is peppered with moving crevasses that go mostly undetected but for ground-piercing radar.

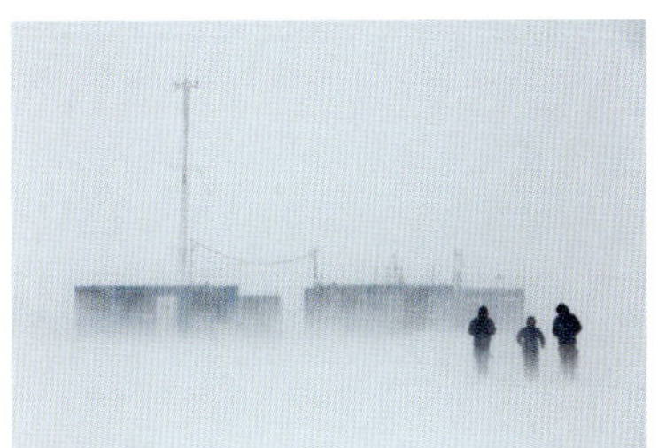

WEATHER STATION AT UNION GLACIER (Page 168)
This communications and weather station from Antarctic Logistics & Expeditions delivers daily forecasts for the ever-changing summer season. It services the West Antarctica sector, making calls for when flights can take off and land. Weather and visibility can ground flights for days. This can leave missions stranded until a system lifts.

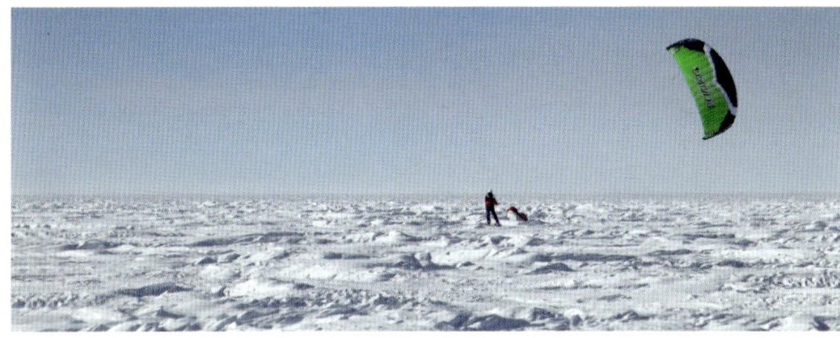

CROSSING ANTARCTICA (Pages 170–171)
Kite skiing enables long-distance travel in Antarctica, when topography allows it. Ascending terrain is generally dominated by descending airflow. These winds can be extremely powerful and prevent the use of kites when headed uphill. Alternatively, the flatter plateau makes for generally light winds.

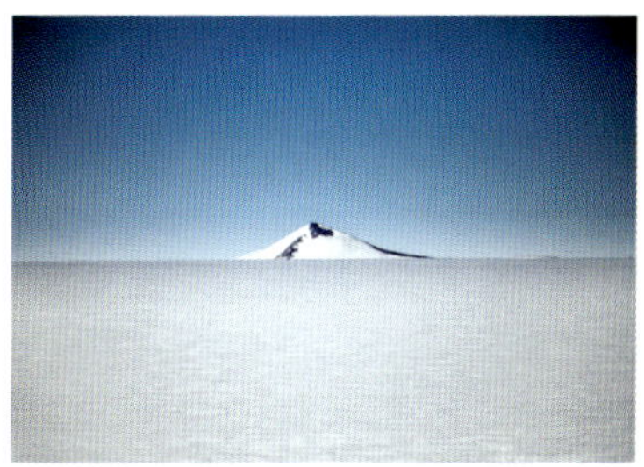

NUNATAK, QUEEN MAUD LAND (Page 175)
Queen Maud Land in East Antarctica was the first region of the continent to be sighted in 1820. Dynamic mountain peaks in this area reach 10,328 feet in elevation, but many have been buried below the rising ice sheet. On occasion, only a nunatak peeks through the ice, belying the scope of the range.

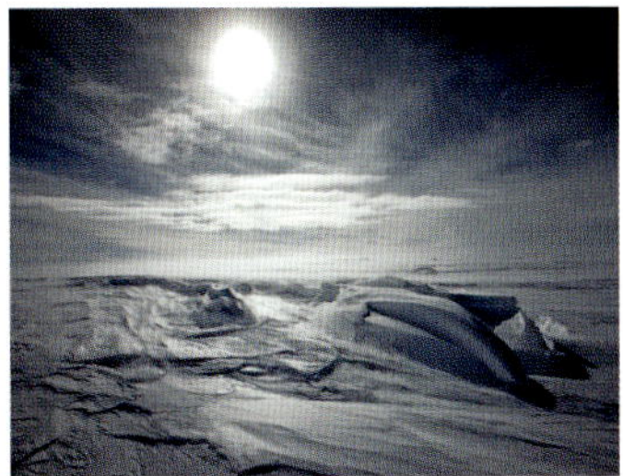

STORM ON THE EAST ANTARCTIC ICE SHEET (Page 184)
Sastrugi are shapes sculpted on the ice by wind erosion. Katabatic winds, a term describing winds flowing down a slope, will reach speeds exceeding 200 miles per hour in the winter in Antarctica, where sastrugi heads can reach six-and-a-half feet high. Those winds, combined with very little precipitation, define the Antarctic landscape.

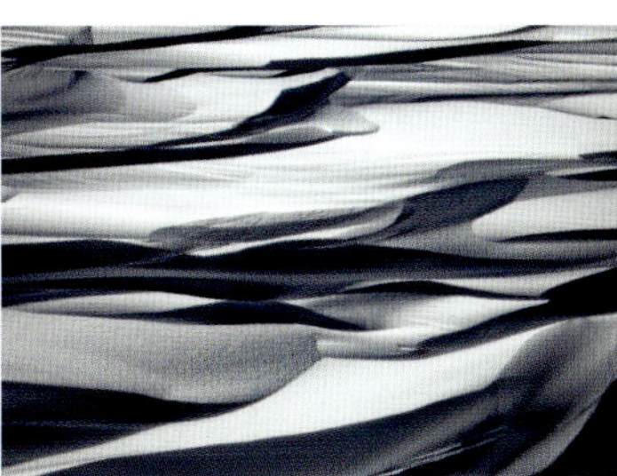

SASTRUGI, EAST ANTARCTIC PLATEAU (Page 186)
Katabatic winds sculpt the surface of Antarctica. Cold winds increase in mass as they drop onto an ice sheet. They also gain velocity when they roll down a slope, following gravity. Consequently, winds can be fairly predictable on an ice sheet from studying topography and elevation variants.

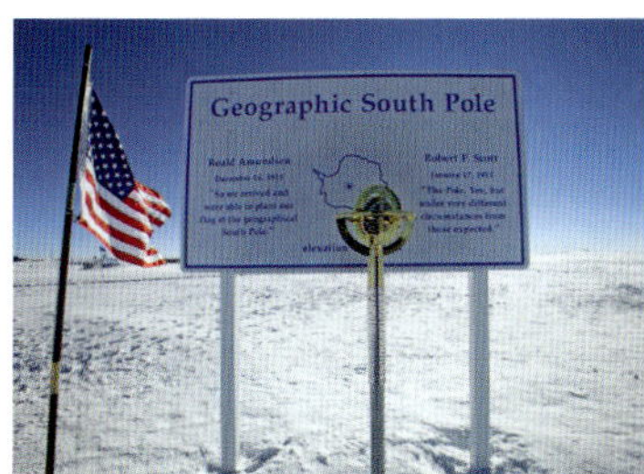

THE OFFICIAL SOUTH POLE (Page 188, Left)
The South Pole, 90° south, is one of two locations where the Earth spins on its axis. Since all longitudinal points meet at the poles, walking around this point effectively means you can cross all of the world's time zones in just a few steps. Given the motion of the ice sheet, the official post must be repositioned every year.

ACKNOWLEDGMENTS

In his book *The Worst Journey in the World*, Apsley Cherry-Garrard shared that in the bleakest moments of his harrowing trek to Cape Crozier, in the pitch blackness of the Antarctic winter, he "did not forget the please and the thank you." To a large extent, upholding that etiquette is what anchors the exploring fare into its gentleman—and, lately, gentlewoman—tradition. With that in mind, any effort to make a book such as this one could not be remotely possible without the help, support, inspiration, or leadership of the following individuals.

First are Frank Hurley, Herbert Ponting, and George Lowe, who pioneered image capture in the brutally inhospitable Antarctic environment with tools that were short on convenience but long on historical significance. Their images made a dreamer out of a tender me at a time when I needed dreaming. Furthermore, it must be noted that nothing happening today in exploration would have happened without the giant Fridtjof Nansen.

Any expedition, whether solo or otherwise, requires a team, a partner, a teacher, a friend. The following people have been that to me and more. Keith Heger, Eric McNair-Landry, and Luc Hardy—I learned more from you than you probably know. My late friends Henry Worsley, Marc Cornelissen, and Dixie Dansercoer—you are still alive in my heart when I revisit the places that we traveled. Will Steger, Doug Stoup, and Sarah and Matty McNair—your friendship is the currency of this trade and my privilege. John Quigley, Bryan Miller, Mark George, Jorge and Guillermo May, and the whole crew from Asociación de Exploración Científica Austral—we laughed and cried, we conquered and lost. And we're still standing! Thank you for your trust. Dr. Huw Lewis Jones, thank you for your unbeatable knowledge of polar history. Børge Ousland, thank you for showing everyone—and I mean everyone—how it's done.

Thank you to Victor Serov and the team at Antarctic Logistics Centre International (ALCI); Steve Jones, Nick Lewis, Peter McDowell, and the whole support crew at Antarctic Logistics & Expeditions (ALE); Tom and Tina Sjogren (what will I do without you?); Marc De Keyser, for your spot-on weather analysis; Chris Imray, for your great handling of my frozen toes; my physiotherapists and trainers Oliver Schmittlein, Aman Abye, Jeffrey, and Ron and Yumi, for showing me a world beyond pain.

Expeditions cannot happen without the help of friends and sponsors. Thank you Lawrence Benenson, Todd Goergen, and Gillian Sandler for your unwavering support. Thank you to Martino Guerrini, for the faith you have placed in me, and your steadfast commitment to field-tested excellence and the decade-long endorsement of my adventures; Petra Hilleberg, for the best nylon house on the ice; Dr. Jack Singh at Organic Food Bar; Karen Cage at Hewlett Packard; Amy Kawadler and Claire-Anne Devillard at Canon; Patrick Pruniaux and the team at Ulysse Nardin; Mark Lewis and Joey Lewis at Lexar Media; Jason Newell at Rossignol; Matt Taggart at Ozone; my great friend Luigi Gratton at Herbalife; the team at Harvest Foodworks, for keeping me fed on the ice; Rob Striker and my friend and fellow peaceful warrior Matt Petersen; and Julie Uggen and the whole team at Norrøna—your gear is core, and it gives me the confidence to go further. Thank you to associate publisher Jim Muschett for your faith in me and the purpose of this mission, and everyone at Rizzoli who worked so hard to make this book, once again, everything I hoped it would be—Candice Fehrman and Susi Oberhelman, your work is on every page!

Thank you to my grandfather John Copeland, for lighting the adventure spark of my younger self; my father, who has taught me that art without discipline is like a mission without purpose; my mother, whose endless support and tireless belief in me has given me the greatest gift of all—the wings of self-expression; and my wife, Carolin, and our two little angels, whose patience and sacrifice during the many months of absence this project required are the lifeblood of my work. Ladies, this one is for you!

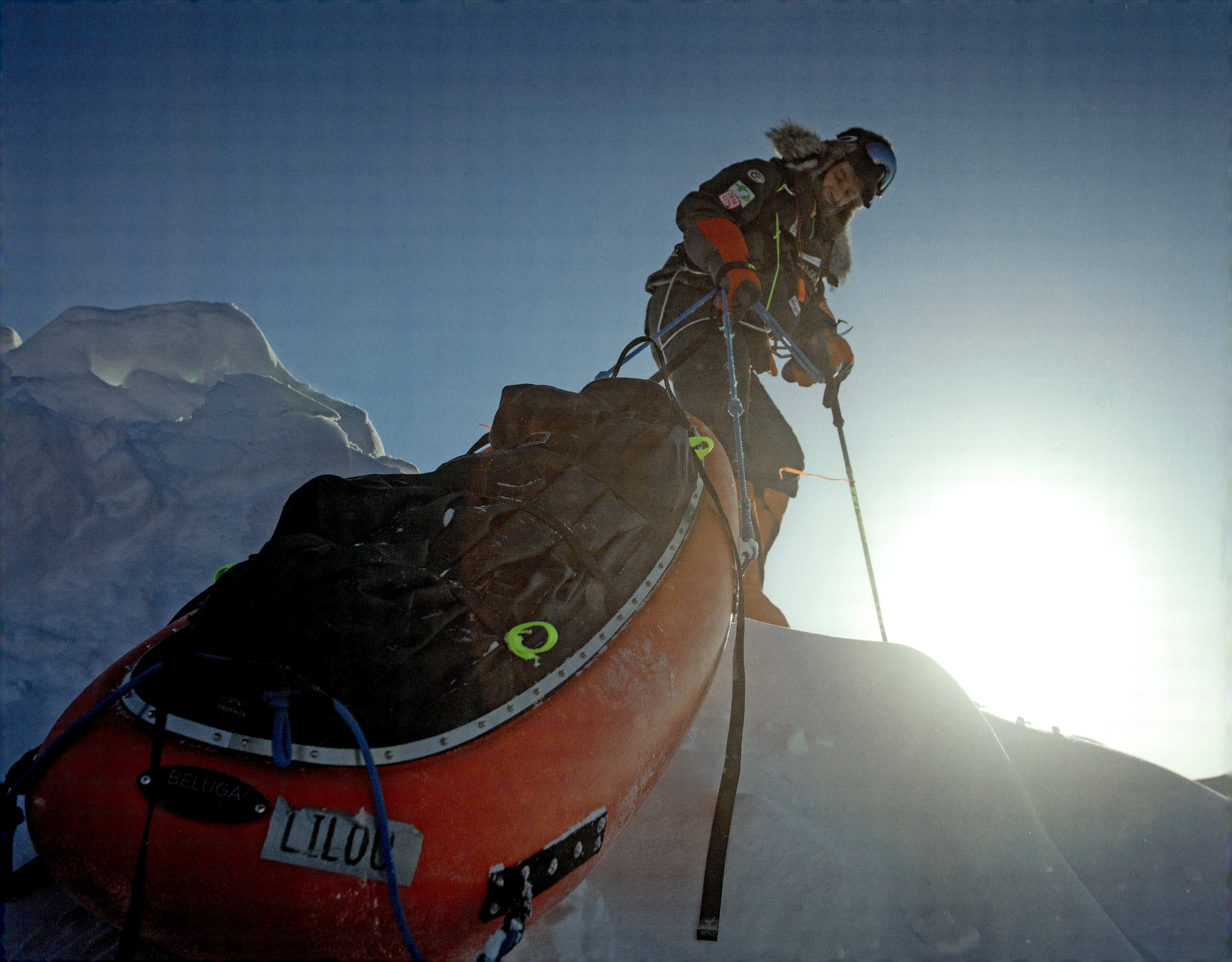
BELUGA
LILOU

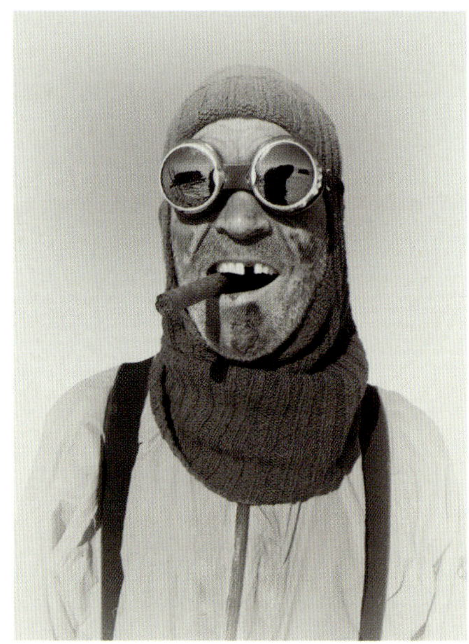

In memory of

Henry Worsley (1960–2016)

Husband, father, soldier, friend

First published in the United States of America in 2022 by
Rizzoli International Publications, Inc.
300 Park Avenue South
New York, NY 10010
www.rizzoliusa.com

I would like to thank the photographers who provided additional images (of me) for this book: Keith Heger: pp. 37, 45, 50, 58, 71, and 78; David Heisler: p. 13; Walter Mather: pp. 4–5 and 56–57; Peter McCabe: p. 44; Eric McNair-Landry: pp. 25, 122, 136–137, 173, and 185; and Bryan Miller: pp. 32–33, 36, 38–39, 46, 55, 61, 62, 76–77, 80, 84–85, and 207.

Publisher: Charles Miers
Associate Publisher: James Muschett
Managing Editor: Lynn Scrabis
Editor: Candice Fehrman
Design: Susi Oberhelman
Foreword: Jimmy Chin
Maps: Yulan Studio, with data from NASA

Printed in China

2022 2023 2024 2025 / 10 9 8 7 6 5 4 3 2 1

ISBN: 978-0-8478-7087-5

Library of Congress Control Number: 2022936328

Visit us online:
Facebook.com/RizzoliNewYork
Twitter: @Rizzoli_Books
Instagram.com/RizzoliBooks
Pinterest.com/RizzoliBooks
Youtube.com/user/RizzoliNY
Issuu.com/Rizzoli

This book and all expeditions featured within it were made carbon neutral by ClimatePartner.

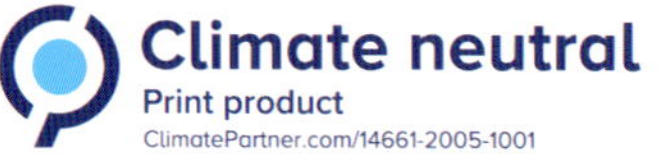

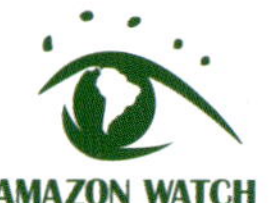